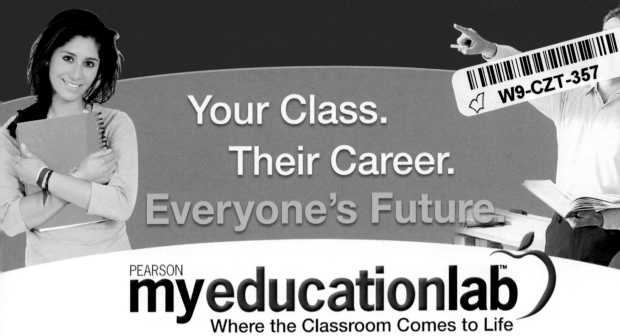

Your Class.
Their Career.
Everyone's Future

PEARSON
myeducationlab™
Where the Classroom Comes to Life

Helping today's students become the teachers of tomorrow.

"Teacher educators who are developing pedagogies for the analysis of teaching and learning contend that analyzing teaching artifacts has three advantages: it enables new teachers time for reflection while still using the real materials of practice; it provides new teachers with experience thinking about and approaching the complexity of the classroom; and in some cases, it can help new teachers and teacher educators develop a shared understanding and common language about teaching. . . ."[1]

As Linda Darling-Hammond and her colleagues point out, grounding teacher education in real classrooms—among real teachers and students and among actual

PEARSON
myeducationlab™
Where the Classroom Comes to Life

examples of students' and teachers' work—is an important, and perhaps even an essential, part of training teachers for the complexities of teaching today's students in today's classrooms. For a number of years, we have heard the same message from many of you as we sat in your offices learning about the goals of your courses and the challenges you face in teaching the next generation of educators. Working with a number of our authors and with many of you, we have created a website that provides you and your students with the context of real classrooms and artifacts that research on teacher education tells us is so important. Through authentic in-class video footage, interactive simulations, rich case studies, examples of authentic teacher and student work, and more, **MyEducationLab** offers you and your students a uniquely valuable teacher education tool.

MyEducationLab is easy to use! Wherever the **MyEducationLab** logo appears in the margins or elsewhere in the text, you and your students can follow the simple link instructions to access the **MyEducationLab** resource that corresponds with the chapter content. These include:

VIDEO ■ Authentic classroom videos show how real teachers handle actual classroom situations.

HOMEWORK & EXERCISES ■ These assignable activities give students opportunities to understand content more deeply and to practice applying content.

BUILDING TEACHING SKILLS ■

These assignments help students practice and strengthen skills that are essential to quality teaching. By analyzing and responding to real student and teacher artifacts and/or authentic classroom videos, students practice important teaching skills they will need when they enter real classrooms.

CASE STUDIES ■

A diverse set of robust cases drawn from some of our best-selling books further expose students to the realities of teaching and offer valuable perspectives on common issues and challenges in education.

SIMULATIONS ■

Created by the IRIS Center at Vanderbilt University, these interactive simulations give hands-on practice at adapting instruction for a full spectrum of learners.

STUDENT & TEACHER ARTIFACTS ■

Authentic student and teacher classroom artifacts are tied to course topics and offer practice in working with the actual types of materials that teachers encounter every day.

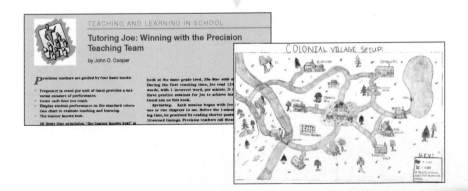

READINGS ■ Specially selected, topically relevant articles from ASCD's renowned *Educational Leadership* journal expand and enrich students' perspectives on key issues and topics.

Other Resources

LESSON & PORTFOLIO BUILDERS ■ With this effective and easy-to-use tool, you can create, update, and share standards-based lesson plans and portfolios.

NEWS ARTICLES ■ Looking for current issues in education? Our collection offers quick access to hundreds of relevant articles from the *New York Times* Educational News Feed.

MyEducationLab is easy to assign, which is essential to providing the greatest benefit to your students. Visit **www.myeducationlab.com** for a demonstration of this exciting new online teaching resource.

[1] Darling-Hammond, L., & Bransford, J., Eds. (2005). *Preparing Teachers for a Changing World.* San Francisco: John Wiley & Sons.

PEARSON
myeducationlab™
Where the Classroom Comes to Life

SEVENTH EDITION

Elementary Social Studies

A Practical Guide

June R. Chapin

Notre Dame de Namur University

PEARSON

Boston • New York • San Francisco
Mexico City • Montreal • Toronto • London • Madrid • Munich • Paris
Hong Kong • Singapore • Tokyo • Cape Town • Sydney

Series Editor: Kelly Villella Canton
Series Editorial Assistant: Christine Pratt Swayne
Executive Marketing Manager: Krista Clark
Composition Buyer: Linda Cox
Manufacturing Buyer: Linda Morris

Editorial Production Service: Omegatype Typography, Inc.
Electronic Composition: Omegatype Typography, Inc.
Interior Design: Omegatype Typography, Inc.
Photo Researcher: Omegatype Typography, Inc.
Cover Administrator: Kristina Mose-Libon

For related titles and support materials, visit our online catalog at www.pearsonhighered.com.

Between the time website information is gathered and then published, it is not unusual for some sites to have closed. Also, the transcription of URLs can result in typographical errors. The publisher would appreciate notification where these errors occur so they may be corrected in subsequent editions.

Library of Congress Cataloging-in-Publication Data

Chapin, June R.
   Elementary social studies : a practical guide / June R. Chapin.—7th ed.
         p. cm.
   Includes bibliographical references and index.
   ISBN-13: 978-0-205-59352-1 (pbk.)
   ISBN-10: 0-205-59352-6 (pbk.)
   1. Social sciences—Study and teaching (Elementary)—United States.
   I. Title.
   LB1584.C47   2009
   372.83'044—dc22   2007039941

Printed in the United States of America

10 9 8 7 6 5 4 3 2 1   12 11 10 09 08

Photo Credits: p. 1, Jonathan Nourok/PhotoEdit; p. 33, Michael Newman/PhotoEdit; p. 73, Bob Daemmrich/Bob Daemmrich Photography, Inc.; p. 110, Tony Freeman/PhotoEdit; p. 142, Brian Smith; p. 183, Robert Harbison; p. 211, Richard Hutchings/PhotoEdit; p. 239, Jose L. Pelaez/Corbis; p. 276, Tom Stewart/Corbis/Bettmann; p. 307, Myrleen Ferguson Cate/PhotoEdit

Allyn and Bacon
is an imprint of

www.pearsonhighered.com

ISBN-10: 0-205-59352-6
ISBN-13: 978-0-205-59352-1

Contents

Chapter 3

Instructional Strategies   73

Chapter 4

Using Multiple Assessments to Evaluate Student Learning in the Social Studies   110

Chapter 5

Aiding Our Students to Interpret History   142

Chapter 6

Teaching Geography   183

Chapter 7

Teaching Economics   210

Chapter 8

Teaching Civic Education   239

Chapter 9

Helping All Our Diverse Students   276

Chapter 10

Linking Social Studies and Literacy   307

Preface

What's New in This Edition

The revisions of this new seventh edition reflect the recent trends affecting the teaching of social studies across the nation.

Technology topics, interspersed throughout all chapters, are indicated by the marginal technology icon. Technology revisions also include new websites and coverage of cyberbullying, video games, blogs, Wikipedia, and stages for using a computer for research.

TECHNOLOGY

Chapter 1 (The Elementary Social Studies Curriculum) brings up to date the challenge of narrowing the social studies curriculum as a result of No Child Left Behind, as well as new material on the status of social studies and textbook changes.

Chapter 2 on planning gives increased attention to Understanding by Design, the backward curriculum model starting with goals clarified and assessment designed before looking at student activities.

Chapter 3 (Instructional Strategies) updates Bloom's taxonomy and concept mapping, includes an increased number of structures for cooperative learning, and discusses pros and cons of banning Wikipedia.

Chapter 4 on assessment includes value-added assessment, best practices with regard to testing, e-portfolios, team testing, more attention to formative assessment, and a summary of characteristics of a good assessment/evaluation system.

Chapter 5 on teaching history emphasizes better quality history instruction for all, including more emphasis on relating topics to present-day issues, improving the holiday history curriculum, National History Day, and debating sources.

There are now full chapters each on the teaching of geography (Chapter 6) and economics (Chapter 7), with new material on projects and lesson plans showing more attention to environment concerns and financial literacy.

Chapter 8 (Teaching Civic Education) further stresses the six goals of the Civic Mission of Schools as well as Constitution Day and global education.

Chapter 9 on diversity emphasizes the changing school population and gives more material on the "boy crisis," overweight children, and elders.

Chapter 10 on literacy has more attention on writing in the social studies, as well as ways to improve readings and listening in the social studies.

The 2001 No Child Left Behind (NCLB) legislation mandated that all students have the right to learn. The increased accountability required by the federal and state governments with their standards and testing has changed how often social studies is taught and evaluated in the elementary school (Chapters 1 and 4). The text makes a case for inclusion of social studies in the elementary curriculum by illustrating how social studies can improve reading, writing, and critical thinking.

After the events of September 11, 2001, and considering the war in Iraq, the issue of teaching patriotism and controversial issues has come to the forefront. Chapter 8 addresses these topics and their implications for developing teaching strategies.

Organization of Text

The first chapter of this reorganized text discusses the basic elementary social studies curriculum. Then Chapters 2 through 4 highlight three interrelated aspects of curriculum development: planning, instructional strategies, and assessment. The next four chapters hone in on the main content and skill emphases of the state standards: teaching of history, geography, economics, and civics. Finally, special attention is given to diversity (Chapter 9) and literacy (Chapter 10), topics that should be diffused throughout the social studies program and emphasized daily. Since teachers are facing increasing diversity in classrooms with ELL students, students with disabilities, as well as differences in ethnic and racial groups, cultures, and social class of the students, related discussion and strategies appear throughout the text.

The importance of the role of the teacher is reaffirmed throughout the chapters. It is the teacher who makes a difference in a social studies program.

Focus of Text

To help educators focus on important concerns, the scope of the text is limited to topics that are *basic, specific,* and yet *critical* to the teaching of the social studies in the elementary and middle school years, kindergarten through eighth grade. To help conceptualize the core information on social studies education, vignettes and other features enrich teachers' knowledge about classroom instruction and curriculum in general. Chapter introductions and definitions of terms provide links to other courses in the area of curriculum and learning. Small group discussion topics, lesson plans, and other activities suggest instructional resources to use when teaching.

The small group and individual exercises integrated into all the chapters, if pursued as part of class time, will help future teachers more thoroughly examine key issues in the text. Time spent doing these exercises with peers enriches critical thinking and reflection about issues related to social studies instruction. Lesson plans, unit outlines, instructional resources, and websites throughout the text suggest activities to try in elementary classes and ideas to build on when planning more extended teaching sequences.

This revision reinforces the primacy of civic education in a democratic society. Too many students grow into adults unable or unwilling to use the knowledge and skills needed to become contributing civic-minded members of their local and wider communities. All the methods and resources necessary to teach participatory democracy to today's students are essential. I believe that the social studies can help make dreams a reality for children, and I invite you to work toward that goal.

Supplements to Accompany the Text

Instructor Manual/Test Bank, prepared by June Chapin, has been updated for the new edition. It includes suggested student activities, resources, and test items for each chapter as well as a "Suggestions to the Instructor" section with general information about journals, standards, organizations, critical autobiographies, service learning, and portfolios.

Your Class. Your Career. Everyone's Future.

"Teacher educators who are developing pedagogies for the analysis of teaching and learning contend that analyzing teaching artifacts has three advantages: it enables new teachers time for reflection while still using the real materials of practice; it provides new teachers with experience thinking about and approaching the complexity of the classroom; and in some cases, it can help new teachers and teacher educators develop a shared understanding and common language about teaching. . . ."[1]

As Linda Darling-Hammond and her colleagues point out, grounding teacher education in real classrooms—among real teachers and students and among actual examples of students' and teachers' work—is an important, and perhaps even an essential, part of training teachers for the complexities of teaching today's students in today's classrooms. For a number of years, we have heard the same message from many of you as we sat in your offices learning about the goals of your courses and the challenges you face in teaching the next generation of educators. Working with a number of our authors and with many of you, we have created a website that provides you and your students with the context of real classrooms and artifacts that research on teacher education tells us is so important. Through authentic in-class video footage, interactive simulations, rich case studies, examples of authentic teacher and student work, and more, **MyEducationLab** offers you and your students a uniquely valuable teacher education tool.

MyEducationLab is easy to use! Wherever the MyEducationLab logo appears in the text, you and your students can follow the simple link instructions to access the **MyEducationLab** resource that corresponds with the chapter content. These include:

- **Video.** Authentic classroom videos show how real teachers handle actual classroom situations.

[1] Darling-Hammond, L., & Bransford, J., Eds. (2005). *Preparing Teachers for a Changing World.* San Francisco: John Wiley & Sons.

- **Homework and Exercises.** These assignable activities give students opportunities to understand content more deeply and to practice applying content.
- **Building Teaching Skills.** These assignments help students practice and strengthen skills that are essential to quality teaching. By analyzing and responding to real student and teacher artifacts and/or authentic classroom videos, students practice important teaching skills they will need when they enter real classrooms.
- **Case Studies.** A diverse set of robust cases drawn from some of our best-selling books further expose students to the realities of teaching and offer valuable perspectives on common issues and challenges in education.
- **Simulations.** Created by the IRIS Center at Vanderbilt University, these interactive simulations give hands-on practice at adapting instruction for a full spectrum of learners.
- **Student and Teacher Artifacts.** Authentic student and teacher classroom artifacts are tied to course topics and offer practice in working with the actual types of materials encountered every day by teachers.
- **Readings.** Specially selected, topically relevant articles from ASCD's renowned *Educational Leadership* journal expand and enrich students' perspectives on key issues and topics.

Other Resources

- **Lesson and Portfolio Builders.** With this effective and easy-to-use tool, you can create, update, and share standards-based lesson plans and portfolios.
- **News Articles.** Looking for current issues in education? Our collection offers quick access to hundreds of relevant articles from the *New York Times* Educational News Feed.

MyEducationLab is easy to assign, which is essential for providing the greatest benefit to your students. Visit www.myeducationlab.com for a demonstration of this exciting new online teaching resource.

Acknowledgments

So many students, classroom teachers, and university colleagues throughout the country have been instrumental in shaping this textbook, and a great debt is owed to them. From them, I have seen teachers make a positive difference in the lives of children and feel privileged to watch children gain opportunities through education. Our reviewers, in particular, served an important role in improving and updating this text for the seventh edition: Barbara Perry-Sheldon, NC Wesleyan College; Roger D. Wolf, University of South Dakota; and Jacquelyn A. Lewis-Harris, University of Missouri.

June R. Chapin is a professor of education at
Notre Dame de Namur University. She is the author or co-author
of over a dozen textbooks ranging from the fourth grade to the
university level. Civic education is her greatest interest and primary
research area.

CHAPTER 1

The Elementary Social Studies Curriculum

In this chapter, we examine the many factors that are transforming the social studies curriculum, including the impact of No Child Left Behind, state standards, renewed interest in civic education, textbook changes wanted by different interest groups, technology, and more diverse students. The following topics are considered here:

- What Are Your Images of the Social Studies?
- What Is Social Studies and What Are the Goals of Social Studies?
- What Should Be Taught? State Standards and No Child Left Behind (NCLB)
- Should Values Be Taught?
- What Are the National Curriculum Patterns?
- Why Are Textbooks and Technology Important?

Why is social studies more than maps and globes?

What Are Your Images of the Social Studies?

Welcome to the world of social studies! What do you remember about your elementary social studies program? If any of the following activities seem familiar, jot down on a piece of paper whether the memory is pleasant.

Clipping out items from a newspaper for Friday current events

Doing a research report on Daniel Boone from your school's encyclopedia

Finding out the latitude and longitude of a long list of cities

Learning about the Pilgrims at Thanksgiving

Going on a field trip to a site where your state's American Indians lived

Answering the questions at the end of a textbook chapter

Writing to foreign consuls and embassies for information about your assigned country

Reenacting pioneer life

Singing patriotic songs

Preparing and serving different ethnic foods

Writing a personal history book

Drawing neighborhood maps

Working on a committee for a group project

Learning about the immigrant groups from which you came

Viewing films

Writing a book report on a famous American

Small Group Work 1.1

What Works Best?

I have used this exercise with classes many times. Often I have heard I loved doing . . . , but sometimes it was *I hated.* . . . This exercise points out that your days as an elementary student years ago are influencing your image of the social studies. Your images act as a filter as you make judgments about what a good social studies program is and what methods should be used to achieve social studies goals.

Now add to this list the activities that you remember experiencing in elementary social studies. Try to include both pleasant and boring times. Compare with others in the group your list of what you liked and didn't like. Are there activities that everyone remembers enjoying? Are there other activities that everyone disliked? Your image of elementary social studies stems mainly from your own experiences. Can you now draw a simple picture or graphic that summarizes either positively or negatively your experiences as a social studies student? What one descriptive word best pulls together your image of the social studies? Do you think teachers teach much in the way they were taught? ●

Role-playing a character

Finding new information

In North Carolina during the 2005–2006 school year, over 300 elementary teachers rated social studies as their third priority after reading/language arts and mathematics. The authors were worried that with the new implementation of a science test, social studies would be relegated to fourth place.[1]

Elementary teachers often have negative attitudes toward the social studies as a result of their own school experiences, perhaps because of the following:

Learning about social studies largely emphasized trivial facts.

The dominant instructional tool was the textbook.

Most social studies activities concentrated on large group recitation and lecture.

Emotional or affective objectives were not included as part of the curriculum.

Small Group Work 1.2

How Important Is Social Studies to You?

How do you rank the importance of social studies in the elementary curriculum? Look at the following list of traditional subjects taught in elementary school.

Health/physical education (PE)
Mathematics
Reading/language arts
Science
Social studies

Now rank these subjects, 1 through 5, in order of their importance to you. Share your list with other members of your group. Most elementary teachers and students rank social studies third or lower. If your ranking was within this range, what influenced your response? ●

In addition, although students on a national survey looked forward to social studies and were not afraid to ask questions in social studies, they did not think social studies was as useful as math, English, and science. Many students do not see the link between their social studies program and social participation in the classroom, school, community, nation, and the world.

Two other reasons may account, at least in part, for the less than enthusiastic attitude that many elementary teachers have toward the social studies: lack of preparation and lack of interest. Many of you have taken only a few social science or history courses in college. You may feel underqualified or reluctant to tackle the sometimes controversial subject matter of the social studies. Many of you may feel strongly that reading and math programs are basic in elementary education; however, a social studies program is also basic. In fact, a good social studies program can go far toward improving students' skills in other subjects, including reading, writing, and math.

The basic purpose of social studies is **civic education** or **citizenship education.** The terms *citizenship education* and *civic education* are used interchangeably but *civic education* is now becoming the more popular term. A good social studies program can contribute to producing good citizens. I believe in the *vital* importance of social studies instruction, both to prepare students to become responsible, thoughtful, participating citizens and to provide

---

[1]Tracy Rock, Tina Heafner, Katherine O'Connor, Jeff Passe, Sandra Oldendorf, and Amy Good. "One State Closer to a National Crisis: A Report on Elementary Social Studies Education in North Carolina Schools." *Theory & Research in Social Education* 34, no. 4 (Fall 2006): 463.

students with the basic skills that they need to function in our society. If I am successful in transmitting these beliefs to you, then social studies teaching at least in your classrooms may not suffer the neglect that otherwise often occurs at the primary level.

This text will help you find ways of teaching powerful social studies that you and your students will find enjoyable, rewarding, and meaningful. Social studies *can* be taught creatively and thoughtfully. As a result of your efforts, students may find that social studies is their favorite subject. More important, through *your* social studies instruction, your students will acquire the necessary knowledge, skills, and values to participate as active citizens in our society and the global community. It is also important that you as a teacher exhibit a personal interest in the social studies, show enthusiasm for the content, and model intellectual curiosity.

What Is Social Studies and What Are the Goals of Social Studies?

What Is Social Studies?

From your images of social studies, you can see that teachers have different understandings of what social studies is and how social studies should be presented to students. In particular, the aftermath of September 11, 2001 (9/11), with the war against terrorism and the conflict in Iraq has evoked concerns about the teaching of patriotism and how teachers should teach controversial events such as globalism (more in Chapter 8).

The differences among teachers also include disagreement on what should be the appropriate **content** or defining attributes of social studies. Look at your state's framework or curriculum documents. Is the title *Social Studies*? Or is it *History/Social Sciences? Social Studies* implies an integrated approach whereas *History/Social Sciences* connotes a separate subject approach.

The National Council for the Social Studies (NCSS), established in 1921, is the national professional organization of teachers concerned about social studies. The national organization publishes *Social Education* and, for the elementary grades, *Social Studies and the Young Learner.* In addition, NCSS also has many state and regional councils. Most state councils also publish journals and newsletters for their members, in addition to holding annual conferences. NCSS is the major advocate for the teaching of social studies and along with the state councils tries to influence legislation concerning social studies, such as No Child Left Behind (NCLB). Your membership in NCSS and your state or regional council could help your professional development; they would welcome your membership. In 1992 the NCSS adopted its integrated definition of the field.

> Social studies is the integrated study of the social sciences and humanities to promote civic competence. Within the school program, social studies provides coordinated, systematic study drawing upon such disciplines as anthropology, archaeology, economics, geography, history, law, philosophy, political science, psychology, religion, and sociology, as well as appropriate content from the humanities, mathematics, and natural sciences. The primary purpose of social studies is to help young people develop the ability to make informed and

Table 1.1	NCSS Curriculum Themes/Standards

1. Culture (anthropology)
2. Time, continuity, and change (history)
3. People, places, and environments (geography)
4. Individual development and identity (psychology)
5. Individuals, groups, and institutions (sociology)
6. Power, authority, and governance (political science)
7. Production, distribution, and consumption (economics)
8. Science, technology, and society
9. Global connections
10. Civic ideals and practice

Source: Expectations of Excellence: Curriculum Standards for Social Studies, Task Force of the National Council for the Social Studies, Bulletin 89, Washington, DC, 1994.

reasoned decisions for the public good as citizens of a culturally diverse, democratic society in an interdependent world.[2]

In addition, when NCSS published its national standards in 1994, it reaffirmed its commitment to an integrated approach drawing its content from seven disciplines: history, geography, political science, economics, psychology, sociology, and anthropology (Table 1.1). The first seven standards were based on the major concepts of the social sciences and history. The last three standards were broadly based themes that included several subject areas. An integrated approach assumes that many issues such as health care and crime are multidisciplinary in nature. In other words, you need knowledge from several disciplines, not just one social science or history, to think intelligently about the subject.

These themes/standards will be elaborated more in Chapters 5 though 8. In addition, going to NCSS's own website (www.ncss.org) gives more detail on each of the standards. Bulletin 89 with 178 pages containing the full NCSS standards illustrates the spirit and essence of NCSS's commitment to an integrated approach and the need for powerful social studies (Figure 1.1).

Note that these NCSS Standards were published in 1994 and are many years old. Therefore, NCSS is in the process of revising these standards, but they certainly will keep true to their integrated approach. In particular, there has been criticism that the NCSS themes/standards are too broad to be helpful for individual day-to-day planning. Also, many want explicit connections to content standards developed by other academic disciplines through national organizations such as the National Council on Economic Education and the National Center for History in the Schools, to be linked to the NCSS Standards.

[2]Task Force of the National Council for the Social Studies, *Expectations of Excellence: Curriculum Standards for Social Studies*, Bulletin 89 (Washington, DC: National Council for the Social Studies, 1994): 3.

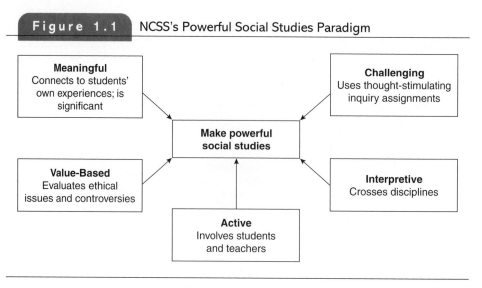

Figure 1.1   NCSS's Powerful Social Studies Paradigm

What Are the Goals of Social Studies?

The main purpose or rationale for teaching the social studies is civic education or citizenship education. There are four major goals for civic education. Goals are very broad and general. Therefore, almost everyone agrees with these expansive aims and there is no controversy about goals.

1. To acquire **knowledge** from the social sciences, history, and humanities
2. To develop **skills** to think and to process information
3. To develop appropriate democratic **values** and **beliefs**
4. To have opportunities for **citizenship/social participation**

These four goals are not separate and discrete. Usually they are intertwined and overlapping (see Figure 1.2). You may find in some state standards or frameworks that two goals are combined. Social participation may be regarded as a democratic value or the goal may be stated as "skill attainment and social participation." The knowledge goal can be referred to as "knowledge and cultural understanding" or "democratic understanding and civic values." Values may sometimes be called **civic** values to differentiate them from **personal** values. But regardless of how the goals are combined or written, together they form the basic goals of a social studies program. Although these goals may take several years of student learning, the schools can and should focus their social studies program on these four main social studies goals, realizing that goals are not achieved in one day, one week, or even one year. Goals such as good health and good citizenship are pursued by individuals for decades and in a certain sense are never completely achieved.

As these goals indicate, social studies is about people and, thus, builds on an inherently high interest. Each of us is concerned about self, family, and friends, and social

Figure 1.2   Goals of the Social Studies

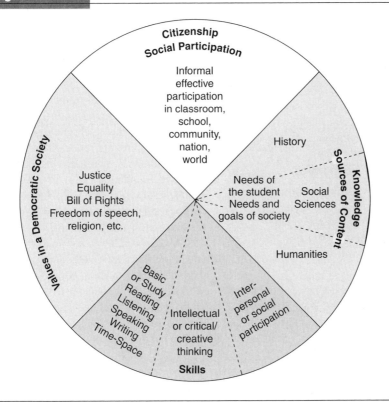

studies is designed to help us understand ourselves and our nearby neighbors as well as those who live halfway around the world. Creative social studies instruction offers the possibility of humane individuals who incorporate basic American values such as equality, freedom, and respect for property and who are able to put these values into action through effective participation in the classroom, school, community, nation, and the world. Again, this emphasizes the main purpose of the social studies curriculum: citizenship education.

Frequently, the process of learning has emotional values attached to it. Did you *hate* math in school? Did you *love* music? For example, when students study pollution, they usually acquire opinions or attitudes about it. Emotional concerns such as racism in the community can have a striking impact on both subject area and students' skill development. Certain skills such as writing or thinking may be taught in school, but there is no guarantee that students will make use of them. Unless students have a commitment to, a need for, or a willingness to use the skills they have learned, those skills will be of little value either to the students or to society. All this underlines the connections among the four main goals of a social studies education; although we may speak of each one separately, we must not forget their inherent interrelationships.

More Emphasis on History

Especially after 9/11 (2001), critics of the integrated NCSS social studies approach became more vocal about what they considered wrong with the social studies. In their view, instruction should be divided into academic disciplines like history or geography. They view the social studies approach as academically flabby, "dumbing down" the content. In addition, for these critics, social studies teachers do not emphasize American values enough. These detractors of the social studies approach generally want more emphasis on history, particularly history with a chronological approach. These viewpoints are reflected by Chester Finn[3] of the Thomas B. Fordham Foundation (a conservative foundation) who in 2003 described social studies as "long on multiculturalism, feelings, relativism, and tolerance but short on history, civics, and patriotism."[4]

On Your Own **1.1**

Social Studies or History, Civics, Geography, and Economics

What is your response to Chester Finn's remarks on social studies? Do you think his viewpoint is reflected by many of the parents in the schools in which you are teaching or will teach? ●

At a general level everyone espouses civic education, but individuals and groups vary on their definition of civic education and what a good citizen does. Chester Finn's views are most closely associated with the citizenship transmission model. Robert Barr, a social studies educator, and his colleagues defined the first three main social studies traditions, shown in Table 1.2. Note that all the approaches emphasize the broad goal of citizenship education but differ on how to achieve this goal.

[3]James Leming, Lucien Ellington, and Kathleen Porter, eds., *Where Did Social Studies Go Wrong?* (Washington, DC: Thomas B. Fordham Foundation, 2003).

[4]Chester E. Finn, Jr., "Why This Report?" in *Terrorists, Despots, and Democracy: What Our Children Need to Know* (Washington, DC: Thomas B. Fordham Foundation, 2003).

| Table 1.2 | Different Approaches to Civic Education |

Approach	Goals of Civic Education
1. Citizenship transmission	Students are taught traditional knowledge and values as a framework for making decisions.
2. Social science/history	Students master social science/history concepts, generalizations, and methods.
3. Reflective inquiry	Students use knowledge and thinking to make decisions and to solve problems.
4. Social action/justice	Students develop understanding and skills needed to critique and transform society; often a focus on injustice/inequality.
5. Child-centered	Students develop a positive self-concept and a strong sense of personal efficacy.

Source: Robert D. Barr, James L. Barth, and S. Samuel Shermis, *Defining the Social Studies,* Bulletin 51 (Washington, DC: National Council for the Social Studies, 1977). Reprinted with permission of the National Council for the Social Studies.

In a more recent analysis of civic education approaches, Westheimer and Kahne[5] outlined three main conceptions of the "good" citizen.

1. personally responsible citizen—more the character education approach
2. participatory citizen—active member of the community
3. justice-oriented citizen—critically assesses structures

Note that each of these conceptions differs on what skills and values students *need* to become good citizens.

Your Choice

You can see now that definitions of social studies content will vary depending on the value system or philosophical orientation of the teacher or curriculum planner. The citizenship-transmission approach tends to emphasize U.S. history and our nation's high ideals and achievements. The social science/history approach uses content from the various social science disciplines and history with a view to understanding the major concepts and the respective methods of gathering data. The reflective-inquiry and informed social action/ justice approaches use almost any content as long as it encourages thinking on the part of students. The child-centered/character education approaches focus on personal development.

On Your Own **1.2**

Compare the Approaches

Which approach or model (see Table 1.2 and consider the other civic education approaches mentioned) do you feel most comfortable with? List the strengths and weaknesses of each approach on a piece of paper. Which approaches are seen most frequently in elementary classrooms? ●

What Should Be Taught? State Standards and No Child Left Behind (NCLB)

*P*rodded by the 1983 federal report, *A Nation at Risk*,[6] which questioned American students' ability to compete in a global economy, and conferences by the nation's governors in 1995, the fifty states in our nation embarked on a standards-based education reform effort. Reform implies something is wrong and changes are needed. **Standards** are what teachers are supposed to teach and students are expected to know (content) and be able to do (performance). Standards are useful for the following reasons:

1. To guide curriculum planning to improve student learning
2. To encourage best practices

[5]Joel Westheimer and Joseph Kahne, "Educating the 'Good' Citizen: The Politics of School-Based Civic Education Programs." Paper presented at the Annual Meeting of the American Political Science Association, Boston, MA, 2002.

[6]*A Nation at Risk: The Imperative for Education Reform.* Prepared by the National Commission in Education (Washington, DC: U.S. Department of Education, April 1983).

3. To guide professional development for teachers where it is needed
4. To prioritize resources such as money for texts, media, and the like.

National Standards

In response to the need for national standards, professional organizations related to the field of social studies then published their national standards. The National Council for the Social Studies (NCSS) had ten broad curriculum themes/standards with five process (skill) standards (see Table 1.1). Four other groups wrote separate discipline standards for history, geography, civics and government, and economics. (These will be discussed more in Chapters 5 through 8.) Much later in 1999 the American Psychological Association published its standards for the teaching of high school psychology, which has had little impact except on high school psychology classes.

At the heart of the reform-based standards effort was the question: *What is the most essential knowledge of the discipline or the social studies?* Answering this question has led to a greater emphasis on students' understanding the major concepts or the big ideas of the subject area and learning the ways of thinking of the discipline, the particular methods used for investigation of knowledge.

The 1994–1995 political outcry over the proposed national history standards ended any possibility of national consensus on history standards (Chapter 5). In addition, conservatives feared increased federal control over the state and local boards of education. Liberals, in turn, worried that the standards movement would stifle educators, be culturally biased, and lead to further standardization. These concerns shifted the development of standards to the states. The states took corrective action to reform schools.

Raising standards presently has widespread approval and strikes a responsive chord with the public and political candidates. Who can argue for low standards? Parents want their children to be adequately prepared for the world of work in the twenty-first century, which means having knowledge and basic skills such as reading and math as well as being technologically literate. Parents are also exposed to the media focusing on urban and rural low-performing schools with little coverage on successful students and schools. These increased perceptions about the "failed public school system" have led to a debate about charter schools, vouchers, and the rapid rise of home schooling. Parents want the power to make choices about the type of school their children attend. Given these anxieties and fears, the standards movement to reform the schools by requiring students to demonstrate by tests certain knowledge and skills makes sense to parents and the public.

State Standards

Now almost every state has adopted standards for the social studies. States have faced two problems in developing standards for the social studies. First, should there be one set of interdisciplinary social studies standards, such as Wisconsin's standards, or should standards be developed in each of the related areas, such as history, geography, economics, and civics? Many states choose to list four separate standards for history, geography, economics, and civics. Second, how should the standards deal with the many value issues and political interpretations so common in the social studies? Here to avoid the firestorm of the detailed national history standards, most states have moved into broad statements. But they have also included more civic standards compared to the national standards.

The state standards for social studies often built on a compilation of national standards developed by NCSS and the four subject areas—history, geography, civics, and economics. The other behavioral sciences such as sociology and psychology were deemphasized. The work on the state's standards often was then repeated by groups at the school district level that prepared their own local versions of the standards because of the desire to keep local control, meet the needs of the community, and to give teachers a stake in the ownership of the standards. To avoid political controversy, the standards were often loosely defined.

To understand this better, let us first discuss the many meanings of the term **curriculum.** In the most general sense curriculum consists of both the **plans** for learning and the actual **delivery** of those plans. Standards are really **curriculum or learning standards** or guides for use in curriculum planning. Your state with its standards or local district may have a **required or recommended curriculum,** which can be mandatory for all teachers. This required curriculum is typically written and spelled out and is often called the **official curriculum** or framework. It has been formally adopted by the state or local board. But what teachers actually do in their classrooms is the **taught curriculum.** The **tested/assessed curriculum** is the curriculum that is revealed in tests and other assessments given to students. Sometimes these are called **performance standards,** which measure mastery or levels of attainment in a given content topic or skill.[7]

Changing States' Roles and NCLB

By 2001, President George W. Bush and Congress were not satisfied with the progress that states had made. For them, state standards had failed to produce significant gains in the academic achievement for four subgroups of students: low-income students, minority students, English language learners (ELLs), and students with disabilities. These students had the right to learn but were challenging to educate, and it appeared the goals of equity were not being met.

By a vote of 87–10 in the Senate and 381–41 in the House, a bipartisan Congress then passed the biggest education reform act in a quarter century. The No Child Left Behind Act (NCLB) was a commitment to standards-based reform. Through NCLB, all schools were to be held to high, measurable standards set by the individual states to raise student achievement for all groups. The NCLB Act mandated broad accountability, requiring all states to test children in grades three through eight in reading, math, and science. Furthermore, schools failing to achieve specific performance targets faced serious sanctions, including providing vouchers to parents for out-of-school programs and eventually replacing the school staff or converting failing schools to charter schools.

This ambitious act required states to establish *their own* annual tests aligned with *their own state standards.* Standards were to be clear, with measurable goals focused on basic skills and essential knowledge. This has resulted in great diversity among state standards and what a given state considers to be proficient students.

---

[7]Allan A. Glatthorn, *Curriculum Renewal* (Alexandria, VA: Association for Supervision and Curriculum Development, 1987).

By 2004 a revolt against NCLB was building in state legislatures. Although most parents expressed support for the concept of school reforms, many were reluctant to punish schools for failure, especially if only one subgroup in the school did not make progress. Parents also believe that it is unrealistic to expect students with disabilities and English language learners to successfully pass tests. Legislatures were upset over the stringency of testing requirements, the large number of schools put on probation, and the cost of implementation. Tension existed between the educational policies of the federal government and the control of education at the state and local level. The states were not entirely free to control their own educational policies because opting out of the NCLB framework caused them to lose funds from the federal government. This unfunded mandate caused an outcry. There was pressure on the federal government's Department of Education to modify some of the rules. In response, some of the regulations of NCLB were relaxed. It is expected that there will be future changes in the law or changes in the interpretation of the mandates by the Department of Education. Many believe that NCLB could be simplified and improved while still holding public education accountable for student learning. However, many state and federal policies also need to change. In particular, state standards should be reduced in number. Too-long lists of standards for many subjects are daunting for even the most dedicated teachers. Hopefully as states prepare for the next cycle of review for standards, they will identify fewer goals for each grade level.

Narrowing the Curriculum?

Many believe with testing of students emphasized in reading/language arts and math, social studies and other subjects like music and art have received less attention than in the past. Science also has often been neglected but this may change with the required testing in science. From newspaper accounts, the narrowing of the curriculum is probably most prevalent in schools with a rating of "In Need of Improvement" or at the primary-grade level.

What evidence is there for social studies being neglected? The Center on Education Policy in a national survey in 2004 showed that 27 percent of districts reported social studies "reduced somewhat or to a great extent" whereas 69 percent of the districts reported social studies as minimally or not at all reduced.[8] You can at once see the difficulties in estimating the time spent on social studies or any other subject due to variation in how much time teachers spend on different subjects from day to day and week to week. In addition, a further difficulty in interpretation is that social studies is often integrated with reading or other subject areas, and the time devoted to social studies may therefore be underestimated.

Time Spent

Large surveys of what teachers report are valuable, but even here teachers' reports on how much time they spend on different subjects may be overestimates. I looked at the data from the Early Childhood Longitudinal Study, a national sample of 20,000 kindergartners and first graders. There were about 8,000 teachers in this study who were asked to give their estimates on time allocations for social studies topics. The most popular topic taught in the first grade

[8]Center on Education Policy, *NCLB: Narrowing the Curriculum?* (Washington, DC, Center on Education Policy, 2005).

was Key Events in American History. Given the popularity of the holiday curriculum in the social studies, probably this topic included attention to Thanksgiving (Pilgrims and Indians), Presidents in February, Columbus Day, and the like. For first-grade social studies, 42 percent reported 1 to 30 minutes a day and 32 percent 31 to 60 minutes a day. Given the wide range of 1 to 30 minutes, it is difficult to ascertain if most first-grade teachers taught social studies an average of 5 minutes a day or 20 minutes a day.[9]

A national survey of about 1,000 teachers in the second, fifth, and eighth grades indicated that fifth-grade teachers spent much more time devoted to social studies than second-grade teachers. Only 8 percent of the fifth-grade teachers spent less than two hours a week devoted to social studies. Time for fifth-grade social studies was indicated by the following results: two to three hours (23 percent), three to four hours (26 percent), four to five hours (22 percent), and five hours or more (22 percent). In contrast, 34 percent of second-grade teachers spent under two hours a week teaching social studies. The most popular second-grade category was 29 percent of the social studies in the two to three hour range, followed by 16 percent at three to four hours and then decreasing amounts of time. Asked about the influence of state testing, 24 percent of the second-grade teachers and 28 percent of the fifth-grade teachers reported spending less time teaching social studies. On the other hand, 62 percent of second-grade teachers and 60 percent of fifth-grade teachers[10] reported about the same amount of time for social studies.

What do surveys of states indicate about the status of elementary social studies? Let us look at surveys of teachers in Indiana and North Carolina that do not have statewide social studies assessments. In a total sample of 594 Indiana teachers, K–3 teachers, on the average, were spending about 12 minutes per day or about one hour per week on social studies. Intermediate Indiana teachers doubled the amount of time spent with at least 120 minutes (two hours) per week or more than 24 minutes per day on social studies instruction. In North Carolina, most teachers reported that students received social studies instruction two or three days a week (39.7 percent). Surprisingly, daily instructional time was the highest in kindergarten and the fifth grade. However, on the whole, K–2 North Carolina teachers spent less time teaching social studies than grades 3 to 6 teachers. In terms of teaching the North Carolina state standards, 36 percent of the K–2 teachers devoted time to the standards compared to 55 percent of the grades 3 to 6 teachers. Both the Indiana and North Carolina researchers expressed great alarm about the crisis in the teaching of social studies.[11] On the whole, it appears that there are justifiable concerns about social studies being crowded out of the curriculum, especially at the primary-grade levels.

A Need for Even Higher Standards?

While the debate continues on what should or should not be done about NCLB and whether or not social studies is being neglected, a high profile group of education, business, and

[9]June R. Chapin, "The Achievement Gap in Social Studies and Science Knowledge Starts Early: Evidence from the Early Childhood Longitudinal Study, *The Social Studies* 97, no. 6 (November/December 2006): 231–238.

[10]James S. Leming, Lucien Ellington, and Mark Schug, *Social Studies in Our Nation's Elementary and Middle Schools: A National Random Survey of Social Studies Teachers' Professional Opinions, Values, and Classroom Practices* (Storrs, CT: The Center for Survey Research and Analysis, 2006).

[11]Phillip J. Van Fossen, "'Reading and Math Take So Much of the Time . . .': An Overview of Social Studies Instruction in Elementary Classrooms in Indiana," *Theory and Research in Social Education*, 33, no. 3 (Summer 2005): 376–403. Tracy Rock et al., "One State Closer to a National Crisis: A Report on Elementary Social Studies Education in North Carolina Schools," *Theory and Research in Social Education* 34, no. 4 (Fall 2006): 455–483.

political leaders announced that aiming for NCLB competency in reading and math is just a meager beginning. Globalization requires much greater changes for all schools. In their report, the National Center on Education and the Economy, a nonprofit group partly financed by the Bill and Melinda Gates foundation plus other foundations, urged an even more drastic redesign of the American K–12 public schools to make the nation more competitive globally.[12] For the 21st century, students need to be competent in traditional academic disciplines but also know more about the world, become smarter about new sources of information, and develop good people skills, as well as being able to think outside the box. Here is a partial list of their recommendations: universal preschool, extra resources for at-risk students, state control of school finances to equalize funding, exams in the tenth grade, increasing salaries with merit pay to attract talented young teachers. Many agreed with the shortcomings of the present system but felt that some of the recommendations were too radical. Thus, it appears that there will be a continuing debate even beyond the accommodations to weaken NCLB on what the schools should be like in the 21st century. What should be the highest priorities of the schools? Stress equity by removing achievement gaps by focusing on the lowest-performing schools as in NCLB? Or prepare for our nation's future competitiveness and well-being with more attention on higher-ability students?

The goals of NCLB are beyond reproach, and it has brought a modicum of academic progress, especially for students who otherwise might receive little attention. NCLB has shown a wider audience which students are not making progress. In terms of this book, however, the most serious negative impact of NCLB has been that in many classrooms the social studies program has been neglected. Unfortunately, too many teachers are not connecting reading and writing skills to the social studies program and are not using trade books on social studies topics, areas which would help learning both in language arts/reading as well as the social studies program (more in Chapter 10).

Examples of Social Studies Standards

There are strengths and weaknesses to having social studies content standards. First, the standards movement has placed greater emphasis on the major concepts or key ideas along with the methodology of the discipline. This could help to focus the elementary curriculum. Some states have reported increased scores on achievement tests. Second, by focusing on every student and not just the brighter students, the standards movement could improve education, especially if there were a financial commitment to create the proper educational conditions for achievement. Too often in the past, in a given state or even in the same district, two different classrooms on the same grade level had wildly different social studies content or too little content, violating students' equal access to the curriculum. There has been little consistency in how much time students spend on a given subject or the knowledge or skills emphasized within that subject area. The real challenge of reform is reaching all students.

In addition, standards can help teachers and their students to be clear about their purposes by developing coherent goals for learning. Students can find standards to be helpful when teachers spell out criteria for high-quality work, explain how the work will be assessed, and give examples of what the work looks like. Students then have a better idea of what to do and how to do it. When goals and expectations are very clear, more students can meet them.

---

[12]National Center on Education and the Economy, *Tough Choices or Tough Times: The Report of the New Commission on the Skills of the American Workforce* (San Francisco, CA: Jossey-Bass, 2006).

Teachers also have found that some standards encourage them to expand the traditional elementary social studies content, especially geography and economic content, as well as giving a benchmark for teaching successfully. Standards need not limit the creativity of teachers. Teachers still can use a wide range of approaches to have their students meet the standards. Furthermore, looking carefully at students' work in comparison to standards can help teachers, students, and students' families understand what students know and what can be done to support further learning. Standards have also encouraged closer cooperation among teachers, especially those on the same grade level, to share and to critique the work of students and promising lesson plans. Although few teachers "have learned to love the test," teachers now pay more attention to the alignment of curriculum and instruction to the standards and assessment.

However, critics of the standards movement cite negative consequences of the standards movement: teaching to the test, more student dropouts, rigid curriculum, cheating, more grade retention that does not help students' motivation, and more pressure on students who need the most help. Teachers note the following specific criticisms about state standards:

1. Standards are not age appropriate.
2. There is too much content specified for the grade level.
3. In contrast to being too specific in content, standards may be too general.
4. There is less attention to multicultural/global education.

Let us check some of these criticisms by examining Virginia's history standards for grade 3 as shown in Table 1.3. For the third grade in Virginia there were also geography, economics, and civics standards.

Table 1.3   Virginia's History–Social Science Standards, Grade 3

The standards for third-grade students include an introduction to the heritage and contributions of the people of ancient Greece and Rome and the West African empire of Mali. Students should continue developing map skills and demonstrate an understanding of basic economic concepts. Students will explain the importance of the basic principles of democracy and identify the contributions of selected individuals. Students will recognize that Americans are a people who have diverse ethnic origins, customs, and traditions, who all contribute to American life, and who are united as Americans by common principles.

History

3.1 The student will explain how the contributions of ancient Greece and Rome have influenced the present world in terms of architecture, government (direct and representative democracy), and sports.

3.2 The student will study the early West African empire of Mali by describing its oral tradition (storytelling), government (kings), and economic development (trade).

3.3 The student will study the exploration of the Americas by

    a) describing the accomplishments of Christopher Columbus, Juan Ponce de Leon, Jacques Cartier, and Christopher Newport;

    b) identifying reasons for exploring, the information gained, and the results from the travels.

Source: Virginia Board of Education, *History and Social Science Standards of Learning for Virginia Public Schools* (Richmond, 2001). These standards are presently being revised but minimum changes are expected.

On Your Own **1.3**

What Is Your Reaction to State Social Studies Standards?

Looking at the brief descriptions of Virginia and California's standards, do you think the standards are age appropriate? Too much content? Will the standards promote creative thinking? Or will they be a list of facts for students to memorize? Or will it depend on the teacher? Realize that you are seeing only a small part of the description of the standards and there is wide variation among the states in terms of their level of detail and degree of prescriptiveness. Check the social studies standards and state assessment (if any) of your state. These are usually available on the Internet. Search by using your state's name followed by Department of Education (e.g., Alabama Department of Education) or Department of Public Instruction (e.g., Delaware Department of Public Instruction). In a few cases the title may be different (e.g., Minnesota Department of Children, Families, and Learning). ●

Another pattern is illustrated by California in its content specifications for statewide assessment by standard (Table 1.4).

Should Values Be Taught?

Role Model

*Y*ou are an important role model. Your actions in and even out of the classroom are carefully observed by your students. Students make judgments on whether you really like them and whether you are fair. In effect, your behavior shows a "proper" way of how to act. Thus, a teacher has been described as a moral compass pointing out to students the accurate direction and the way to act. All values education approaches acknowledge the importance of the teacher as a role model.

Everything you do reflects your values. This leads to the importance of teaching **values**, the strongly held standards or criteria we use in making judgments about people, places, and things. Sometimes the phrases *beliefs and values*, *attitudes*, or *dispositions* are used. Surveys show overwhelmingly that the public and parents want the schools to teach basic values such as honesty, respect, and responsibility. But how, as teachers, do you do this?

Values

Schools have always taught values and moral development through textbooks, teachers, and school rules. Values are presented by the way teachers treat students and the way students are allowed to treat teachers and each other. There is a **hidden curriculum** of what is right and wrong, even when questions of right and wrong do not come up directly in the classroom. Every classroom has rules that embody values. "Children should put or store their possessions in certain places in the room." "Raise your hand if you wish to speak." These rules are more than just classroom management techniques. They communicate to children what is required to be good students. These rules teach important lessons about authority, responsibility, caring, respect, punctuality, working in teams, and so on.

Teaching values directly often becomes restricted to teaching broad civic values such as justice and public responsibilities—voting, obeying the law, paying taxes, and serving on a jury. These public values have a high level of acceptance at an abstract level by almost all members of the community, although concrete issues such as capital punishment and police rights engender wide controversy. The primary organization in the field of social studies, the National Council for the Social Studies, lists thirty-one democratic beliefs and values grouped in the following four categories:

| Table 1.4 | California—Grade Two: People Who Make a Difference |

2.1 Students differentiate between things that happened long ago and things that happened yesterday. (A History Standard)

   1. Trace the history of a family through the use of primary and secondary sources, including artifacts, photographs, interviews, and documents.
   2. Compare and contrast their daily lives with those of their parents, grandparents, and/or guardians.
   3. Place important events in their lives in the order in which they occurred (e.g., on a time line or storyboard).

2.2 Students demonstrate map skills by describing the absolute and relative locations of people, places, and environments. (A Geography Standard)

   1. Locate on a simple letter–number grid system the specific locations and geographic features in their neighborhood or community (e.g., map of the classroom, the school).
   2. Label from memory a simple map of the North American continent, including the countries, oceans, Great Lakes, major rivers, and mountain ranges. Identify the essential map elements: title, legend, directional indicator, scale, and date.
   3. Locate on a map where their ancestors live(d), telling when the family moved to the local community and how and why they made the trip.
   4. Compare and contrast basic land use in urban, suburban, and rural environments in California.

2.3 Students explain governmental institutions and practices in the United States and other countries. (A Civics Standard)

   1. Explain how the United States and other countries make laws, carry out laws, determine whether laws have been violated, and punish wrongdoers.
   2. Describe the ways in which groups and nations interact with one another to try to resolve problems in such areas as trade, cultural contacts, treaties, diplomacy, and military force.

2.4 Students understand basic economic concepts and their individual roles in the economy and demonstrate basic economic reasoning skills. (An Economic Standard)

   1. Describe food production and consumption long ago and today, including the roles of farmers, processors, distributors, weather, and land and water resources.
   2. Understand the role and interdependence of buyers (consumers) and sellers (producers) of goods and services.
   3. Understand how limits on resources affect production and consumption (what to produce and what to consume).

2.5 Students understand the importance of individual action and character and explain how heroes from long ago and the recent past have made a difference in others' lives (e.g., from biographies of Abraham Lincoln, Louis Pasteur, Sitting Bull, George Washington Carver, Marie Curie, Albert Einstein, Golda Meir, Jackie Robinson, Sally Ride) (An Ethical, Value Standard)

Source: History-Social Science Framework for California Public Schools Kindergarten Through Grade Twelve. Updated Edition, California State Department of Education, Sacramento, CA. 2001, pp. 46–47.

Table 1.5	Approaches to Major Values Education	

Approach	Purpose	Method
Caring (Noddings)	Care for self Care for others	Modeling, dialogue, practice, and confirmation
Moral development (Kohlberg)	Students develop higher set of values	Moral dilemmas, small group discussion, teacher in devil's advocate role
Values clarification (Simon et al.)	Students become aware of their own values Students identify values of others	Variety of methods, self-analysis exercises
Social action	Students have opportunities for social action based on their values	Projects in schools and in community
Indoctrination	Values of students change in desired direction	Variety of methods, selective data provided
Analysis	Students use logical thinking to decide values issues	Rational discussion, research

Note: Difficulties arise when trying to place certain programs such as substance abuse approaches like the Drug Abuse Resistance Education (D.A.R.E.) program, which stress self-esteem and drug-free behavior. Some would classify these programs as indoctrination while others would put them in the analysis approach since they may use medical research as a data source. There is a similar problem with many of the character education approaches.

1. Rights of the Individual (life, liberty, justice, security, privacy, etc.)
2. Freedoms of the Individual (worship, thought, assembly, etc.)
3. Responsibilities of the Individual (honesty, respect rights of others, etc.)
4. Beliefs Concerning Societal Conditions and Governmental Responsibilities (elections, civil liberties, minorities protected, common good, etc.)[13]

Few educators or parents would dispute the inclusion of teaching these general public values in the classroom, but more controversial are social/moral issues and personal values. The differing viewpoints of community members as well as different teachers make teaching controversial issues a contentious subject (see more in Chapter 8). Ultimately, it boils down to whose values will be taught.

There are many approaches to values education in the school (Table 1.5). Let us look at these various values education approaches. Even though moral development has generally received little attention by educators, Nel Noddings and many others have advocated that more attention be given in the schools to developing caring individuals who have a knowledge

[13]John Jarolimek, Chair NCSS Task Force on Scope and Sequence, "Social Studies for Citizens of a Strong and Free Nation," in *Social Curriculum Planning Resources* (Washington, DC: National Council for the Social Studies, 1990), 31–32.

of self and a moral recognition that they can do both evil and good. According to Noddings, restructured schools need to teach students not to harm each other.[14]

Lawrence Kohlberg sought to help students develop more complex reasoning patterns based on a higher set of values. Kohlberg called for students to discuss the *reasons* for their value choices, not merely to share with others, but to foster change in the students' stages of moral reasoning. His main method was to present artificial moral dilemmas (whether you should steal a drug to help some family member, whether you should tell on a friend who has stolen a sweater in a department store, etc.). Students then would take positions (such as whether you should tell on a friend) followed by group discussion and relatively structured argumentation in a Socratic dialogue format.[15] Carol Gilligan criticized Kohlberg for omitting a feminine perspective. She believed that females had a different but equally valid way of arriving at moral decisions.[16] Along with a consideration of gender differences, others maintain that more attention also should be paid to the importance of race and sociocultural factors in moral development. Critics of this approach have argued that the moral dilemmas were unrealistic and not the problems that most students presently face in everyday life.

However, the most severe criticism about values education in the schools was directed against Sidney Simon and his colleagues, who advocated a nonjudgmental approach called *values clarification.*[17] These authors wanted to help students become aware of and to identify their own values and those of others. They wanted students to communicate honestly with others about their own values even if their beliefs might be supportive of using drugs or other socially unaccepted values. Simon's methods included using both rational thinking and emotional awareness to allow students to examine their personal feelings, values, and behavior. Often these exercises were contrived situations (deciding who should be chosen to stay in a fallout shelter, writing your own obituary) and self-analysis exercises (writing about two ideal days, jotting down twenty things you love to do). Although critics raged against the values clarification approach for not teaching "good" values and allowing any value system to be acceptable, teachers purchased handbooks of values clarification exercises by the hundreds of thousands and most students enjoyed working with the "fun" exercises.

Critics of the values clarification approach were also concerned about invasion of privacy issues as students talked about their own personal behavior. Some parents also felt that the schools were teaching the wrong values or not correcting students who had "bad" values; many were horrified at Simon's conception of values as relative rather than absolute.

In addition, the few teachers who implemented *social action*—changing or reforming the community—were also criticized when students were encouraged to take social action based on their values. Usually no one complained if the students cleaned up the local park, and student campaigns to protect the faraway whales usually did not engender much controversy. Citizens were upset, however, when the students began a public information campaign about a local factory that was polluting the environment or when students tried to protect local endangered species such as the spotted owl in an area economically dependent on logging. Value analysis and indoctrination approaches are discussed in Chapter 8.

[14]Nel Noddings, *The Challenge to Care in Schools* (New York: Teachers College Press, 1992).

[15]Lawrence Kohlberg, "Moral Education in the Schools: A Developmental View," *School Review* 74, no. 1 (Spring 1966): 1–30.

[16]Carol Gilligan, *In a Different Voice: Psychological Theory* (Cambridge, MA: Harvard University Press, 1982).

[17]Sidney B. Simon, Leland W. Howe, and Howard Kirschenbaum, *Values Clarification* (New York: Hart, 1972).

All these approaches to values education—caring, Kohlberg's moral development, Simon's values clarification approach, and social action—raise the question of whether the values education classes in the schools really work (see again Table 1.5). The evidence is inconclusive partly because of the problems of doing research in the field. If you teach students to think and reason about important values, do they *behave* according to their reasoned values? Does formal teaching about values always translate into action? Measuring the effectiveness of any values education approach in the schools has always been difficult. What do you count? A reduction in the number of student referrals or suspensions? The number of children who report more smiling faces?

Classroom Episode

Cheating by Using the Internet: A Value Question

Ms. Kim Camera, a teacher with a fourth–fifth grade combination class, has successfully taught the unit on "Early Explorers and Pioneers" for many years. But she has noticed that on student projects and reports that there is a growing number of students whose written language is way above their typical level. Ms. Camera thinks they are using whole paragraphs and even articles without getting permission from the source or citing the source. She suspects that the copying is from the Internet and CD-rom adult encyclopedias, but she has no definite proof. Ms. Camera wants students to cite the sources of their information at all times and thinks copying without permission is a bad habit for students to get into.

Being careful not to accuse any student, Ms. Camera talks privately to each student she suspects of "cheating." Students grudgingly report the following: "Mom helped me." "I don't remember how I got the information." "I forgot to put down where I found the stuff." "The Internet is free and you just take it."

At parent conferences Ms. Camera then speaks to these students' parents about this alleged copying. Ms. Camera is amazed at most of the parents' responses. Most defend their actions with the following sentences. "You should be glad that I am helping Benjamin; I work long hours and I am giving him my time." "Get with it;

there is a real world out there and that's the way the Internet works." "Other teachers do not object and are glad to see better reports." "Our Gina needs special accommodations to do the work you require." "Boys do not write as well as girls and they need the help from the Internet."

Ms. Camera realizes that there is a difference between her values and that of parents and their children. She is unsure what to do next. She is also aware that the principal wants to improve school–family relationships.

What steps do you think Ms. Camera should take? Speak to the principal? Bring the issue up at teacher meetings? Talk more to the students about not copying and needing to cite sources of information? What would you do? Does your opinion change if the teacher has tenure?

Ms. Camera knows that there is a standard called "Digital Citizenship." Maybe she should use one of the many websites to teach students about ethical behavior on the Internet (NetSmartz, i-Safe, NetAlert). Or would it even help if she posted a list of computer rights and responsibilities?

TECHNOLOGY

Your Decision on Values

Your values influence how you teach. Your definition of the social studies, civic education, treatment of controversial issues, and culture education springs from your position on values and the way they should be explored in the classroom. Are democratic values and how these values relate to living in a democracy central to teaching social studies? You will make the decision about whether you want to formally teach values, moral education, or character education.

On Your Own **1.4**

What Are the Sources of Your Values?

What do you think have been the main sources of your values? How do you think your values may affect your teaching? ●

What Are the National Curriculum Patterns?

The United States has thousands of local school districts. Although each one is autonomous and can organize a curriculum to suit its own needs and meet state requirements, a national social studies curriculum exists. There are two reasons for this. First is the dominant role that textbooks have had in social studies instruction. In fifth- and eighth-grade classrooms across the nation, you will find in some form U.S. history being taught from books published by only a handful of large companies. About five probably control nearly 90 percent of the textbook market, which ensures a certain similarity in course offerings throughout the nation. Second, most teachers follow guidelines produced by their state, and the states have been influenced by the recommendations of the National Council for the Social Studies. In the past some state standards and frameworks were very broad, requiring only that history, geography, and the social sciences be taught in some manner from kindergarten through twelfth grade. The recent trend with standards-based reform is to provide standards with considerable detail for each or some grades.

State standards and frameworks in turn influence textbook publishers, who want as broad a market as possible. State frameworks of the largest states, particularly California and Texas, help to determine what focus textbooks have. For these interrelated reasons, we see a certain amount of uniformity in elementary social studies programs throughout the nation.

In 1980 Project SPAN (Social Studies: Priorities, Practices, and Needs, funded by the National Science Foundation) found a pattern to the social studies curriculum in most U.S. schools (Table 1.6). Is this the pattern that you followed when you were in school? The basic structure of social studies content at both elementary and secondary levels has changed little during the past fifty years, but a careful reading of the list in Table 1.6 reveals some problems in the traditional social studies curriculum.

Notice first that U.S. history is taught at three grade levels. Too often all three courses are surveys, covering repeatedly everything from Columbus to the latest space shot. There is little differentiation of content and a minimal attempt to build from one course to the next.

Table 1.6	Topics in Social Studies by Grade Level

- Kindergarten/First Grade
    Self
    Family
    School
- Second Grade
    Neighborhoods
- Third Grade
    Communities
- Fourth Grade
    State history, geographic regions
- Fifth Grade
    U.S. history, culture, and geography
- Sixth Grade
    World cultures, history, and geography
- Seventh Grade
    World cultures, history, and geography
- Eighth Grade
    U.S. History
- Ninth Grade
    Civics
- Tenth Grade
    World history
- Eleventh Grade
    U.S. history
- Twelfth Grade
    U.S. government/problems of democracy

How did this come about? It happened partially for historical reasons. In the early years of this country, children attended school for only a few years. Because it was important to teach children U.S. history before they ended their school careers, it was taught in the fifth grade. Then, as more children remained in upper elementary school, the course was taught again in the eighth grade, just before students left school to go to work. Finally, as more students continued on through high school, educators again wanted to make sure that they remembered their U.S. history. So history was repeated in the eleventh grade.

Concerns about patriotism continue to favor the inclusion of U.S. history in elementary and secondary schools. It would be unpopular for a local district or a state framework committee to suggest dropping a U.S. history course—how unpatriotic or un-American! Thus, the impact of tradition and patriotic concerns has led to the entrenchment of three separate U.S. history courses.

Notice also the problem area in the sixth and seventh grades. Both grades cover the same broad topics, but there is little agreement about what the content should be at these levels. In some schools, ancient civilization is taught in the sixth grade; in others, this topic is found at the seventh-grade level. Thus, world history/world cultures courses also have a similar problem of duplication as U.S. history courses. Usually the high school course covers everything again, from early human history to the latest world crisis.

Some social studies educators believe that the primary-grade topics are not sufficiently differentiated. The content is thin and redundant—repeating families and communities several times. Too often the textbook content is already known by students or likely to be learned through everyday experiences. Topics are stressed in the first, second, and third grades without new material being introduced or higher levels of thinking being required.

In particular, Janet Alleman and Jere Brophy, in their many publications, call for retaining most of the topics of the traditional elementary social studies curriculum but putting the emphasis on the fundamentals of the human condition.[18] For the primary grades (K–3) the following units contain the powerful ideas for the curriculum: food, clothing, and shelter (Book 1); communication, transportation, and family living (Book 2); and childhood, money, and government (Book 3). This organization of these units not only connects better with students' prior knowledge and experiences but allows these topics to be examined in depth. Thus, the unit on shelter goes beyond just showing photos and video clips on the various types of shelter found throughout the world. Students can examine whether their families own or rent their homes along with the advantages and disadvantages of each. If their parents/guardians owe their own home, are children aware that most likely there is a mortgage? Or students can examine how homes and apartments that are being built in their neighborhood take into account the location and climate of the area. As you can see these activities that draw on all of the academic disciplines, such as economics and geography, and avoid the often superficial coverage of the family and the community.

But perhaps the heaviest criticism of primary social studies content focuses on the "holiday curriculum." In many schools, holidays such as Thanksgiving, Christmas, Presidents' Day, Valentine's Day, Easter, and Mother's Day dictate what is covered in the primary social studies program. These holidays do offer the opportunity to explain much about our cultural heritage, but reliance on them suggests that many teachers feel more comfortable teaching these topics than ones that require more thoughtful preparation.

The holiday curriculum, however, need not be narrow. Holidays can be used as springboards for teaching about cultural diversity by showing how they are celebrated (or not celebrated) in this country and throughout the world. In many cases, though, holiday activities are simply repeated grade after grade, with little attention paid to learning beyond entertainment. Valuable social studies time is wasted. Furthermore, teachers are not always sensitive to the feelings of children from different backgrounds who may be offended or excluded by

[18]Janet Alleman and Jere Brophy, *Social Studies Excursions, K–3. Book One: Powerful Units on Food, Clothing, and Shelter.* (Portsmouth, NH: Heinemann, 2001). Janet Alleman and Jere Brophy, *Social Studies Excursions, K–3. Book Two: Powerful Units on Communication, Transportation, and Family Living* (Portsmouth, NH: Heinemann, 2002). Janet Alleman and Jere Brophy, *Social Studies Excursions, K–3. Book Three: Power Units on Childhood, Money, and Government* (Portsmouth, NH: Heinemann, 2003).

On Your Own **1.5**

Your State Curriculum

How does your state or local curriculum compare with the traditional social studies curriculum patterns? Is there more emphasis on diversity? On global education? ●

the holiday focus. In the same manner, children may not understand why particular religious holidays are not mentioned or are celebrated in ways unrelated to their religious meanings. The separation of church and state in the United States means that children may *learn* about different religions but religious beliefs may not be practiced in the classroom (more in Chapters 5 and 9).

As you can see, there *is* a national social studies curriculum pattern. But your state's pattern may vary from this model in several ways. Each state generally requires that its own state history be taught at the fourth-grade level. Check on what your state recommends for the sixth- and seventh-grade levels as well. Information about social studies content guidelines can be obtained from your state department of education and the Internet. Your state may also have *legal requirements*—observance of holidays, positive and accurate portrayal of the roles of women and minority groups, or the protection and conservation of the environment—that dictate to some extent what will be taught in the social studies.

Scope and Sequence

Almost all elementary social studies textbooks use what is often called the **expanding communities pattern** or the **expanding horizons** or **widening world scope and sequence model.** All three terms are used interchangeably. **Scope** refers to the list of topics covered in a program. **Sequence** is the order in which these topics are covered. Usually, the two words are used together to indicate what is being taught, whether in the social studies or in any other area of the curriculum.

Scope and sequence issues are important. You need to know when students are ready for certain difficult concepts, such as time or chronology. Most primary students have great difficulty trying to imagine what life was like 2,000 years ago. They may think that we have always had television, airplanes, and cars. The eras designated by B.C. and A.D. pose conceptual difficulty for most primary students. Determining at what grade level you might successfully try to teach time concepts is a scope and sequence issue.

The traditional scope and sequence pattern for the elementary grades—the expanding communities—is based on a consideration of the developmental needs of the child. Children usually learn better about real things and life around them than about abstract topics that they cannot see or feel. Therefore, the expanding communities concept begins where children are when they enter school. The focus in the primary grades is first the self, then families, communities, cities, the region, and finally the nation and the world (Figure 1.3).

This pattern of expanding communities made a lot of sense years ago. But now, with computers, mass media, and especially television, children are exposed to events and issues taking place far from their homes. Children also travel more. Primary-grade children are aware of international relationships and domestic crises, wars, terrorism, and pollution

| Figure 1.3 | The Expanding Horizons Curriculum |

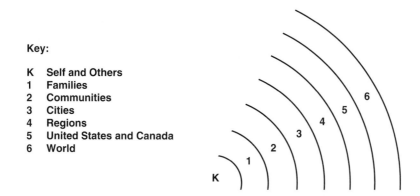

Key:

K   Self and Others
1   Families
2   Communities
3   Cities
4   Regions
5   United States and Canada
6   World

Source: Robert D. Barr, James L. Barth, and Samuel Shermis, *Defining the Social Studies*, Bulletin 51. Reprinted with permission of the National Council for the Social Studies.

problems. They come to school with a greater knowledge of the world and a far wider range of interests than the expanding horizons curriculum envisioned.

Critics believe that the expanding horizons curriculum does not present an accurate view of the interrelationships among the different communities (e.g., family, local community, state, nation, and world). It may also discourage using current and controversial events that take place outside of the community being studied. For critics, the focus on the here and now can be replaced with other learning experiences if children can connect with the topic through personal experience or interest.

The 1990s were awash with new curriculum ideas. The national standards in history, geography, civics, and economics all stressed more attention to their respective fields including the primary-grade area. Some advocated a greater focus on children's literature integrated into the social studies curriculum whereas others wanted more integration of subject areas within a theme. Alternative assessment ideas also attracted attention. However, these recommended changes were all within the existing expanding horizons model.

One older alternative pattern is the **spiral curriculum** advocated by Hilda Taba (see Figure 1.4). In this model, basic concepts and processes from the social sciences such as interdependence or cultural change are taught each year on a higher level of abstraction. For example, first-grade students might learn how families depend on one another for natural resources and manufactured goods. By the fourth grade, they might study the first pioneer families that settled in their state. Care must be taken in using this pattern to ensure that the topics are truly moving to higher levels and not just repeating topics such as "community workers" or "food." The spiral curriculum can be used to support the rationale for repeating U.S. history three times—each time it is taught at a more complex and more meaningful level. The NCSS ten learning themes are also an example of a spiral curriculum.

Figure 1.4	The Spiral of Concept Development

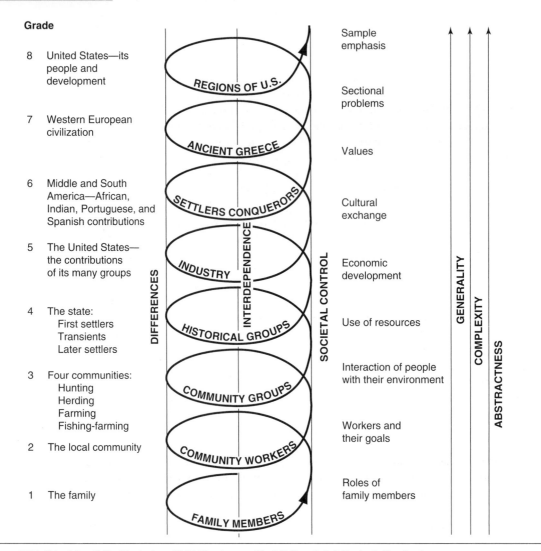

Source: Hilda Taba, Mary C. Durkin, Anthony H. McNaughton, and Jack R. Fraenkal. *A Teacher's Handbook to Elementary Social Studies*, 2nd ed. (Reading, MA: Addison-Wesley, 1971). Copyright © 1971 by Addison-Wesley Publishing Company. Used by permission of Pearson Education, Inc.

Why Are Textbooks and Technology Important?

The adoption of social studies textbooks and programs has had a great influence on what is taught in elementary social studies. If you compare a new social studies textbook series with the one you had in elementary school, you will notice that today's textbooks are much more colorful and attractive.

Due to the growing number of diverse students, almost all textbook series now show content and pictures of a wide diversity of ethnic, gender, racial, and religious groups, in response to demands to eliminate racism and sexism in our society. Publishers now can tailor the number of photos of ethnic/racial groups to match the percentages of particular states. For example, Hispanics in a California social studies textbook account for 35 percent of the photos and illustrations, but Hispanics are only 6 percent in the same text in North Carolina. However, African Americans make up 22 percent of the people in the North Carolina text, compared to 7 percent shown in the California edition. In general, publishers are interested in getting their textbooks adopted in large states such as California and Texas along with large urban districts. This has increased the percentage of images devoted to minority groups. Publishers also have guidelines to reflect the disabled and the elderly in their textbooks. As an additional sales technique, publishers may also give away a lot of free material—tests, workbooks—with each purchase of a set of classroom books.

Typically the large publishers offer a series (often called a *basal series*) of textbooks and related supplementary materials from kindergarten through grade 6 or 7. Even if you follow a basal series closely, you will have some choices about what you teach. One choice occurs at the fourth-grade level, where state history and geography are generally taught. The major publishers issue specially prepared state textbooks for large states, and regional books are available for smaller states. Smaller publishing firms may also offer state history textbooks.

The next choice occurs at the sixth- and seventh-grade levels. Because there is no standard curriculum pattern at these levels, publishers often offer two or more textbooks that can be used for either grade, thus providing a wide and varying range of topics—the Eastern Hemisphere, the Western Hemisphere, or the world, for example.

Each publisher has a text for the pupils and a teacher's edition. A Spanish pupil text is also frequently available. The Big Book format is often used in kindergarten and primary grades instead of a pupil text. There also may be a separate Big Book format for geography or a special theme or subject area.

Recent trends found in elementary social studies textbooks include the following:

- Standards-based social studies content, organized around big ideas or concepts (in large adoption states, the state's standard may be written in each section of the student's textbook so that students are more aware of the purpose as they read.)
- Reading support built into the text with more strategies for struggling readers and English language learners as well as suggestions for the gifted/talented and special education students
- More technology components
- Students as "historical thinkers" using primary and secondary sources and multiple perspectives
- More visuals and maps

Publishers have looked carefully at the various standards to insure that their texts in general can meet as many state standards as possible. In addition, the testing required under the No Child Left Behind Act has put a prime focus on reading improvement. In fact, some critics are worried that the social studies texts are becoming more like reading texts and are not emphasizing enough social studies content. Reading skills are also reinforced by a wide

On Your Own **1.6**

Compare the Series: Identify Differences

At a curriculum library, examine three different social studies textbook series at one particular grade level. Note carefully what content is covered in the textbook. Also, look at the teacher's guide for suggestions on how to teach the program. How are the series similar? How are they different? ●

array of supplemental materials. Each grade level usually has literature books, adventure books, vocabulary books, a primary source anthology (usually for the teacher to read aloud), vocabulary cards, and various types of workbooks. Help for English language learners (ELLs) also is common. Nontechnology aides include transparencies, outline maps, atlases, posters, and foldables (graphic organizers). The emphasis on testing also is shown by supplemental materials on tests for chapter, unit, and performance assessment. In addition, practice for taking tests is available.

Technology abounds with almost all publishers having a CD or DVD for an oral presentation of the text. Software may also be used to increase writing skills, another area of emphasis along with reading. Songs, poems, and games on CD or DVD can enliven the text, as can software for making time lines, maps, and graphs. Videos and video clips on CD or DVD are also correlated with the text. The publisher can offer services using the Internet for current events as well as professional training in using their products.

Of course, all of the supplemental materials cost money on top of the initial purchase price of the pupils' textbooks. Publishers' representatives informally state that if a teacher or district buys the supplemental materials, then the teacher is more likely to have and to use the materials. This will result in more time spent in achieving a better social studies program. But in many classrooms, teachers feel fortunate if they have enough pupil textbooks and a teacher's guide for their own use.

Some critics argue that the basal social studies textbooks are very similar. This concern may stem from the similarity of titles; the word *family*, for example, shows up frequently at the first-grade level. But a careful examination of the textbooks will show considerable differences. Some textbook series are better for struggling readers. Others emphasize global education. Still others, although they bear recent copyright dates, really have changed very little from those of twenty years ago. Map skills are found in all textbooks, but some series also emphasize skills in reading, fact-finding, and thinking.

Textbooks may be better than ever but it is the teacher as a planner who uses the textbook to make it an effective resource and tool. The teacher's instructor guide can inspire teachers to do a better job of helping their students to learn. For that reason, it is a good idea to get copies of both textbooks and teacher's guides from several publishers. That way you have an abundance of ideas for student learning on a given topic.

Educators complain about overreliance on the textbook. Often it has been the only instructional tool used, and this limitation has resulted in narrow, restricted programs. Applied creatively, however, the textbook can be a very valuable resource. It is important for teachers and committees concerned with the selection of textbooks to look very carefully at the possible choices. There are many differences among the textbook series. The wide range of activities suggested in a teacher's guide may make a social studies textbook series unique. Teachers stuck with unsuitable textbooks for their classes work at a disadvantage in trying to provide a good social studies program.

Technology

TECHNOLOGY

The widespread use of computers and associated interactive multimedia tools is continuing to change what happens in many classrooms as well as in our homes and the outside world. Technology has unlimited possibilities for enriching and enlivening the social studies and our lives. Most classrooms now have a few computers. With the increased use of handhelds, some classes have moved to individual computing with each student having computer capacity. More frequently both teachers and students use e-mail and search the Net for information about historical or current events. For example, primary sources from data collections, art museums, and historic places can locate photos, documents, and music that can help students visualize the past.

Teachers increasingly use teacher portals and other websites to find repositories of lesson plans, assignments, links, and ideas. From these many sources, they then use word processing to make their lesson plans and activities for their students. More teachers send e-mail to parents and colleagues. In addition, there is greater use of class management systems for student information such as attendance records and grades/report cards. In the classroom, students use software to learn basic skills in reading and math and word processing for writing. Assessment of students is increasingly being done online, especially teachers monitoring during the year how well students are doing in reading and math. There may be a class blog.

However, students spend more time at home than school using the Internet for e-mails, sending messages to friends, or playing games. A few even write blogs. Even primary students are now more computer savvy as they watch their family members use computers and realize that often their parents/guardians use computers at work. Children have positive attitudes toward technology. They want to play with the computer too. However, while it appears that everyone is online, there is still a "digital divide" for lower-income children. About four-fifths of children have access to the Internet at home and those without access need special attention to help them develop computer literacy. Solutions include loaning materials such as computers, printers, and software to students and providing a safe and convenient place for students to access computers and the Internet at school.

Although teachers are using computers to make their everyday teaching lives easier, it appears that many in teaching social studies are using the computer mainly to locate lessons, information, photos, and videos. Much less frequently are teachers designing lessons in which their students use the computer other than to find information. It is a challenge for busy teachers to find the time to incorporate technology into their lesson plans. As an example, collaboration and communication with students other than classmates is less common. Seldom is there a blend of online and classroom teaching.

Small Group Work 1.3

Check Where You Stand

Do you think any changes should be made in what is taught (topics) and when it is taught (specific grade levels)? Should there be a greater emphasis on certain disciplines such as history? Do you think the expanding community pattern is the best way to organize the elementary social studies curriculum? ●

Summary

A good social studies program should help students become informed citizens capable of making wise decisions. Advocates of NCLB and state standards encourage teachers and schools to strive for higher achievement. However, the social studies program could be neglected by the current emphasis on reading, math, and science, unless teachers integrate and highlight the social studies. Your values and background influence the decisions you make in teaching the social studies. National curriculum patterns and textbooks influence greatly how social studies is taught.

Suggested Readings and Websites

Barr, Robert D., James L. Barth, and S. Samuel Shermis. *Defining the Social Studies*, Bulletin 51. Washington, DC: National Council for the Social Studies, 1977.

Hundreds of stories to help children understand and develop character. An example of building character education approach. See also Bennett's two other books: *The Book of Virtues for Young People: A Treasury of Great Moral Stories* (New York: Simon & Schuster, 1997) and *The Children's Book of Heroes* (New York: Simon & Schuster, 1997). Other advocates of the character education movement are the following: William Kilpatrick, *Why Johnny Can't Tell Right from Wrong* (New York: Simon & Schuster, 1992); Thomas Lickona, *Educating for Character: How Our Schools Can Teach Respect & Responsibility* (New York: Bantam, 1992); Edward Wynne and Kevin Ryan, *Reclaiming Our Schools: A Handbook on Teaching Character, Academics, and Discipline* (New York: Macmillan, 1993).

Cuban, Larry. "History of Teaching in Social Studies." In James P. Shaver, ed., *Handbook of Research on Social Studies Teaching and Learning*, New York: Macmillan, 1991, pp. 197–209.

Summary of history of social studies teaching.

Evans, Ronald W. *The Social Studies Wars: What Should We Teach the Children?* New York: Teachers College Press, 2003.

History of attacks on social studies.

Evans, Ronald W., and David Warren Saxe, eds. *Handbook on Teaching Social Issues*, NCSS Bulletin 93. Washington, DC: National Council for the Social Studies, 1996.

Rationale and activities for issues-centered social studies.

Haas, Mary E., and Margaret A. Laughlin, eds. *Meeting the Standards: Social Studies Readings for K–6 Educators*. Washington, DC: National Council for the Social Studies, 1997.

Excellent source of journal articles designed to help teachers using the NCSS standards; other curriculum issues also discussed.

Jenness, David. *Making Sense of Social Studies*. New York: Macmillan, 1990.

A publication of the National Commission on Social Studies in the Schools.

Kaltsounis, Theodore. "Democracy's Challenge as the Foundation for Social Studies." *Theory and Research in Social Education* 22, no. 2 (Spring 1994): 176–193.

Democracy and democratic citizen education should be the logical foundation on which to structure the social studies program. Previous models of democratic education have failed.

Kirschenbaum, Howard. *100 Ways to Enhance Values and Morality in Schools and Youth Settings*. Boston: Allyn & Bacon, 1995.

Traditional methods for inculcating and modeling as well as the values clarification approach.

Munroe, Susan, and Terry Smith (The Casados Group). *State Geography Standards: An Appraisal of Geography Standards in 38 States and the District of Columbia*. Washington, DC: Thomas B. Fordham Foundation, 1998.

Authors funded by a conservative foundation find most state geography standards faulty.

National Commission on Social Studies in the Schools. *Charting a Course: Social Studies for the 21st Century*. New York: National Commission on Social Studies in the Schools, November 1989.

Rejection of expanding communities pattern by four organizations.

National Council for the Social Studies. "Fostering Civic Virtue: Character Education in the Social Studies." *Social*

Education 61, no. 4 (April/May 1997): 225–227.

Policy statement on character education.

Noddings, Nel. *The Challenge to Care in Schools.* New York: Teachers College Press, 1992.

Alternative approaches to education organized around the theme of care.

Posner, George T. *Analyzing the Curriculum.* New York: McGraw-Hill, 1995.

Basic understanding of how curriculum has been organized and developed in America.

Saxe, David Warren. *State History Standards: An Appraisal of Standards in 37 States and the District of Columbia.* Washington, DC: Thomas B. Fordham Foundation, 1998.

Author funded by a conservative foundation reviews state history standards and is very disappointed in their quality.

Social Education 49 (March 1985), article by S. Samuel Shermis and James L. Barth followed by response of James Shaver on indoctrination in the social studies.

Social Education 54 and 55 (November–December 1990 and January 1991), special issues devoted to pros and cons of *Charting a Course: Social Studies for the 21st Century.*

Stern, Sheldon M. *Effective State Standards for U.S. History: A 2003 Report Card.* Washington, DC: Thomas B. Fordham Institute, 2003.

Funded by conservative foundations, the author reviews state standards for U.S. history. For more on the Thomas B. Fordham Institute, see www.fordhaminstitute.org.

Task Force of the National Council for the Social Studies. *Expectations of Excellence: Curriculum Standards for Social Studies,* Bulletin 89. Washington, DC: National Council for the Social Studies, 1994.

NCSS's curriculum standards.

Journals

The three journals of social studies that teachers should become familiar with are *Social Education, Social Studies and the Young Learner*, and *The Social Studies.* In addition, publications such as *Learning* and *Instructor* may have social studies materials.

Websites

Education Week
www.edweek.org

Weekly stories and features about educational issues.

ERIC
www.eric.ed.gov

ERIC is the world's largest source of education information with more than one million abstracts of documents and journal articles on education research and practice.

National Council for the Social Studies
www.ncss.org

Site of the most important organization in the field of social studies, the National Council for the Social Studies. Material on its associated groups, conferences, workshops, standards, and resources.

Public Education Network
www.publiceducation.org

A wide variety of topics about public education.

PEARSON
myeducationlab
Where the Classroom Comes to Life

RESEARCH ARTICLE READING EXERCISE

The Values Manifesto

Go to MyEducationLab, select the topic **NCSS Standards,** and read the research article entitled "The Values Manifesto" by G. Euvrard.

This article is an exciting case study of the NCSS standard "civic ideals and practices." Teachers and their students in Nambia worked to develop their own values manifesto. As a result of this activity, teachers found that class participation increased, and students expressed their opinions more freely. Teachers also reported that they began adhering to the classroom values more closely.

Complete the homework questions that accompany the article. You may print your work or have it transmitted to your professor as necessary.

CHAPTER 2

Planning for Social Studies Instruction

*T*eacher planning is necessary to increase student learning. Planning is also necessary to meet the wide range of abilities and diversity among our students. Good planning helps to achieve good classroom management for effective student learning. Traditional curriculum planning of units and lesson plans includes standards/objectives, activities to achieve the objectives, and assessments to evaluate if objectives have been achieved. In contrast, the backward design starts with the desired results and assessment evidence. Chapter topics are organized from the general, broad planning to specific daily lesson plans.

- Planning
- Goals, Long-Range Planning, and Standards/Instructional Objectives
- Treasury of Resources and Technology for Planning

- Units
- Lesson Plans

Why is it helpful to plan with another teacher?

Planning

$\mathcal{A}$ teacher is the key to the social studies program. In their role as **decision makers,** teachers decide on what units to include during the year or what tomorrow's lesson plan will be. Planning is especially important to meet the needs of all our students in the **inclusive classroom.** Thought-out planning is better than decisions made on the spot. If you do not know what to do next, the classroom experience can be very frustrating for both you and your students. Lack of planning can waste time and also create class management problems. In contrast, thinking about what you are going to do can contribute to student learning.

Good planners actively seek materials. You should systematically build your own collection or library of resources for teaching social studies. Continue this throughout your teaching career. Having a variety of unit plans and instructional resources for students will pay dividends. Organize your collection under standards, themes, or categories so that you can retrieve your resources as you need them.

Successful planning needs to be detailed enough to help you organize what actually happens in the classroom. It is inaccurate to suggest that only drudges and drones plan; planning is a vital and basic skill for all effective teachers. Research indicates that teachers who plan are more likely to be satisfied with their teaching and are more likely to remain in the teaching profession. Careful and flexible planning makes you a professional who builds on students' backgrounds and experiences.

On Your Own **2.1**

Your Concept of Planning

Concept maps are useful ways of organizing ideas. Jot down the words *teacher planning* in the center of a sheet of paper. Think of the various subtopics such as lesson or books. Now try drawing the relationships you see among the topics. Compare your concept map of teacher planning with the maps of others in your class. ●

Busy Teachers

Sometimes elementary schoolteachers resist planning, especially writing out their plans, because they are so busy with immediate responsibilities—filling out forms, grading papers, checking homework. Planning is often a low-priority task. But there is an important psychological benefit to planning and especially to working out and writing down daily lesson plans: confidence. With a plan in front of you, you feel organized and prepared to face the class. A plan a day keeps disaster away. Planning can often help you anticipate management problems in the classroom, and it enables you to have better control of the situation. As the old saying goes, "An ounce of prevention is worth a pound of cure."

Some teachers argue that planning encourages rigidity. Having a written plan, they suggest, prevents them from taking advantage of unexpected instructional opportunities. Serendipity is always welcome! Your lesson plan, however, is meant to be a guide, not a prison sentence. Always be ready to bend it to take advantage of student interest or some recent and unanticipated event.

Value of Written Lesson Plans

Writing out lesson plans helps you to better remember what is supposed to happen since you have used multiple senses in writing the lesson plan.

You may find that you have no choice about writing out lesson plans. Some school districts and principals require teachers to submit lesson plans for the coming week throughout the year. Frequently, administrators ask only for brief statements of topics and textbook pages to be covered. Most plans written for administrators show very little detail. Written lesson plans are valuable to administrators if they need a substitute teacher for you or if there ever is a parent who challenges what you are teaching. The fact that a lesson plan must be submitted, however, acts as an incentive for many elementary teachers to plan ahead, if only to list the subject areas they will cover in a given week. Writing in topics under subject-area headings—science, social studies, math—may suggest areas of potential integration: How can language arts or science work with this week's social studies lessons?

There are often differences between what is listed on the plan handed in to an administrator and what actually goes on in the classroom. Some differences are inevitable, since lesson plans should always allow for flexibility. In a few cases, subjects are listed that are never taught. Frequently, this happens because the teacher does no planning in depth and, therefore, has no real plan to implement.

The Reflective Teacher

Sometimes a new teacher will say, "I did a lot of planning for a lesson on our local transportation system, and the whole thing fell flat. But the next day I walked in 'cold' and taught a terrific lesson on neighborhoods. So why plan?" This can happen. Planned lessons do not always go as well as expected. Instead of abandoning planning, however, you should go over an unsuccessful lesson at the end of the day, when you are less emotionally involved. At what points did it go off track? Were the students bored? Unable to keep up? Confused? What actually was wrong with the lesson? Make notes on your lesson plan to help you with future planning. Using a word processor for your lesson plans is ideal because you can easily revise them. In effect, you are **reflecting** on your teaching, a highly approved method to improve your teaching.

Even if a lesson *is* successful, you should critique your written plan. What would have made the lesson better? Write down proposed changes so that you won't forget them. Having both the original plan and your notes on how to improve it will provide you with an ever-expanding resource file in years to come.

Now more emphasis is on teachers sharing and collaborating with their colleagues. The whole school now works together to improve test scores. A teacher shares data from a lesson, and other teachers reflect on the lesson in a supportive manner. This is called *lesson study,* a professional development approach credited to Japan. Sharing teachers' work and expertise can improve student learning. Teachers gain knowledge of subject matter, instruction, and capacity to observe students.

Getting Started: Locating Resources

How do you go about planning? First assemble all available planning tools and resources. They include the following:

- Social studies state framework and standards along with district curriculum guides (standards for language arts and other subject areas may also be useful)

Small Group Work **2.1**

Issues That Affect Social Studies Planning

Some of the many issues in curriculum planning that teachers must consider are meeting the needs of an increasingly diverse student population, using technology in the classroom, and improving test scores. Note if these issues apply to where you are teaching or are expecting to teach. ●

- Mandated social studies test requirements (if any)
- Your adopted textbook, the teacher's guide, and ancillary materials
- Media catalogs for your district and county
- Recommendations from your school media specialist (usually your librarian) for stories, trade books, reference books, map and globe collections
- Computer resources including virtual field trips, WebQuests, lesson plans from the Internet, and simulations
- Ideas from other teachers in your school
- Parent resources
- Community resources, guest speakers, field trips, and local newspapers
- Information on the backgrounds and abilities of your diverse students
- A school calendar (essential for holidays, changes in schedule)

Once your resources are assembled, you are better able to see your options. Then you can choose units and activities for which you have appropriate materials and which you think will interest your students and be appropriate for their backgrounds. Try to choose a program that fits your abilities and talents. A lack of interest on your part will surely be conveyed to your students. However, do not ignore your state standards.

Goals, Long-Range Planning, and Standards/Instructional Objectives

*L*et us now go through the process of planning a social studies curriculum following the outline in Figure 2.1. *First, read carefully the standards or curriculum framework of your state and local district.* These documents are published by your state education agency and/or your local school district. Then look at the framework's **goals,** which are the broad statements of desired outcomes.

Promoting good citizenship, which is often found on district lists of educational goals, is also generally listed as a goal for social studies education. The social studies program does not have sole responsibility for teaching citizenship skills; other areas of the curriculum also contribute. But an elementary social studies program should be designed to do as much as possible to move students toward effective citizenship participation (see Chapter 8). As an elementary teacher, you will plan the entire day or most of the

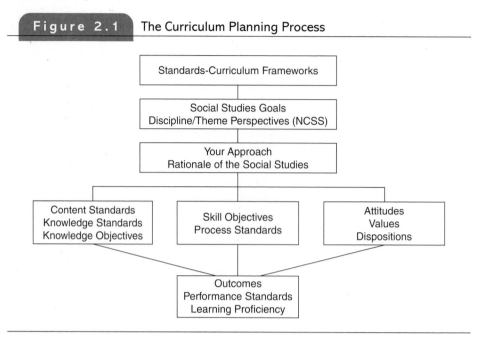

Figure 2.1   The Curriculum Planning Process

day for your students. In looking over the day's program, you will want to be alert to those activities that best promote both broad educational goals and specific goals of the social studies.

In Chapter 1, we mentioned the four basic social studies goals:

1. To acquire **knowledge** from the social sciences, history, and humanities
2. To develop **skills** to think and to process information
3. To develop appropriate democratic **values** and **attitudes**
4. To have opportunities for **citizenship/social participation**

In some states, instead of the term *goal, essential questions, guiding questions, fundamental questions,* or *overarching understandings* is used. These interchangeable terms identify what is to be learned at a broad level. Regardless of the terms used, almost all districts have some set of general goals (lifelong learning skills and habits, health, responsible behavior at school, etc.) as well as goals for certain subjects.

These goals provide the framework for planning in the social studies and also fit easily into the general goals of most states and school districts. In some cases, the Ten Themes of the National Council for the Social Studies (NCSS) or the goals and standards of the separate social science/history disciplines might be included because they often list the key discipline concepts on which the social studies curriculum should focus.

The problem with goals is that they are so broadly stated that any social activity you plan to teach could be listed under at least one of them. Goals are useful in defining broad objectives but they lack the specificity necessary for effective day-to-day teaching.

Long-Range Planning

What are the next steps in planning after you have gathered and skimmed over your resources and looked at goals? Most elementary teachers begin social studies planning by roughing out an outline of the entire curriculum. Given the number of weeks in the school year, how would you divide the subject matter normally covered in, say, the fifth grade using standards? See how a fifth-grade teacher using California's standards could broadly block out a year's work (Figure 2.2). In general, the teacher in Figure 2.2 used about one month for each of the major standards. Note that in Chapter 1 the California grade two standards (p. 17) are organized into five major standards. For broad long-range planning, a teacher could decide that she might want to spend three months on Standard 2.5 on heroes but only one month or so on Standard 2.3 on governmental institutions and practices. Or the teacher could decide to spend approximately two months of each of the five standards. What would be the most important ideas or concepts? What would make reasonable, manageable sections?

Many teachers when planning for the year like to make a list under the three headings of Social Studies, Language Arts, and Science. As they think about the months of September and October, they see if correlations offer any possibilities such as literature selections or science experiments. As teachers do monthly planning, they again see if other subject areas can be correlated with standards, learning activities, and resources.

As you do this, your own approach or rationale to the social studies comes into play, whether it is conscious or not (Chapter 1). Teachers' personal beliefs as liberals and conservatives also influence their teaching. This affects how you make some decisions: Will you select only certain units from the textbook, or will you try to cover all of them? Will you use the district's curriculum guidelines, or will some of your units be from specific curriculum packages—an economic unit on choices, perhaps? Once you begin to make these basic determinations—what you will cover and how much time you will devote to each topic—you can focus your attention on the individual chunks of time, frequently called **units,** the main divisions of the curriculum. Long-range planning is vital because there is usually far more content (and resource material) available than there is time to teach it. By making these tentative choices, you are now doing long-range planning.

Figure 2.2　　Broad Long-Range Planning Using California's Standards

Month	Grade 5—The Nine Standards for Making a New Nation
September	5.1　Native Americans—major pre-Columbian settlements
October/Nov.	5.2　Early explorers and explorations of the Americas
December	5.3　Cooperation/conflict among American Indians, settlers, Europe
January	5.4　Colonial life—political, religious, social, economic institutions
February/March	5.5 & 5.6　Causes and consequences of the American Revolution
April	5.7　Development and significance of the Constitution
May	5.8　Colonization, immigration, and settlement patterns, 1789 to 1850
June	5.9　Location of 50 states and names of their capitals; review

The Textbook

Textbook use increases as children advance from one grade to the next. We include the adopted textbook as a prime resource for instructional planning, acknowledging and agreeing with the criticisms leveled at textbook-centered teaching. In our view, a good program needs structure and topical direction. Most textbooks provide this. Taking advantage of the content outline, activities suggested, and enrichment ideas need not condemn you to a rigid chapter-by-chapter, lesson-by-lesson coverage. Instead of thinking of the text as a novel to be read from beginning to end, we need to see the text as a tool to help us conceptualize and speed up our long-range planning. If you use the textbook as your main guide in long-range curriculum planning, you should typically follow these steps:

1. Skim the text, looking at broad unit titles. Decide which ones you will use. (The author's recommendations about how much time a unit will typically take may be helpful.)

2. Decide which units will receive major emphasis or minor emphasis.

3. Examine the teacher's guide. Look for activities for you and your students.

4. Find other activities to supplement the text. The teacher's guide may suggest some; the publisher may also provide other materials, such as literature books.

5. Decide whether you will use the tests supplied by the publisher for evaluation.

What you are doing at this stage of the game is thinking about what you want students to gain in content, skills, and values. There should be challenging subject content that aims at higher-level thinking. This necessity forces us to consider sound education practices for the age group we are teaching. Normally we want high student involvement with a connection to real life. In addition, to show us that they have achieved these goals, we have to plan assessments as an ongoing process, integrated with instruction, as well as at the end of the unit.

Adjust to Promote Student Learning

Because a major part of your long-range planning will be done early in the school year or even before it begins, you probably won't know your students' full range of talents and abilities. Once you begin to learn more about your students, you will need to modify the learning activities in your curriculum to fit your classroom, where student abilities may range from those of students with disabilities to the gifted. Following constructionist ideas, you will want to find out your students' prior knowledge. What do they already know about a topic or idea and what do they want to learn about it? Some teachers involve students in planning what is to be learned.

Remember always that the purpose of planning is not to just focus on the teacher but *to promote student learning*. In other words, this makes every teacher's planning and classroom unique. You as the teacher, your students,

On Your Own **2.2**

Facilitate Child-Focused Planning

Interview three students—a high-achieving student, an average student, and a struggling student. Ask what teaching approaches they like and which seem to help them most. ●

and your school are all influences on your planning. Consider your students' motivation and prior knowledge. In addition, your school's staff, parent, and community involvement are affecting your planning, as well as your own values, background, experiences, content knowledge, teaching methods, and classroom management.

Content Standards and Instructional Objectives

Whereas a *goal* is a broad statement of purpose, **content standard** or **instructional objective** is a specific accomplishment that you want your students to achieve in a specific period. Often the terms *knowledge objective, knowledge standard, standard, content standard,* and *instructional objective* are used interchangeably. The standards movement has greatly increased the number of educational terms because states often have used different terms.

You know that a well-written objective specifies the level of acceptable performance and the conditions under which a student must perform. Typically, objectives are focused on specific content mastery or skills that are more easily measured or evaluated. Many teacher education programs advise their students to use Bloom's taxonomy. For many state standards the objectives are listed but without the level of acceptable performance necessary on the part of the students.

The objectives approach affirms that it is not enough to love and nurture children. It is not enough to have fun activities. The teacher needs to guide students toward learning objectives. You are no doubt familiar with the traditional process of curriculum planning. Typically, there are three main questions to answer:

1. What are your standards or objectives?
2. What learning experiences will be used to achieve the desired objectives?
3. What evaluation procedures will be used to determine whether the objectives have been achieved?

You hear the term **alignment** more often. Pleas are made to teachers to align classroom instruction to the state/district standards in methods, materials, and assignments. Administrators want to ensure that all students are developing the knowledge and skills needed to meet the standards. In many cases, professional development is provided to help teachers in this process. This may reflect the desire to have higher test scores.

There is now also more attention given to the goal that objectives, instruction, and evaluation should all be connected or coordinated with each other. This is called **curriculum alignment**—meaning that both instruction and evaluation should be based on the objectives. Poor alignment can occur because of various circumstances—for example, when the objective is improved thinking skills but the learning activities do not involve the students in thinking, or when the objective is improved thinking but the students are tested with low-level factual questions that do not assess their thinking skills.

Examples of Alignment

As an example of the instructional cycle in Figure 2.3 for the primary grades your **objectives** in a law-related education/civic education unit would be:

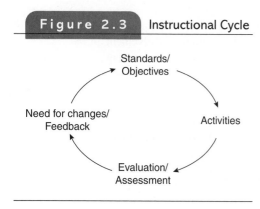

Figure 2.3   Instructional Cycle

- To understand the need for rules and laws
- To understand the need for fair consequences for inappropriate behavior
- To develop rules appropriate in a given situation

Your activity to accomplish these objectives is to read *Goldilocks and the Three Bears* (any of the many versions) to the class. As an introduction to the story, have students make a sad face on one side of a paper plate. Tell them that you are going to read the story *Goldilocks and the Three Bears* and that they should raise a sad face each time Goldilocks does something they believe she should not do.

As you read the story, you notice that many children do not raise a sad face (the assessment) when Goldilocks does something wrong, such as entering someone's house without permission, breaking the chair, sleeping on the bed, and running away without an apology. This assessment/feedback alerts you to the fact that perhaps some of the students enjoy the charm of this old classic, especially as you change your voice for the three bears' dialogue, but they really do not understand the need for rules and laws.

This assessment/feedback leads you to engage the students in a discussion, listing on the board what Goldilocks did wrong and why it is wrong. Ask students to suggest a fair penalty for each wrong action. Should Goldilocks's parents be involved? Does the fact that Goldilocks was hungry and tired excuse her actions?

As another activity, you might as an extension read another classic, *Jack and the Beanstalk.* Again ask if Jack did anything wrong. Has the giant done anything wrong? Discuss what has happened from the giant's point of view. Again the instructional cycle is repeated with the same objectives and the same activities of reading the story and discussion, with evaluation of students' responses to see if they truly understand the objectives. As another activity you could also discuss a variety of situations on "What's Fair." Some of these could be experiences from your own students. You could also ask the students to give a report card grade (A to F) on how good the characters were. You would then make an assessment based on students' responses to see if further changes in the curriculum were needed. Perhaps the objectives need to be modified if students still do not see that Goldilocks or other characters did anything wrong. New objectives would be formulated based on the previous feedback. Or you could conclude that the objectives for your students had been achieved.[1]

Evaluation/assessment should be both aligned and an integral part of the learning experience (see Figure 2.3). It may occur during a given day's lesson. If assessment is embedded within a lesson, students receive immediate feedback and can better understand that testing is part of learning and that it is to their advantage to recognize their strengths and weaknesses.

---

[1]The activity described was adapted from *Goldilocks, The Trial,* video and leader's manual (Maryland State Bar Association, 1990).

Table 2.1	Comparison of Traditional versus Standards-Based Planning
Traditional Practice	**Standards-Based Practice**
Formulate objectives	Select standard(s) that students need to know and skills are needed
Design instructional activities; what resources will I need?	Design an assessment that allows each student to demonstrate what he/she knows or can do
Plan and give an assessment; often summative assessment	Design appropriate learning activities with resources needed for all students to achieve the standard
Check to see if objectives have been reached; if necessary reteach, modify next lesson or unit	Give assessment(s); use rubrics
Give grades to students	Use data from assessment to give feedback, reteach, or move to a higher level of the standard or a new standard

Backward Design

A more innovative approach is to turn the traditional planning model upside down into the standards-based practice (simplified in Table 2.1). This model, often called backward design or planning, is based on the work of Grant Wiggins and Jay McTighe in *Understanding by Design* (UbD).[2] It calls for delaying the planning of classroom activities until the goals have been clarified and assessments designed. Thus, the three main stages in this model are as follows:

1. Desired results (big idea, enduring understandings, essential questions)
2. Assessment evidence (how will students demonstrate what they have learned or can do)
3. Learning activities (what opportunities will the student have to learn)

Examples of Using the Standards-Based Practice or Backward Design Approach

After an overview of your state's framework and standards, you need to clarify what a given standard really means for teaching and student learning. This is sometimes called unlocking or unpacking the standard. Let's see how this would work, breaking it down into

---

[2]Grant Wiggins and Jay McTighe, *Understanding by Design,* 2nd ed. (Alexandria, VA: Association for Supervision and Curriculum Development, 2005). This expanded edition includes the Wiggins & McTighe first edition (1998) as well as other supplementary materials.

steps. Assume that for your third grades you have chosen the following standards from West Virginia's history objectives for grade three:

Students will:

SS.3.5.3   compare and contrast present cultures to the cultures of people of other historical time periods (e.g., source of food, clothing, shelter, products used)

SS.3.5.4   make historical inferences by analyzing artifacts and pictures.

These standards or closely related standards are found in almost all state standards. For example, Colorado State Standards for Student Learning include the following:

History
- Describe the economic reasons why people move to or from a location (for example, explorers, nomadic people, miners, traders).
- Recognize the presence, interactions, and contributions of various groups and culture have affected the school, neighborhood, community, and states.

Geography
- Identify the causes of human migration.
- Identify the factors that affect where people settle.
- Identify how people depend upon, adapt to, and modify the physical environment.
- Describe how places and environments may have influenced people and events over time.

Reading and Writing
- Read to locate, select, and make use of relevant information from a variety of media, reference, and technological sources.

How do you proceed?

1. Unpacking the Standards   The *overarching understandings* or big idea could be as follows:

There are basic needs in all societies, past and present, such as food, clothing, shelter, communication, transportation, government, and so on.

We can interpret how people lived in the past by analyzing artifacts and pictures and see the *changes* that have occurred in time.

You could also name the important concepts and skills that will be developed in this unit.

2. Designing the Assessment(s)   Using West Virginia's standards, you must now decide what assessment you will use to determine whether your students have achieved the standards. You think that having the students produce a community almanac is a good idea. This will also fit in with literacy needs and use other standards for the social studies. In effect, the product, the community almanac, will be the assessment tool of how well students have achieved these specific history standards as well as other standards.

You have to make some additional decisions about the unit. First, you decide to limit the comparison in your community to 1940 to the present. Otherwise, the students may be confused. Choosing 1940 compared to the present also allows you to get data (maps, newspapers, and so on) more easily than for earlier periods. Using 1940 as a benchmark means also that students can interview older, long-term community members to gain data.

You also have to articulate or make clear the *criteria* or rubric that will be used to evaluate student work/performance. *Rubrics* are clearly described performance levels for student tasks. Typically, there are four levels in using a rubric. In other words, Level 1, the lowest level for this unit, means that a student(s) did not complete the project, made almost no effort for the assignment, and produced a minimum amount of work. For Level 4, the highest level, students successfully wrote two or three pages of well-organized paragraphs and photographs describing their significance (more on rubrics in Chapter 4).

3. Design the Activities to Ensure Learning for All Students   What activities will have to be done to achieve these standards? Students will learn that an almanac is a publication of miscellaneous information. You will share with them samples of different almanacs such as *The World Almanac* and *The Farmer's Almanac*. In addition, you need to write to parents that their help is needed for the community almanac project with photographs of their family and the community. Students then will be divided into groups and each group will produce two or three pages, including photographs, about their topic for the community almanac.

In Table 2.2 are some topics and in parentheses are concepts that students will use to compare the changes from 1940 to the present. Although the students will all have learning experiences in history as they compare the changes from 1940 to the present, you can see that students in this unit will also learn about other social studies standards and concepts as well as literacy skills. Another alternative is a podcast as the assessment. Thus, starting with selecting a specific standard and then choosing the type of assessment will lead into the topical development of the curriculum and instruction for this unit.

Table 2.2	Compare 1940 to the Present
1940	**Present**
Immigration (migration)	
Land Use (human–land relationships)	
Food Produced (economics)	
Transportation (economics, technology)	
Businesses (economic systems)	
Clothing (culture)	
Recreation (culture)	
Homes and Appliances (culture, human and environmental relationships)	
Time Line of Important National and International Events Such as World War II (change)	

Let us review the steps we made in this example.

1. *Standard Number and Description* (in some states more description is given). Unpack the standard. What are the major understandings outlined in the standard.
2. *Essential Key Concepts and Skills for This Standard.* The most important concepts are change, a history concept, and community, a civics concept. Skills include research skills for gathering a variety of primary sources for student topics, reading maps, interpreting photographs, constructing time lines, using the Yellow Pages to find specific types of businesses, working cooperatively in groups, and writing.
3. *Secondary or Optional Topics for This Standard.* Economic and geography standards are also used for the student topics, such as location, land use, and the relationships among geographic factors, available resources, and transportation in determining how people make a living.
4. *Interdisciplinary Opportunities/Connection.* Strong connection with writing.
5. *Activities for Student Learning.* Lesson plans with resources plus getting feedback on how students are doing
6. *Review of What Student Learning Has Occurred.* Use data from assessment to give feedback to students. Is any reteaching needed? Gaps in students' understanding?

What seems the hardest step? Often it is breaking down a standard and planning the assessment. Let look at another example to further break down a standard by taking California's state standard 5.5, "The Causes of the American Revolution," which could be used when U.S. history is taught. The overarching understanding could be as follows:
Economic, political and social differences may lead to conflict.

Essential Questions
1. How did economic interests influence the revolution?
2. How did politics influence the revolution?
3. In what ways did individuals influence the revolution?

What assessment(s) will be used by students to demonstrate their understandings of the standard/essential questions? The key understandings and skills could be as follows:

1. Students will identify and explain key events and people leading up to and during the revolution.
2. Students will identify loyalists and patriots and explain their beliefs.
3. Students will analyze the Declaration of Independence for its core ideals

What assessment could be used? Some that are tied into the above three understandings and skills are presented below. Always check with a pretest what students already know.

1. Make a timeline of key events and people. After reading a chapter of historical fiction on the American Revolution, students record what is happening to the protagonist coordinated with a timeline.
2. Role-play loyalist and patriot viewpoints on the Boston Tea Party.

3. Write a statement of independence from something, someone, or a group. This could be an actual situation or one made up. Include four parts: introduction, beliefs, wrongs, final decision.

You can see that many learning activities could flow from the planning done for the all students.

Of course, some districts will request even more detail. Examine the Los Angeles Unified School District guidelines (Table 2.3). Whew! After glancing at the Los Angeles Unified School District's standards-based instruction model, do you want to teach there? It will take time to design an instructional unit using this standards-based instruction model. However, with such detailed planning and sharp focus, there is also a much better chance that the students will learn more. Note that this model is a combination of new ideas about standards and assessment with the older practice of instructional objectives using clearly defined verbs (e.g., student *will identify* . . . or student *will compare* . . .). In some schools, specific state standards are used instead of objectives. This appears to be a growing trend. However, realize that standards-based practices mean different things to different people. Furthermore, different states' standards have different emphases for their content standards.

On Your Own **2.3**

Students Need to Know the Standard?

Especially in schools defined as "failing," principals and other trainers have asked that teachers post the standard that they are teaching and that students, when asked, know the standard. In a few cases, students actually write the number of the standard on their assignments. Why is this being done? Do you think this is a good idea? ●

Table 2.3	Los Angeles Unified School District

Guidelines for Developing a Standards-Based Instruction Model

1. *Culminating Task/Assignment for a standard.* What will the individual student produce to demonstrate achievement of the standard(s)? Begin the task with a verb. The student *will* . . .

2. *Assessment.* What criteria or rubric will be used to evaluate/score student work/performance of the culminating task? The statement of the product to be scored is followed by a verb. Task to be scored by four levels (highest score to lowest score).

3. *Instructional Activities.* What learning activities will the student be involved in to acquire content knowledge and skills to achieve the standard? Consider alternative strategies and modifications to promote equal access for all learners. Begin each learning activity with a verb describing what the student is to do.

4. *Time.* How much time will be required for the student to complete each of the activities?

5. *Resources.* What materials, textbooks, supplies, documents, and so on will support the student doing each instructional activity?

Source: Model developed, refined, and field-tested by Task Force on Standards-Based Instruction (no date).

Treasury of Resources and Technology for Planning

You probably have already gathered some resources for your unit. However, it is helpful to try to especially locate the following resources to help with better planning of your social studies program.

Student, Parent, and Family Resources

Because the social studies are about people, students and their families can often be used as resources. A grandmother may be able to tell what it was like to live on a farm fifty years ago. A parent may be able to describe his or her job when the class is studying community workers or the job market. A student may have lived in another part of the country or the world. There may be artifacts from different nations in the homes of students that would be of interest to the class. Many teachers find that these resources add sparkle to the class. Use special events such as open house and media presentations by the class to talk to and ask for help from parents. Try newsletters or e-mails to parents outlining what is going to be covered in the coming social studies unit and asking if they can help in any way.

Community Resources

The community is the neighborhood beyond the family. There are three important community resources: local publications, field trips, and guest speakers. Use the community as a resource for field trips, especially if the students are able to walk to see something such as the local bakery or police station. If this is not feasible, resource people from the community (e.g., probation officers or park rangers) can come to the classroom. Community resources can also include free local newspapers or materials from the local bank or other community institutions, especially government agencies. In particular, community programs such as Healthy Start, After School Partnerships, Healthy Kids, and School-Health Connections desire more cooperation and attention from the school in their goal to improve the health of all children.

Your school may also have a partnership arrangement with a local company or institution such as the local college or university. This can be an important resource because the partnership often provides funds, tutors, and other resources. Explore in what ways the partnership could help your class. To be successful, however, partnerships must be a two-way street. Both sides need to contribute. Students should not just be on the receiving side. For example, can the teacher and the students put together a short musical performance or skit for the other half of the partnership? Communication with the partner as well as parents can also be increased by e-mail and websites of the school or the individual class.

In addition, students can serve the community in projects ranging from helping senior citizens to cleaning up local parks. Community service provides a bridge between students and the community and can be an important resource in building toward the goal of citizenship (see Chapter 8). Be certain to clear such projects with your school principal.

Computer Resources

More and more teachers are using the Internet for ideas, units, and lesson plans. **Teacher portals** with their repositories of lesson plans, assignments, and links are becoming more popular even though some include advertising and fees.

TECHNOLOGY

Blue Web'n	www.kn.pacbell.com/wired/bluewebn
The Internet Public Library	www.ipl.org
The Gateway to Educational Materials	www.thegateway.org
MarcoPolo	www.marcopolo-education.org
One Stop Research	www.nationalgeographic.com/onestop

For educators, the leading computer journal is *Learning & Leading with Technology,* produced by the International Society for Technology in Education (ISTE). In addition, they publish many helpful general resources, such as *Resources for Assessment* or *Multidisciplinary Units for Prekindergarten Through Grade 2* (www.iste.org/bookstore). Check if your media center subscribes to this journal or has some of their publications. This organization also has the most widely accepted computer literacy standards for students. These standards can be divided into three main areas:

1. *Basic skills or operations.* Use a word processor, use e-mail, use developmentally appropriate multimedia encyclopedias, find pertinent reliable data and information, use technology systems and software responsibly, operate equipment such as a VCR, audiotape player, DVD player, and interactive books.
2. *Critical thinking skills.* Select and evaluate information resources; distinguish between fact, opinion, and point of view; evaluate accuracy, relevance, appropriateness, and bias.
3. *Construction skills.* Use a variety of media and formats to communicate information and ideas effectively, prepare publications, apply problem solving and decision making to tasks.

When using computer and related resources, keep these student literacy standards in mind.

Video Clips   If your school/district can afford it, using commercial services that offers thousands of educational videos and video clips on demand is very convenient to quickly find a video clip on the Statue of Liberty or archaeological sites of ancient Egypt. It is even better if the video can be projected directly on a whiteboard. By pausing, students can then identify the important details. Free video clips are available from The History Channel (www.historychannel.com) and other sources, often public institutions such as universities.

If you are not as fortunate to have commercial services, you need to look carefully at the videos, photographs, slides, and television series that can be obtained in your district. Typically, the sooner your order is placed, the better will be your chance of securing the items because other teachers also may want to use these resources. These media, especially with visual components, can add meaning to otherwise abstract ideas that a teacher's voice cannot provide. Technology such as the digital versatile disc (DVD) or digital video disc is also becoming more available, adding an additional resource to enrich your teaching.

Free or inexpensive posters and other materials may be obtained from the consulates of foreign nations in large U.S. cities. Order the materials as early in the school year as possible to allow time for shipment, and make arrangements well in advance for speakers, especially those on tight schedules, such as government officials.

Current Events/Current Affairs

The social studies are unique among elementary-school subjects because they deal with events that are continually happening in the local community and the wider world that have an impact on students and their families. Often these events are directly relevant to what you are trying to achieve in your social studies program. The goal of encouraging social participation in community affairs should lead you to consider how current events can be used to enrich the social studies program.

Weekly papers, prepared by publishers at the appropriate reading levels for students in different grades, can be helpful. But in real life, newspapers, magazines, and television are not as neatly balanced and objective as educational products, and students eventually need to become familiar with regular news reports. In addition, students living in an environment dominated by television must understand what the news reporters on television are talking about. Discussions on television are often incomplete. Students need more background to understand the issues. Also, television news is frequently weak on analysis. Students need to understand how all elements of the mass media including the Internet are important and be able to analyze the messages that are being given and received.

TECHNOLOGY

All these elements make the social studies unique among subject areas and should be part of your consideration in planning. See Chapter 8 for more detail on teaching current events/current affairs.

Units

A **unit** is the unifying structure focus on which lessons and assessments are prepared. Basically it is time allocated to teaching a major subdivision in the year's course. The unit is a plan that organizes a sequential progression of lessons related in theme, topic, issue, or problem, as well as how assessment will be handled. Typically, a social studies unit covers the main concepts of a particular subject area. In addition, the unit has provisions for teaching skills, values, and, if possible, social participation. A unit consists of three parts: (1) an introductory activity designed to activate students' prior knowledge and to stimulate interest; (2) a series of sequenced lesson plans; and (3) one or more culminating activities that reinforce, bring closure to the unit, and allow students to demonstrate what they have learned. Using this planning model, teachers can determine student strengths and weaknesses in the context of daily learning activities rather than waiting for the unit test/assessment.

Why do experts recommend teaching in units? Students learn less if on Monday they have a map exercise on latitude and longitude, on Tuesday they have a value exercise on twenty things they love to do, on Wednesday they visit their local fire department, on

Thursday they read their social studies textbook on American Indian tribes in the northeastern part of the United States, and on Friday they study current events. Each lesson may be worthwhile by itself, but the lessons do not build sequentially. A unit should tie skills and knowledge together under a theme so that learning is not isolated and fragmented. Learning is more likely to take place when topics are not fragmented or isolated. Learning takes place when we introduce a unit, have a progression of lessons to develop a theme, and conclude with an activity. We can characterize the many different types of units as textbook units, commercial units, and teacher-prepared units.

Textbook Units

Textbook units are found in most texts in use today. Almost all social studies textbooks are organized by major units such as *Africa Today* or *The New Nation Faces Many Problems.* There are usually several big units in the book and under each unit are several chapters. Then within each chapter are several daily lessons. The publishers generally predict or project a given time for how long a unit will last and offer many suggestions for teaching or enriching the unit. Probably the greatest advantage to using the units in the textbook is that they reduce the amount of planning a teacher needs to do, especially if the teacher's background in the content is not strong or current. However, we should use textbooks with caution. Some students may not be able to read the textbook, or they may find the concepts are described too briefly, making the ideas seem artificial and abstract. Often the textbook's lessons and chapters are written in a repetitive format, requiring students to read and answer questions posed by the textbook. The students' reaction: boring, boring, boring. With few hands-on experiences or discussion of the topics, the social studies program is lackluster.

Textbook units cannot accomplish every aspect of planning in the classroom. Specifically, they may cause teachers to make the following instructional errors:

- Teacher makes all the decisions on what will be learned and when.
- All students must learn the same body of knowledge despite individual differences, prior learning, culture, and disabilities.
- Students do not always understand the purpose of an assignment.
- Texts may encourage fragmented connections with other subject areas.
- Content is not connected with students' interests and experiences.
- Texts may encourage the teachers to ask lower-level factual questions based only on the textbook.
- Texts may not focus on changes and problems in the students' real-life community.
- Students will see social studies as just facts and figures from a textbook.
- Texts may not be related to state and local standards.

Commercial Units

Commercial units are similar to textbook units but are prepared by a specific group. For example, the Anti-Defamation League has prepared workbook units with the objective of reducing bias and discrimination in our society. Professional organizations also make units available for a fee. The National Center for History in the Schools (University of California,

Los Angeles, CA, 90024-4108, FAX: 310-825-4723) sells units developed by teachers who have spent a summer developing and then trying out units.

Often these commercial units are designed by teachers or consultants who are trying to meet a special curriculum need or a desire of the sponsoring group to get its point of view into the classroom. For example, since 9/11, the war in Iraq, and changes in population, new state curriculum directions may ask sixth-grade teachers to cover Islam, a topic that has rapidly achieved high interest and importance. Many experienced teachers would feel unprepared to teach a unit on Islam or other unfamiliar topics. Although websites do offer lessons on current issues, they may not have enough content and skills for a unit. Teachers are often willing to pay or have the district pay for a unit that can specifically help them to include a topic new to them in their program. Buying commercial units is common in the teaching of novels, especially classics such as *The Adventures of Tom Sawyer* and *Little House on the Prairie.* Groups such as those trying to introduce more economic education into the curriculum may find one of the easiest ways to do so is to produce a unit that teachers can immediately implement.

Commercial units, often free, are also produced by associations or companies with the goal of exposing students indirectly to the organization's ideas. Organizations ranging from the Dairy Council to the National Association of Newspaper Editors and the National Rifle Association produce units and free or inexpensive instructional materials. For example, Procter & Gamble for years has produced social studies units on ecology, the economy, and advertising. These free materials may include reproducible lessons, videos, teaching tips for each lesson, and colorful posters. A teacher, of course, needs to be aware that a given company may be introducing subtle bias into the unit and should carefully alert students to the source of the data. Commercially sponsored units or kits are especially common in the areas of nutrition, the environment, and the economy.

Teacher-Prepared Units

Teachers can develop or adopt from a variety of resources to organize their own units. Unlike the typical textbook or commercial units, **teacher-prepared units** can be based on the concepts, generalizations, and themes generated by the social sciences. For example, economics focuses on how individuals and groups use the resources available to them. Therefore, both individuals and groups make economic decisions every day. Using this major economic generalization, a teacher can ask primary students to keep track of what they spend their money on during a given time period. Then they can classify which expenditures were for goods and which ones were for services. Which is the larger category? Children often see their parents paying by check, credit card, or money when they buy goods, but they seldom see them pay for the dentist, and they are even less likely to realize that their families pay indirectly through taxes for public services such as those given by teachers or other employees of the schools. Children can be asked to list people who provide services that are paid for by taxes. Shifting from services to goods, students can classify the materials that were used to produce the goods they purchased, such as candy bars, or the tools that workers used to deliver services. For example, what resources are needed to make candy or bread? Another resource is time. How are students spending their time when they are out of school? What choices are they making? What are the implications of their research? What do the data reveal about themselves and their community? This one economic generalization can lead to a variety of interesting lessons focused on the children's lives while also helping the children make sense of the complex world in which they live. Most textbook or commercial units would not be as focused on the lives of the students and their communities as would be possible with a teacher-made unit.

Teachers can experience several advantages from making their own units:

- Having a sense of ownership and pride in the unit if it is successful
- Integrating the curriculum easily across subject areas because the teacher knows what will be taught during the rest of the day and can link subject areas
- Individualizing the unit to match students' abilities and experiences
- Using the teacher's own talents and experiences
- Using local community resources

Other Teacher-Made Units

Check with the website of your state's department of education. Many states have online units as well as lesson plans. For example, the California Department of Education has course models for teachers in grades 1 through 12 keyed to the California state standards (www.history.ctaponline.org) Another source of teacher-made units are WebQuests (Chapter 5), a problem solving inquiry that mostly uses resources from the Internet. Both your state's department of education resources and the WebQuests, found on the Internet, are free of charge.

TECHNOLOGY

Integrated Curriculum/Interdisciplinary Thematic Units

How Common Is an Integrated Curriculum?   What is an integrated curriculum? Definitions may vary but an **integrated curriculum** cuts across the subject areas or academic disciplines. It is a combination of two or more subjects areas. An integrated curriculum tends to go beyond the typical textbook treatment for a given subject area. The most likely pattern is targeting social studies and reading/language arts as a successful combination for student learning (more in Chapter 10). *This curriculum pattern is especially advocated now when social studies is being crowded out of the curriculum.* The rationale for integration is that since students need to read, why not have them read social studies content. In this manner, social studies is taught but it also strengthens reading, writing, and communication skills. However, the opposite viewpoint is that reading and math as skills subjects need to be taught separately since reading and math are tested whereas an integrated curriculum is not.

How commonly is social studies taught as an integrated subject? A national survey of elementary teachers showed the vastly differing patterns at different grade levels (Table 2.4). In general, the second grade had the most integrated social studies programs whereas the eighth grade had the least. In the eighth grade, social studies is most often taught as a separate subject since it is most likely taught in a departmentalized setting and not in a self-contained classroom.

Interdisciplinary thematic units typically try to combine history and the social sciences with other academic subjects such as science, literature, music, arts, and other areas. An interdisciplinary thematic unit has a theme (or concept or generalization) that organizes the learning around central ideas. Thus, in an integrative social studies unit, reading/

Table 2.4	Amount of Integration at Different Grade Levels, as Percentages		
	Grade 2	Grade 5	Grade 8
Stand-alone	18	37	67
Partially integrated	54	49	27
Mostly integrated	27	14	6

Source: Modified from Question 27 in James S. Leming, Lucien Ellington, and Mark Schub, *Social Studies in Our Nation's Elementary and Middle Schools: A National Random Survey of Social Studies Teachers' Professional Opinions, Values, and Classroom Practices,* p. 67. (Storrs, CT: The Center for Survey Research and Analysis, 2006).

language arts and mathematics are not seen as ends in themselves but should become tools students use to study the social studies content. Thus, some skill development in these subjects flows from the tools needed in the unit, such as reading the text or reference books and newspapers, leading to a more natural sequence of instruction. Thus, advocates of integrated curriculum want to avoid the compartmentalization in which subjects are taught without students making connections about what they are learning. In other words, too often the science unit on plants or energy is not related to what students are learning about pioneer families' food production and their preparation of food. In addition, integration helps to cut down the "bloated curriculum" of the many different subject areas. Advocates say it provides a way young children learn naturally.

In an interdisciplinary approach, subjects are interwoven instead of being taught as separate subjects at different times of the day. This approach also goes by a variety of other names: *curriculum integration, integrated curriculum, interdisciplinary curriculum, thematic instruction, multidisciplinary teaching,* and *integrated studies.* The terms *integrated curriculum* and *integrated instruction* are also used interchangeably. All of these terms and synonyms refer to a way of planning and teaching so that the separate disciplines are brought together in a meaningful unit.

Concerns about Integrated Curriculum   Critics such as Brophy and Alleman[3] have raised questions about whether curriculum integration is a boon or a threat to social studies. They are concerned that social studies goals get lost in the process of integration and academic content is trivialized. In particular, important content is not taught when students read a literature book about an immigrant family or the Civil War and, thus, students do not have the background to understand why the historical events in the book are occurring. In other words, sometimes in practice an integrated curriculum often avoids difficult content and low-quality learning experiences are the result.

Another concern about integrated curriculum is that it leads to confusion on the part of students because they only partly understand the various subject disciplines introduced. For

[3]Jere E. Brophy, and Janet Alleman, "Is Curriculum Integration a Boon or a Threat to Social Studies?" *Social Education* 57, no. 6 (1993): 287–291.

example, in studying Benjamin Franklin, students may not understand enough about electricity to appreciate Franklin's experiments with electricity or have enough background in U.S. history to comprehend Franklin's important roles before and during the American Revolution and his crusade in later life against slavery. He was just someone flying a kite during a storm. In some classrooms, Franklin might be best studied with the emphasis on the historical period.

These criticisms of integrated curriculum are worth taking seriously. There is little research presently on student learning from integration. The whole point of an integrated unit is how students' learning can best be encouraged. Does this happen most of the time? For example, a fifth-grade class studied a unit on the American Revolution by reading theme literature, but the students could not tell which side was victorious in the American Revolution. It did not appear that the students learned much about history. A strong argument can be made that each discipline or school subject has important contributions to make to student learning and that an integrated unit is not always desirable.

These comments emphasize that during a given year all units do not have to be integrated or need to be taught as separate subjects. Professional judgment is necessary to evaluate when it is best to integrate a unit and how much integration is needed. Good interdisciplinary thematic units have many advantages if they are well thought out and result in high student interest and achievement. Normally in the social studies some degree of reading, listening, and writing is found. These skills then can be infused into the social studies unit. In many cases, social studies is the most logical area for integration of a theme. Reading/language arts as well as art and drama are often easily incorporated into an interdisciplinary thematic unit. But at times it is artificial to try to integrate a subject or subjects into a theme and the results are a jumbled mess in terms of students losing sight of what the theme or central idea is.

How are thematic units put together? In practice, units are integrated in varying degrees—ranging from some that are barely blended to completely integrated units with no subject boundaries.

Designing Integrated Units   Let us look at a possible primary grade topic: transportation. A common standard might be "Study transportation today (and in the past)." The major theme or generalization is that transportation is moving people or things from one place to another.

Sometimes changing the theme into a question makes planning easier. What kinds of transportation exist in the world today? By brainstorming ideas that fit this broad question, you will develop a list of concepts, definitions, and questions relating to the theme. Here are some possibilities:

Animals that provide transportation

People power, such as walking

Machines that provide transportation

Transportation on land, air, and water; different kinds; classification

Why it is important to have good transportation

Safety; roads and highways; traffic rules and signs

What is a vehicle? A wheeled vehicle?

What makes a vehicle run or go?

Trucks

Trains

Some teachers like to think in terms of subjects. How might art contribute to the theme? Science? Math? Language arts? More teachers are now using the four basic social science disciplines found in their state standards to guide their planning.

History: What was transportation like long ago?

Civics: What are the government regulations/rules for different types of transportation? Safety rules? Taxes for roads and highways?

Economics: How much does it cost to go to the same place by car, bus, taxi, and so on? What jobs are found in transportation?

Geography: What geographic features cause difficulties for building transportation systems?

The next step is to look over these ideas and questions. Which ones seem logically connected with each other? Drawing these connections on a large sheet of paper using the technique of concept mapping will help you visualize ways that topics can be linked and sequenced. Once the topics or questions are diagrammed, the next step is to focus on what objectives you wish to achieve from the unit. They might be as follows:

1. Students will identify examples of transportation on land, air, and water (a content objective).
2. Students will create a graph of the different types of transportation their families use within a week (a skill objective).
3. Students will give reasons why it is important to have a transportation system in their community (content and appreciation objective).

Once the objectives are sketched, the next task is to think of all the learning activities and resources that will help develop each objective. Trade books, songs, tapes, and records need to be surveyed as a first step. You can then list other resources and activities:

- Possible guest speakers such as pilots and animal control officers
- Class surveys of different transportation used by students
- Field trips to airports and truck depots to see these systems in operation
- Observation and discussion of correct ways of crossing streets
- Figuring out distances to school
- Getting lost, or the value of helpful maps

You can add a lot more. The difficulty usually comes in deciding when to stop and selecting the ideas you will use.

This type of unit would have the usual introductory activities as well as a final culmination activity. The learning activities and resources come from a variety of academic areas. With no artificial divisions between time periods in the classroom, students can put together and reconstruct their own ideas more easily. Students can express their ideas through drama-tization, writing projects, visual arts, or music. Assessment and evaluation could include portfolios of student-produced projects, observations, as well as paper-and-pencil tests.

The formal process for developing interdisciplinary thematic units can be summarized in a few logical steps:

1. Select a standard/theme/important idea.
2. Brainstorm different ideas, activities, and resources that fit the theme.
3. Formulate unit objectives.
4. Locate resources.
5. Organize activities that allow students to make connections among ideas and experiences.
6. Evaluate and assess progress and achievement (may be done throughout the unit).

The sample unit plan "Grasslands: A National Resource" is an example of how the NCSS geography theme/standard, People, Places, and Environments, used Grasslands as an interdisciplinary unit. One key concept for the students to learn is *region,* an area with one or more common characteristics or features that give it a measure of unity and make it different from surrounding areas.

Look carefully at this briefly sketched unit. Do you like it? Is it a good interdisciplinary unit? Its strengths are that the assessment is built into the learning experiences and is not divorced from it. There is also a beginning (providing background), a middle (with numerous sequenced activities), and a final culminating experience.

The designer of this unit, a teacher from Colorado, used Colorado as one of the two regions of grasslands. You might want to use the common characteristics of the region in which your students live and make some comparison with a similar or different region. Some teachers have used different regions of their own state. You can identify the animal and plant life indigenous to your region, or the products your region produces and where they are marketed. Perhaps you may want more time to show that regions change or that a region has common characteristics. Or you may want to include more group work or to use photographs to describe ways in which your local area has changed. Note that any teacher can modify and emphasize different key ideas in the concept of region in this unit, especially through the selection of resources and materials.

Small Group Work **2.2**

Identify Academic Disciplines and Skills in Grasslands

1. Make a list of the disciplines (science, art, and so on) that appear to be used in each activity and assessment.
2. Write down the skills that are developed in each activity and assessment.
3. Each group member should decide if this is a good interdisciplinary unit. ●

UNIT PLAN

Grasslands: A Natural Resource

Overview

Grasslands are the world's best places to grow food. Grasslands have less than 20 inches of rain per year. Getting food becomes a problem as our population increases and land is plowed under to make room for people. This unit teaches about two grasslands (in Colorado and in Kenya) and ends with the class analyzing the future of one of the earth's most precious natural resources.

NCSS Themes/Standards

Culture (1) and Geography (3)

Integration

Social studies, science, language arts, art

Activities

1. Utilize a number of books/resources about the grasslands to provide background knowledge.
2. Begin dioramas that will be used in assessment. Plant grasses from Colorado prairie and Kenya savanna NOW so these will be growing at assessment time.
3. Review concepts of region. Discuss if grasslands are a region. Use primary atlases to investigate if (and where) grasslands are found on various continents.
4. Using a variety of resources, identify and analyze past and present use of both grassland areas. Develop a chart or graphic organizer to display information gathered.
5. Investigate what food products come from grasses.
6. Investigate and analyze how weather and climate affect grasslands in these two areas.
7. Discuss present use of both areas and theorize on the future. Discuss conservation/preservation practices.
8. Do the treasure map activity that takes students through a grassland to practice map skills.

Assessments

1. The task is to make the previously planted container into a recognizable ecosystem by adding plants, animals, people, homes, etc., in some art form. Each diorama is to be divided in half, to show both past and present.
2. Present diorama to class and justify contents orally using information gathered in this unit. Weather and climate are factors to be discussed. State why grasslands are a "region."

Source: Abridged version of a unit for grades 1–5 by Janet Pommrehn, Denver Public Schools Elementary Teacher.

What are some sources of themes? Besides traditional themes such as transportation, the American Revolution, and the environment from content areas, sources might include biographies, local events and history, world events, or family histories. Teachers have successfully used such themes as Egyptian mummies, architecture of a given community, or a book such as *Sarah, Plain and Tall.* Popular primary themes are foods, friends, grandparents, folktales, and famous people. Themes for the middle grades might focus on immigration, courage, and prejudice. Themes could be selected by the teacher or could emerge from the experiences and current needs of students.

Beginners often ask how long a unit should last. There is no fixed answer to this question, but younger students probably profit more from shorter units, perhaps two or three weeks, and older students gain more from units that are longer, up to six weeks. If the unit goes on too long, students may lose interest. Some teachers, however, find that students beg for more after interesting units, such as the economic simulation called *Mini-Society,* which lasts a full six weeks. The ideal time depends both on the age of the students and the material being taught.

Units may vary in length depending on how many other areas of the curriculum are included in them. A social studies unit that incorporates art, music, literature, and science usually lasts longer than one that includes no other disciplines. In planning a unit, try to incorporate as many relevant curriculum areas and skills as possible.

Two Units on Hawaii

Now let us look in more detail at some other units. Units about states may include the following NCSS themes/standards: Culture (1); Time, Continuity, and Change (2); and People, Places, and Environments (3).

Elizabeth A. Gelbart reported about the unit "Travel Day to Hawaii," which she had designed, at a social studies conference.[4] In addition to the previous outline, Gelbart provided ten pages describing in more detail worksheets with topics such as "A Hawaiian Volcano Erupts."

The sample unit plan "Travel Day to Hawaii" has many strengths; many classes would learn from and enjoy it, especially the final day's culmination activity. Check how assessment is handled. Does it flow naturally from the activities? But there is one serious concern: Is the unit reinforcing stereotypes about Hawaii? Will students learn about the large city of Honolulu with its wide diversity of people? Will students find out about the problems Hawaii is facing today as its land usage changes? The unit focuses on the tourist

On Your Own **2.4**

Analyze the Unit

In the sample unit plan "Travel Day to Hawaii," are the theme and content appropriate for the age group? Are there provisions for teaching skills and values? Is there a variety of activities for the children? Is there integration with other subject areas of the curriculum? Do you think the class would enjoy the unit? Is there a progression of experiences and activities that leads to a culmination in the unit? ●

[4]Elizabeth A. Gelbart, "Travel Day to Hawaii." Presented at the California Council for the Social Studies Conference (Los Angeles, 1986).

UNIT PLAN

Travel Day to Hawaii

The following unit is planned to last one week and is prepared for the primary grades. Usually, such a unit has a broad objective and specific daily objectives. Although it might be inappropriate to use verbs such as *know, value,* and *understand* in behavioral objectives for individual lessons, such words are appropriate at the beginning of a unit where they provide overall guidance and organization to the instructional process.

NCSS Themes/Standards

Culture (1), History (2), and Geography (3)

Unit Goals

1. Students will understand the geography, history, and traditional culture of Hawaii.
2. Students will identify different types of transportation.

Day 1

> *Objectives:* Students will distinguish an island from a land mass.
> Students will describe their experiences about Hawaii.
> Students will draw the Hawaiian Islands.

1. Introduce the vocabulary term *island.* Brainstorm with the class: What is an island? Have the children look at a map of the United States and find a state that is a group of islands.
2. Discuss the history of Hawaii. Share past experiences of children or their parents who have visited there.
3. Tell the children that the class will go on a "pretend" trip to Hawaii in five days. Discuss different modes of transportation.
4. Draw the islands on brown butcher paper and label them according to shape. Have the children pin up the product on the bulletin board with a blue background for water.

Day 2

> *Objectives:* Students will differentiate the various types of transportation.
> Students will calculate distances from their state to Hawaii.

1. Brainstorm with the children as to the different ways the class could travel to Hawaii (airplane, ship, sailboat, etc.).
2. Design an airplane ticket. Include the date, time of departure, and so on.

Day 3

> *Objective:* Students will describe the traditional cultures and history of Hawaii.

1. Read "Palm Tree" from *Young Folks Hawaiian Time.*
2. Discuss the term *luau,* as well as foods usually eaten, dances, and so on.
3. Have children make drawings of Hawaiian traditions for a mural.
4. Learn the hula from a community member.

UNIT PLAN continued   Travel Day to Hawaii

Day 4

Objective: Students will depict the sequence of volcano formation.

1. Brainstorm the term *volcano*. Discuss how volcanoes formed the islands.
2. Have the children divide paper into four squares. Illustrate an eruption of a volcano in sequence.

Day 5

Objective: Students will simulate a travel day in Hawaii. This lesson plan is part of a full day's activity: a "pretend" in-classroom flight to another state. Hawaii is used as an example in this lesson, but other states or nations could be used as well. This travel day combines all subjects in a *fun* educational setting. The following is an example of such a day.

1. "Takeoff"
   a. Collect children-made airplane tickets at the door.
   b. Review the flight route (ocean to be flown over, etc.).
2. Math-macaroni leis
   a. Design a simple count pattern (two reds, one yellow, and repeat) with dyed macaroni and construction-paper flowers. Save for the luau.
   b. Count the number of leis made.
3. Language/letter-writing skills
   a. Write and design a postcard to a friend or family member.
   b. Discuss how to address a postcard, the purpose of a stamp, and how to use descriptive language.
4. Reading/vocabulary skills
   a. Share "Hawaiian Alphabet" from *Young Folks Hawaiian Time*.
   b. Complete a worksheet on Hawaiian terms.
   c. List terms in alphabetical order.
5. Science: parts of flowers
   a. Label a hibiscus flower.
   b. Discuss the climate needed for it to grow and the stages of plant growth in general.
6. Art and music
   a. Learn the hula and Hawaiian folktales.
   b. Design a scrapbook of the day's events. Draw scenes of Hawaii with brief written descriptions.
7. Social studies: culture and foods of Hawaii
   a. Finish with a luau in Hawaii. Poi, coconut, and pineapple juice are a few suggested foods to share. The children should eat with their fingers.
   b. "Reboard" for the return flight home.

world of Hawaii. Attractive as that may be, it is not the whole picture. Note that the basic plan of this unit could be used for other nations or even states within the United States, but a teacher must be certain that students understand there is more to a region than the tourist view.

Let us now look at another unit on Hawaii, "Living in Hawaii: Now and Long Ago," using more of the **constructionist** or active learning on the part of the learner. Constructionist theory and instructional practices:

- Stress the importance of students' prior learning by asking what students already know
- Posit that learning occurs when the student is able to tie newly acquired information to previous understandings
- Organize learning and instruction around important ideas
- Challenge the adequacy of the learner's prior knowledge
- Assess a learner's knowledge acquisition during the lesson

Critiquing the Two Units

Comparison of the two units certainly shows the variety and creativity that can be developed with the same topic. Both units encourage an integration with other areas of the curriculum and use skills and content from a variety of subject areas. Both also try to make the activities interesting and meaningful for students. By comparison, both can make connections with previous units.

Both units have the power to expand student knowledge and skills. Both units could also be used to compare life in Hawaii with the student's own community or state. The uniqueness of Hawaii with other states often makes for a strong contrast.

Compared with the first unit, "Living in Hawaii: Now and Long Ago" goes beyond tourist stereotypes and pushes students beyond their first, and probably inaccurate, images of Hawaii. The second unit also fosters more respect for the daring and brave Polynesians who made the trip to Hawaii. This emphasis on the native culture and its history probably also encourages a more multicultural view of the history of Hawaii.

Are there any weaknesses in "Living in Hawaii: Now and Long Ago?" Checking your state standards might suggest that the geography focus is not as sharp as it could be. It is implied by media used in the unit that the students would learn about Hawaii's tropical climate and volcanic origins but this is not explicitly taught. In the second unit, are economic data on jobs as interesting as those in the first unit, "Travel Day to Hawaii"? Both students and the teacher might like the "Travel Day to Hawaii" unit more and this might contribute to its success.

TECHNOLOGY

But perhaps the greatest challenge (both a strength and a weakness) is that "Living in Hawaii: Now and Long Ago" requires sufficient reading skills in finding information in media and the Internet and higher-level skills in comparing now and long ago. Even with a strong media component, for some pairs the only way to find the necessary information (for example, the data on jobs) would be by reading. That is why the suggestion is given that students work in pairs, chosen by the teacher. It is hoped that one strong reader will be in each pair. In addition, "Living in Hawaii: Now and Long Ago" requires that the students become familiar with taking turns at the computer(s) and helping each other. For these reasons, this unit might be more appropriate for older primary children or children who have some skill in finding information. In addition, some pairs will finish their assigned tasks sooner than other pairs. If they finish earlier, they can be encouraged to

UNIT PLAN

Living in Hawaii: Now and Long Ago

The following one-week unit is prepared for primary grades.

NCSS Themes/Standards

Culture (1), History (2), Geography (3), and Economics (7)

Unit Goals

1. Students will understand the geography, history, and traditional culture of Hawaii (same objective as first unit, "Travel to Hawaii").
2. Students will compare the traditional Polynesian culture of Hawaii with the present (different objective compared to the first unit)

Day 1

Objectives: Students locate Hawaii on a globe.
Using a KWL chart, students tell what they know (K), want (W) to learn, and later did learn (L) on Hawaii.

1. Locate Hawaii on the globe as well as on maps. As a review, compare the location and size of Hawaii to the state where students live.
2. Ask: What do you *know* about Hawaii? Explore individual experiences.
3. Ask: What *would* you like to learn about Hawaii? Record answers.
   Although there would be a lot of variation, let us presume that the class narrowed down the "would like to know" to the following:

   A. What plants and animals are found on Hawaii today? Long ago?
   B. What jobs do workers have today? Long ago?
   C. Why do people in Hawaii do the hula?

Day 2

Objectives: Student will view a section of "Holo Mai Pele," a sixty-minute *Great Performances* video from 2001 or video clips on Hawaii.
Each pair will choose a topic.
Students will review computer skills and how to find evidence for their questions.

1. The teacher lists the following topics for investigation; students will work in pairs.

Long Ago	*Today*
Voyages of the Polynesians	Transportation
King Kamehameha I	Population/ethnic groups
Queen Liliuokalani	Cities/high cost of living
Population/social structure	Macadamia nuts
Small farms/self sufficiency	Alien plants and animals
Taro (poi)	Tourism

(continued)

UNIT PLAN continued   Living in Hawaii: Now and Long Ago

Pigs and chickens	Imports
Sugar cane	Exports
Yams	Hula today/contests
Coconut	Military presence
Hula (chants, instruments)	Land ownership
Fish ponds	Jobs

Note that there are probably more topics (twenty-four) than student pairs. However, though some of the topics are essential for answering the questions, the easier and less important topics such as coconut and sugar cane could be omitted.

2. Teacher and students review how to use sources of information: encyclopedia, library resources, and media, including skills using the Internet. Before Day 2, the teacher has already prepared the websites on Hawaii or has printed from the Internet fact sheets on Hawaii, data from Hawaii's Agriculture Department, pictures of Hawaiian plants and animals from museums and gardens, and the like. These data are put into labeled folders for the children. In turn, children using the Internet also make an extra copy for possible use by other pairs and place them into the appropriate folders.

3. Students who need to use the Internet rotate by pairs into the computer area while the rest of the class uses library resources. If needed, the teacher (or any other available help) observes what students can do and coaches students on how to find their information for their topic. In the process of working with pairs, the teacher assesses what evidence a given pair has already found and what they have learned from the activity. The teacher keeps track of student work.

Day 3

> *Objectives:* Students search resources and the Internet for information.
> Students find evidence to answer their topic questions.

1. View a section of "Holo Mai Pele" or other videos on Hawaii.
2. Show and explain pictures from the Internet on Hawaii that students/teacher have found as well as other colorful books on Hawaii.
3. Students in pairs work on researching their topic. Teacher coaches pairs on how to find information and how they will present their data on Friday.

Day 4

> *Objectives:* Students search resources and the Internet for information.
> Students find evidence to answer their topic questions.
> Students work on their presentation of their evidence.

1. Show pictures from the companion book that coordinates with the video "Holo Mai Pele."
2. Teacher coaches pairs on how they will present their data. Can they role-play whether to build more hotels on beaches? Can they role-play a Hawaiian descendent demanding land rights? Can posters be used to present the most important imports and exports? Can they perform the basic foot steps of the hula (sway, sway walk, and kahola)? Oral presentation?

UNIT PLAN continued   Living in Hawaii: Now and Long Ago

Day 5

Objectives: Using a variety of formats, pairs will take turns presenting their evidence.
Students will complete the KWL chart.
Students will assess their own work.
Students will review what they have learned.

1. Teacher leads students in filling out the KWL chart and drawing conclusions.
2. Teacher asks if students would like to share their Hawaiian unit with another class. If affirmative, students practice using a variety of formats (role playing, hula performance, oral presentations, video segments, etc.).
3. Self-assessment by pairs on their contribution to the KWL chart and what they learned. Teacher also makes an assessment.

tackle other topics that have not already been assigned. Thus, there may be more management problems with the second unit. In addition, days with using the media and computer may be more physically demanding as the teacher moves around from one pair to another.

Notice that the two Hawaiian units used the more traditional planning model of objectives, activities, and then assessment. Given the same first unit goal—"Students will understand the geography, history, and traditional culture of Hawaii"—think how you would plan using the backward design model. You would be looking immediately at assessment before planning activities. Do you think the backward design model would contribute more to student learning?

"Living in Hawaii: Now and Long Ago" also illustrates the advantages of using the Internet for finding resources on Hawaii. It would be very unwise, however, to have young children search the Internet for general topics such as *Hawaii*. It is the teacher's responsibility to find the websites before Day 2 or print out the material from the Internet beforehand (see Figure 2.4). Before the unit starts, the teacher assembles the general resources on **TECHNOLOGY** Hawaii but cannot anticipate whether the students will want to learn about the symbols of Hawaii (state bird, flag, state flower, state tree) or whether they want to learn more about the independent monarchy (1795–1894). Will the children want to learn more about the Hawaiian language or the USS *Arizona* Memorial that they may have visited? The second unit forces the teacher to be able to find resources quickly.

Note that for younger children the teacher initially found a lot of the resources for the children to use. Harder is for older students to figure out "How am I going to find out what **TECHNOLOGY** I need to know," or in other words, how can good information be located. Often there are many sources and the student has to select the best sources of information. This requires critical thinking skills to assess the relevance and reliability of Internet-based information. Often, students rely on use visual images as being the most important in determining the meaning and significance of the information. This is often easier for them to do than to read the large amount of printed information. This means students need supervision in developing search skills and also critical thinking skills.

In addition, this unit, like other units, illustrates the importance of the teacher's knowledge, background, and experiences as well as those of the learners. Try to build on your own strengths. During your vacations as well as during the year, round up as many resources as possible for current and forthcoming units.

Research Computer Skills

TECHNOLOGY

Along with reading skills, the needed research skills using computers for some of the information (Figure 2.4) in the second unit make it more difficult to teach this unit. Kids get stuck! Weaker readers have even more difficulties (Chapter 10). Even after a review on how to use sources of information, the teacher may have to show students individually how to find information more effectively. If students ask questions such as whether there are poisonous snakes in Hawaii or do men do the hula, the teacher tries not to give the answer but shows the students how to find the information. This way the teacher is a guide and hopes the students will become more independent and not rely on the teacher for all of the answers.

Once students find the information, they must jot down a few words from the resources regarding pictures, text, videos, and the like. It is helpful for students to use graphic organizers to fill out information. Animals could be grouped into categories such as birds, insects, and so on.

Figure 2.4 Stages for Using a Computer for Research

---

1. **Teacher**
   - Locates background information for both the teacher and students.
   - Google is most popular, but often more helpful are specialized social studies aids such as One Stop Research, a website sponsored by the National Geographic Society (www.nationalgeographic.com/onestop). This site's results are organized by type: photos, art, maps, pictures, articles, video, games, and so on.

2. **Teacher to Student**
   - Gives articles, photographs, graphs, maps, books, and so on to students
   - Assign "computer assistants." Those with greater computer experience can help keep computer use moving in an efficient manner.
   - Teaching students the value of planning. Discussion and brainstorming are best done before starting research on a computer.
   - Post list of computer rights and responsibilities. Give key commands near the computer station. If necessary, use a timer and a sign-up sheet.

3. **Students and Teachers**
   - Students do research to answer their questions.
   - Information organized into a format (written, oral, and so on.)
   - Possible publication or presentations investigated.
   - Check if penpals would work. The largest free K–12 electronic penpal network is ePals Classroom exchange (www.epals.com) or KeyPals Club (www.teaching.com/keypals)

Travel Day

Having more resources available has led in some schools to a more complex form of Travel Day. It is called Passport Day when each classroom at a school represents a different country, state, or time period that students have learned about in their social studies program. For example, the sixth-grade class studied India while a third-grade class studied the American Indians in their area. Students may wear attire representative of the culture on Passport Day as they explain their work and artifacts to visitors. Students holding passports in their hands visit the different classrooms according to an arranged time schedule. Passport Day makes a good culminating experience for completion of a unit. Exchanges between classes also encourage more of a school community feeling and students may even look forward to the next grade levels when they see the results of interesting social studies units. Increasing use of computer networks should make access to teaching materials easier.

TECHNOLOGY

In some communities, the exchange is called It's a Small World or International Day. Each class studies a different country, decorates the halls, and the PTA organizes a celebration with passports, crafts, and entertainment with an International Food Tasting. This is often the highlight of the year. During the class period, each student may be given a number that signals the time for their presentation so there is no competition within a class on who is being given attention.

A more economic focus is a Bazaar Day where students sell the crafts they have made for a given culture. Typically, each entrepreneur with a team of their fellow classmates make products, often at home with the help of their families. Parents as well as the whole community are invited to the Bazaar Day where the bargaining begins. Evaluation of the project usually finds that students have gained understanding of running of business as well as understanding more about a given culture. For this type of project to be successful requires careful planning and cooperation from teachers, students, parents, and the community.

Elements of a Unit

What does a unit contain? The typical elements found in a unit are shown in Figure 2.5. No set format exists for writing units. Some teachers prefer to divide a page into three columns—the first for objectives, the middle for teaching procedures, and the third for materials. Others like to put each lesson plan on a separate page so they can eliminate or modify individual lesson plans more easily.

What criteria can be used to choose units? Here are some ideas:

- *Construction of knowledge:* Will students organize, interpret, or explain information? Will they consider different points of view and alternative solutions?
- *Thinking and other skills:* Will students use and extend their skills?
- *Value beyond school:* Will the knowledge and skills be used outside the classroom? Will citizenship skills and values be likely to increase?
- *Link to state standards:* Will the unit help students to achieve state and local standards?

> ## Figure 2.5   Sample Unit Format
>
> **Elements of a Unit**
>
> 1. Description
>   Title
>   Description of a grade level, target student population
>   Rationale/overview for the unit; significance of topic; tie to standards
>
>   Estimated time
>
> 2. Goals and objectives (number each for ease of referral)
>   3. Lessons
>   Introductory and initiating activities
>   Series of sequence lesson plans with enough detail on procedures so that the teaching strategies and activities are clear. Worksheets and similar handouts should be included.
>
>   Concluding activities to encourage students to apply what they have learned
>
> 4. List of resources (textbooks, people, media, library books, speakers)
>
> 5. Assessment, including procedures used during the unit as well as tests.

On Your Own 2.5

What Are the Strengths of These Activities?

In many cases, teachers incorporate the ideas from resource units or guides into their own teaching. Do you think any of these ideas on foods are helpful? Might you incorporate them into your own unit? ●

What is the difference between units (sometimes called *teaching units*) and resource units? **Resource units** are units designed (e.g., by the Census Bureau to help teachers teach about the census) for use by a great many teachers. Districts may design a resource unit for a given topic. Usually resource units contain more ideas and activities than any one teacher can use. See, for example, the sample unit plan "Foods."

What are some special considerations that teachers should be aware of in designing and implementing units in the social studies? One is *variety*. Look at your lesson plans. Are you using the same techniques (e.g., worksheets) every day? Are you showing three videos three days in a row? Is content emphasized without consideration of the importance of skills, values, and civic education?

To spot these problems more easily, some teachers like to jot down in broad outline what they are doing throughout the course of a week. Seeing a whole week's schedule often points out the need for more variety in teaching strategies and more attention to skills and values.

After you have completed a unit, evaluate it from your students' point of view. What was their favorite activity? What did they like least about the unit? Most important, what did they learn from it?

Food

The following resource unit, designed to promote global education, is from the *Indiana in the World* teaching activities packet.

Activities

The pupils may:

Draw a two-column chart. Head one column "Animals" and one "Plants." List in the columns the foods students eat that come from plants and animals.

Make a list of their favorite foods.

Make a collage of their favorite foods.

Make a list of junk foods.

From a list of favorite foods, categorize the foods according to the six groups of the nutritional pyramid, identifying those that qualify as junk foods.

Discuss the nutritional value of the food they eat.

List and discuss health problems that can be prevented through adequate nutrition.

Describe and discuss their individual family eating patterns and compare them with those of other members of the class.

Divide into groups, each group choosing a foreign country; research and list the foods of their chosen country.

Find pictures and make a picture chart of the foods of their chosen country.

Discuss the eating utensils of a country (e.g., chopsticks in Asia).

Visit a supermarket that features foods of many countries. List the foods that are featured from the country they are studying.

Take a field trip to a restaurant featuring food of a chosen country.

Research and make a picture story chart on the influence religion may have on the diet of a country.

Plan a balanced diet from the foods of their chosen country.

List five or more foods eaten by people of other countries. State the countries (e.g., octopus, Italy).

Research and report on the history of some foods eaten in the United States.

List some of the foods eaten in the United States that were brought here from other countries. Name the countries.

Find pictures of children suffering from malnutrition in other countries.

Research and report on the diseases prevalent in these countries because of malnutrition.

Write two story paragraphs, one explaining plankton and the other hydroponics.

Lesson Plans

A **lesson plan** is an outline of what you expect to teach in a given day's lesson. (See the daily plans in the sample unit plan "Travel Day to Hawaii" for examples.) Many teachers begin by creating and photocopying a blank form with several headings (see Figure 2.6). This form can be filled in at the beginning of each week or each unit.

Lesson plans are constructed within the general framework of a unit and should reflect the goals of that unit. You need to be alert in constructing daily plans to how activities can move your students toward an understanding of the unit's general goals—how daily activities can make those goals more meaningful. This requires a careful match between student readiness and interest and the activities you plan.

Planning for the Inclusive Classroom/Adaptations

Teachers face a diverse group of students who have a variety of learning styles and abilities. Students may have many commonalities but they also bring differences that make them individuals. Yet all students can learn. The first step is to *plan your lesson for the whole class.* Activities such as prereading and prewriting can help all students. You can also adapt your lesson plan to specific learners by pairing up students, allowing alternatives, giving more time, rewriting questions, using graphic organizers, reducing complexity, and so on. For the gifted, you may want to make the lesson more challenging. If available, use resource teachers or aides to help certain students.

Sometimes this is called **differentiating instruction.** Students in classrooms with differentiating instruction find there are multiple ways to acquire content, make sense of ideas, and then express what they have learned. The teacher is willing to modify instruction to help the diverse group of students. Typically, this means that there is a blend of whole-class instruction, small-group instruction, and individual instruction (more in Chapters 3 and 9). One important group that often needs more attention are the growing number of English language learners (ELLs), sometimes called ELs.

Almost every teacher supports the goals of differentiated instruction. The problem comes in trying to implement this important strategy. One of the most common techniques is to place students into small groups according to their abilities or readiness (more on small groups in Chapter 3). However, sometimes groups are formed on the basis of

---

Figure 2.6   Lesson Plan Format

Subject Area _____ Date _____

- Objective/standard
- Materials/resources
- Initiating activity/interest building
- Procedures/teaching strategies/lesson development
- Assessment
- Possible follow-up/expansion/integration

student interest. Often this arrangement involves assigning different materials to the different students or think-pairs. For example, in studying medieval Japan, individual biographies like Minamoto Yoritomo or Antoku, the boy emperor whose grandmother drowned herself and the boy to avoid being captured, are easier for challenged students. Other groups could be formed for each of the social classes: emperor, shogun, daimyo, samurai, peasants, merchants, and artisans. Or in studying the spread of Islam in West Africa, students could study Sunni Ali Ber, or Askia Muhammad, rulers of Songhai, while others study the social structure: emperor, noble families, traders, free people of towns, skilled workers, slaves.

TECHNOLOGY

As you can see from these examples, the teacher must gather up a wide variety of resources or at least check if the content is easily accessed from websites. Always give the websites to the students to avoid long searches on the Internet by students. Another difficulty is that it may take the groups different amounts of time to complete their assignments to describe each social class, especially if the data are to be put into a chart or graph. Differentiated instruction does take the time of the teacher. For this reason, one recommendation is for a teacher to start slowly, one unit at a time, to implement differentiated instruction. Differentiated instruction may be more easily implemented when there are large blocks of time versus shorter periods of time.

Tips for Writing Lesson Plans

The first consideration in making a lesson plan is the objective or purpose. Is there a special concept that you hope students will acquire? The next step is motivation. What can you do to capture students' attention? This may involve relating the experiences of students to your objectives. Student interest and involvement in the lesson may be triggered by an artifact, a learning game, or a planned classroom experience.

Beginnings are important. They help to shape the motivation of students. Teachers should try to effect a smooth transition from what students already know to the new material. In general, sequence your instruction from the simple to the complex. Sometimes a brief review by a student of what was done in yesterday's social studies lesson is helpful. Try to create an organizational framework for ideas or information so that students know where things are going. It is often valuable simply to state the purpose of the lesson. Some teachers turn lessons into guessing games for their students, who must figure out where they're going and why. This generally does not help the learning process, especially for slower learners.

In writing out procedures, teachers often do not use enough detail. What does "read and discuss the textbook" mean? Read aloud? Read silently? Read one paragraph silently and then discuss? Will students discuss questions in small groups? You can see that "read and discuss the textbook" is open to a wide variety of interpretations. Often more planning could turn the lesson into an exciting and useful learning experience for the students.

During the lesson, be attentive to the responses of the students. Is there a sense of accomplishment among them? Finally, think about closure, or ending the lesson. Will you depend on the bell to close the lesson? That can leave students dangling in mid-thought. A better way is to draw attention to the end of the lesson, to help students organize their learning, and to reinforce what they have learned. Have a student summarize the lesson for the class, or do so yourself.

Small Group Work **2.3**

Locating Interesting Lesson Plans

It would be exhausting to develop all your lesson plans by yourself in the area of the social studies. Look at teachers' guides, professional literature, the Internet, and resource units for ideas for lesson plans. Find three lesson plans you like. Explain why they appeal to you. See websites at the end of the chapters or use quotation marks around "social studies lesson plans in you Internet searches." ●

In summary, these are planning practices that help students to learn.

- Have clearly defined yearly, semester, unit, weekly, and daily plans.
- It is better to overplan than underplan. But be flexible.
- Start lessons with openers that relate to students' experiences or arouse their curiosity.
- The textbook is only one tool. Be careful not to overuse it.
- Use the humanities—music, art, literature—as much as possible.

Organizing and Scheduling

Time for teaching is a valuable resource. Many elementary students attend school for more than six hours a day, and the trend in the reform movement is to increase the number of minutes that elementary students spend in school. But when you subtract lunch time and recesses, most teachers probably have only about four hours a day actually to teach. Some studies show that one-third of all time is absorbed by nonteaching responsibilities.

How much time should be spent on teaching the social studies? Many school districts give recommendations. The minimum usually is fifteen minutes a day for the first grade with an increasing time allotment each year. By the fourth grade, around thirty-five minutes a day is usually recommended, and by the sixth grade, social studies usually occupies a full period of approximately forty to forty-five minutes.

These time allocations, however, presume that subjects are not integrated. Typically, first-grade language arts (reading, writing, listening, speaking, spelling, handwriting) are allotted *two to three hours* each day. This means that if you integrate different areas, such as language arts (reading stories about the culture you are studying, writing a thank-you note to a community worker who spoke to your class), you can greatly increase the number of minutes devoted to social studies instruction. Integrating science and social studies is also worthwhile; studying the geography of a given area lends itself easily to the study of that area's plants, animals, climate, and the like. Integrating social studies with music, art, dance, and drama is natural, especially when you are studying a particular culture. More middle schools are using **block scheduling,** a longer period of time.

TECHNOLOGY

When is social studies typically taught during the school day? In many schools the basic subjects, reading and math, are taught in the morning "prime-time" hours. In terms of computer use in elementary schools, there is a surge of computer activity from about 10:45 to 11:45 in the late morning before lunch. Teachers appear to only allow computer time before going to lunch and later before going home. Social studies is generally relegated to the afternoon in such programs. By integrating subjects, however, you can bring social studies content into the morning hours when students are fresher and better able to learn.

You may not have complete control over scheduling block time and subject areas. In most schools, physical education, music, art, and other such subjects are taught by specialists whose schedules will dictate part of your own scheduling. In addition, students are often grouped for reading and math and may go to different rooms for these subjects. Again, you may have to follow prescribed time allocations for such classes.

Most teachers, however, can make decisions on how to use the time available. You will probably want to set up a "normal" daily and weekly schedule. You may decide that you would rather teach social studies on Monday, Wednesday, and Friday for a longer block of time than every day for a shorter period. Time allocations may change depending on the activities. A field trip or a local guest may dictate changes in the normal schedule. However, most classrooms eventually move into routine scheduled times for different subject areas or learning periods. Teachers differ on how to schedule and organize their class time. As long as time is used wisely, these differences are probably not important.

Summary

Planning is important for effective teaching. Teachers usually block out a year's social studies curriculum by determining what units will be taught during the year. The unit approach with a theme, sequential lessons, and assessment provides better learning experiences for students. Ideally, daily lesson plans should be detailed enough to make teaching of the social studies effective and interesting. Teachers also have to plan so that citizenship and multicultural education as well as other goals and skills are treated as a day-long concern (see especially Chapters 8 through 10).

Suggested Readings and Websites

Davis, James E., ed. *Planning a Social Studies Program: Activities, Guidelines, and Resources,* 4th ed. Boulder, CO: ERIC Clearing House for Social Studies/Social Science Education, Social Science Education Consortium, 1997.

Good tool for schools changing their social studies program.

Eisner, Elliot W. *The Educational Imagination.* New York: Macmillan, 1985.

Sees much of teaching as an artistic enterprise.

Fredericks, Anthony D., Anita Meyer Meinbach, and Liz Rothlein. *Thematic Units.* New York: HarperCollins, 1993.

Theory of thematic approach and examples of thematic units.

Lindquist, Tarry. *Seeing the Whole Through Social Studies.* Portsmouth, NH: Heinemann, 2002.

Strong on integrating learning, grades 3 through 8. See also her earlier books, *Social Studies at the Center: Integrating Kids, Content, and Literacy* (2000) and *Ways That Work: Putting Social Studies Standards into Practice* (1997), all published by Heinemann.

Roberts, Patricia, and Richard D. Kellough. *A Guide for Developing an Interdisciplinary Thematic Unit.* Englewood Cliffs, NJ: Prentice-Hall, 1996.

Purposes, initiating an interdisciplinary thematic unit, developing objectives and learning experiences plus assessment.

Websites

Awesome Library K–12 Lesson Plans
www.awesomelibrary.org/social.html

Lesson plans and downloadable readings.

A Curriculum Site
http://discoveryschool.com/schrockguide

Categorized list of sites useful for the curriculum.

Federal Resources for Educational Excellence (FREE)
http://free.ed.gov

U.S. Department of Education's website that serves as a repository of school-related resources from the federal government such as Library of Congress, Endowment for the Humanities, Smithsonian Institute, National Science Foundation, and the like. Excellent with many primary source documents and photos and also suggestions on how to teach. Probably best for upper elementary and middle schools.

Gateway to 21st Century Skills
www.thegateway.org

Thousands of educational resources of the National Education Association

Kathy Schrock's Guide for Educators
http://school.discovery.com/schrockguide

Updated by topic for K–12. Useful also for ELLs.

National Center for History in the Schools
www.sscnet.ucla.edu/nchs

The National Center for History in the Schools has the national history standards and over sixty world and U.S. history teaching units of reproducible primary sources and materials. Best for fifth grade and above.

Social Studies Lesson Plans
www.csun.edu/~hcedu013

Select from the lesson plans and teaching strategies to plan classes or complete projects.

A Teachers' Website
www.teachers.net

A gathering place with lesson plans, curriculum, supplies, and chat center.

The WebQuest Page
http://webquest.sdsu.edu/webquest.html

A WebQuest is an inquiry-oriented activity in which most or all of the information is drawn from the Web.

myeducationlab
Where the Classroom Comes to Life

VIDEO HOMEWORK EXERCISE

Opportunities for Learning

Go to MyEducationLab, select the topic **Cross Curricular Connections**, and watch the video entitled "Opportunities for Learning."

In the video, a first-grade teacher teaches a lesson integrating both math and social studies to demonstrate the importance of presenting concepts in ways that facilitate mastery by children with different learning styles.

CHAPTER 3

Instructional Strategies

This chapter illustrates the use of various instructional strategies with social studies topics. One instructional approach is not appropriate for all types of content and all types of learning. Remember that teaching strategies should be challenging, flexibly applied, and responsive to students. The following areas are highlighted in the chapter:

- Different Methods
- What Happens in Real Classrooms?
- Direct Teaching: From Passive to Active Learning
- Problem-Based Learning and Thinking
- Inductive Thinking and Questioning
- Cooperative or Collaborative Learning
- Role Playing
- Simulations

What makes a cooperative learning experience successful?

Different Methods

An artificial distinction for the sake of clarity has been made between planning (Chapter 2), how to teach (Chapter 3), and assessment (Chapter 4). As soon as you start planning *what* to teach, you need to think *how* the content and skills will be taught. You also have to think about what type of assessment will be used to see if students really have mastered the content and skills.

Typically the terms **methods, strategies,** or **instructional strategies** are used interchangeably. Once you gain competency in a teaching method, it is referred to as a **teaching skill.** The difficulty of looking at methods is that there is no "right" method that works in all cases. Any method can be more or less effective depending on the teacher, the students, and the environment of the school. Therefore, to teach effectively you need to have a wide repertoire of teaching methods. Using a variety of strategies will help you meet the varying needs of students who have different styles of thinking and learning.

Learning Styles

Learning style is the student's dominant or best way to learn. Students vary in the unique ways they learn and prefer to learn. Although there are other theories of intelligence, Howard Gardner is the best known for emphasizing the importance of matching learning styles to instruction.[1] Gardner initially identified seven basic intelligences:

- Verbal/linguistic (language)
- Logical/mathematical
- Visual/spatial
- Body/kinesthetic
- Musical/rhythmic
- Interpersonal (understanding of others)
- Intrapersonal (understanding of self)

Later Gardner added naturalistic intelligence, the ability to identify plants and animals, and the possibility of an intelligence to ponder questions about life, death, and ultimate realities. Gardner believes that individuals possess all of these intelligences but differ in the relative strengths of each. However, schools tend to focus primarily on only the first two. This means that teachers need to provide experiences that use and extend all the intelligences of children. Gardner also is critical of a curriculum based on facts and advocates more of a focus on depth and understanding.[2] Although critics report that applications of the theory of multiple intelligence (MI) in schools have not improved achievement in formal research studies, Gardner's ideas that each child may have important abilities offers hope for learning when teachers use a variety of methods.

Strong Management Skills

Regardless of what method you use, do not allow it to exceed your management skills. A quiet signal by the teacher should be in place to control chaos and to prevent students from being off

[1]Howard Gardner, *The Unschooled Mind: How Children Think and How Schools Should Teach* (New York: Basic Books, 1991).
[2]Howard Gardner, *The Disciplined Mind: What All Students Should Understand* (New York: Simon and Schuster, 1999).

Small Group Work **3.1**

Using Gardner's Intelligences

Take the topic of the Renaissance and describe an activity for each type of the intelligences. (Hints: make a simulated craft for each guild, sketch artwork using perspective, etc.) Or take any given nation or culture as a topic for multiple intelligences. ●

task. Underlying what you are teaching should be a structure that makes sense to both you and your students. Clear and agreed-on classroom rules are necessary for student learning.

In addition to the learning needs of students, certain environmental factors may also influence your choice of teaching methods. Large class size might make some methods inappropriate. The physical environment of the school or the social climate of a given class may not be conducive to certain methods. Simulations and team chants, for example, may be noisy. If the walls are thin and a simulation would bother other classes, using this activity would not be a considerate choice. In addition, each class has its own personality. Often you hear experienced teachers say, "No group reports this year. My kids just don't mesh well enough." Each particular mix of students in a class is unlike any other. Experienced teachers know that one lesson or approach will not always work the same way in a different class. Each class has its own personality and its own needs.

Example of Using a Wide Variety of Methods

To meet the wide diversity in student backgrounds and learning styles, it is wise to use a range of teaching methods. For example, with a fifth-grade class studying the history of the U.S. West, you could begin with an exercise on planning a trip to the pre–Civil War West. Have the students, organized in small groups, decide how much they should spend on various supplies and which articles they should put in the covered wagon. (There are computer programs such as *The Oregon Trail* that work on a similar theme, but if you do not have the computer game in your classroom, the small group exercise can work very well.)

Ask students to analyze their findings. In a whole-class discussion, they can gain insights from the experiences of other groups about priorities for the trip. The class can rank the important items for moving west. (Discussion and list-making favor verbal students.)

Then you could check on how often students themselves have moved and the positives and negatives about moving. Introduce literature and songs about the pioneers to enhance the students' understanding of the settlement of the West. Learn or listen to songs such as "Oh, Susannah" or "Sweet Betsy from Pike;" talk about the *Little House* books or television shows; teach students square dancing. To use another strategy, give a short lecture on abstract concepts such as freedom and lawlessness on the frontier. Have students read the appropriate textbook pages and do workbook assignments. Involve nonverbal students in a range of art projects or activities: putting together a short play on the West, making maps of wagon-train routes, and so on. More verbal students might write "pretend" diaries, songs, or poetry on the West. All might gain from films that show the perspective of American Indians whose land was being taken away from them. Finally, have students evaluate their own efforts to see how these projects could serve as stepping-stones for future learning.

The variety of activities in this unit on the West provides channels for a wide range of learners and their abilities. Students start with a concrete experience (planning a trip to the West) and move into concept development (lawlessness, freedom, etc.). Furthermore, the students find applications for the materials and concepts as they develop their own projects. In the process of evaluating their projects, the students engage in analysis and also move into the affective domain by sharing their projects with other members of the class. You will meet many needs in this series of lessons.

What Happens in Real Classrooms?

Most experts believe sound education practices include depth as well as breadth, student involvement, and connectedness to curriculum and life skills including being technology literate. We want students to gain critical thinking and problem-solving skills, effective communication skills, and responsible behavior toward self, community, and citizenship. But what happens in actual classrooms?

There is a focus away from teacher to student learning. A majority of elementary teachers believe that they and their school administrators want a student-centered classroom rather than a teacher-centered one. However, when asked the methods used in their most recent social studies class period, more teachers of grades 2, 5, and 8 reported using more whole-class teacher presentations/discussion (90%) than any other methods. Well over half of the teachers had students reading textbook (64%) and working in workbooks or handouts (58%) during this period. But teachers also reported students were working in small groups (85%) and engaged in critical thinking activities (86%). Computer-based activities and video-based activities were used about half of the time in the last social studies class.[3] What interpretation can be made about these reports? On the positive side, it appears that teachers are using a wide variety of methods, including technology. A blend of traditional (a systematic linear, basic-skills curriculum) and progressive ideas (child-centered) is often successful. This combination will better meet the different needs of students. However, teacher effectiveness for these methods was not evaluated in this study.

There may also be a disconnect between teachers viewing themselves as student-centered while actually using teacher-centered methods. One factor is that teachers, like the rest of the adult world, are now much more casual in their dress and manner. Today's teachers compare themselves to their own teachers who often were more formal both in dress and manner and may conclude that they are student-centered. Nevertheless, a long-standing criticism of teachers is that they spend too much time in talking and asking questions of students. In fact, many studies have found teachers talk to students at least 75 percent of the classroom time.

Teachers' Decisions

Teachers are making countless decisions daily regarding what instruction or methods they will use. *Remember:* If we really believe that each student has individual styles of learning,

[3]James S. Leming, Lucien Ellington, and Mark Schub, *Social Studies in Our Nation's Elementary and Middle Schools: A National Random Survey of Social Studies Teachers' Professional Opinions, Values and Classroom Practices.* (Storrs, CT: The Center for Survey Research and Analysis, 2006.)

Table 3.1	Methods of Teaching
Model	**Goal/Objective**
Direct Teaching	Present information
Problem-Based Learning, Inquiry	Increase thinking, analytical skills
Inductive Thinking (Taba Model)	Development of inductive processes and reasoning
Cooperative Learning	Both increase interpersonal (group) skills and content knowledge
Role Playing	Introduce students to inquiry into personal and social values
Simulation	Help students experience various social realities and examine their reactions to them

there can be *no best method of teaching* that works for every student. However, in considering various practices, methods or strategies can be divided into two main categories: **direct teaching** such as lecturing in which the teacher has a prominent role and **indirect methods** of teaching such as cooperative learning, role playing, and simulations in which the teacher's role changes. Let us now examine these various methods in depth to help you make sound core curriculum decisions (Table 3.1). Most students benefit from being taught by both direct and indirect methods.

Many factors need to be considered when you think about teaching methods. Each method represents one possible route to more successful learning for your students, and different methods may be more appropriate for different topics and skills.

TECHNOLOGY

All teaching methods, however, have some common elements. Each one involves teacher direction of student thinking processes. All require preparation, concern with motivation, setting up the learning experience, and the creation of some evaluative technique to assess whether students have gained in knowledge, skills, values, and social participation—the four goals of social studies.

On Your Own **3.1**

Checking Out Strategies

Type *social studies strategies* in an Internet search for more strategies that could be used in teaching social studies. ●

Direct Teaching: From Passive to Active Learning

Correcting the Faults of Talking All the Time

Most teachers feel more comfortable using the term **presentation/discussion,** a combination of talking and asking questions of students, instead of **recitation. Lecturing** also has a more negative connotation. Although lecturing is one of the oldest teaching methods, the "talk and chalk" method has many critics. To improve lecturing, a method called **direct**

teaching or **direct instruction** is employed. Direct instruction presents information directly through lecturing, questioning, and demonstrating/modeling. It makes explicit to students at the beginning of the lesson what students are to learn. The main purpose of direct teaching is to present knowledge and skills that will enable *all* students to *master* the material being taught. Sometimes this method is called *direct explanation teaching*.

Direct teaching advocates argue that this approach—which includes structured content, the carefully explained introduction of new material, demonstration, considerable student practice (both guided and independent), and frequent recall and comprehension questions—can improve achievement, especially for lower socioeconomic status students.

Direct teaching has been successful in part because it begins from a realistic assessment of what goes on in many classrooms, including social studies classrooms. It recognizes that the textbook is still the major vehicle for social studies instruction. Unfortunately, teachers often simply assign sections of text and worksheets without much explanation of the material covered. Direct teaching or lecturing can be used to help teachers convey content more effectively.

Figure 3.1 illustrates one model of the direct teaching method: the five-step lesson plan. What are the key elements of direct teaching? *Pacing* and *learning for mastery* are important. Students spend a high percentage of their time on tasks that they will successfully complete. In contrast, regular instruction too frequently skips many of the elements of direct teaching and leaves students frustrated, either because they are not sure *what* they are supposed to have learned or because they don't know *why* they are learning it.

The direct-teaching model may remind you of what a public speaking instructor would say: Tell them what you're going to say, say it, and then tell them what you've said. That is, in fact, a large part of direct instruction. In addition, the emphasis on *set* is an attempt to relate actual student experiences to the objectives—to bring students into a more active participation in learning. Direct teaching attempts to stimulate interest and involvement in the lesson by explaining to students the importance of what they are learning and by presenting the content clearly. Furthermore, the lesson is planned in detail, so the teacher avoids meandering along trivial or personal paths. Finally, direct teaching gives students an opportunity to practice what they have heard and then to reinforce it with further assignments.

When is direct teaching appropriate in the social studies? Certainly, teachers need to explain ideas and concepts to students whenever instruction begins on a new unit of work, a new concept, or a new project. Direct teaching methods can help. Here is how direct teaching might work if a textbook is being used.

Teaching a Concept: Organizations

In this section, we show how Mr. Smithy, a third-grade teacher, wants to explain the concept of *organization*—a group that has at least two members who have common interests and rules. Note in teaching a concept, Mr. Smithy uses the classic method of examples and nonexamples. See Figure 3.1 on the steps used to explain concepts including identifying critical attributes of the concept and giving many examples. Note how frequently Mr. Smithy is using this technique.

Mr. Smithy's teaching objective is for students to distinguish organizations from nonorganizations. To *set* the lesson, Mr. Smithy points out that many members of the class belong to organizations: José is a Cub Scout and Sarah is a Brownie. What other students,

Figure 3.1	Five-Step Direct Teaching Plan

1. Anticipatory set
   a. Focus students
   b. State objectives
   c. Establish purpose
   d. Establish transfer (if possible)

2. Instruction
   a. Provide information
      Explain concept
      State definitions*
      Identify critical attributes*
      Provide examples*
      Model
   b. Check for understanding
      Pose key questions
      Ask students to explain concept, definitions, attributes
        in their own words*
      Have students discriminate between examples and nonexamples*
      Encourage students to generate their own examples*
      Use active participation devices

3. Guided practice
   a. Initiate practice activities that are under direct teacher supervision
   b. Elicit overt response that demonstrates behavior
   c. Provide close monitoring
   d. Continue to check for understanding
   e. Provide specific knowledge of results

4. Closure
   a. Make final assessment to determine whether students have met
        objective
   b. Have each student perform behavior on his or her own

5. Independent practice
   a. Have students continue to practice on their own
   b. Provide knowledge of results

Note: The starred items are particularly critical when you are teaching an abstract concept (e.g., democracy). They may not be relevant or appropriate when teaching a practice-oriented concept (e.g., state capitals). Thanks to Bill Crandall for the development of this material.

he asks, belong to these or other organizations? Mr. Smithy explains that religious or after-school sports groups are also organizations.

Mr. Smithy then tells his students that they are going to learn about organizations, which form important parts of our society. It is, thus, useful for the students to be able to identify them. In other words, Mr. Smithy has explained the *objective* and *purpose.* In the *input* stage, he may give examples of organizations. The city council is an organization; it has more than two members, rules, and common interests. The local gardening club is also an organization. Members have common interests, pay dues, and come to meetings to find out more about how to garden. The Parent–Teacher Association (PTA) is another organization, as are computer clubs and after-school soccer teams.

Mr. Smithy then gives examples of *non*organizations. The local shoe repair store employs only one person. It is not an organization. A group of individual shoppers in a mall is not an organization; the group includes more than two people but the shoppers do not meet regularly or follow common rules.

Mr. Smithy explains to his students the main characteristics of an organization. He continues to provide examples of organizations and nonorganizations. He summarizes the main distinctions again, then has the class read the pages in their textbooks about organizations.

After the class finishes reading, Mr. Smithy *checks their comprehension* by asking questions about what is and what is not an organization. Then he gives a worksheet to the class and has students check the words on a list that represent organizations and those that do not. The list may include people at a movie theater, the Sierra Club, or people walking in the park. Mr. Smithy supervises this activity, providing *guided practice.*

After allowing time for this exercise, Mr. Smithy and the class go over the correct answers on the list. During *closure,* the students summarize again the main characteristics of an organization.

Finally, for homework, Mr. Smithy has students ask their parents what organizations they belong to (unions, churches, clubs, and so on). Students then create, independently, lists of organizations to which their parents belong. This provides *independent practice.* Mr. Smithy may check these lists to be certain that students have an accurate understanding at this point of what an organization really is.

In the foregoing example, Mr. Smithy assumed that all students could read a textbook, which is not necessarily true of all class members. By identifying the key ideas before giving students the reading assignment, however, he ensured that even students who were not good readers would find the assignment easier. In effect, he had built in "readiness" for the reading experience. He used the textbook to reinforce his own teaching and to help students understand a concept.

Evaluating Direct Teaching

Simply creating all the elements of a good direct teaching lesson is not sufficient. You must *communicate* those elements to your students. Breakdowns can occur in direct teaching as well as in any other teaching method. Because much of the instruction in this method depends on your speaking to your class, your vocal delivery is important. If you use poor diction, mannerisms, or digressions, or show a lack of clarity, these may interfere with your delivering the information effectively to your students. The level of abstraction may be too great for a particular group, and students may simply "tune out." Students may also ignore what you are saying if the lesson goes on too long. Their attention may be diverted by physical distractions in the room or by other students. Concrete examples will always help maintain student interest, as will having students use their other senses by employing visual aids or requesting a written response. Too often lecturing is a passive activity for students, who remember little of what they have heard. If you follow a direct teaching model carefully, you won't fall into the trap of delivering a poor, ineffective lecture.

Direct teaching emphasizes the teacher, rather than the student, as a decision maker. However, used exclusively, direct teaching can stifle creativity in teachers and prevent them from exploring different teaching strategies in different situations. Direct teaching obviously has many good points. Whenever you explain a concept or lecture to a class, you would do well to check the steps of the direct teaching model. Introducing lessons with clear goals and making ideas logical and cogent are helpful principles in conveying knowledge and skills. As with any teaching strategy, however, direct teaching should not be employed day after day in the social studies program. Daily repetition of the same process is dull for both student and teacher unless you are an exceptionally enthusiastic advocate of this method. Direct instruction may be particularly effective for teaching facts and skills to low-ability classes, but the teaching of higher-level thinking skills may best be done by other methods.

Small Group Work **3.2**

When to Use Direct Teaching

How did you learn to use e-mail or any other computer application? How did you learn about what to do in a power shortage or how to find information in a reference book? Make a list of student social studies knowledge and skills best learned by direct instruction. You may wish to refer to one of the units in Chapter 2 for a list of activities. Share your list with your group. ●

Problem-Based Learning and Thinking

Problem-Based Learning

What do the words **problem-based learning, WebQuests, project-based learning, discovery learning, inquiry, problem solving, inductive thinking, thinking** and **thinking skills** have in common? They are ways of thinking that can be organized as indicated in Table 3.2. All these terms refer to the processes that everyday citizens as well as scientists and scholars use to discover knowledge, make decisions, and solve problems. The schools have always claimed to do more than just teach the three Rs. One goal of education has been to foster the thinking skills that are universally needed outside the classroom by all members of society. Many critics believe, however, that thinking is a process rarely encouraged or manifested in most classrooms. This is indeed a dismal finding.

How many times have you wished you could have done something differently after things have gone awry? "If only I could do things over again" is frequently heard as we discuss our personal problems with others. This human capacity to learn from experience is our greatest potential resource for building a better personal future. Instruction in the

Table 3.2	Three Kinds of Thinking
Type	**Example**
Analytical Thinking	To analyze, critique, judge, compare and contrast, evaluate, assess; what most teachers think of as "critical thinking"
Creative Thinking	To create, invent, discover, imagine if, suppose that, predict
Practical Thinking	To apply, use, put into practice, implement, employ what students know

Source: Robert J. Sternberg, "What Is an 'Expert Student'?," *Educational Researcher* 32, no. 8, p. 5.

processes of thinking is even more vital for the future of our lives as citizens. Teaching decision-making skills is essential in the curriculum of the social studies. When making decisions, ranging from minor ones such as what book to choose from the library for recreational reading to major ones such as evaluating what is the best way for the nation to have good health care services, children as well as adults must determine the alternatives and then choose wisely among them. Decisions made without careful consideration of the alternatives and the consequences of each can be costly in terms of the quality of our lives.

When thinking skills are not taught, many students (and inevitably, many adults) lack confidence in their own abilities as thinkers. For most, thinking is a *learned,* not an *innate,* skill. Those without it feel unsure of themselves and believe that they cannot generate good ideas. This lack of confidence is true even of those students who receive high grades in all subjects on their report cards.

A reform movement recognizing the need to teach thinking skills began in the 1960s. More than fifty new social studies projects were created at that time, and many of them had some emphasis on teaching thinking, most commonly called *inquiry.* Although educators in the 1970s showed greater concern with values and relevance of materials to students, an interest in teaching thinking skills has manifested itself again today for many reasons. Our society in general is more concerned about being able to compete in a global market. Only if our youth are educated to think, this argument goes, can the United States survive as a leading industrialized nation with a high standard of living. In addition, citizenship goals have always emphasized the need for teaching all children to think.

Thinking Everyday in the Classroom

Thinking does not occur in a vacuum. Good thinking is a coordination of strategies and knowledge, a product of a number of factors interacting with each other—from well-developed language skills and short-term memory capacity, to well-controlled emotions and appropriate confidence. You can borrow a student's backpack, perhaps from another classroom, filled with items. Exhibit the items one by one to the class. Have the students first by themselves make a profile of the backpack's owner and try to guess how the owner became separated from the backpack. Then move the students into pairs to discuss their ideas.

The constructivist model of teaching and learning places a high priority on the importance of thinking because understanding is developed through **discussions** in which problems are posed, clarifications are sought, and dialogue is promoted. The student tries to make sense of new information by relating it to prior knowledge and participating in discussions guided by teachers.

Every day try to make students summarize what you and others have stated. Ask students to evaluate the consequences of judgments and reasoning. What would happen if . . . or what would have happened if . . . (an event in history). Helpful also are thinking programs such as HOTS (Higher Order Thinking Skills) that use technology to teach by questioning. Employing computers, HOTS moves toward less teacher talk and increasing student talk.[4]

Although in practice, thought processes differ from one person to the next and the steps are not uniform, the following sequence outlined by John Dewey is a good starting

TECHNOLOGY

---

[4]Stanley Pogrow, "Restructuring High-Poverty Elementary Schools for Success: A Description of the Hi-Perform School Design," *Phi Delta Kappan* 88, no. 3 (November, 2006): 223–229.

| **Figure 3.2** | Dewey's Steps for Problem Solving |

1. Define the problem.
2. Suggest alternative solutions to the problem; formulate hypotheses for testing.
3. Gather data to support or negate hypotheses. Try to use a variety of sources.
4. Select supportive hypotheses or reject unsupported ones.

point for "thinking about thinking."[5] The sequence shows the importance of dividing the problem into steps (Figure 3.2). Attacking the broad problem straightforwardly is too difficult for most children and adults. The first step may be to gain an understanding of what students know about the problem and what new knowledge is needed to solve the problem.

Formal Steps in Thinking or Inquiry

Dewey's sequence translates into the following steps for teaching thinking skills:

1. Introduction—problem, question, or dilemma posed
   Example of activities:

   What are our images about Mexico?

   Small groups brainstorm; chairpersons report back to the class.

   Teacher presents items on Mexico gathered from media and the Internet.

2. Developing a hypothesis (tentative answer)
   Example of activities:

   Teacher leads a discussion of ideas generated from brainstorming and teacher and class select the best one; hypothesis could be that our images of Mexico are not accurate or it could be the more specific hypothesis that Mexico is facing serious financial (or political or social) problems.

3. Developing a plan to collect and analyze data
   Example of activities:

   TECHNOLOGY

   Students extract data from textbooks and other references.

   Students collect data (group or individual research) from the Internet.

   Students classify and interpret data.

4. Accepting or rejecting hypothesis; presenting findings
   Example of activities:

   Class and/or teacher evaluates data and methods of research.

   Class and/or teacher states a conclusion.

   Students suggest further questions for investigation.

[5]John Dewey, *How We Think* (Boston: D. C. Heath, 1933), 72.

We use these processes of problem solving in our everyday lives. Assume that you go to your car in the morning and it does not start. Definitely a problem! You listen and it seems to be making a funny noise as you try to start it. You form a hypothesis: The battery is dead. Then you get help from a friend or neighbor who charges the battery. It works! Your hypothesis (the cause of the problem was a dead battery) has been supported.

Students also face decision making or problem solving on many different levels in their own lives. They may make plans for a birthday party and have to decide whom to invite or what activities to plan. They need to decide how to use their leisure time. Should they watch television, read a book, or play soccer? They may need to resolve problems in getting along with classmates or siblings. They may need to figure out a way to earn money. Students may also have more weighty concerns about how they should behave in school or outside the classroom.

Problem-solving skills, then, have universal value. Anything that the schools can do to sharpen students' thinking skills now will have a big payoff in the future. Certainly, our society and its citizens face many problems that can be solved only through informed and logical thinking. But developmental stages are important, and there are limits to what children can do in thinking and problem solving. Young children, for example, cannot think abstractly. In addition, children who are impulsive and not motivated toward intellectual tasks may not show much interest in thinking activities in school. In teaching students to think, you need to consider the formal process as well as the specific needs of your students.

Defining the Problem

To resolve any problem, we must first be able to recognize it and define it. This is a thinking ability that you should encourage in your students. A good way to approach this first step at the elementary level is through **inductive reasoning,** in which an individual perceives a particular pattern of relationships based on a finite number of items or events. It is a way of generalizing from experience or data. The inductive model gives students the opportunity to construct their own ways of learning by building on what they already know. Read more on inductive thinking later in this chapter.

To encourage inductive thinking to help students recognize that culture influences art, you might bring in pictures of the art and architecture of a particular society, such as the Mayans or ancient Greeks. After they have seen a series of art "products" from that culture, have the children try to state something about that culture's beliefs. How are women and men depicted? Does most of the art represent gods and goddesses? What does that suggest about the importance of religion? By beginning with the concrete objects and encouraging students to generalize from them, you will help students grasp the concept that culture influences art. In contrast, simply asking your students how cultural beliefs affect a society's art will present a far more difficult problem for them. Other inductive activities include bringing in artifacts from earlier time periods, such as buttons, toys, tools, photographs, or postcards from various states or nations—or even full wastepaper baskets—to allow students to make inferences about the culture.

Many forms of problem solving begin with inductive reasoning. Teachers often try to trigger student thinking by presenting a discrepancy between what students *think* they know and some new data. Ask your students what images they have about a given nation. Contrast this with actual data. Or raise a controversial question such as what a community should do about housing the homeless or controlling pollution. Contrast the students' solutions with what is actually being done.

Generating Ideas

The second step in thinking is to generate ideas or hypotheses (tentative answers) to help explain why a problem is occurring. Try to draw forth as many ideas as possible without making any judgments. Even silly ideas should be accepted to encourage all students to participate.

You might ask individual students to jot down as many different ways as they can think of to improve the common bathtub or, for more of a social studies flavor, their local transportation system. We recommend that students work by themselves for a minute or two before moving into small groups to share ideas. Always have students do some individual thinking first. Students should not get into the habit of believing that they can think only when they are part of a group. A good strategy is to have students think alone, then form pairs or small groups and share ideas. This is called the **think-pair-share strategy.** The steps are first to brainstorm yourself by making a list. Second, compare your list with that of someone nearby. Third, make a whole-class list from the contributions of the pairs.

Within each group, students will usually encounter a variety of ideas. Some students might think that public transportation should be increased; others might think that workers need to arrive at their places of employment at different times to avoid commuter congestion. It is good for students to learn that not everybody perceives the world and solves problems in the same way. In some exercises, especially at the beginning, you may not want to focus on determining the *best* ideas. In fact, students should be encouraged to brainstorm and generate ideas without making judgments about which ones are best. Students who are accustomed to questions with only one right answer (e.g., what is the capital of Chile?) may find the notion of many right answers both confusing and exciting.

All students bring into the classroom their ways of looking at the world that have been formed by their environment and personal experience. Students may come from homes in which the teacher's authority of telling and directing students is considered more important than promoting students' exploration or alternative solutions. In addition, some groups freely incorporate emotion and personal beliefs to come to a conclusion instead of developing arguments based on evidence and logic. This does not mean that students cannot generate ideas or do problem-based learning but may need to be explicitly taught how to do so.

Class activities can help students learn to select good ideas, decisions, or solutions. In the lesson plan "Deciding Which Ideas Are Best," students take the role of an explorer and try to determine solutions to particular problems. The exercise encourages cooperation rather than competition. Notice also that the lesson plan tries to break down the steps of thinking. It does

Small Group Work **3.3**

Take the Student Role

First, pretend you are a student. Work out the exercise on Captain Portola. Then share your responses with a small group or with the class. Do you think the foregoing exercise helps students to think? What if a student decides that Portola should have done something other than what he actually did? Should the student's idea be accepted? How would you respond? What if the student takes the perspective of an American Indian? ●

LESSON PLAN

Deciding Which Ideas Are Best

In 1542 the Spanish had a claim, or right, to the land in California. This was a land in which 300,000 American Indians lived. But in the 1700s the Russians were moving down from Alaska. They wanted the rich otter fur trade. The British were also coming closer to "Spanish" land.

Around 1700 the Spanish had settlements in Baja, California (now part of Mexico). To protect its claim, the Spanish government decided to send soldiers and missionaries to California to teach the Californian American Indians and to create a permanent Spanish settlement.

The military leader of the group sent to California was Captain Gaspar de Portola, the governor of Baja, California. The religious leader was Father Junipero Serra, a Spanish priest and missionary.

Captain Portola had to decide how to move his group to San Diego, 640 kilometers (400 miles) north of Baja, California. He had two choices: to go by water or by land.

1. Put yourself in Captain Portola's place. List the most important consideration he should think of in making his journey._____

_____

Ships at that time were small, about thirty meters (100 feet) long. A crew might number twenty. The winds might blow the small ship off course. The captain had poor maps. The crew and passengers might get ill from not eating the proper amount of fruits and vegetables, especially if they were at sea for a long time.

By land there was possible danger from the natives. The group had to bring enough food since they could not depend on living off the land. They had to find water. The trip was also slow since most people walked only a few miles (kilometers) each day. There were not enough mules and horses available to carry everyone and all the group's supplies.

2. Captain Portola had to consider an additional problem. In 1769, the year the trip was to start, Father Serra was fifty-five years old. He was short and walked with a limp. How do you think Father Serra should travel? Why?_____

_____

3. Captain Portola also wanted to bring some cattle and horses with him to California. The animals would be useful in the new settlement. What would be the best way for them to travel? _____

_____

4. Now, with these considerations, what choice do you think Captain Portola should make on how to travel to California? Why? _____

_____

5. Captain Portola decided to "hedge his bets." He would use three ships and two land groups, one land group going ahead of the other land group. Was this the best plan? Why? _____

_____

(continued)

LESSON PLAN continued | Deciding Which Ideas Are Best

6. Captain Portola had to decide whether he, the leader, should go by land or by the sea route. Portola was a skilled army leader. Which way would his talents be best used? _____

_____

7. Captain Portola and, surprisingly, Father Serra went by land. Walking with much difficulty and riding, Father Serra, with great determination, made it to San Diego. There the land group met the group that had gone by sea. One of the three ships was lost at sea, and many from the voyage were sick and died. The land party also had lost men from illness. But even with these hardships, Captain Portola was successful in establishing the first permanent European settlement in California. Had he used the best ideas in his decision making? What would you have done differently? _____

_____

_____

Another thought exercise is to ask students about the effects of this exploration and settlement on the lives of the American Indians.

---

not simply pose the problem but first provides background information. Unfortunately, teachers often pose problems too broadly. In this exercise, the student is led step by step through the process to see which ideas will work best in the particular situation.

Students need a lot of practice in generating ideas and then in deciding which ones are best. Usually, if a student's explanation of events or situations considers all the relevant facts, it is an idea worthy of consideration and should not be rejected. Ask your students to make sense of or generate ideas out of puzzling things, such as why Stonehenge in England was built or why American Indians called Mound Builders built their large structures in certain parts of the United States. Most students will enjoy thinking about and looking at data on the Bermuda Triangle and drawing conclusions about the possible explanations of events there. Or children's own experiences can be used to generate ideas. What can be done about the big kids in other classes who bully younger children? Or what do we do when all students want to use the computer. Students can also be given more formal social studies exercises, such as trying to account for the growth of large cities in their state. All these examples can serve as springboards for thinking and for generating ideas (i.e., hypotheses) to be tested.

Concept Maps

More attention is now being given to **concept mapping,** a method to represent information visually. Concepts maps are used to stimulate the generation of ideas, as well as seeing and developing connections. There are many different formats for making concept maps. One is hierarchical (top of the page is the king/ruler and other social classes are put below). Or in the center of the page is the basic concept such as prejudice with branches and arrows going from the center box. Another format is to make a spider map to represent pros and cons of an issue. For example, using the issue of abolishing capital punishment, the pros are on one side of the page and the cons on the other. Using software, more students are becoming familiar with concept maps, especially as a prewriting task. The use of this software is especially helpful for students with lower verbal proficiency. In addition, many students benefit from working with visual aids to generate ideas and review work, thus encouraging the use of concept maps.

Gathering Data

After identifying the problem and suggesting promising ideas to explain or solve it, the third important step in problem solving is gathering data to support or reject the hypothesis. It is important for students to acquire data from a variety of sources. Finding information often involves skills best taught directly, as with the direct teaching model. Thus, in teaching the more creative thinking skills, you may find yourself using direct teaching methods.

Information Skills
1. Finding information in a book
   - Using a table of contents
   - Using an index
   - Using a glossary
   - Using an appendix

TECHNOLOGY

2. Finding information in a library/media center
   - Using online computer reference services and websites
   - Using a card catalog or a computer to find books
   - Using the Dewey decimal system
   - Using an encyclopedia
   - Using an atlas
   - Using an almanac
   - Using other reference books
   - Using a telephone directory

In many cases, before students can find information and data to support their hypotheses, they must be able to use the library and a computer appropriately. In the second Hawaii unit (Chapter 2), students could not answer the three "want to learn" questions unless they knew how to use library and computer resources. Usually, a school librarian will be helpful in explaining how to use the library and how to collect information, including using a computer.

Ban Wikipedia?

TECHNOLOGY

More and more students are now using the Internet to find resources. Why not use Google and other Internet sources instead of walking to the library? Convenience wins hands down. However, use of Wikipedia, the free encyclopedia, is controversial. Citing its poor quality, some teachers and schools have banned Wikipedia both as a source or citation. Nevertheless, those in favor of using it believe that it offers a representation of how knowledge is changing. In addition, Wikipedia offers far more articles than printed encyclopedias. Those against using Wikipedia affirm that is a cheap imitation of a scholarly resource, containing a proliferation of misinformation. Unwary young students, according to this viewpoint, do not recognize the inaccurate information and suffer the consequences. Perhaps the best compromise is to use Wikipedia and other websites to start research to get a general picture of the topic. Then students need to check the facts they find in Wikipedia against other sources.

In other words, students should always be encouraged to think how the "experts" got their data. This is especially important in looking at the information from some websites and Wikipedia. This may include looking at traditional resources found in the library or the Internet versions of scholarly encyclopedias. In other words, students need to blend both computer and traditional library skills along with using critical thinking skills to evaluate data.

Evaluating Data

The importance of evaluating the data was shown in a study when a group of students investigated unsolved "mysteries" such as the Loch Ness monster, bigfoot, alien autopsy, and Stonehenge by using computer searches. The children reported that they found most sites were convincing in the way they presented information or, as one said, "If you didn't believe in bigfoot, why would you waste your time creating a website for it?" The conflicting information made the students look at "expert opinions" on the Internet and how to determine which ones are truthful and honest. In addition, students reported that they liked visual images more than text and tended only to scan the written information, which could influence their conclusions. To do this exercise on the Internet, as with all Internet searches, students must have good reading skills.[6]

Students can ask the following questions to evaluate a website.

- What is the purpose or intent of the site?
- What persons or organizations develop and maintain the site?
- What values and points of view are represented? Any important omissions?
- What is the copyright date or the last update? Is the matter current?
- How well does the site work? Is it easy to navigate around the site? What is the reading and interest level?

TECHNOLOGY

Practice Information Activities

Here are other examples of activities that encourage information skills. Photocopy for each student the one-page Quick Reference Index of *The World Almanac and Book of Facts*. Then ask students to give the *category* in which you would look to learn about major earthquakes, the population of Canada's provinces, where nuclear reactors are located in the United States, and so on. Similarly, prepare an abbreviated copy of the telephone numbers of government offices. Although government agencies now have information and forms available online, sometimes it is best to ask questions over the phone if you need an interpretation or the law/regulation is complex. "How long does my neighbor's dog have to bark before I call the police?" "If I sell my used textbooks, do I have to report that as income?" Then explain how to find government office telephone numbers in the pages of a telephone

---

[6]Mark E. Brown and Tracy L. Riley, "Internet Investigations," *Learning and Leading with Technology* 26 (November 1998): 28–34.

directory. Finally, ask students to find and write down the telephone numbers for offices such as animal control, birth records, or building permits.

Students may also assemble their own data from interviews and questionnaires, but they must be taught to ask questions in an objective manner and to communicate clearly what is being asked. Most students will need your assistance in designing an interview sheet or questionnaire to gather data, for example, on how local residents view traffic problems in their neighborhood. Poorly designed interview forms and questionnaires may yield misleading information that is of little value in proving or disproving a hypothesis. Such questionnaires may also reflect unfavorably on the school and the teacher.

Accepting or Rejecting a Hypothesis

After students gather data and ask questions, they need to classify and organize the information. Finding relationships and classifying facts under main headings requires skill. Students must be able to see, for example, that data on immigrants might belong in several categories, such as the problems immigrants face and the successes they have had. In addition, students will often have to analyze and interpret their information to decide what it really means. Only then are they in a position to accept or reject their hypothesis, the final step in the thinking process. Do the data support the hypothesis? Discuss and debate the conclusions.

On Your Own **3.2**

Just the Facts!

How much thinking do you believe goes on in a typical social studies classroom? Does it occur during the entire day? If you believe that little thinking takes place in most classrooms, list three reasons why many teachers concentrate on having students recall facts instead of emphasizing thinking. •

We have shown here that you will probably have to use a variety of methods to teach problem solving or thinking. Questioning is almost always part of the process as well as discussion. Discussion, either in small or large groups, requires skills in observation (seeing the nonverbal communication), listening, and questioning. Discussion can take many formats. Some elementary teachers like using the **council discussion format.** Here students sit in one large circle and a talking stick is passed from student to student. You can speak only if you have the stick. The speaker's comments are usually brief and limited to one minute.

Thus, sometimes students will work in small groups; other times, they will work alone. In some cases, your role will be indirect as you try to encourage students to generate as many promising ideas as possible. In these cases, your role is not to judge but to encourage an atmosphere in the class in which ideas are welcome and not subjected to ridicule by other students. On the other hand, for specific skills, such as how to find information in an atlas, direct teaching may work best. But it is not enough just to drill students in these skills. Worksheets or other teaching material should be as entertaining as possible so that students will want to use the skills after they do the required assignments. Teaching skills that students will not use in the future is not beneficial for either the students or the school.

In teaching thinking, then, present a variety of open-ended problems or questions that students can use to practice their thinking skills. Make sure the students become interested in the problems, and don't pursue a problem if most children seem bored by it. Also, don't foster dependency in students by giving them too much help. Be positive about their ideas, and remember that many children have not had much experience in thinking and will not become creative thinkers in merely a few weeks. Remind students that making mistakes is part of the learning process and that they should not be discouraged if their first ideas do not work out. Finally, make the encouragement of thinking a goal in everything you do and every lesson you teach, throughout the year.

In summary, here are some hints for teaching thinking:

- Teach for meaning, not just memorization.
- Ask thought-provoking questions.
- Explain your thought processes.
- Have students explain their thought processes; promote metacognition—knowledge of when and where to use thinking strategies.
- Encourage and accept all ideas and viewpoints.
- Summarize main ideas.

Inductive Thinking and Questioning

Inductive Thinking

Inductive thinking moves from several examples to a concept or generalization. Among the several strategies devised to help children acquire inductive thinking skills is the simple scheme developed by Hilda Taba, an outstanding elementary educator who made significant contributions to social studies teaching.[7] This classic strategy has three basic steps:

1. Teacher enumerates and lists students' responses to an opening question.
2. Students group the responses.
3. Students label or categorize their groupings.

In this strategy teachers promote group discussion through questions that follow these steps. For example, to explore the concept of rules, a teacher might ask, "What comes to your mind when you hear the word *rules*?" Recording student responses as they are given, the teacher tries to elicit a variety of responses, accepting all without regard to whether they are accurate. Working from the original responses, the next question would be "Can we group any of these?" "What is the reason you put these together?" Finally, "What title can we give to this list?" This line of questioning can also be used for guiding students in the formation of generalizations.

Look how this inductive procedure works in the lesson plan "Geographic Regions."

Teacher Questioning

As you can see from problem-based learning and inductive thinking, questioning is an integral part of thinking and learning that is common to all methods. Teachers need to ask a variety of appropriate questions—multiple responses as well as application, evaluative, and factual questions. Frame the questions carefully so that they are adapted to the cognitive

[7]Hilda Taba, *Teaching Strategies and Cognitive Functioning in Elementary School Children,* Cooperative Research Project no. 2404 (Washington, DC: U.S. Office of Education, 1996).

LESSON PLAN

Geographic Regions

NCSS Standard III: Peoples, Places, and Environments

Grade Level: Third grade

Objective: Students will group various items into categories through analysis of common characteristics or attributes of a region. (Presume that the class has studied four regions.) Students will then justify and label the groups.

Materials: Cut up sets of words in envelopes. Words to include: *mesa, timberline, tornado, grain, ocean, coyote, lizard, moose, snow, cactus, cedar, swamp,* and the like.

Procedures

1. Teacher provides words in envelopes to be grouped by small groups. Teacher tells the class that the terms on the cards have to do with things they have been studying.
2. Students put words into categories that they feel go together with reference to the regions.
3. One group at a time writes their words assembled into categories on the chalkboard, whiteboard, or overhead projector.
4. Other students guess why this particular grouping was made and label the group.
5. Teacher asks if other words belong in the group.
6. Each student group explains their grouping and how the categorizing relates to what they have studied about the four regions. If differences, each group justifies their rationale for grouping.

Source: Armin C. Pearson, pp. 9–10 in Fontana (CA) *History-Social Science Professional Development Program,* Inland Area History Social Science Project, no date.

levels and affective needs of your students. Use wait time of at least three seconds to give students more time to reflect. Remember that such wait time has payoffs for students: Participation increases, responses are longer and more complex, and confidence rises along with academic achievement. Teachers also gain by not having to repeat questions.

Handle incorrect responses with prompts such as restating the question at a lower level, and avoid negative statements and nonverbal cues. The modeling of questions should in turn encourage students to ask their teacher as well as classmates questions as they work in small groups with discussion, simulation, and role playing (Figure 3.3). However, teachers should avoid always asking low-level factual questions because they do not stimulate students to think. For students doing research, try to avoid "Go Find Out About." Instead of saying, "Find out about our state," ask "Which of the cities in our state would you like to move to?" Try to ask "Why" questions. Why was Mohandas Gandhi (or any other historical figure) important? Why do people around the world want to emigrate to the United States? Why do people in the United States not live as long as in other nations like Japan? Asking such questions instead of just finding out about Gandhi also reduces student copying straight from the Internet.

| Figure 3.3 | Questions to Improve Thinking |

Questions of clarification
What do you mean by _____?
Can you give me an example?
Can you explain further?
Why do you say that?
What do you think Ellen meant?
Can you summarize what José said?
José, is that what you meant?

Questions that probe for reasons and evidence
Do you have evidence for that?
Why do you think that is true?
How can we find out whether that is true?

Questions about viewpoints or perspectives
How would other groups respond?
What objections might these other groups make?
Can you see this in another way?
What would someone who disagrees say?

Questions that focus on consequences
Which individuals/groups will gain? Which individuals/groups will lose?
What will happen if that goes into effect?
Will this always happen?

Bloom's taxonomy has a hierarchy and requires more cognitive skills as a student moves from one level to another. This format for planning, thinking, questioning, making test items and curriculum has been used for around fifty years. The use of Bloom's taxonomy is such a well-established procedure that you will encounter it in lesson plans and it may be used by some of your instructors. However, in 2001 Bloom's taxonomy was revised, as illustrated in Table 3.3. You may see either framework used in education but the newer version also emphasizes that more thought be given to how learners process information and how they think about their own cognition.

The questions in Figure 3.3 are based on Bloom's taxonomy (Table 3.3) with its six levels of cognitive processes. Each level of the taxonomy includes the verbs that indicate the level of thought involved in answering questions at that level. Primary-grade teachers almost always spend time each November on Thanksgiving. But too often teachers only ask lower-level questions about Thanksgiving and each grade level only repeats what has been taught in the previous year. Yet good questions by the teacher could help students to think about this holiday.

Student Questioning

Young children ask lots of questions. Often they are yes or no questions or short-answer questions. "What is this?" "Can I wear this t-shirt?" By the time students are in the upper grades, most questions asked of the teacher are housekeeping questions: "Where do we put our worksheets?" "What pages do we read?" Students are often afraid to ask questions so they will

Table 3.3	Different Levels of Questions Using Bloom's Taxonomy

Level	Verbs	Examples
1. Remember	who, what, where, when recall, identify, define, describe, locate	Who were the Pilgrims? When did they come to America?
2. Understand	describe, compare, rephrase, contrast, summarize	Compare what happens at Thanksgiving with activities of other U.S. holidays
3. Apply	apply, classify, use, choose, demonstrate	Are there similar Thanksgiving holidays in other parts of the world?
4. Analyze	tell why, analyze, identify the cause of, infer, categorize, detect	Why is Thanksgiving celebrated in the United States?
5. Evaluate	evaluate, judge, appraise, decide, support, criticize, determine which is better	Should Thanksgiving be changed in any way(s) in the United States?
6. Create	design, construct, plan, develop, predict, draw	Design a Thanksgiving celebration for the class

Source: Lorin W. Anderson and David R. Krathwohl, eds., *A Taxonomy for Learning, Teaching, and Assessing: A Revision of Bloom's Taxonomy of Educational Objectives* (New York: Addison Wesley Longman), 2001. See also older version, Benjamin S. Bloom, ed., *Taxonomy of Educational Objectives: The Classification of Educational Goals: Handbook I: The Cognitive Domain* (New York, David McKay), 1956.

not appear dumb to their peer group. On the other hand, a few students may constantly ask questions that often are not on target with the discussion. Yet students can be encouraged to ask meaningful questions, especially open-ended questions, that aid in their thinking.

Many teachers have used versions of Twenty Questions to help students ask categorical questions. "I am thinking about an historical event (or person)." "I am thinking about something concerning the Inca Civilization (or any other group)." "I have in this bag something related to our study of our local community." Students almost always enjoy playing Twenty Questions and can generalize this learning to other tasks. Remember to support students who ask meaningful questions in this game and throughout the day.

Cooperative or Collaborative Learning

Importance of Small Group Discussion Skills

Cooperative learning is a popular instructional strategy in which small groups work together toward a common goal. In the literature, it can take a variety of forms such as jigsaw, student team learning, group investigation, complex instruction, and learning together. Common characteristics of cooperative learning are holding each individual in each group accountable for his or her learning, assigning complementary roles and tasks to each individual, and communicating with each other and rewarding members for achieving their goal. Spencer Kagan, a well-known expert in cooperative learning, defines cooperative learning as PIES: positive interdependence, individual accountability, equal participation, and simultaneous interaction. In contrast, **collaborative learning** is a more unstructured process in which the group members negotiate goals, define problems, develop procedures, and produce knowledge. Collaborative learning is probably best done at higher levels of education but in usage the terms *cooperative* and *collaborative learning* are interchangeable. Sometimes cooperative learning is confused with **group work.** Here the teacher may say: "In your groups, list as many reasons as you can why cell phones should or should not be allowed in classrooms." Guess what normally happens! One or two verbal students do all of the talking, ignoring the others. All students in the group did not have to cooperate to complete the task.

There are compelling reasons for using cooperative learning. Students may learn from peers and increase their academic knowledge. They may increase and learn skills in listening to others, offering ideas, asking questions, compromising to resolve conflicts, and improving intergroup relations. Cooperative learning may be especially favorable in helping English language learners and increase cross-ethnic/race relations. The class climate can improve with both the teacher and students liking the class more. Although not necessarily the only way to teach, and certainly not a panacea to all the problems of education, cooperative learning is a viable strategy you can use to deliver content and to teach skills.

Definitions of Cooperative Learning

Cooperative learning has many definitions. Some educators include peer teaching and cross-age tutoring as examples of cooperative learning. But these forms of tutoring lack an important element of cooperative learning: *individual accountability.* In cooperative learning, each member of the group must learn the subject matter or complete the task and is evaluated on his or her performance. This accountability seldom occurs in tutoring, as the tutor is normally not tested in the subject area that she or he is teaching. Tutoring also implies an unequal status relationship in which the tutor knows the material while the person being tutored is presumed to be less able academically.

In contrast, cooperative learning presumes that all students will make distinct contributions to the group's task. In other words, they are *all* members of the group and each is dependent on the other group members (i.e., one member of the group does not have all the answers).

Some definitions stress the size of the group. Cooperative learning consists of three or more students who are united in a common purpose to complete a task and to include every group member. Elizabeth Cohen suggests that the group size be limited to no more than five members, whereas Spencer Kagan believes four is the magic number (see suggested readings at the end of the chapter).

In summary, cooperative learning is a method in which a heterogeneous group is given a task to do that should include the efforts of all the students in the group. Students directly interact with each other. They do not just sit silently working on their own assignments. In addition, cooperative learning includes the element of individual accountability. There should be no "free ride" or "social loafing" in which any student does not contribute to the group's efforts. Instead, each student is held accountable for learning the subject matter or contributing to the task. Lack of student accountability is probably the biggest problem in

Table 3.4	Teacher Evaluation of Cooperative Learning			
Group	**Work**		**Presentation**	
Name	**Used Time Well**	**Encouraged Others**	**Quality of Information**	**Effectiveness in Delivery**
1.				
2.				
3.				

using cooperative learning. Accountability is often determined by tests or teacher evaluation of group work and presentations (see Table 3.4). To encourage group effort, some teachers assign a group grade on a test as well as the presentation (if given) so that the more able members of the group take some responsibility for teaching the material or skills to all members of the group.

Why do experts recommend cooperative learning? During the typical classroom discussion, the average student has only one chance out of twenty (or whatever the class size may be) of having the opportunity to speak at a given moment. But if she or he is in a small group of four, the probability of speaking goes up to one in four. This means that there is more interaction among students, an important factor in learning both content and social skills.

Adults spend a great deal of time in small groups. Most of us interact with our families and friends. In community affairs, organizations, and clubs, a task is frequently assigned to a small committee. For teachers, it is almost impossible to avoid being put on a committee to work on some project to help improve the school.

In order to function in our society, everyone needs the skills to participate in small groups. Usually the activity is pleasant; most of us enjoy the socialization and companionship. But this is not always true. Have you ever been in a three-person group in which the other two members "ganged up" on you and tried to impose their views? In real life, three-member groups are often unstable regardless of the setting—three people sharing an apartment or three people on an outing. Or have you been in a small group that was unpleasant because one person knew all the right answers and would not listen to others? Just putting individuals or students into a small group is not a guarantee that students will automatically become more involved, thoughtful, tolerant, or responsible when working with a group.

Decisions for Cooperative Learning

With these cautions, the first task for a teacher is to identify appropriate lessons for cooperative learning. Ideally, there should be more than one answer or more than one way to solve the problem. If just factual answers from a textbook are asked, students will look to the brightest member of the group for all the answers and the rest of the group will just copy them. The task must be challenging and rewarding, requiring a variety of skills such as reading and writing. After **planning,** the teacher may also have *to teach the skills* necessary for successful participation in cooperative learning. Like other methods, the teacher also has to explain the goals and objectives of the activity while also monitoring the small groups.

The format or the structure for the group also has to be decided. **Brainstorming** focuses on group ideas, such as "List the ways to get more citizens to vote." Or will one of the snazzy structures of Spencer Kagan (or modifications) be used, such as the following:

- **Round robin**—taking turns orally, sometimes timed to give each student equal time
- **Round table**—each student adds something to a paper or project passed around
- **Think-Pair-Share**—write your ideas to a question, pair up with another student to discuss it, and then share with the whole class
- **Numbered Heads Together**—students on a team each have a number (1, 2, 3, or 4); the group put their heads together to come up with a best answer; teacher calls on a number (1, 2, 3, or 4) and only that student in each group can respond. This strategy forces all members of the team to know the correct response.

Size of the Group

The teacher's second task is to make organizational decisions in five areas: group size, team formation, use of roles, room arrangement, and materials. Group size, as noted previously, is an important characteristic of cooperative learning. In the past, some group work has divided the class into three more or less equal groups, typically with seven to ten members. This is far too large for effective small group work. In general, younger children profit most from smaller groups. In fact, two children is the proper group size for many primary children. Groups of three, four, or five are appropriate for more mature children. Group members must be able to see the nonverbal clues that other group members give as well as hear what everyone is saying. If the group is too large, members cannot monitor what is happening. Five should probably be the largest size for a group.

In assigning groups, especially early in the year, you need to look carefully at the academic achievement and the personalities of the class members. Initially all experts recommend heterogeneous grouping—mix students by ability, gender, ethnic groups, and so on. One way to do this is to make a list of students by academic achievement, from the highest to the lowest. If there are to be groups of three, put into each group a high-ability member, a middle achiever, and a low achiever. Some experts think it may be wise not to put high- and low-ability students in the same group if the differences are too extreme. Here the recommendation is to mix lower and middle students in small groups and middle and high students in other groups. Ensure that the gender and ethnic distributions are mixed. That means there should be a fairly equal distribution of girls and boys and of minority students. If you know that two students don't get along, do not, at least initially, place them together. However, later in the year, after their small group skills improve, you might *want* to assign them together. Avoid placing best friends on the same team. They will tend to talk and interact only with each other and ignore other members of the group. As a final suggestion, many teachers color code the groups. The names of all members of the blue team or group are posted under blue. These color-coded materials allow all students to easily find their team.

The traditional approach by experts was to recommend heterogeneous grouping. But now tentative research findings have pointed out some dilemmas for teachers. The below-average student gains in achievement test scores if she or he had access in the group to a high-ability student who has correct answers and high-quality explanations. However, in general high-ability students gain more if they are grouped with other high-ability students.[8] In addition, high achievers grouped together are more focused on getting work done, offering better conceptual explanations, and engaging in superior problem-solving strategies. This may be due to the high-ability students having greater oral facility and more experience in providing explanations than lower-ability students. The net result is that teachers will have to make decisions and struggle with balancing the needs of low- and high-achieving students in their classrooms. It may also be a problem if there are not enough experts, or high-ability students, to spread around to each group.

However, teachers who deliberately used a mix of criteria in forming groups by taking into account students' achievement levels as well as compatibility and interest reported stronger outcomes. This suggests you get inferior results by using grouping strategies such as random assignment (count off 1, 2, 3, and so on), groups of convenience (seated near each other), and self-selected groups. The teacher's judgment in forming groups increases achievement levels of the small groups.

Even with your best judgment in assigning groups, some groups may have difficulty working together. There may be personality clashes, ranging from minor bickering to insults that end in tears. Another problem is lack of participation. Often there are recognized stable hierarchies of "smart" and "slow" students. Most students in most classes within a short time categorize every member of the class as smart, average, or dumb, usually based on verbal ability (such as reading). These attitudes about ability can carry over into students' small groups. Groups frequently take less advantage of the contributions and skills of students who are labeled dumb, despite your plea that everyone participate and that all work together.

Thus, students may quarrel about who is to do what and who should make decisions. In effect, they play power games, just as adults do. Higher-status students want to have leadership roles, and lower-status students resist being in a group that does not seem to appreciate their talents. In many cases, "slower" students withdraw by physically moving away from the group or by disrupting it.

Roles

To mitigate these problems, some teachers assign roles to each member of the group. This is the third organizational decision. One student is the chairperson, another is the secretary, a third is responsible for getting the supplies to the group, and a fourth is charged with seeing that the group stays on task. Some teachers prepare cards with the title of the role—"chairperson" or "secretary"—to emphasize that each member of the group is to perform a certain role.

Here are some roles that students can play in small groups:

Chairperson or Facilitator

Organizes the group's work

Makes sure the group understands its job

Takes the group's questions to the teacher *after* trying to get answers from the group

[8]Norren W. Webb, Kariane M. Nemer, Alexander W. Chizhik, and Brenda Sugrue, "Equity Issues in Collaborative Group Assessment: Group Composition and Performance," *American Education Research Journal* 35 (Winter 1998): 646.

Recorder or Secretary

Writes down the group's answers on the group's answer sheet

Checker

Checks that everyone can explain and agrees with the group's answer

Supporter or Encourager (eventually all members should be this)

Keeps people feeling good about working together

Shows interest and excitement about the group's work

Some teachers include other roles such as reporter, but often it is easier for the secretary to read his or her own writing than to give it to another student to try to decipher. Of course, these roles should be rotated throughout the group so that each student has a chance to assume each of the roles. You need to monitor what is going on. Occasionally, students do not take their assigned roles and, thus, allow leadership, for example, to pass on to another student who has not been assigned that role.

Roles may have to be taught and evaluated. You should explain clearly what is expected in each role. Sometimes a teacher may want to use the role of a student observer who checks carefully what is happening in the group. Another way is for group members, at the end of the work session, to process how they have worked together. One way to do this is for the teacher to ask whether everyone in the group participated and to ask the group to consider this question; another way is by using a group self-evaluation form (Table 3.5). Students should be given an opportunity to process how the group is working. This does not have to be done every day but is often a neglected element in cooperative learning.

Room Arrangement

The teacher's fourth organizational decision concerns the room arrangement for the groups. Ideally, the groups should be in a circle, preferably without tables or other obstructions. The group members should be close enough to each other to communicate and be removed enough from the rest of the class so that they do not get distracted by the noise and activities of the other groups. In addition, the teacher needs to be able to circulate among the groups without encountering physical obstacles.

You should consider what materials are needed for the group to complete its task. Will the members have to share one set of materials per group or will there be a textbook for everyone? Do students need a place to write or will oral discussion be the focus of the

Table 3.5   Group Self-Evaluation

	Usually	Sometimes	Never
1. Every group member participated.			
2. Our group used its time wisely.			
3. Every group member did his or her job.			
4. Group members encouraged each other.			

group's activity? Your decisions can influence the amount of interaction that the students have in their group.

Team Building

These are the general steps for implementing cooperative learning. Usually it is wise at the beginning of the year to set up group learning experiences so that students can get to know one another better. Some teachers find it wise to start gradually with students in groups of two (dyads) for several weeks and then move into larger groups. At this point, the lessons do not have to include academic social studies content. Have the students in groups make collages, illustrating things they like to do, or have them share information about themselves with other members of the group. A favorite task is to develop a team name or sign to identify the group such as "The Experts" or "All-Stars of Room 2." Small groups might make poems on topics such as birthdays or a holiday. To do this, have individual students first jot down ideas or short phrases on the topic. These ideas can be incorporated into the group poem, which one member of the group might then read to the class. You might also want to post a copy of the poem, signed by all members of the group. The purpose of these activities is to teach students to use the ideas of *everyone* in the group and to take pride in *the group's final product.* In effect, this is team building in which each member develops a respect for everyone in the group.

As students get to know each other in the group, you may want to move into different formats of cooperative learning. One is group investigation, which requires each student to find material and decide how to communicate his or her learning to the remainder of the class. Perhaps you have decided that for the whole class to cover all the material in the textbook on American Indians would take too much time. Instead, you decide to divide the students into cooperative groups, having each group study in depth a single nation or tribe. You can assign the nation or tribe, or let the group, with your approval, select the one they want to study. After being directed to the appropriate sources of information (with the help of your school librarian), the groups share with the rest of the class what they have discovered.

Jigsaw

A more complex form of cooperative learning utilizes the *jigsaw technique* (Table 3.6). Here students teach each other factual content. Each child is assigned to both a learning team (the original home team) and a study group. Typically, content or a textbook chapter is divided into sections. On the elementary level, this probably should not be more than four pages. On the topic of the American Revolution, content could be divided into the following sections: the American Army, the American Navy, foreign aid, Loyalists, and prisoners. Often the teacher prepares a list of questions to be answered on each section.

In every home team, each team member is assigned a number. For example, all of the "1's" get together to study the same materials, such as the content on the American Navy. All of the "2's" study the content on foreign aid. Each group becomes an expert in the content it has been given and thinks of ways to teach its content. Then these experts return to their home team to teach their topics to the other home team members. Within the group, members take turns teaching the information in which they have become experts. Thus, each member teaches his or her assigned content to the rest of the group and learns from the others the content they were assigned to teach. Finally, after studying the content in their

Table 3.6	Jigsaw Technique

Steps

1. Design a lesson with a clear objective for the task. The task should be communicated both orally and in writing.
2. Choose the group size and composition.
3. Assign roles, divide learning materials into small portions.
4. Have students do individual reading of information of their group.
5. Have each expert group study the information and decide how best to teach other groups.
6. Send experts back to home teams to teach their information.
7. Assess learning on all the material.
8. Process how well the groups did (expert and home teams).

own home group, all students in the class are tested on content from all of the chapter sections. Typically, each student receives two grades from the test: an individual score as well as a team score. Realizing that their grades are partially dependent on the achievement of the home team, students are encouraged to do their best in group work.

The teacher acts as a timekeeper; sometimes this can be a problem in the expert group, in which material may not be covered. Students often request more time. Each phase of jigsaw need not be done on the same day.

In jigsaw as well as other forms of cooperative learning, grading can be a problem. Sometimes the "smart" students overparticipate, and the less-able students contribute little (or find their contributions undervalued by the group). Often students see the teacher's insistence that all members of the group be given the same grade as unfair. If you explicitly require that all students in some way participate in the group's efforts, the "able" students will be more likely to make sure everyone is included so their grades will not be lowered. Some teachers use the whole group's score on tests to determine whether there is improvement and give extra points to the groups that improve. Other experts are completely against the use of group grades in cooperative learning because they create resentments and appear unfair.

Other Problem Areas

Teachers also have to decide how long a given group stays together. Some teachers like to change the groups after a number of weeks so that students will learn to work with a variety of different personalities. Others keep the same groups for months, especially if the focus is on teaching social participation skills, such as having members encourage each other. These skills take time and practice, and often they can be applied more effectively if the group members already know each other.

Cooperative learning, like any other method, can be used in inappropriate ways. In the worst cases, cooperative learning can exacerbate status differences and create dysfunctional relationships among students. When teachers do spend the time needed to teach the skills of group work, specify tasks, and use time allotments and roles for group work sessions, cooperative learning can be a productive and powerful method. The class atmosphere may

Small Group Work 3.4

Trying Out Small Group Tasks

The best way to learn how to use small-group or cooperative learning is to do it yourself. Experience first-hand what it is like to be a member of a small group. Try the following format called **corners.** Each student moves to a corner of the room representing a teacher-determined alternative. One corner could be "We need (or should keep) a state social studies test." Another corner could be "We should not have a state social studies test," and another corner, "Our state should make the social studies test voluntary." The fourth corner could be "The state social studies test(s) should only be given in high school." Students discuss the reasons for their point of view, and then paraphrase ideas from the other corner. This activity forces students to listen to alternative arguments. ●

improve as students get to know one another better and learn to work together. Everyone enjoys the class more. Furthermore, the academic achievement level of the class may increase.

Cooperative learning does require special attention and planning by the teacher. Make your assignments and instructions clear so that the group does not take too much time trying to determine what has to be done. If there is to be a group product, do students know the criteria or rubric that will be used to evaluate their work?

In addition, you must monitor carefully what is going on and that the group is on task with all the students participating. Are some students passive? Is one group constantly bickering? Is one student always ordering the other members of the group around? If these problems persist, even after processing, you may have to show students how to make improvements in the group. Role-playing "being bossy" or demonstrating other problems can also provide a rewarding opportunity for students to become aware of how to improve their small-group skills.

Teachers also need to think about students who have attention deficit hyperactivity disorder (ADHD) when using cooperative learning. It is important that all students understand the team rules. Team rules alert all students to expected behavior without targeting students with ADHD as potential "troublemakers." You may need to prepare and alert students to an alternative assignment or "time-out" area for students needing to remove themselves temporarily from their groups.

Role Playing

What is role playing and how does it work? *Role playing* is a method of problem solving that enables participants to explore alternative solutions to a given problem. It is an *unrehearsed* dramatic presentation, usually more appropriate for children age 9 or older. Role playing is especially useful for dealing with controversial issues.

The impetus for role playing can be provided by reading the class a story or a law case or by having students view an open-ended film or photograph showing conflict. Classroom problems such as lack of sharing or breaking school or class rules can also be used for role playing. When you use problems in your own class such as dealing with the class bully, however, do not use actual names, and disguise the incident on which the group is focusing.

The basic steps in role playing are outlined in Table 3.7. Role playing can be a safe way of exploring alternative behavior. It allows us to express feelings or opinions without risking disapproval. Many of us, when we are driving on the freeway or sitting at our desks at the end of the day, have said to ourselves, "If only I had said this or that, the situation

Table 3.7	Steps in Role Playing

1. Present the open-ended problem. Set the stage by asking, "Have you ever . . . ?" or "How did you feel when you were . . . ?" Then say, "Today we're going to hear a story about Kyle (or any name other than that of a member of your class) who got into a similar mess. Think about how you would feel if you were in such a situation." Next, read the story up to the conflict point. Encourage students to identify the problem and talk about how the people in the story feel.

2. Select the participants or role players. Ask for volunteers to play the various roles. The rest of the class will serve as observers.

3. Begin the role play. Enact an ending for the story. Have students pretend to be characters with the feelings and ideas of the people in the specific situation.

4. Discuss the solution, especially in terms of its realism. Ask the observers if there are alternative ways of solving the problems.

5. Explore the alternative possibilities in further role playing.

6. Discuss the several role-playing experiences and, if possible, summarize what has been learned.

would have been better." Students need to know that sometimes alternative ways of acting lead to better solutions. Role playing offers a safe opportunity to explore.

Role playing also can help prepare students to cope with conflict resolution and problem solving. Role playing is used, for instance, to help students "say no to drugs." Proponents of this approach in substance-abuse education believe that it is not enough just to tell a student to say no to drugs. It is better to act out situations, such as a party at which one student offers alcohol to another student. Showing different ways in which a student can refuse alcohol while still remaining "friends" with the offerer may be important to students. In addition, this approach can suggest to the "straight" student that it is possible to find activities other than alcohol use to share with the user—a step to help the substance user.

Using role playing in substance-abuse education also illustrates another value of role playing. Role playing can deal directly with issues on which students might be reluctant to give their opinions in other formats, such as what to do if you see two children fighting or if you meet a friend after hearing that this friend told lies about you. By providing a situation in which students are and yet are not themselves, you give them a chance to bring out feelings and opinions they might otherwise not be willing to express.

Most students enjoy participating in and watching role playing. It provides an opportunity for more active involvement than many other classroom learning experiences, and it is more personalized. Acting out the dilemma of a pioneer child who must decide if he will report to his American Indian friend that the tribe's camp will be raided the next day involves the students in what has happened in the past. Many teachers say they are using role playing to play out historical events (e.g., the Constitutional Convention of 1787) much as they actually occurred. Technically, when students act in a prescribed fashion and merely duplicate the historical event, they are doing *dramatic play,* not role playing. *Mock trials,* often used with older children who are already familiar with the procedures used in courts, are also an example of using drama. For example, students can reenact the Salem witch

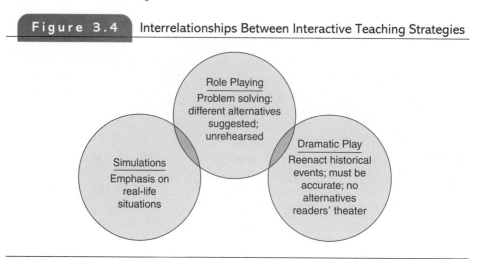

Figure 3.4   Interrelationships Between Interactive Teaching Strategies

trials, Socrates' trial, or other important trials in history. To be successful, students need a good background in the time period as well as knowledge of court procedure. *Readers' theatre* is another dramatic presentation in which the lines of the students, as in a play, are already fixed and not given as alternatives. This is not to deny the value of reading a play or script, especially if students themselves have made the script. It merely points out the differences in dramatic play and role playing. The focus of role playing is the concept of *alternatives,* or other ways the story or historical event might have ended (see Figure 3.4).

You may encounter students who are reluctant to volunteer for role play, especially at first. Others are often born hams who want to play roles every time. Do not let these "actors" take over the stage completely. Start with less controversial or emotional issues so that students become more at ease in role playing. Continue to encourage the shy students to volunteer, and as students get used to the format of role playing, they will become more eager to play a role. However, be careful not to cast students in the roles they occupy in the minds of their classmates. Do not put the class clown in a role in which he or she plays the class clown. Instead, put each student in someone else's shoes. The class bully should play the role of the weaker student who wants to have a turn in a game. Continually emphasize the role that the student is playing and avoid calling the student by his or her real name. Refer to the police officer or the landlady rather than to the specific student.

Sometimes students have a difficult time maintaining their roles. They start to giggle and often are distracted by the audience response. Audience members, too, must play their role appropriately. You may want to comment on this before or after the exercise. Usually, with time and practice, students are better able to maintain their roles.

Initially, you may find that many students want to play the enactment as it "should" be. In other words, they will play a role in a kind and loving manner and do all the right things. You need to ask if this is how it really happens. Some teachers are bothered if students enact negative, although realistic, behavior. They think that the class may model the wrong pattern. This is especially true, for example, if a student role involves pretending to take drugs or acting according to some other behavior that the community strongly opposes. But this should not be a major concern if you have an appropriate discussion and debriefing on what was going on. You can ask students who acted in negative roles how they felt. Often they will say that they were uncomfortable about how they acted. Thus, the debriefing stage is one of the most important parts of role play-ing. By sharing feelings and answering ques-tions at the end of the enactment, students may see further alternative ways to act.

Teachers sometimes believe that they must force a generalization from the role-playing ex-perience. They want the group to come to a conclusion—for example, "If you are not hos-tile in a situation, there is more chance that you can solve a problem." But sometimes students are not yet ready to reach that conclusion. In those cases, it is best to drop the matter. Perhaps in a later experience, the group will come to that or a similar conclusion.

Small Group Work **3.5**

Develop a Role Play

Try role playing in your class. You might use the scenario of a principal walking into a class when every-thing is confused and disorderly. Assign roles of the principal, student teacher or teacher, and a few students in the class. ●

Role playing in the social studies offers the possibility of moving into the affective do-main. It can help teach children to empathize with others by showing them how it feels to be in someone else's place. It can tap the emotional responses of students to certain situa-tions while still moving toward a rational solution of a problem. This is one of the values of role playing. Often role playing can be a springboard for further study on a given topic. For this reason, it can be a successful method for the social studies teacher.

Simulations

Simulations are learning activities that present an artificial problem or event. The situation described tries to duplicate reality but removes the possibility of injury or risk. Pilots, for ex-ample, learn to fly by using a simulator, whereas both the military and business worlds may use simulations to learn how to win a campaign or where to locate a new factory. In many cases, a computer records the responses of the trainees or participants in the simulation.

Like role playing, a simulation allows the trainee or the player to try out a role and make decisions in a safe environment. But unlike role playing, which focuses on problem solving, simulations have a gamelike quality in which there are players, roles, and an end goal, such as winning. Because of this, many students think that simulations are fun, and they are moti-vated to do their best. Often they are put in a conflict or crisis situation, such as a political sit-uation in the Middle East, and are asked to play high-ranking political and military leaders or other important roles. Usually, they compete with others. Simulations such as "Seal Hunt" encourage cooperative behavior, but most simulations are based on competition.

In education, simulations were used initially without a computer. Students played sim-ulations such as "Star Power," which set up an unequal division of power and resources, and students were supposed to learn what it was like to be a member of certain power groups. In another social studies simulation, "Farming," set in western Kansas in three different years, students acting in teams of two made economic decisions on what to invest in—hogs, wheat, livestock, and so on. The simulation tried to duplicate the reality of farm-ing in the 1880s, and at the end of the simulation, many of the couples (students) found that they had lost their money. Part of the purpose of this simulation was to bring to life the problems that farmers were facing after the Civil War. For the colonial era "Sail America" and "The Pilgrims" from Interact are popular. Interact also has many simulations for 19th-century U.S. history ("Mountain Men Rendezvous," "Cattle Drive") and even more for the 20th century ("Ford Assembly Line," "Lindbergh Solo Flight"). One of the advantages of well-designed simulations is that they can make abstract concepts such as oversupply or power more meaningful for students. In addition, simulations provide almost immediate feedback to the students on how they are doing, which is a key to motivation.

TECHNOLOGY

We are now seeing more computer-based social studies simulations. They are probably most common in teaching economics ("Stock Market"), history ("Civil War"), and politics ("President-Elect"). In most of them, the individual student interacts with the computer program, playing the role of the king-priest of an ancient city making economic decisions, for instance, or trying to win a political campaign in the United States. Other examples are the well-known "Oregon Trail" or the "New Oregon Trail," where players travel on the Oregon Trail making decisions faced by the original pioneers. There are many variations of this as children pretend to travel on the "Santa Fe Trail" or go to the gold mines of California ("Golden Spike"). In a few games, such as "Geography Search," students act in teams to try to locate valuable resources. In these cases, there is often competition between different teams in the same classroom.

Neither computer nor noncomputer simulations in the social studies are usually designed commercially for the primary-grade levels; they are for middle grades and beyond. However, primary teachers may design their own simulations, setting up, for instance, a post office, hospital, or other community institution. For example, primary students have taken the roles of park planners as the students design a visual park. Decisions on where activities are to be located and what plants should be used helped children understand the human/environment interaction as well as skills in working with each other.

Along with many advantages, there are also pitfalls in using simulations in the classroom:

1. In some cases, especially at the middle school level, students may have to learn complex rules in order to play. They may be unable or unwilling to listen to a long explanation, and you may find it best to have students learn by doing, even if some encounter frustration.

2. Some students are motivated in simulations only when they have important roles to play. They find it unfair that they have to play poor people or members of a group who are discriminated against. You may find that students are reluctant to accept these roles, although the roles are necessary to the simulation.

3. Simulations can have management problems. They are often noisy. Occasionally, students get so involved in playing the simulation that they actually become hostile and even start fights. You must constantly scan the classroom to monitor what is going on.

4. Teachers sometimes believe that simulations misinform students by oversimplifying. If a student plays the role of a United Nations delegate, for example, the student may then believe that he or she knows all about the United Nations. Some teachers also worry that simulations encourage unethical or immoral behavior, as when students choose to drop bombs and start wars or to take resources from poorer players.

As you can see, some of these concerns are similar to those associated with role playing. As with that approach, discussion and debriefing are essential to clarify what actions players choose to take and what effects those actions have on other players. Thus, in "Seal

Hunt," students must realize that their decision not to share resources may have forced other students to starve. In the "Mercantilism" simulation, which is set in colonial America, students, eager to make money, find they are often engaging in both slavery and smuggling. It is important in debriefing to clarify what the students are actually doing and to explore the consequences of such behavior.

The strong advantage of a simulation is that students are often highly enthusiastic and motivated. There is a minority of students, however, who would rather read the textbook and answer the questions at the end of the chapter; not all students are the same. You must, therefore, determine whether a simulation has achieved the desired objectives. Do the students now know more about understanding different cultural groups? Do they feel more empathy for disadvantaged people or developing nations? Like any other method, a simulation is worthwhile only if it conveys knowledge, skills, or changes in feelings and attitudes.

On Your Own **3.3**

Research by Doing

Acquire a simulation. Your curriculum library or computer library may have some to choose from. Good sources of what is available are Interact, P. O. Box 997, Lakeside, CA 92040 (www.interact-simulations.com) or Social Studies School Services, 10200 Jefferson Boulevard, Culver City, CA 90232-0802 (800-421-4246; FAX 800-944-5432; www.socialstudies.com). Secure the teacher's manual. Review the simulation, step by step, to see how it works. Do you see possible difficulties? What does it seem to teach? Secure reviews, if possible, from teachers or from the Internet on how the simulation is rated. ●

Other methods do exist for teaching the social studies. Some teachers individualize instruction and set up learning centers. Others assume the role of a coach to the students. The teacher as a coach helps students master particular skills through the use of practice and prompts such as questioning. Sometimes questioning is listed as a distinct method, although questioning is part of almost all methods. In particular, the Taba approach, which uses teacher questions to move students to concepts and generalizations, is often recommended (see Chapters 5 and 10). Different methods are more appropriate for certain students and for achieving certain objectives; no method will work all the time for all teachers and all students. Since you are the decision maker, you must decide what combination of methods is best suited to achieving your objectives.

Summary

Teaching strategies should be challenging, flexibly applied, and responsive to students' needs. Each teaching method has certain advantages. The direct teaching learning model can be useful to impart certain information and concepts. Inductive and problem-solving methods are extremely important in teaching students how to think. Cooperative learning or other small-group activities can teach knowledge *and* social skills. Role playing and simulations are more interactive methods that can touch the affective domain. Questioning skills are an integral part of all methods. The choice of methods depends partly on what you are trying to achieve. In general, by using variety in your teaching methods, you will be more successful in adapting to content differences and the diverse learning styles of your students.

Suggested Readings and Websites

Armstrong, Thomas. *Multiple Intelligences in the Classroom,* 2nd ed. Alexandria, VA: Association for Supervision and Curriculum Development, 2000.

Strategies for implementing multiple intelligences in the classroom.

Baum, Susan, Julie Viens, and Barbara Slatin. *Multiple Intelligences in the Elementary Classroom.* New York: Teachers College Press, 2005.

How to design a curriculum for diverse student learning abilities.

Boostrom, Robert. *Thinking: The Foundation of Critical and Creative Learning in the Classroom.* New York: Teachers College Press, 2005.

Too often teachers unintentionally promote nonthinking. Suggestions to improve thinking.

Borich, Gary D. *Effective Teaching Methods,* 5th ed. Upper Saddle River, NJ: Prentice Hall, 2004.

Reviews teaching methods.

Clegg, Ambroise A. "Games and Simulations in Social Studies Education." In James Shavers, ed., *Handbook of Research on Social Studies Teaching and Learning.* New York: Macmillan, 1991.

Reviews games and simulations for the social studies.

Cohen, Elizabeth G. *Designing Groupwork,* 2nd ed. New York: Teachers College Press, 1994.

Good pointers, step-by-step approach.

DeLisle, R. *How to Use Problem-Based Learning in the Classroom.* Alexandria, VA: Association for Supervision and Curriculum Development, 1998.

Erickson, H. Lynn. *Concept-Based Curriculum and Instruction for the Thinking Classroom.* Thousand Oaks, CA: Corwin Press, 2007.

How to develop a thinking classroom.

Freiberg, H. Jerome, and Amy Driscoll. *Universal Teaching Strategies,* 4th ed. Boston: Allyn & Bacon, 2005.

Divided into three main sections on organizing, instruction, and assessment.

Hunter, Madeline. *Mastery Teaching.* El Segundo, CA: TIP Publications, 1982.

Advocate of direct teaching.

Johnson, David W., and Roger T. Johnson. *Learning Together and Alone,* 5th ed. Boston, MA: Allyn & Bacon, 1999.

Excellent on cooperative learning techniques.

Joyce, Bruce, Emily Calhoun, and Marsha Weil. *Models of Teaching,* 7th ed. Boston: Allyn & Bacon, 2004.

Different chapters on various models/methods used in teaching.

Kagan, Spencer, *Cooperative Learning.* San Clemente, CA: Kagan Publishing, 1994.

Detail on cooperative learning structures with helpful examples and practical tips.

Orlich, Donald C., Anne L. Remaley, Kevin C. Facemeyer, Jerry Logan, and Qin Cao. "Seeking the Link Between Student Achievement and Staff Development," *Journal of Staff Development* 14, no. 3 (1993): 2–8.

A critical report on the effectiveness of the Hunter model.

Shaftel, Fannie R., and George Shaftel. *Role Playing in the Curriculum,* 2nd ed. Englewood Cliffs, NJ: Prentice-Hall, 1982.

Best text available on role playing.

Slavin, Robert E. *Cooperative Learning—Theory, Research, and Practice,* 2nd ed. Boston: Allyn & Bacon, 1995.

Reviews research, theory, and applications of cooperative learning.

Stahl, Robert J., ed. *Cooperative Learning in Social Studies: A Handbook for Teachers* Menlo Park, CA: Addison-Wesley, 1994.

A set of fourteen articles on cooperative learning as applied to the social studies.

Stahl, Robert J., and Ronald L. Van Sickle, eds. *Cooperative Learning in the Social Studies Classroom,* Bulletin 87. Washington, DC: National Council for the Social Studies, 1992.

Good examples.

Taba, Hilda. *Teacher's Handbook for Elementary Social Studies.* Palo Alto, CA: Addison-Wesley, 1967.

Excellent on thinking strategies.

Thornton, Stephen J. *Teaching Social Studies that Matters: Curriculum for Active Learning.* New York: Teachers College Press, 2004.

Teachers need curriculum skills.

Yeager, Elizabeth Anne, and O. L. Davis, Jr., eds. *Wise Social Studies Teaching in an Age of High-Stakes Testing: Essays on Classroom Practices and Possibilities.* Greenwich, CT: Information Age Publishing Inc., 2005.

How to bring creativity, higher-order thinking and meaningful learning into the classroom.

Websites

Cooperative Learning Center
www.co-operation.org

Good for research on cooperative learning plus practical procedures.

Score

http://score.rims.k12.ca.us

A good source for lesson plans is the Schools of California Online Resources for Education (SCORE). Lessons and resources are organized by grade level as well as topics. Although the website is organized for the standards and framework of California, most of the content is valuable for all teachers.

Spencer Kagan
http://www.kagononline.com

List of free articles by well-known author on cooperative learning. Advice and essays on cooperative learning

Note: Many of the websites for problem-based learning focus on the university level such as www.udel.edu/pbl where they are used in medical schools and other departments.

VIDEO HOMEWORK EXERCISE

Inquiry Method

Go to MyEducationLab, select the topic **Teaching Strategies,** and watch the video entitled "Inquiry Method."

In the video, a fourth-grade class uses an inquiry chart in a unit on World War II.

CHAPTER 4

Using Multiple Assessments to Evaluate Student Learning in the Social Studies

Assessments and evaluations can tell if students have achieved social studies standards/objectives. Three main categories for assessing student learning are highlighted: performance-based assessment, paper-and-pencil tests, and informal evaluations. Conferences, grades, and report cards are shown as ways of communicating the results of assessments and evaluation.

- Perceptions of Testing
- Federal and State Roles in Testing
- Performance-Based Assessment
- Paper-and-Pencil Tests
- Informal Evaluations
- Conferences, Grades, and Report Cards

Why is it necessary to talk to a student about her work?

Perceptions of Testing

Tests and testing evoke a wide variety of emotions. Few are likely to be neutral about testing in the schools. Let us examine the attitudes and beliefs about testing among six groups concerned with education. The key issue is finding the best ways to determine what students have learned. Knowing how to design a wide variety of assessments can assist you in diagnosing student learning difficulties and using appropriate corrective teaching strategies.

Definitions

First, you need to be precise about terms such as **assessment, evaluation,** and **testing,** because often these terms are used interchangeably. Assessment is the process of gathering information about students' learning. Assessments are the many ways used to check if students have achieved certain objectives. Often the first image of assessment that comes to mind is a paper-and-pencil test. However, students ideally should be assessed in many different ways, not just paper-and-pencil tests, so they can show what they have learned.

Often assessment is confused with evaluation. Evaluations are the judgments and interpretations made on how well students have achieved. By itself, a score of a sixty or eighty tells little. It could be a "good" score or a "poor" score; it has to be interpreted. The most common form of teacher evaluations are **grades** (A, B, C) or **rankings,** such as proficient (P), in progress (I), or not yet (N) on report cards. The report card shows that teachers have reviewed a variety of tests and other assessments and have made their evaluation of student learning.

A **test** is a procedure for gathering data to check if the learning objectives have been achieved. A test is getting a sample (and thus, a limited amount) of information about what a student knows or is able to do. Tests should be measuring the objectives we want students to know and be able to do. In other words, the tests should be aligned with the objectives.

A newer term is **value-added assessment.** *Achievement* is the level of proficiency of students at the end of the year. *Growth* refers to the progress made by students on their end-of-year tests. You can see the problems using annual yearly progress. Some students at the top levels may show high achievement but actually have had low growth during the past year. On the other hand, a few low-achieving students may exhibit high growth during the year even though their test scores are still below the norm.

Value-added assessment compares a student's current level of achievement with his or her past achievement. Individual students are tracked over time instead of just using the scores of the whole classroom or school. Value-added assessment focuses on growth during the year for all students, not just NCLB's concern for low-performing students. Since it is individually based, value-added assessment can provide diagnostics to improve instruction, which is especially helpful if a few years of test scores are accumulated. For these reasons, it is expected that the popularity of value-added assessment will continue to grow along with requiring related diagnostic tests. A few states are now requiring diagnostic tests so that student needs are identified early enough to be addressed.

The Student

The effects of testing on students can be positive or negative. Students who perform well usually are not fearful of tests, and, in fact, a few may even look forward to taking a test.

These students usually have enough confidence in how they will perform. These competent students generally are proud of the high grades they receive on their report cards. Testing translates in their minds, as with most students, into grades or rankings they receive on their report cards. For students, grades can emphasize competition rather than personal improvement. If there is a **high-stakes, standards-based test** that influences their promotion or need to go to summer school, then the high-stakes test becomes more important than grades.

How their peer groups and families regard grades, as well as the motivational climate in their own schools, also influences students. Some students feel thankful that their grades are about average compared to the rest of the class. For struggling students, however, testing and lower grades may be a negative experience pointing out to them and others that they are not "good learners" like other students. Some may regard themselves as failures who lack the ability to learn. These older elementary students often say "I don't care about grades." This usually is not an accurate statement. Grades affect how students perceive themselves and how they are viewed by their friends, parents, and teachers. However, frequently students who get poor grades interpret this as a sign that the teacher does not like them and has something against them.

As children get older, they often get the idea that the teacher's written tests are the most important parts of the school learning. Older elementary students frequently ask, "Will this be covered on the test?" If the content and skills will not be tested, they are less concerned about learning the content or skills. This points out that for some students tests and grades are a motivating force. Students often try harder if they know it will be tested. Even first graders who have spelling tests quickly learn that it pays to study for the spelling test given each Friday. Thus, tests and grades can be an incentive.

The Parent or Guardian

Parents want the teacher to appreciate the special uniqueness and talents of their child. They want the teacher to give their child as much attention as possible. A child's grades are important to parents since it gives an indication on how well the child will succeed as an adult. In addition, many times parents see their child's grades as a refection of their own ability to be a "good" parent.

Parents like to see high marks on report cards. In fact, sometimes they would rather see high marks than see a lower grade because of a "harder" curriculum. In addition, parents always want to know how their child compares to the rest of the second-grade class. A few parents go beyond this and want to know how their child compares to other second-grade classes in the local school district, state, or nation. Also, more parents with children in failing schools are aware that they may seek tutoring or extra help after school or may even be able to transfer their children from the failing school.

Often parents welcome suggestions from the teacher to improve their child's grades. However, parents send a mixed message about homework. Some parents want their child to have more homework while others want less. Similarly, some parents can set aside time to make sure their child is reading or doing homework. However, teachers are well aware that, especially in families where both parents work or a single parent heads the household, a parent or parents may be stressed by the end of their working day and attending to their child's homework may be difficult.

The Teacher

Due to the No Child Left Behind Act and state testing, more teachers are worried about how their class will do on standardized state tests. A few teachers actually have resorted to explicit cheating to get their classes' scores higher. Their principal may regard getting high state test scores as vital to the success of the school. Even when the principal is supportive and trying to help teachers, teachers may feel pressure to have their students do well on local and state tests. However, about half of all teachers have not had a test and measurement course in their teacher education program, so some teachers are not confident about how they should test and evaluate their students.

Assessment is one of a teacher's most important tasks. Effective teachers are skilled in the diagnosis of student learning needs and adapting instruction to their needs. However, teachers may not always look forward to designing assessment tasks for their students. Some teachers may see assessment as taking time away from "real" teaching. Also, busy teachers do not always spend time thinking how test scores and other assessments could lead to improvement in planning the curriculum or helping individual students, essentials for improving student learning.

Administrators

Principals and the superintendent are well aware that low test scores have serious consequences on their own job security and for the school district. Because of mandated state testing in many subject areas, the results of state test scores are now available from many sources—newspapers, websites, real estate offices, local school offices. The annual publication of state test scores frequently sets offs a debate on "what is wrong with our schools."

When administrators receive the data from test scores, they sort test results by gender, race/ethnic group, languages spoken at home, school lunch status, ELLs and special education students, number of years in the school district, and more. This enables a closer look at student achievement. This has lead administrators to ask for more formative assessment throughout the year to measure how students are doing so that changes can be made during the current school year, not waiting until the next year.

Under pressure, a few administrators encourage giving more resources to students who are just below passing and ignoring the needs of the lowest performing students and the gifted and those who can easily pass tests. Administrators also have been accused of trying to exclude low-performing students from testing. Furthermore, in failing schools, administrators have the responsibility to give parents information about supplemental services and the option for the children to change schools.

The Community and the State

Besides parents living in a community, the other residents of a community know that their property values are influenced by the reputation of the local public schools. Parents want to send their children to "good" schools and are reluctant to buy or to rent housing in a neighborhood with "poor" schools, where tests show that the children are not achieving as expected. Because of the importance of school performance, many real estate agents are armed with the published test scores of various schools to show prospective buyers or renters. Furthermore, local and state governments levy taxes to pay for public schools and test scores of schools can become an important public issue. Should there be more effort to reform education? In what ways? Thus, test scores get the attention of the public. For example, employers seeing test scores stress the need for a skilled labor force.

Measurement and Evaluation Experts

From Chapter 2, you know that the most important function of assessing/testing is to check if the standards/instructional objectives have been achieved. Therefore, student assessment is an essential task of every single teacher. Measurement and evaluation experts agree with this function. However, it should be noted that state-mandated standardized testing is a very small amount of the total time that is devoted to assessment. Much more time is spent with teachers' own assessments. So, experts want teachers to make good use of teacher-constructed tests. This also includes other student activities that are evaluated, such as worksheets, homework assignments and projects, small group discussions (see Chapter 3 for checklists), responses to oral questioning, and informal observation by the teacher. These day-to-day assessment techniques can contribute to improving the quality of instruction and helping individual students.

Measurement and evaluation experts also are concerned about the validity of tests, especially the use of scores for high-stakes decisions about students and schools. Another source of worry for experts is the inclusion of students with disabilities and with limited English proficiency in the state tests. They are troubled about poor testing practices that misidentify school status and cause difficulties in measuring annual yearly progress.[1] Furthermore, experts want to ensure that the state-mandated standardized tests do not result in poor teaching practices such as "drill and kill" instruction or cheating. In addition, experts also strongly advocate the following recommendations for assessment and evaluation:

- Determine if standards/objectives have been met
- Use multiple measures to assess student achievement
- Use assessments to make curriculum decisions and help individual students
- Make **formative** evaluations, checking constantly on progress during instruction
- Make **summative** evaluations, a formal evaluation at the end of the unit or important component of the student's grade

Small Group Work **4.1**

Accountability

How do you feel about being accountable as a teacher for the test scores of your students? Do you think this type of accountability improves teacher performance? Do the students that you are familiar with work harder if they know they are to be tested? ●

Now that we know how various individuals and groups perceive testing, let us look briefly at the role of federal and state requirements for testing. This is followed by an analysis of the many types of assessments in the following order:

- performance-based assessment
- paper-and-pencil tests
- informal evaluations

[1]W. J. Popham, *The Truth about Testing: An Educator's Call to Action* (Alexandria, VA: Association for Supervision and Curriculum, 2001). Robert L. Linn, "Assessments and Accountability," *Educational Researcher* 29, no. 2 (2000): 4–16.

Federal and State Roles in Testing

Federal Role

The No Child Left Behind Act allows individual states to choose what tests should be used to assess reading, math, and science. This has resulted in a significant variation in both the design and effect of accountability systems in different states. What is proficient in one state is not proficient in another state. For example, in 2004 Nebraska persuaded the U.S. Department of Education to allow school districts to use portfolios to measure student progress. Portfolios are an expensive and time-consuming process for teachers and make comparisons among districts difficult, but this was the system that Nebraska had been using. NCLB has also greatly increased public awareness of accountability issues, especially for schools with low scores.

National Assessment of Educational Progress

Another role of the federal government in testing is the **National Assessment of Educational Progress (NAEP).** Since 1969, NAEP, as mandated by Congress, measures student growth in various areas of the school curriculum by doing testing on a very large sample of American students in grades 4, 8, and 12 so that the results can be generalized to the whole nation. It is the nation's foremost (and only national) ongoing educational survey, allowing all to see the strengths and weaknesses of American students.

NAEP has two assessments: the main NAEP in various subject areas, such as history, geography, and civics, and the long-term-trend NAEP in four subject areas: reading, mathematics, science, and writing. These two assessments use separate data collection procedures, samples of students, and test instruments. Student and teacher background questionnaires also vary between the main and long-term-trend assessments. Chapters 5, 6, and 8 will report on the NAEP test results in history, geography, and civics, respectively.

State Testing

Along with mandated testing from the No Child Left Behind Act, many states have also mandated state testing in the social studies. States are also piloting or implementing computerized high-stakes tests, a trend that probably will continue. Computer adaptive tests (CATs) can custom design the test items depending on the ability of the student, for students below grade level as well as for those above grade level. The difficulty of questions increases or decreases on computer-based adaptive tests based on student performance along the way. In this way the test is individualized for each student and probably causes less frustration.

Let us first carefully define the terms used in the state accountability assessment programs.

High-stakes, standards-based testing means that rewards and penalties are directed at students, administrators, schools, and districts tied wholly or in part to test scores. The groups that are affected vary among the states. For students, this could affect high school graduation or grade-level promotion at certain grade levels such as fourth and eighth grades. For administrators, it could mean a transfer, or in states that do not have tenure for principals it could mean the loss of their position. For schools and districts, continued low scores without improvement (annual yearly progress) could mean that the state takes over control of the school or district. In most states, the high-stakes focus is directly on students and individual schools and indirectly on districts.

Types of State Tests

What tests will a state use to test social studies? One choice is **off-the-shelf standardized tests.** Off-the-shelf tests are basic, generic, national tests such as the Iowa Test of Basic Skills, Stanford Achievement Test, and TerraNova, which are available by catalog. Their questions are based on national standards, regional curriculum, and testing research. In the politically charged education environment at the present time, publishers are very careful in developing their tests. Lawsuits, especially if the test is unfair to minority students, make publishers mindful of the consequences of having a poor test. But even with carefully constructed questions, a particular state's standards may not be aligned to a national test, meaning it is not truly measuring what is being taught.

Of course, the advantage of off-the-shelf testing is low cost. To create a custom-made test for states is expensive; however, it is being done, for example, in Wisconsin for its social studies tests. A custom-made test can use the state's own standards, control the rigor of the test, and adjust to any distinctive customs and mores. Some states are putting increased emphasis on problem solving and on items with more than one right answer. These are desirable goals and may be the most important impact of standards-based reform. Traditional tests have been criticized for prompting teachers to emphasize basic, factual information and for providing few opportunities for students to learn how to apply knowledge.

Most national tests are scored by **norm-referenced testing,** which compares students' results with a national norm. The result for individual students are expressed in percentiles from 1 to 99, comparing student performance to a national sample of students on the same test. To determine norms, test makers give exams to a representative national sampling of students. Typically the norms are reconfigured every seven years. This means that progress toward state standards cannot be assessed with norm-referenced exams because they test how students compare with each other and not how much they know or can perform measured by the standards.

In contrast, **criterion-based testing** or **performance testing** measures students' performance based on standards of what they should know. Such tests can answer the question of how particular students compare with the criterion or standard that educators expect them to know or to demonstrate. NAEP tests are an example of criterion-based tests. Frameworks for the subject area are established by educators and state education officials and reviewed by a wide range of committees, public hearings, scholars in the fields, and so on to establish the subject standards. Test items are then produced that elicit whether the student knows or can perform according to the standards. Scores are then reported as levels—not proficient, basic, proficient, advanced. Although performance scores are a better measure of what students know than percentile scores, they are also somewhat arbitrary and subject to the judgment of the experts who establish the cutoff points. The cutoff score that is used to indicate failure or nonproficiency is extremely critical because it influences the number of students who fail the test.

Let us remember that among students individual differences are immense. Some can easily pass a social studies test whereas others will have difficulty. Furthermore, the accuracy in testing means that there is always a small degree of error.

The problem is to **set standards that are high but obtainable.** Holding all students, however, to the same standards will lead to lowering standards or untenable retention and failure rates. Just as Goldilocks wanted something not too hard or too soft and not too warm or too cold, standards should not be set too high or too low. This is easier said than done. This also means that students need the opportunity to learn the content and skills, and teachers need professional development opportunities so that their students can meet the standards. Professional opportunities allow teachers and administrators to analyze instruction, assessment, and achievement. They can learn about effective practices and set goals for improvement. In addition, options such as untimed tests need to be examined.

Teachers Research Their State Tests

What, as a teacher, can you do about state social studies tests? A concern for high test scores should not drive the curriculum, but there is an overlap of good teaching of social studies and good social studies test scores. In fact, teaching higher-level skills improves test scores. It is wise to become familiar with the test. Analyze the test to understand the knowledge and skills needed to succeed. For example, in a fourth-grade test, what proportion of the test is comprised of geography items versus economic items? How are the items formatted? Multiple choice? Bar graphs? Time lines?

Then infuse the goals of the test in your ongoing social studies program. Through reading, listening, speaking, and writing activities plus instruction, test preparation occurs throughout the school year. In contrast, teachers who confine test preparation to the week or two before the test focus more on how to take the test rather than on how, over time, to actually gain and retain the knowledge and skills that underlie what is being tested. Also in your regular assessment give your students the opportunity to become familiar with the content, skills, and formats of the test items. Students should not be exposed to a new test item format on the day of the exam. They should be able to meet the challenge of the predictable test items they will face. Practice taking tests with a similar time period as the state test.

Check if some or all of your ELL students or those students with disabilities (SD) will be required to take the test. The trend is for more inclusion in testing except for those with severe disabilities. Press for all possible accommodations for these students so they can show what they know.

What can a teacher do? Most of all tell your students what achievement targets they are expected to know and do. For example, they must understand a time line or be able to interpret a map. Students are helped if the objectives are given at the beginning of the learning process, for example. "Today, we are going to find out how the environment influenced which crops were grown in the Middle Colonies." Then think about assessment in this way:

- Is a test the best way to find out whether students learned the information or skill?
- In what different ways can students show their understanding? Which will be meaningful for them?

Frequent assessments should be made to show student achievement. This should help to build students' self-confidence. Avoiding assessment and not giving the results back to students does not help to build student confidence. Constantly give feedback to students on how to improve. This should be done in a nonjudgmental, non-blaming manner. All of these steps will help make students better prepared to show what they have learned.

Small Group Work **4.2**

What Are the Effects of State Testing?

What effects do state or district testing have in your area? Examine both positive and negative effects. ●

Best Practices

In schools with higher achievement on tests, it is more likely that the curriculum and instructional materials are aligned closely with the state social studies standards. Teachers map the standards into their weekly lesson plans. In addition, teachers ensure curricular alignment both within grades (e.g., all of the sixth-grade classes) as well as using curriculum alignment from grade to grade by examining the scope and sequence of curriculum topics. Principals frequently review and discuss student assessment data from multiple sources. Since administrators now can disaggregate data by each classroom, you could be identified as a teacher whose test scores are above average, average, or below average for the school.

Not all students have the same degree of motivation when taking tests. Some want to do their very best. Others are competent but they do not see themselves as doing well on tests. Still others are just content if they do not fail. Test anxiety may interfere with some students not performing up to par. All these student reactions suggest frequent formative assessment to help students get adjusted to taking tests and learn about their strengths and weaknesses.

Using Technology for Formative Assessment

TECHNOLOGY

Summative assessments at the end of the unit or the end of the year are nothing new. But increasingly more attention is being given to formative assessments during the unit and throughout the year. Instead of waiting for summative test results, teachers can better target each individual student's understandings and skills by having the student take an assessment chosen by the teacher on a computer.

There are two types of computer formative assessment tools: Web-based and software-based. The major vendors for these tools are the major publishers of school textbooks such as Pearson, Harcourt Brace Jovanovich, Houghton Mifflin, and McGraw-Hill. This makes sense because these publishers already had thousands of test items already developed for coordination with their textbooks. In addition, especially in states that are embarked on "one-to-one" computing resources for each student, free customized tests and quizzes aligned to the state standards and grade levels are available.

Of course, reading and math are the popular subject areas for formative assessment tools. But social studies is also included. In some cases, there is even state-specific software available that makes curriculum alignment less of a problem. The test items include multiple choice, short-answer questions or performance tasks. The results of the test are usually communicated online. Then the most important step is for the teacher to understand what the test results mean and what steps the teacher should take. Students should also be informed about their strengths and weaknesses immediately so they can be aware of what steps to take to improve their learning. Feedback to students is essential. Unless this is done, computer formative assessment is a waste of time.

Legalized "Cheating?"

TECHNOLOGY

Although most students are honest, student surveys indicate that students do confess to cheating on tests. Furthermore, new technology means students can access Internet information from their cellphones and PDAs. For this reason, some teachers now have more open-book tests, especially for writing essays. Students can use their notes, textbooks, and the Internet. The rationale for this approach is that in real life adults use resources ranging from a dictionary to the Internet for projects. An adult is seldom placed in a sealed room without being able to use resources. In addition, it is argued that students should learn how to access information and just rote memorization test items do not do much good after the test is given. Teachers report better essays when students are allowed to use resources and that it cuts down cheating. Another format is using a small group for testing instead of individual testing to improve group skills and critical thinking.

On the other hand, critics believe that until advanced placement tests and the SAT allow one to use resources, it is not good practice for students to use resources while being tested. In addition, in real life, you interview for a job as an individual, and not as part of a group. Often an individual has to perform their work solo instead of with a group.

Regardless of your stance on open-book exams and using resources during testing, it is important that students explicitly know the rules about cheating. This also means, in most cases, monitoring the class during tests periods by standing in the back of the room rather than marking student papers at your desk. But more than the mechanics of preventing cheating, it is important that the teacher try to have a class atmosphere where the values of honesty and integrity are encouraged.

Performance-Based Assessment

*A*ssessments are the ways we collect data about student learning. Assessments can be divided into three main categories: (1) performance-based assessment, (2) paper-and-pencil tests, and (3) informal evaluations. Each type of assessment has its own advantages and disadvantages (see Table 4.1). First let us clarify what is meant by the term **performance-based assessment** or **authentic assessment**.

As the school-age population has become more diverse culturally and linguistically while needing more advanced higher-order thinking skills, assessment tools must expand beyond multiple-choice or short-answer tests in order to measure progress accurately. **Authentic** or **performance-based assessment** is based on the idea that students should perform tasks that replicate the standards and challenges of adult life. Sometimes the equivalent terms are **performance assessment** and **authentic assessment**.[2] Regardless of the

[2]Some do not like the term *authentic*, which implies superiority to more conventional assessments and fear that *authenticity* denigrates the importance of knowledge and basic skills as legitimate educational outcomes.

Table 4.1	Comparison of Assessments
Authentic Assessments	**Paper-and-Pencil Tests**
Examples: essays, open-ended problems, portfolios, hands-on problems	*Examples:* short answer, matching, true-false, multiple choice
Subjective evaluation	Objective evaluation
Small sample of tasks	Can tap a large number of content items
Time-consuming evaluation	Easy to grade
Student directly involved in own learning/assessment	Tend to separate assessment from learning

term used, performance-based assessment requires students to create products or to perform, not simply to answer paper-and-pencil tests. The assessment may call for writing (the familiar term paper used in higher education) or problem solving, or the students' learning may be measured from the oral presentations or projects they produce as a result of their studies. Although performance-based assessment is not new, in the past it has been pretty much reserved for art, music, and physical education teachers who have always evaluated their students on the basis of their products and performance and not on paper-and-pencil tests.

Portfolios

Probably the most popular form of performance-based assessment in the social studies is the **portfolio**—a file or folder of selections of student work collected over a period of time that provides evidence of student learning, achievement, and progress in the social studies. Portfolios can furnish a broad picture of individual performance assembled over time. Although not without controversy, portfolios have been promoted as an assessment strategy that allows teachers to evaluate higher-order, complex skills and also to provide opportunities for student goal setting and self-evaluation of progress. Portfolios are now very popular, with reports of almost three-quarters of primary-grade teachers and 60 percent of intermediate-grade teachers using portfolios in at least one subject area. They are most common in writing and language arts.

What should a portfolio include? Look at Table 4.2. You may see different items in some portfolios. This depends partly on the purpose and the audience for the portfolio. Roughly, portfolios can be teacher or administrator centered when they serve in school accountability and grading. Or portfolios can be student centered by students collecting most of the items and being involved in self-assessment. Mixed models seem to be becoming more popular. Self-assessment by the student is still encouraged but more teachers are combining portfolios with traditional assessment strategies such as tests, worksheets, and homework assignments so that multiple measures will be offered by students to parents. The portfolio might also include peer assessments by fellow students. In the future, electronic portfolios containing a student's work for several years may really demonstrate growth over time.

More teacher education programs now have candidates do an electronic portfolio, often to show that they have met the standards of the course or the program. There can be different audiences for the portfolio, whether for the higher education faculty or for the elementary school where they are applying for a position. The student candidates often

Table 4.2	Elements of a Portfolio

- Learner goals or objectives/standards
- Guidelines for selecting material—example, best work
- A table of contents—valuable to find work
- Work samples chosen by student, usually good work
- Work samples chosen by teacher—not all agree this should be done
- Teacher feedback, sometimes tests
- Student self-reflection pieces
- Clear and appropriate criteria for evaluating work (rubrics)

highlight, emphasize, or change parts of the portfolio depending on the audience. With the use of computer programs such as Microsoft PowerPoint pre- and in-service educators can create effective, visually rich portfolios. In many cases, you will want to keep your own portfolio "alive" after you secure a teaching position.

Are Student E-Portfolios the Wave of the Future? Student electronic portfolios have the advantage of documenting the work of a semester, year, or several years. E-portfolios also can encourage self-assessment by students and show them what they have to work on. However, there are two disadvantages presently to student e-portfolios. One is the time necessary to assembly them. Probably e-portfolios can only be effectively used by students at age ten or older. Even then, the teacher will have to include regularly scheduled e-portfolio days in which the students archive artifacts, perhaps every five to ten weeks. Most teachers are unlikely to "give up their classroom time" to do this. Unless students can archive artifacts as homework, which presumes all have access to computers, student e-portfolios presently appear to be too time consuming.

TECHNOLOGY

The second disadvantage is the time needed by the teacher to give feedback in the e-portfolios. Now most portfolios are organized by standards and subparts of standards. The student selects material and shows how it meets the standard. This means that the teacher should give a rating of the work submitted on the e-portfolio and comment on the student is progress. In addition, the teacher should read the reflection the student has written, showing their growth in the standard. Given these time-consuming processes, it is unlikely in the near future that e-portfolios for students will be popular until high-stakes testing is reduced.

Small Group Work **4.3**

What Are Your Experiences with Portfolios?

In what classes were portfolios a requirement? What did you like about the experience? Was it fair? Any disadvantages? ●

Essays

After a long period of eclipse, the essay is emerging as a technique for assessing a student's knowledge. Previously, teachers were persuaded that a more objective assessment of students' knowledge was one that could be counted and quantified, permitting them to compare individuals and groups. Some teachers welcomed objective tests as a time-saving way to avoid correcting essays. We now recognize the centrality of written expression in all curricular areas for assessing higher levels of thinking. Students who can talk about or write about facts and ideas show that they have structured new information. They not only recall and classify information as an objective-type test item would require, but they can also put the information into a context.

Examples of Essay Questions

You are Columbus. Write a letter to King Ferdinand and Queen Isabella to convince them to finance a voyage. Be sure to include the following points:
- Benefits to Spain from trade
- Spreading Spain's Catholic religion
- How technology has improved safety on voyages
- Increases in Spain's power

Notice that the essay question is not vague but helps the student to focus on what should be covered in the question. In a similar manner, look at this essay question:

> Benjamin Franklin was known as a "man of ideas." He was influential during his time and well respected. Explain how he contributed to the people of his time in the following roles:
>
> - Inventor/scientist
> - Writer
> - Diplomat

This question could also be changed from Benjamin Franklin to Thomas Jefferson or some other historical figure by easily adding or subtracting categories.

Some essay questions are called *short-answer essay questions*. These often ask students to justify or explain their answers within a specified length, normally one paragraph or so. Here are some examples:

> Explain why Americans did not want their new leader to be called a "king."
> Explain why most American Indians lost control of their lands.
> Why was the scholar-official class important in China during the Song Dynasty?

All of these formats illustrate the value of good essay questions to promote student thinking and reasoning.

Scoring

New York is one of the few states that is also using a **document-based question (DBQ)** at the fifth-grade level examining primarily fourth-grade social studies work. A document-based essay question typically uses primary sources, cartoons, photos, and the like. It asks the writer to use the majority of these documents as supporting evidence in their essay. At the elementary level this typically includes a lot of visual clues like sketches of American Indians. The DBQ can test higher-level thinking since the students need skills of analysis to understand the documents. It allows different interpretations. Thinking is stressed more than just memorization as students use data to back up their interpretation. The DBQ on a state test can encourage teachers to use this format so their students will be familiar with document-based essay questions. Writing skills may also improve as students become familiar with this type of essay question.

Teachers using holistic scoring estimate the overall quality of the performance. They then assign a grade, often using the A–F rating scale or using three divisions (such as below average, average, and clearly outstanding) to judge quality rather than assigning specific points for specific aspects of the performance. Holistic scoring may be easier for the teacher to do compared to rubrics or rating scales but may not be as reliable nor provide as much feedback to the students.

More teachers are using **rubrics** in grading essay questions. Typically there are four different levels ranging from very proficient to notice level. If the rubric is explained to students before they write, many students benefit and can better focus on what is desired. The rubric makes clear the criteria that are being used to evaluate the essay questions.

Holistic scoring of a learning product such as an essay, map, videotape, or audiotape is useful when the goal is an overall assessment of student performance. As with a rating scale, the assessment must focus on the most important instructional goals that prompted the learning product. One way to use the holistic approach in evaluating essays and other open-ended learning products is to separate them into stacks of good, average, and poor, and then to reread or review each stack, further separating products into smaller stacks according to the grading scheme. When evaluating learning products, teachers must decide how to disentangle the evaluation of content, or "message," from form, or "medium." One way is to assign two grades, one for content and another for form.

To assist students, models of excellence should be made available and analyzed. Saving good examples of student work from one year to the next can assist you in aligning instruction with evaluation. Do remember privacy concerns when showing student work. When students analyze an excellent student product, they learn what is expected of them in a very concrete sense, and they recognize that these expectations have been met by others at their level of instruction. Cooperative analysis of excellent learning products empowers students to recognize the characteristics of quality. Even more important than sharing examples and recognizing what is good about them is a teacher-led discussion of how the former students went about producing the product. For some students, understanding the process of how to do the "assignment" is sufficient motivation. For even more students, participation in the dialogue about how their work will be assessed is crucial to their motivation to do the work. For nearly every student, participating in cooperative assessment of their own work and that of their classmates is highly motivating. Furthermore, students probably will be gratified that a teacher values student learning products enough to show them off.

Team Testing

One innovative approach to testing is *team testing* or *group testing*. In this type of assessment, students are put in groups of three or four, or in some cases pairs (dyads). All students are given a copy of the test. Then one student is assigned the role as "reader" and the rest are "judges." The reader reads the test item aloud and calls one at a time on each group member for the correct answer and an explanation of his or her rationale for the correct answer. If all agree, they go on to the next question. If they disagree, the process is repeated. If there still is not agreement, each member marks his or her test with what they believe is the correct answer.

Team testing is especially valuable the day before a "regular test." Students, by listening and talking with each other, feel more confident about being tested. Students often become aware of areas where they are confused or deficient. However, this format must be monitored by the teacher to make sure the format is being followed and the brightest student does not do all of the work.

Outside Assessors

Many teachers report that they are frustrated by the lack of motivation of students who are responsible for a project or a performance. What can be done? It has been found that if students know that their project or performance will be evaluated by an outside person or audience, they are more likely to produce a work of higher quality. They do not want to be put on the spot or appear to be inadequate. This may include putting their work online. Science and art fairs have been using this principle of outside evaluation for years.

Most students want to be proud of their work. Students derive more pleasure from their higher-quality work. Students are aware of an audience beyond their regular classroom teacher. This also means that the teacher needs to be more of a coach to help students when they encounter problems and difficulties.

Scoring of writing assessments by teachers other than one's own teacher are also valuable. Perhaps you can do a trade-off. You grade the written assignments from a colleague's class and in turn he or she will score your set of written work. You will find that even if you have been informing a given student time and time again about the need for a topic sentence, having it pointed out by another teacher or outside assessor often has more of an effect.

Written Assessment Tasks

In designing assessment tasks, what student **products** can provide evidence of student learning in the social studies? You can see all the great possibilities in Table 4.3. In addition, many times the written is combined with the visual as shown in the following: cartoon, chart, data table, graph, map, model, outline, Venn diagram, and webbing/mind map. See the lesson plan "Hero or Villain?" for an example. Any of these assessment tasks can indicate what the students have learned. A rubric is essential so that students know what is expected and for students to be graded fairly.

Short Constructed-Response Questions

Along with the wide diversity of products possible for assessment, probably the most commonly used product for formal authentic assessment is a short constructed-response

Table 4.3	Designing Assessment Tasks	
Written	**Oral**	**Visual**
Advertisement	Advertisement	Advertisement
Biography	Debate	Banner
Book report	Dialogue	Cartoon
Diary	Discussion	Chart
Editorial	Dramatization	Collage
Essay	Interview	Computer graphic
Journal	Newscast	Data table
Letter	Oral report	Drawing
Notetaking	Role play	Graph
Poster	Skit	Outline
Questionnaire	Speech	Photograph
Reader's theater	Teach a lesson	Poster
Research report		Time line
Script		Venn diagram
Test		Webbing

Source: Adapted from handout of Dr. Priscilla Porter at the California Council of the Social Studies State Convention, San Diego, 2000.

LESSON PLAN

Hero or Villain? An Example of a Student Product

Especially in teaching history, students encountered the lives of many important rulers and individuals. To encourage thoughtful reflection about an individual, try the following hero or "Wanted" poster strategy.

Chairman Mao, A Hero	WANTED for

For the first square, create a hero's plaque for contributions to his or her nation or to democracy. Then construct a jail "Wanted" poster that condemns the same individual. Include the following:

1. Two sketches of Chairman Mao.
2. Two sentences for his achievements placed below the hero's sketch.
3. Two sentences explaining why Chairman Mao should be labeled as a villain or enemy.
4. Then a short paragraph giving your opinion whether Chairman Mao was more of a hero or a villain.

Note how easily this assessment format can be used for a wide variety of people: Lenin, Genghis Khan, Caesar, Ho Chi Minh, Elizabeth I (queen of England), Napoleon, Nat Turner, Robert E. Lee, or American presidents Andrew Jackson, James K. Polk, or Harry S. Truman. Try to pick controversial figures neither too saintly nor too evil. Note how this assessment taps higher-order thinking, inviting different perspectives of an individual as well as writing skills.

question test item or short write-in item. Sometimes it is called a short-answer question. A **constructed-response question** requires students to produce an answer to a question. A short constructed-response item is a good compromise between the multiple-choice question and an essay. It can test for factual knowledge and critical thinking without putting a heavy writing burden on students or a time-consuming grading task on the teacher. In constructed-response items, questions may have just one correct answer or they may be more open-ended, allowing a range of responses. Common in the social studies are **identifications.** Here in a few sentences students need to describe why the person, event, or idea is significant. Try to encourage students to write more about Columbus to tell of his importance as an explorer.

Look at the following fourth-grade NAEP test item.

Your teacher has asked you to teach your classmates about *one* of these famous places where an important event in American history happened:

the Alamo
Pearl Harbor
Gettysburg
Roanoke Island

My famous place in American history is _____.
Write down three facts about the place you have chosen that will help you teach your classmates about this place.

Again, as in all performance assessment, the use of a rubric is essential. Responses to this question were scored according to a four-level rubric as (1) inappropriate, (2) partial, (3) essential, and (4) complete. Look at Figure 4.1 to see how the responses were marked. Note the format which forces the student to answer in terms of three separate sentences. This makes it easier to score.

As a compromise between full essay questions and multiple-choice items, the short-constructed response test items are becoming more popular on state examinations.

Summary

What are the advantages and disadvantages of performance-based assessment? An advantage is that often performance-based assessments are integrated in the social studies unit. The natural flow of unit teaching produces opportunities as the unit evolves to gather data about student progress as students make time lines or write a diary about their experiences as a pioneer. Performance assessment can measure some important kinds of outcomes but often does not have the potential for generalizability. If a student does well on one particular essay or problem-solving exercise, will she or he do well on the next one? Even advocates of performance assessment point to difficulties and limitations.

Performance assessment tends to rely heavily on ability to read and write standard English as shown in portfolios, essays, written assessment tasks, and short constructed-response questions. Yet young children's thinking abilities transcend their ability to write. Furthermore, this is a particular problem for students learning English as a second language or those who come from nonstandard English backgrounds as well as those with various learning difficulties. They may know the content but not be able to express it adequately.

Because of cost, most states are using multiple-choice items with a short writing sample. It may be that more authentic forms of assessment

Small Group Work **4.4**

Your Reaction to "My Famous Place in History"

Do you like this question? Is it too hard for fourth graders? Do you agree with the scoring? Did you see that the student with the high score of 4 has many spelling errors? Are the three facts accurate and their relevance and chronology deserving a high score even with poor spelling? ●

| Figure 4.1 | NAEP Short Constructed-Response History Item |

Sample Response (Score of 3):

My famous place in American history is ____ *Gettysburg* ____

Write down three facts about the place that you have chosen that will help you teach your classmates about that place.

Fact 1 *It was during the civil war.*

Fact 2 *Many people died in this battle!*

Fact 3 *It ended the civil war.*

An **Essential** response (score of 3) gives two facts that are relevant to the particular place and that would help another person understand the place.

Sample Response (Score of 4):

My famous place in American history is *Pearl Harbor*

Write down three facts about the place that you have chosen that will help you teach your classmates about that place.

Fact 1 *The Japenes propeld a bome on Pearl Harbor*

Fact 2 *The bome distroed lots of ships*

Fact 3 *The U.S.A. fote back.*

A **Complete** response (score of 4) gives three facts that are relevant to the particular place and that would help another person understand the place, such as that the bombing of Pearl Harbor caused the U.S. to enter WWII, or that the battle of Gettysburg was a turning point in the Civil War.

Source: NAEP 1994 U.S. History Report Card: Findings from the National Assessment of Educational Progress (Washington, DC: U.S. Department of Education, National Center for Education Statistics, 1996), p. 99.

will continue to become a larger part of classroom-level and individual assessment whereas states will still require standardized achievement tests. In actual practice, it appears that teachers are combining both performance assessment and traditional paper-and-pencil tests.

In summary, neither performance assessment nor objective tests can be used as the *sole* indicators of student learning. Many forms of assessment are needed to enable all students to demonstrate accurately their knowledge and abilities. This means that teachers need to be familiar with both the newer performance-based assessments as well as traditional paper-and-pencil tests.

Paper-and-Pencil Tests

*L*et us now examine paper-and-pencil tests both in order to critically review test items designed by others and to learn how to write good test items. Teacher-made tests are strongly advocated because they can be designed to a specific curriculum and meet the special needs of your class. However, try to avoid only using questions that require low-level recall memory—a common fault of teacher-made tests. Check your tests against Bloom's taxonomy categories (Chapter 3) to ensure that you are including some higher-level test items.

Paper-and-pencil tests are the most suited for assessing social studies goals in the knowledge and thinking skills area. In our test-dominated age, the use of paper-and-pencil testing in the social studies is often taken for granted, almost as a cultural imperative. Furthermore, tests provide a relatively easy means to gather data on what children know and what they are able to do. The data from objective-type test items are easily counted for ranking and averaging. Tests included in textbook-series materials make the chore of preparing tests easier. In addition, tests accompanying texts often have better coverage of textbook content and are written more clearly, especially the multiple-choice questions, than most teacher-made tests because of the time and energy required in test construction.

Most teachers use the commercially prepared tests that accompany textbook series. Feeling compelled to provide numerical evidence of student progress pushes many teachers to rely on textbook-related tests. Thus, the content of their instruction tends to be tied to the textbook. You may think this technique for selecting and assessing content is too narrow and limiting. Or you may believe that the content of texts you use is appropriate as a definer of instructional content. Either way, you need to be a critical consumer of prepared commercial tests or tests that accompany a social studies textbook series.

There are several criteria for selecting tests or test items. The principal criterion is to verify that the items are aligned with your instructional objectives. They should be consistent with both the content covered and the level of thinking about the content you have led the students to experience. Providing sufficient items to check individual objectives is still another criterion. That is, we can learn more about a student's mastery of a concept if the student has several opportunities to answer questions about it.

Beyond the general criteria for test and item selection, each type of test brings special considerations.

Short Answer

A short-answer item is typically a statement with a key word or phrase missing. Which of the following pairs are the better items?

    a. Mexico, Canada, and the United States are _____.
    b. The three largest nations of North America are _____, _____ and _____.
    a. _____ invented the _____ in _____.
    b. The inventor of the cotton gin was _____.

Both "a" examples are inferior. Neither cues the student to the desired content. For short-answer items, the content cue is best presented at the sentence beginning and its completion at the sentence ending. The first example requires students to invent, and they may give semantically correct answers such as "fun" or "big" or "all purple on the map" that have no relation to the content studied.

Short-answer items, and all pencil-paper items, can be criticized as testing reading more than knowledge of the social studies content. Should we give children a grade in the social studies that is really related more to their reading ability than, perhaps, to their social studies knowledge? Most teachers are more concerned with learning what a child knows about the social studies content. They find that poor readers of English can respond correctly to the items if these items and the possible answers are read aloud.

Matching

Using the process of elimination is a good thinking strategy. Matching items should prompt students to use this strategy. As with all test-item types, students need practice with this kind of item before they are tested.

Which of the following three sets of matching items is best?

a. You have read about American Indians, white settlers, and the buffalo. Now, draw lines below connecting the part of the buffalo with the way that part was used by the Plains tribes.

hair	bow strings
hide	food
horns	mattresses
meat	spoons
sinew	

b. Match the following countries with the continents in which they are located.

Mexico	South America
Chad	Africa
Finland	Europe
Chile	Asia
India	North America

c. Match the example with the economic category it fits best.

services	skateboard
goods	trip to Disney World
resources	haircut
	gold coins
	farmland
	sleeping
	running a race

The best item is "a," according to test makers, because it has uneven lists. The student must use the process of elimination as well as either direct recall of what has been studied or analysis of what might be possible. Note that in "a" but not "b" or "c" the choices are listed in alphabetical order. Alphabetical order saves the student time when rereading the list. Other pointers for this type of item include not making the list too long and not mixing categories within the lists. Item "c" commits both of these errors.

True-False or Binary Choice Items

Items that are true or false invite students to guess and afford them a higher probability of being correct than any other type of test item. For this reason, and because this type of item tends to be written at a low level of cognitive difficulty, most test-construction experts do not favor true-false tests as reliable measures of what children know.

Writing good true-false items is more difficult than answering them. It is easy to "give away" the answer to this type of item. Even though experts criticize these items, teachers continue to use them, recognizing that they require less time to check. Below is a list of development rules compiled by researchers that you can refer to when evaluating true-false items.

Checkpoints for True-False Items[3]

1. Avoid using specific determiners (*always, never, only*).
2. Avoid use of negatives or double negatives (*not impossible*).
3. Limit statements to a single idea.
4. State ideas as concisely as possible.
5. Avoid exact wording of the text or source material.
6. Make the statement clearly true or false.
7. Test only important ideas.

To extend true-false items beyond the level of factual recall, you can ask students to rewrite false items to make them true, or to tell one more thing they know about true items.

Selected Response or Multiple-Choice Questions

The term **multiple-choice questions** evokes such negative images to some students and teachers that publishers are now calling them **selected response questions.** Multiple-choice questions have a poor reputation because they have often focused only on rote memorization. But they can be designed to test the ability of students to think. The advantage of multiple-choice questions is that they can provide a broad and balanced coverage of the unit. They can also give poor writers a better chance to show what they know.

A multiple-choice question consists of a *stem* (the body of the question before the choices are presented), the incorrect responses, and the correct answer (known as the *key*). Publishers report that they have moved away from old-fashioned multiple-choice testing that isolates factual recall to using more test items that test higher thinking processes.

Multiple-choice items are commonly found on various state-mandated tests. Many states release the spring test items to help teachers and the public to understand that the history/social science test and other subject area tests were based on the learning standards and core knowledge topics required by the state. For example, the released test items of the Massachusetts Department of Education in 1999 gave the specific learning standard and particular core knowledge topic as shown by the following items for grade 8.[4]

---

[3]Adapted from a twenty-one-item list developed by David A. Frisbie and Douglas F. Becker, "An Analysis of Textbook Advice about True-False Tests," *Applied Measurement in Education* 4, no. 1 (1990): 69.

[4]*The Massachusetts Comprehensive Assessment System: Release of Spring 1999 Test Items* (Malden, MA: Massachusetts Department of Education, 1999).

9. A historian in the 1990s is researching life in the Massachusetts Bay Colony in the 1630s. The historian finds a sermon and a diary written in the 1630s and includes them in a textbook. Both the sermon and diary are examples of a

A. primary source.
B. chronology.
C. secondary source.
D. biography.

Study Strand and Learning Standard: *History:* **Research, Evidence, and Point of View (p. 286)**
Core Knowledge Topic: *The United States:* **Early America and the Americans (Beginning to 1650) (p. 289)**

17. By 1815, the United States' land bordered all the bodies of water except

A. the Pacific Ocean.
B. Lake Erie.
C. the Gulf of Mexico.
D. the Atlantic Ocean.

Study Strand and Learning Standard: *Geography:* **Places and Regions of the World (p. 287)**
Core Knowledge Topic: *The United States:* **Expansion, Reform, and Economic Growth (1800 to 1861) (p. 289)**

Note that in Question 9, the student needs to know the meaning of a primary source and apply that knowledge. Use of primary source documents has received increased attention in the past few years and so the question is probably appropriate in terms of content. In Question 17, the student must be able to make a mental map of the United States in 1815, identify major bodies of water, and remember historical knowledge such as the Louisiana Purchase. Both questions require some thinking, an advantage of good multiple-choice questions. They also are tied in or aligned to certain Massachusetts standards.

15. The Maya, Aztec, and Inca civilizations each developed

A. powerful seafaring traditions.
B. monotheistic religious systems.
C. democratic governments.
D. complex architectural structures.[5]

In the preceding sample question, from the California Standards Test the student needs to understand something about three different civilizations and to distinguish what is similar and different about each one. Comparison is a higher level of thinking than rote memorization.

Look carefully at the time line question (Figure 4.2) from NAEP for fourth graders. A test item that requires the student to interpret a primary source, a map, a chart, a time line, or a graph is called an *enhanced multiple-choice test item*. To be able to select the correct option, students had to be able to read and understand the time line, which indicated that the First Thanksgiving was celebrated in October rather than in November as it is today. In order to eliminate the first two options, students needed to understand from the

[5]Sample California Standards Test question. California Department of Education, 2004.

Figure 4.2	Sample U.S. History Question Grade 4—Time Line: *Mayflower* and Thanksgiving

First Year in Plymouth, from Fall to Fall

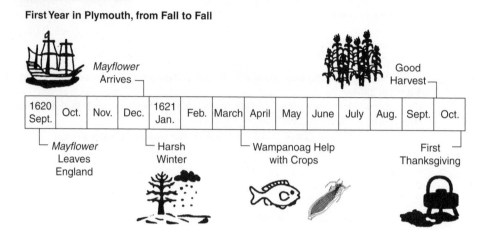

3. What can you tell from the time line?

Ⓐ The *Mayflower* took more than one year to sail to Plymouth.

Ⓑ The *Mayflower* arrived in Plymouth in 1621.

● The first Thanksgiving was not celebrated in the same month as it is today.

Ⓓ The Pilgrims in Plymouth ate mostly fish.

Source: Evelyn Hawkins, Fran Stancavage, Julia Mitchell, Madeline Goodman, and Stephen Lazer, *Learning About Our World and Our Past: Using the Tools and Resources of Geography and U.S. History: A Report of the 1994 Assessment* (Washington, DC: U.S. Department of Education, National Center for Education Statistics, 1998), p. 100.

time line that the *Mayflower* was at sea for about four months and that it arrived in America before the beginning of 1621.

Only a third of the fourth graders were able to answer this question accurately, showing that they were able to read the time line, understand the negative phrasing of the correct response option, and relate it to their outside knowledge that Thanksgiving today is not celebrated in October. Why do you think students found this difficult? Probably most do not really understand how to read a time line.

Look again at these three multiple-choice test items. Do you see any problems with them? Remember these tips in writing and using multiple-choice questions. Use clear language in the stem. Avoid double negatives. Always emphasize important individuals, events, or ideas, not trivia. Avoid choosing or making test items with excessively long sentences or a reading level that is too high for your students. Eliminate trick responses, such as "both *a* and *b*" or "neither *a* nor *b*."

Diagnosis and Corrective Reteaching

When you use objective test items, or any other assessment, it is important for students to find out what they got wrong and why they got it wrong. An error and the right answers must be analyzed as soon as possible for each student. Try not to wait too long to grade tests. Returning tests given two weeks ago reduces the incentive of students to see their mistakes and to learn from them. Taking too long to correct tests also robs teachers of the opportunity to do reteaching right away in areas in which many students are having difficulties.

Informal Evaluations

$\mathcal{M}$ost informal classroom assessment is based on the observation of students by teachers. This can take many different formats.

Students Answering Questions

One of the most common methods of assessment used by teachers is asking students questions and judging how well a given student has learned the content. Normally this is done so frequently during the day that the teacher does not keep a record of how successful the student was in answering the question. Instead, teachers quickly evaluate the accuracy of the response. For example, they may be surprised, considering the ability and interest of the student, that a given student has not correctly answered the question or only partially answered the question. This may move the teacher to ask further questions to clarify why the student has been mistaken (see Chapter 3 on questioning). But the teacher also must maintain the flow of activities in the classroom and cannot always stop just to meet the needs of one student. Nevertheless, diagnosis of individual student needs and modifications in teaching can help student learning. Ideally, later in the day, the teacher can help the student who was having difficulty in answering a question.

"Catching" Observation Data

Collecting data on oral performance is important for social studies. Some of the oral performances that you may have to assess and evaluate include oral presentations and oral reports, skits, newscasts, dramatizations, and class and small group discussions. How can you proceed to assess these areas?

Michigan's Authentic Assessment Project uses skits as a method to set up authentic assessments (see Table 4.4 for a primary-grade example).[6] It is suggested that after viewing the skit, students in small groups will discuss the focus and public policy questions. Do you think this will be interesting to primary students? If you use it, how can you assess it?

Here is the **rubric,** the criteria used for assessing student discussion at different levels of proficiency (Table 4.5). Do you think the rubric is clear? The Michigan Department of Education recommends using a mechanism for recording the discussion, either audio or video, to help with the evaluation. It also suggests that students could be instructed to conduct self-evaluations. But you can see the problems of trying to "catch" all the behaviors that are going on in the many groups. In the future, handheld computers already coded with names of the students and an appropriate rubric will allow teachers to gather this type of assessment quickly and be able to get feedback to students after they finish their discussion.

[6]Michigan Department of Education, *Social Studies Authentic Assessment Project: Conducting Investigations, Group Discussion, Responsible Personal Conduct* (Lansing, MI: Michigan Department of Education, no date), 35.

Table 4.4	Wearing Hats in School

A boy and a girl both wear hats to school. When they come into the classroom, the teacher tells the boy to take his hat off. The teacher says it is polite for boys and men to take their hats off indoors. The girl's hat matches her outfit. The teacher does not say anything to the girl.

The boy asks the teacher why he has to take his hat off but the girl is allowed to leave her hat on.

*Introduce the scenario as a skit, which you rehearse in advance with a boy and a girl from the class.

Related Core Democratic Values: Diversity, Rule of Law, Freedom of Expression

The Focus Question

What should the school do about letting boys and girls wear hats in the classroom?

The Public Policy Issue Question

Should schools allow boys and girls to wear hats in school?

Table 4.5	Group Discussion Rubric for Early Elementary

	Made a Relevant Statement	Responded Appropriately
Performance Level 4	Participated in the discussion by making many relevant and elaborating statements throughout the discussion.	Responded appropriately at all times and made a concerted effort to invite and acknowledge the contributions of others.
Performance Level 3	Participated in the discussion by making at least one relevant statement that supports their point of view or clarifies the issue.	Responded appropriately at all times.
Performance Level 2	Participated in the discussion but statements were only marginally relevant to the discussion or did not support their view.	Responded inappropriately but made some appropriate comments.
Performance Level 1	Did not make any relevant statements during the discussion.	Responded inappropriately and made no appropriate comments, *or* did not take part in the discussion.

Note: The Michigan Department of Education gives further examples of what is appropriate and inappropriate behaviors, p. 20 in *Social Studies Authentic Assessment Project.*

Glancing at Student Work on the Fly: Assessing the Attainment of a Concept

Assessment need not always be a painful experience for students. An assessment that is a fun review for concepts is the game of Yes/No. Sometimes this game is called Twenty Questions or the Animal, Vegetable, or Mineral game. You may have played this game as a child. The teacher has in mind a concept such as a continent. The teacher first gives an example of a yes answer (Africa) and then a no answer (Kenya). Students then generate questions to the teacher and the teacher answers if they are yes or no. Using two columns, yes and no, students place the example in the correct column (see lesson plan "Revolutionary America").

LESSON PLAN

Revolutionary America

History/Social Science Standard: Students will understand the institutions that developed in the colonial era.

Grade Level: Fifth grade

Objective: Students will identify characteristics of the pre- and postrevolutionary United States using yes and no examples.

Procedures

1. Tell students, "I have an idea, and I want you to guess what my idea is by looking at your yes and no lists."
2. Discuss the rules:
   a. Do not shout out the answer.
   b. If you know the answer, raise your hand and suggest an example to put in the yes list.
3. Teacher models the first two examples.
   a. Students write answers in the correct column on their pieces of paper.
   b. Students give examples and teacher answers yes or no.
4. After many examples, students write the idea on their pieces of paper and then tell chorally what the idea is.
5. Trace student thinking. "What did you think first when I put this in the yes column? What changed your mind?"

Possible questions for **Yes** answers	Possible questions for **No** answers
colonies	states
royal governors	Constitution
boycott of British goods	Bill of Rights
Tea Party	Shay's Rebellion

Source: Abridged lesson by Wendy Shapard, p. 28 in *Fontana (CA) History-Social Science Professional Development Program: Models of Teaching*, a funded program of the Island Area History Social Science Project, California, no date.

For example, assume that the teacher is thinking of the concept of cities.

Yes Column	*No Column*
Las Vegas	Florida

The teacher says: "The example of Las Vegas belongs in the yes column." Students write down *Las Vegas* in the yes column on their piece of paper.

The teacher says: "The example of Florida belongs in the no column." Students write down *Florida* in the no column on their piece of paper.

You can have one child who is a good speller at the chalkboard also writing down the names of places if you think spelling will be a problem for some students. The child at the chalkboard then frees the teacher to be able to move around the room quickly instead of the teacher taking time to write the examples.

Students then ask their own questions. "Is Chicago a yes answer?" "Is warm climate a yes answer?" After several examples, and by the teacher walking around glancing at whether or not most students were placing examples correctly in either the yes or no column, the teacher asks the class to tell chorally what the idea (concept) is. The volume and apparent participation in the answer also give the teacher immediate feedback about whether students really know the concept.

Notice that most students will regard this as a fun activity. In fact, they often become so eager that they want to shout out the correct answer. They do not realize that by walking around and glancing at their columns the teacher is really making an assessment about whether most students have mastered the concept. Students are also practicing inductive reasoning as they put together clues and jump to the deductive level, the concept.

This game could use many different concepts from history content. For example, it could be used to identify the American Indians living in the students' area using examples such as buffalo, tipi, hogan, acorns, canoes, Chief Joseph, totem pole, and the like. In addition to these examples, sometimes a teacher will hide an artifact and ask what is covered in the basket or under the cloth. The object could be what students have studied such as a washboard, ancient lanterns, or a Kachinas doll. In addition, this yes/no format is used to identify a wide range of historical persons, places, or things—from the Mayflower to our latest president. Again, as described in the lesson plan on geographic regions (page 187), students can sort word cards, small pictures, and objects as an assessment strategy that the teacher can observe.

The yes/no format is an assessment strategy that really does not take time from instruction since students are practicing concept attainment at the same time they are being assessed. The teacher observes student behavior and makes a judgment on how well the students have learned content. It is often an ideal format for reviewing content as well as assessing what has been learned. It can alert the teacher on what needs to be retaught. Note that it is a good idea to diagnose students' needs a few times a week, even if the efforts are informal. Then, if necessary, change or modify your teaching based on what the assessment has shown.

Self-Evaluation

The ideal situation is for students to take responsibility for their own learning. Encourage students to make frequent self-assessment. Students then can watch themselves grow over

Table 4.6	Unit Evaluation

Instructions: Considering our unit "Our Community" (Name of Unit) mark the one best choice for each statement:

	Often	Sometimes	Never
1. I believe social studies is fun to learn.			
2. I learned a lot during this unit.			
3. I had access to quality social studies materials.			
4. I used technology during the unit.			
5. I made good use of my time.			
6. I used social studies to solve problems.			
7. I was asked to write in the social studies unit.			
8. I was asked to read in the social studies unit.			
9. Other students were helpful to me.			
10. Each lesson lasted too long.			

time. They can realize that they are in charge of their own success. It is not just due to chance or luck that they have learned something.

At the minimum, the end of the unit is an appropriate time to ask students to assess their work. This can be done orally by the teacher asking such questions as "How wisely did you make use of your time?" or "What more could you learn?" Or a simple questionnaire can be given anonymously to students after a unit has been completed (Table 4.6). This can also be used to see how students felt about the unit and about the social studies in general. The form also could be modified for parents. In effect, this questionnaire is also assessing your own effectiveness.

Characteristics of a Good Assessment/Evaluation System

In summary, you can use the following criteria to judge your assessment/evaluation system.

- Assessments are aligned to important standards/objectives.
- Assessments are a mix of performance, paper-pencil tests, and teacher observations.
- Assessments measure different levels of thinking according to Bloom's taxonomy.
- Multiple assessments provide many opportunities for students to demonstrate what they know or can do.
- Assessments consider the varying language skill levels of students (ELLs, etc.).
- Rubrics with clearly described performance levels are provided for student tasks.
- Assessments are reviewed for possible reteaching or extensions.
- Assessments/evaluations provide many opportunities for students to engage in self-assessment and reflection.
- Assessments/evaluations provide parents with insight into their student's learning and progress.

Conferences, Grades, and Report Cards

Conferences

What can be done to make parent/guardian conferences more productive and less frustrating? The first requirement is to be prepared with numerous examples of the student's work. Some teachers have also found it useful to have each student fill out a sheet listing their strengths and their needs. These materials can be shared with the parents.

Parent/guardian conferences are usually very pleasant if the student is making continual progress toward the standards/objectives and is up to grade level. Parents enjoy hearing about the good work and the intellectual and social improvement of their child. Difficulty occurs when you must communicate less-than-positive findings about a child's progress. However, it is important that the parent is informed, especially if there may be serious consequences of the lack of progress such as required summer school or nonpromotion. Parents must know if the child is not passing the state or district standards examinations. This information should be given in a written format as well as orally.

Increasingly more school districts have the student present during the parent/guardian conference, making it a three- or four-way conference. This is an excellent idea because students should not be kept in the dark about what their teacher is saying about them. The student can show his or her work or portfolios and can answer any questions posed by the teacher or the parent. Some teachers ask that the student share the portfolios the night before the conference. This gives the parents a better chance to think about what questions they want to ask. However, samples of work may not be helpful to parents unless they know the standard for the grade level. Parents may regard the samples of work as adequate when this may not be the case.

Small Group Work **4.5**

Student Led Conferences?

A new twist in the middle school is for a student to put together a portfolio of work from every class to show to their parents while the teachers watch from the sidelines. The student also has to tell their parents or guardian what grades they are getting and why. Do you think this increases student responsibility? Self-assessment for improvement? •

One essential requirement for all types of communication is that there should be no surprises at the parent/guardian conference for either the student or the parents. Teachers who keep all of the grades in an electronic or traditional book without communicating the results are not doing anyone a favor. Both the student and the parents should be given frequent feedback. This is why formative evaluation is done continually during a unit.

Work that is sent home weekly (in a few cases, daily) for the parent to sign, e-mails to the parents that are not always negative, and letters sent home are good ways to communicate with parents. Some teachers have students keep track of the books or pages they've read, the scores or grades they've received on each assignment or project, and the spelling or other tests they've taken. It also helps if the parents know at the beginning of the year what the standards and objectives for the year will be. In addition, at the beginning of each unit a communication by e-mail or letter on what is being done in the social studies is valuable in keeping the parent informed and getting their help.

At the conclusion of the conference, whether led by the student or the teacher, there should be a plan of action or suggestions on what to do to improve the situation. Nothing is more discouraging than giving the student and his or her parents lots of dismal information about the lack of progress without some ideas on how to make improvements. Opportunities for improvement are essential. Ideally, these suggestions should be written down as a contract and signed by all interested parties—the student, the parent(s), and the teacher. In effect, all parties involved have agreed on what can be done.

If there are language barriers, using translators is necessary. Although many parent conferences take place in the teacher's own classroom, if the teacher expects to have a difficult time with a given parent, it is best to move the conference to a more public area. However, the needs of privacy should always be respected. Parents waiting for their time allocation should not be exposed to a weeping or upset parent. These parents can infer that the conference was not pleasant and there are difficulties for the student.

Grades and Report Cards

Grades and report cards are ways of communicating with students and their parents. Teachers report that they are often under pressure to award higher grades than students deserve. This may influence and in some cases even distort the communication. The report card is the written format for communicating student learning progress. Districts vary widely on what type of report card they use. The trend is away from awarding grades, whether the traditional A through F or some other letter grade like E for *excellence* and G for *good*. Now more K–8 students are being measured on long lists of knowledge (called benchmarks) or skills. Some are very detailed.

About half of all districts are using or planning to change from the traditional format. Letter grades are being replaced with 1-to-4 ratings with 1 indicating minimal progress and 4 reflecting advanced understanding. It is hoped that the detailed review of progress will make it easier for parents to help their children. Some districts are using performance levels such as "advanced," "proficient," and "basic." Most parents understand what a percentile rank means, but they may not understand what "basic" and the other performance levels means. You may have to educate the parents about how to interpret these scores.

In some cases, the standards are now being used to indicate the progress of students. For example, the Howard-Suamico School District in Green Bay, Wisconsin, uses the following standards:

Grade 4 Social Studies	Knows how the legislative branch passes laws
Grade 8 Social Studies	Understands the key elements and results of the Revolutionary War

What is the impact of this change from letter grades to a rating scale of 1 to 4? One of the most obvious is that the amount of effort put forth by the child is no longer counted. The student is evaluated on how much of the standard has been mastered. Administrators say this change is needed because in the past students received high grades but were scoring low on the achievement tests given by the state or district. In effect, letter grades have probably been inflated and did not reflect what the student actually could do.

The newer rating system has concerned some parents who believe they cannot understand the more extended lists of ratings. However, other parents welcome the detailed information from the newer report card. In effect, however, the new report

Small Group Work 4.5

Tell the "Truth"?

What if you have students who are not able to work at grade level, such as ELL students or challenged students? What grades do you think these students should get? ●

cards do mean more work for the teachers. Ideally teachers are collecting formative assessment frequently and then putting that in a final summative format, the rating on the report card. If anything, report cards aligned with the standards reinforce what learning is expected and if the student has made progress toward achieving the standard.

Summary

Assessment and evaluation are among the most important, although difficult, tasks for all teachers. Testing is an emotional minefield for many of the parties involved: students, parents, teachers, administrators, and the community. Teachers need to use a wide variety of assessments including both performance-based testing and the traditional paper-and-pencil tests. Observation of students also yields valuable data about student progress. Finally, all the data are evaluated and put into a format for communication with the students and their parents: conferences, grades, or ratings.

Classroom assessments can powerfully enhance student learning. But to do so, teachers need to give feedback so learners can advance their understandings. This often means teachers need to provide corrective instruction. The assessments teachers use can also help them evaluate and refine their own teaching practices, because the ultimate goal of assessment and evaluation is to improve student learning and teaching.

Suggested Readings and Websites

Adams, D. M. K., and M. E. Hamm. "Portfolio Assessment and Social Studies: Collecting, Selecting, and Reflecting on What Is Significant." *Social Education* 56 (February 1992): 103–105.

Survey of necessary issues to consider when using portfolios as an assessment tool.

Cervone, B., and K. O'Leary. "A Conceptual Framework for Parent Involvement." *Educational Leadership* 40 (October 1982): 48–49.

Suggestions for involving parents in school learning.

Cramer, Susan R. "Navigating the Assessment Maze with Portfolios." *Clearinghouse* 67 (November–December 1993): 72–74.

Presents rudiments of portfolio content design and use as assessment tool stressing importance of previously agreed-on criteria for assessing quality.

Darling-Hammond, Linda, Jacqueline Ancess, and Beverly Falk. *Authentic Assessment in Action: Studies of Schools and Students at Work*. New York: Teachers College Press, 1995.

Case studies of classrooms and how five schools have developed authentic performance-based assessments of students' learning.

Gallagher, Chris W. *Reclaiming Assessment: A Better Alternative to the Accountability Agenda*. Portsmouth, NH: Heinemann, 2007.

Examines the Nebraska state assessment system.

Glazer, Susan Mandel. "Assessment: How You Can Use Tests and Portfolios Too." *Teaching K–8* 25 (August–September 1994): 152–154.

Brief discussion showing significance for students of portfolios in teacher–student interactive assessment.

McKeon, Denise. "When Meeting 'Common' Standards Is Uncommonly Difficult." *Educational Leadership* 51 (May 1994): 45–49.

Brings educational equity concerns to bear on standards movement that shows little consideration of learners from minority cultures and languages.

Phelps, Richard P. *Kill the Messenger: The War on Standardized Testing.* New York: Teachers College Press, 2005.

Examines the benefits of testing including its necessity.

Popham, James W. *America's "Failing" Schools: How Parents and Teachers Can Cope With No Child Left Behind.* New York: RoutledgeFalmer, 2004.

Testing expert sees potentially devastating effects of No Child Left Behind.

Simmons, Rebecca. "The Horse Before the Cart: Assessing for Understanding." *Educational Leadership* 51 (February 1994): 22–23.

Deals with demonstrating how to interpret evolving jargon used to describe assessment ideas when outcome-based education replaces mastery learning.

Tucker, Mark S., and Judy B. Codding. *Standards for Our Schools: How to Set Them, Measure Them, and Reach Them.* San Francisco: Jossey-Bass, 1998.

Good examples of seeking high standards.

Wiggins, Grant P. *Educative Assessment: Designing Assessments to Inform and Improve Student Performance.* San Francisco: Jossey-Bass, 1999.

Guidance on how to design performance-based assessments for use in classrooms.

Websites

Authentic Assessment
www.nwrel.org/scpd/sirs/6

Information on electronic portfolios, creating rubrics, and self-assessment.

National Assessment for Education Progress
http://nces.ed.gov/nationsreportcard

Can get information on the assessment of several subject areas. Data also organized for different audiences such as principals and teachers.

San Diego County Office of Education
www.sdcoe.K12.ca.us

Assessment information.

PEARSON
myeducationlab
Where the Classroom Comes to Life

VIDEO HOMEWORK EXERCISE

Standardized Tests

Go to MyEducationLab, select the topic **Assessment,** and watch the video entitled "Standardized Tests."

In this video, two measurement and evaluation experts give their views on standardized tests.

CHAPTER 5

Aiding Our Students to Interpret History

This chapter addresses how to help students to interpret history, the predominant subject area of the social studies curriculum. Many consider history the most essential discipline of the social studies curriculum.

- The Central Place of History in the Social Studies Curriculum

- History Wars

- History Definitions and Issues

- Linking History and Trade Books to Students

- Doing History or Being a Historian

- The Promise of the Internet: Primary and Secondary Sources

- Learning about Time and Chronology

What do you think students gained from their Stonehenge project?

The Central Place of History in the Social Studies Curriculum

$\mathcal{W}$hat images does the social studies program from the fourth through eighth grades bring to your mind? It's history! In fact, along with some geography, your own experiences at those grade levels in social studies (Table 5.1) probably have been mostly about history.

As you can see from these topics, history and, to a lesser extent, geography have been emphasized at these grade levels. Within these grade levels, you probably had a wide variety of experiences. Do you recall any field trips, mock trials, artifacts, genealogies, historical reenactments, or time lines? Did you ever make a pretend newspaper for a given time period?

On Your Own **5.1**

What Do You Think About History?

Think about your own experiences when you studied history. Was it mostly memorizing people, events, and dates for recall on tests? Did you ever have to obtain data about a history topic? Do you remember any worthwhile experiences that helped you to understand the past? ●

NAEP History Results

How well are elementary, middle school, and high school students actually learning history? The NAEP 2006 U.S. History Report Card stated that fourth, eighth, and twelfth graders all knew more U.S. history than in the past. Scores were up overall for all three grades and most racial/ethnic groups showed improvements. Over the past dozen years, white, African American, and Hispanic students made gains in all three grades but only grade 4 saw some closing of the gap between white and Hispanic or African American students. The greatest improvement for fourth graders was found for the lowest-performing students. When classifying students as basic, proficient, or advanced, 70 percent of fourth graders performed at or above the *basic* level compared to 64 percent in 1994. There was no significant change in the percentages performing at the *proficient* level or above. Male students scored higher on average than female students in grades 8 and 12 in the 2006 history survey. Knowledge of U.S. history was also higher for children of higher-income parents and parents with more years of education.

According to NAEP, what in particular students know about U.S. history:

Fourth Graders
- 66% understood the symbolism of the Statue of Liberty
- 35% explained how two inventions changed life in the U.S.
- 24% explained why people settled on the western frontier

Table 5.1	Social Studies Topics in Fourth through Eighth Grades
Grade 4	State history, geographic regions
Grade 5	U.S. history
Grade 6	World cultures, history, and geography
Grade 7	World cultures, history, and geography
Grade 8	U.S. history

Eighth Graders
- 64% identified an impact of the cotton gin
- 43% explained goals of the marches led by Martin Luther King, Jr.
- 1% explained how the fall of the Berlin Wall affected foreign policy[1]

Indeed, this was good news that the emphases on language arts/math did not appear to affect the U.S. history scores. One wonders, however, why so few students understood the goals of Martin Luther King, Jr.'s marches or why people settled on the western frontier, subject areas that it could be assume would receive attention in every school, even in a holiday curriculum. Also of concern was that the gains appeared on lower level questions and not on higher level thinking test items.

Better Quality History Instruction for All

From the NAEP test results, you can see that every student, regardless of race, ethnic group, or gender, needs high-quality history instruction. All students should be engaged in a variety of interesting classroom activities to make history alive. Here are just a few general suggestions:

- The arts and music of different time periods can increase understanding and empathy about different cultures.
- Artifacts, field trips, and virtual field trips can help students visualize history.
- Simulations about workers, peasants, and warlords can help students feel how it was to live at a different time period, especially in a crisis situation.
- Media has always been popular for portraying the past; now more free video clips are available from the Internet.

Bringing Issues Up to the Present

Another strategy is to see the relevance of the past to the present by discussion. One way to do this is to bring an historical topic up to the present. This is illustrated by Figure 5.1. You can see that topics such as industrialization suggest issues about unions and consumer protection. The history of ancient and medieval civilizations bring up such issues as whether democracy is the best form of government or whether there should be a separation of religion and the state. Try at the end of each unit to have at least one activity that explicitly brings an issue up to the present. Always remember to consider at least more than one perspective on an issue.

Gender Issues

History is also for girls. However, traditional history texts in the past have been male dominated both in terms of emphasis on males and in political, diplomatic, and military history. Now textbooks do include more about the contributions and importance of women. The National Women's History Project (www.nwhp.org) offers numerous ideas for lessons and

---

[1]*The Nation's Report Card U.S. History 2006: National Assessment of Educational Progress at Grades 4, 8, and 12.* Washington, DC: National Center for Educational Statistics, NCES 2007–474.

Figure 5.1	Topics That Relate to Present-Day Issues

Topic	Issue to Be Discussed
Many groups come to the United States	Should immigration be restricted?
Making of the Constitution; electoral college	Was too much power given to small states?
American Indians or African Americans	Do we owe reparations to American Indians or African Americans?
Cost of colonial exploration	Should we be spending more for space exploration?
Decisions of the Supreme Court	Is the Supreme Court too powerful?
Problems of farm families	Should farmers or corporations be helped with government subsidies?
Settlement of the West; pollution	Will we have enough natural resources like water?

activities. Of course, a supportive environment is necessary for all in the classroom to learn and be involved in learning about history.

History Wars

Almost everyone agrees that history, both of the United States and the world, should be taught in the elementary school. However, given the huge amount of history available, what should be taught? It is impossible to include everything, and every day the amount of history continues to increase. Can you cover U.S. history from Columbus to the latest president in one year? Or from ancient civilizations to the most recent war? Some state standards have tried to divide the content to prevent repetition. Thus, for American history classes in California, the fifth grade studies the colonial and revolutionary periods, the eighth grade studies the nineteenth century, and the eleventh grade studies the twentieth century. This type of division of content allows coverage with more depth and detail than could be possible if covering centuries in one school year.

History Wars

As you are probably aware from the media, the kind of history that features a particular people's story of the past is a controversial issue for the schools. There is a national debate on what history should be taught. In general, liberals advocate multiculturalism in history, trying to include the experience of all U.S. citizens by expanding the traditional Eurocentric perspectives. In contrast, conservatives see "extreme" multiculturalism as a rejection of Western culture and a fragmentation of U.S. society. Thus, the following questions arise: Whose history is to be presented? How much attention should the various groups receive? Should multiple perspectives be presented, such as showing how immigrant women or white male managers saw the growth of the industrial revolution in the United States? If more attention is given to various individuals and groups, will all students be exposed to the core values and cultural heritage of American as well as global society?

There are no easy answers to these questions. Your response partially depends on your values. In general, more conservative educators advocate teaching all children a core of historical knowledge to maintain the mainstream culture and the democratic values that tie together all U.S. citizens and give us our shared heritage and national identity. This group is concerned that there is now too much emphasis on diversity and not as much on teaching mainstream U.S. history. However, more liberal educators tend to believe that the histories of too many groups have been left out of U.S. textbooks and the children from these groups do not see themselves or their groups in the textbooks they study. Thus, they believe that not enough attention has been given to the various individuals and groups that make up the diverse U.S. society and more multiple historical perspectives from people of color and women are needed. In a similar manner, the debate continues over whether the world history/world culture course has too much of a European-centered focus. Should non-European history or cultures be given more attention?

Another issue is curriculum integration in social studies. Some argue that history should be taught mainly as a separate subject in the social studies program. The proponents of the separate subject approach believe that history teaching has been so diluted during the past twenty years by concentration on other social sciences that students no longer learn history as history. They cite research about students' gaps of knowledge, such as when the Civil War took place. Currently some curriculum experts value greater integration in all subject areas, whereas other advocates and scholars recommend teaching academic disciplines primarily as separate subjects, believing students will learn more with this approach. These advocates, if they do recognize other subject areas and the humanities, generally want their subject area to be the primary focus, with the other social sciences and the humanities in a more subsidiary role.

A controversy about the teaching of history immediately arose with the publication of three books in 1994 presenting history standards:

National Standards for United States History: Exploring the American Experience (5–12)

National Standards for World History: Exploring Paths to the Present (5–12)

National Standards for History: Expanding Children's World in Time and Space (K–4)

What history to teach and how to teach it were examined carefully by the National Center for History in the Schools (www.sscnet.ucla.edu/nchs.standards) which produced the National History Standards Project (see Chapter 1). This group proposed an integration of historical thinking (skills) and historical understanding (what students should know).

Even before the publication of the *National Standards for United States History* in November 1994, conservatives and other individuals and groups protested against the report, stating that it was a "politically correct" document concentrating on "multiple perspectives." Lynne Cheney, former head of the National Endowment for the Humanities and wife of Vice President Dick Cheney, in a *Wall Street Journal* editorial October 20, 1994, criticized the document as a too "gloomy" picture of America, one that is too critical of all things white and too uncritical of all things brown, black, and other.[2] As evidence, she reported the number of times historical subjects were cited in the *National Standards*. According to her count, Senator Joseph McCarthy and/or McCarthyism is mentioned nineteen

---

[2]Lynne V. Cheney, "The End of History," *Wall Street Journal,* October 20, 1994, p. A22.

times, the Ku Klux Klan seventeen times, the Seneca Falls women's rights convention nine times, and Harriet Tubman six times, whereas important male heroes such as Paul Revere, Daniel Webster, Robert E. Lee, Alexander Graham Bell, Thomas Edison, Albert Einstein, Jonas Salk, and the Wright brothers were not mentioned at all. She and other critics felt that not enough attention was being given to the positive aspects of U.S. history in its long struggle for liberty, equality, justice, and dignity, and too much emphasis was placed on the country's failures.

The media and their commentators picked up on this controversial topic. Headlines in the leading newspapers and magazines had such titles as "Conflict over a New History Curriculum," "The Hijacking of American History," "Instead of Western Civ, It's Multiciv," "History According to Whom: Let the Debate Continue," "History Rewrites Itself," and "History without Heroes?" In general, the critics condemned the standards for being manifestations of left-wing "political correctness" and extravagant multiculturalism. The criticism also focused heavily on the American history document (at the fifth to twelfth grades) and then the world history standards. The comments were almost exclusively devoted to the examples given of student achievement (the bulk of the document) and not on the standards. Hardly anyone commented on the five historical thinking standards that were to be used from grades K through 12 except to say that they demanded more critical thinking of students than had typically been required in most history courses.

Responding to the harsh criticisms and the recommendations of the Council for Basic Education, the National Center for History in the Schools revised its standards, dropping all student achievement examples, and condensed the three separate volumes into one that focused just on standards.[3] Although the examples of student achievement had brought about most of the criticism, for teachers the examples were probably the most useful part of the three volumes. In terms of practicality of the standards, teachers believe there is not enough time for most students in most schools to meet these ambitious standards. One social studies expert stated that an average fifth-grade teacher would have to teach nothing but history all day long for three years to meet the fifth-grade standards. In addition, some believe that the performance standards have emphasized what students should "know" at the expense of what they should "do," a direction that might lead teachers to require students simply to memorize a lot of facts. Proponents of the standards respond that the purpose of the standards is to raise the level of teaching and learning in U.S. schools.

The history standards do reflect more multiple points of view than most teachers now use, and this is a concern of the conservatives who feel that too much of traditional U.S. history and Western civilization is being left out. On the other hand, the history standards may not be extensive and complete enough to satisfy those who want even more attention to diversity. These standards, thus, clearly illustrate the debate in our society on what children should learn about U.S. and world history. The teaching of these subjects is inherently controversial. As teachers attempt to interest students in how the knowledge of the past informs their present, it is hoped that the content selected will illuminate the ideals that attract and connect us while honoring the diverse experiences of individuals and groups seeking to enjoy the promises of these ideals.

The controversy about national history standards meant that each state had to write its own history standards. However, state standards did not end the controversy. In 2003, the

---

[3]National Center for History in the Schools, *National Standards for History: Basic Edition* (Los Angeles, CA: National Center for History in the Schools, 1996).

Thomas B. Fordham Institute, a conservative group, reviewed the state standards for U.S. history.[4] This group believed that a history education crisis existed and social studies educators had inadequately responded to September 11, 2001. They scored five states' U.S. history standards with the grade of A, but almost half of the states were given an F. In addition, this group published *Where Did Social Studies Go Wrong?*[5] and a critique of high school history textbooks which, among other faults, they considered bland and dull.[6]

Interpretations of History

Summarizing the history wars, we should never forget that historians are constantly changing their views about topics of history. History is not a fixed set of facts. History can only account for a small sampling of the past; the past consists of all the things that have happened for millions of years. History is also influenced by the selection of which aspects of the past have meaning for us today. Historians always interpret evidence and construct tentative versions of what happened in the past. History is therefore socially constructed, debated, and revised. What we know about history today is not the same as what was known twenty years ago and will not be the same in twenty years as new research, new perspectives, and new areas of significance are pursued.

This means that history should include not only what happened in the past, but how history is constructed. This strongly suggests that besides attention to history content, students also need to be aware of how historians go about their work. In addition to studying differences in interpretations of history, some experts in the teaching of history want more attention to citizenship skills. Too often students do not see the connection between what they have learned in history and their responsibilities as citizens.

Small Group Work **5.1**

Are Students Aware of Different Interpretations of History?

Do you think students are aware of the many interpretations of history? Do they accept without question the versions of historical events such as the assassination of John F. Kennedy presented in Hollywood or mass-media history documentaries? ●

History Definitions and Issues

Definitions

For decades experts have emphasized teaching for understanding of history rather than just the rote memorization of historical facts. But what do we really mean by the various terms used in the teaching history? The central aim of teaching and learning history is to make sense of the past. **Historical understandings** refers to the need for all students to know about the history of their nation and the world. It usually includes the idea that students should get a **sense of history,** which means seeing time from a larger perspective.

[4]Sheldon M. Stern, *Effective State Standards for U.S. History: A 2003 Report Card* (Washington, DC: Thomas B. Fordham Institute, 2003).

[5]James Leming, Lucien Ellington, and Kathleen Porter, eds., *Where Did Social Studies Go Wrong?* (Washington, DC: Thomas B. Fordham Institute, 2003).

[6]Diane Ravitch, *A Consumer's Guide to High School History Textbooks* (Washington, DC: Thomas B. Fordham Institute, 2004).

More than just learning facts and dates, a sense of history allows one to understand why political and social conflicts erupt and how they might be resolved. Historical understandings also point to how history includes a wide array of knowledge from what are considered cultural areas: the arts, literature, music, philosophy, religion, science, technology, and social and political knowledge. Historical understandings focus on what has happened in the past but also try to help us make sense of the present world.

One also hears the use of the terms **perspective-taking** and **empathy.** Sometimes these terms are used interchangeably, referring to the ability to see through the eyes of the people who were there or to have the sense of what it was like to be there. Perspective-taking is part of the understandings of history. Different teachers stress either how similar people living in a previous era were compared to people now or how different they were.

In contrast, **historical thinking skills** refer to chronological thinking, historical interpretation, and the methods of historians. Sometimes this is called *historical reasoning* or *historical research*. It is important to remember that historians' interpretations of the past continue to change. Historians also disagree with each other's interpretations. The perspective or point of view of a historian shapes what he or she sees as a problem to be investigated as well as the data sought. Historians, like other individuals, are influenced by their culture, and this determines the significance of historical events. As noted in the holiday curriculum, minority groups can have a different perspective on certain holidays. How many different perspectives and which perspectives should be included throughout the history curriculum have been considerable sources of controversy.

To do historical research, both students and historians use the same methods. They conduct an investigation using primary sources and secondary sources to answer a question. You can immediately see the parallels with inquiry or problem-based learning (Chapter 3). You also recognize at once that historical reasoning and research can be more difficult than just using the textbook and supplementary materials that focus on historical understandings.

Often historical understandings and historical thinking skills are embedded in a given unit. Students may make a time line, a historical thinking skill, while they are studying content. To choose some type of history research, students need some background about the historical period. However, units typically vary in the amount and time devoted to historical understandings and historical skills. The distribution of emphasis of the unit may depend on students' prior knowledge and the amount of desired in-depth coverage of the unit.

Students' Prior Knowledge

More research continues to be done on children and their thinking about history. According to the constructionist theory of learning, children learn a great deal of history outside of school from sources such as family stories, historical films, television historical fiction and documentaries, holiday celebrations, local architecture, and museums. However, students' prior knowledge of history tends to be overlooked. Often there is little connection with what has been learned outside of school and the typical textbook learning in the classroom. Therefore, it is wise to check students' prior knowledge by asking them to write what they already know about a given person or topic such as Davy Crockett at the Alamo or the Underground Railroad. The KWL format (see Chapter 2) also lends itself to finding out what students already know and want to learn. Ask students to list five things they know about a particular topic (e.g., the Civil War) and to underline the two things that they believe are the most important. If students already know a lot about community helpers (people who work in the community) or the ancient Greeks, it suggests that either less time or no time should be spent on the topic or the coverage should be approached in a vastly different manner.

Coverage Versus Depth

Typically, the early primary grades cover little history. Then, suddenly, from the fourth grade on, teachers are covering vast amounts of historical content. Perhaps many teachers have focused more on the memorization of facts because they have felt the need to cover the social studies content for their grade level. In many situations, pursuing an **in-depth approach** instead of a broad coverage is worthwhile, especially if students are already familiar with the content. Remember that not every unit has to be in depth. The difficulty of the in-depth approach is that a teacher needs to know a great deal more than the student textbook about the topic chosen for in-depth study. Examples of in-depth topics might be the American Indians who lived in your community in the past or the immigration patterns in your community.

Drama, Simulation, and Historical Newscast

Dramatic play or reenactments are one of students' favorite activities. In dramatic play, students take the part of historical characters and dramatize the actions, usually in the format of short skits. One problem with dramatic play is that children often do not restrain their imaginations and consequently embellish the facts. Dramatic play or reenactments should be factually accurate. The Texans at the Alamo and the accused people at the Salem Witch Trials are not rescued at the last moment. Because of these concerns, many teachers favor readers' theatre, which already has prepared scripts. All, however, agree that children are most likely to remember the history if there are dramatic activities that make history come alive.

Some classes use a **simulation** for a Renaissance "faire" or market day for a different culture at a different time period. Students explore what a market in a given time period in China (or Africa, etc.) would be like. First, they identify products and services needed in the society to make life function on a daily basis. This would include a wide variety of foods and cooking utensils, clothing, toys, musical instruments, medicines, and furniture. Then students write commercials, slogans, or scripts or draw posters telling why their product or services (e.g., carpenters) improves the quality of life. They may make a price list for the types of items sold. When market day occurs, each student or group has the opportunity to advertise their product or service. Again, the descriptions of the products and services should be accurate and not combine twenty-first-century technology with an older culture. Sometimes this activity stresses more the economic features of supply and demand or is more similar to Travel Day or International Day (Chapter 2).

You can buy reenactments of U.S. history. Among the topics are Great Presidential Decisions (Louisiana Purchase, Fort Sumter), Great National Debates (Women's Rights), Congressional Crisis Sessions (Texas Independence, Mexican War), and important trials (Anne Hutchinson, John Brown, Andrew Johnson, and John Scopes for U.S. history; Socrates, Joan of Arc, Martin Luther, Galileo, and Louis XVI for world history).

Or you can use the TV newscast format for reporting an event in U.S. or world history. Reporters on the scene describe the event, its background, causes, and most importantly, the likely consequences or significance of the event. The reporters can interview witnesses on the scene. Stress the importance of addressing the significance of the event or otherwise you may just get a compilation of factual who, what, and where.

Using a Question or Problem

Many teachers have used focus questions to guide students in understanding history and, in particular, to understand reading the assigned text or other materials. This helps students to think and to read with a purpose. Students have to gather evidence to answer the question. The level of focus questions may vary as indicated for a U.S. history course.

Focus question for the Constitution and Bill of Rights

How does the structure of the federal government protect the rights of people?

One-day lesson focus

In what ways do the rights guaranteed in the First Amendment protect citizens?

Or in a world history course, the great plague of the 14th century could have focus questions such as "How many people did this affect? How many areas of life?" Thus, the key points of the standards are turned into a question.

What about History in the Primary Grades?

But what about history in the primary grades? Should history even be taught in the primary grades? Doesn't the traditional, expanding-horizon curriculum state that children usually learn better about real life around them than about abstract ideas and events far away? Let us look at two different approaches, the holiday curriculum and the history standards, designed to help students at the primary grades understand how to interpret history.

The Holiday Curriculum

Frequently many primary classrooms are decorated during the traditional U.S. holidays. The students extensively decorate the rooms with pumpkins, turkeys, hearts, and the like. Most students look forward to holidays because there is often a classroom party with holiday snacks. Do remember that some parents, including Seventh-Day Adventists, may not want their children to participate in school holiday celebrations. Often student understanding of these holidays is limited to the arts and crafts and party activities that surround them. Furthermore, the important concepts associated with these holidays are not developed to a higher level of understanding for each higher grade.

Particular U.S. holidays, especially federal holidays, do deserve attention: New Year's Day, Martin Luther King, Jr. Day, Presidents Day, Memorial Day, Independence Day, Labor Day, Columbus Day, Veterans Day, Thanksgiving, and Christmas. With the exception of the religious holidays, the fundamental U.S. ideals and shared values are celebrated on our national holidays. These holidays should be examined because they help us remember values and ideals that we share as U.S. citizens. You may find such books as Myra Cohn Livingston's *Celebrations* (Holiday, 1987) to be helpful. Also, use the Internet for investigating local ethnic holidays and festivals.

You can also use **WebQuests,** an inquiry-oriented activity in which learners get most of their information from the Internet (http://webquest.sdsu.edu). There are many WebQuests on holidays such as Halloween, in which students find out the origin of Halloween and how it is celebrated in other countries. Other holiday WebQuests are "Festivals and Holidays in

TECHNOLOGY

Hong Kong," "Pilgrim Life Adventure," and "Presidents Day WebQuest." (There is a very wide variety of WebQuests on history ranging from the ancient world to the Arab-Israeli conflict.) Check that the Internet resources are current before your students begin a WebQuest.

Inductive Strategy on Holidays   The teacher, using the Taba approach, asks, for example, "What comes to your mind when you hear the word *Thanksgiving*?" The teacher records all student responses, including those that are silly or trivial. After getting a wide range of responses, the teacher asks "Can we group any of these?" "Why did you put _____ and _____ together?" Finally, the students are asked to give a title to the list or to form a generalization about the particular holiday. There is a high probability that the students will reveal the essential characteristics of the holiday, including important values.

Another alternative is to ask students to brainstorm a list of holidays. Write each holiday on a word strip or on paper that can be cut into strips. Make several sets. Ask the children to sort the holidays into the following categories: historical, religious, cultural, and other. You may wish to define the meaning of these categories for students. Here are some possible definitions:

Historical: Honoring a person or event in history (Thanksgiving, Veterans Day)

Religious: Celebrating or observing a religious event (Easter, Hanukkah)

Cultural: Celebrating or observing an event with origins from a specific culture (Kwanzaa)

Other: Celebrating someone important in your life or for fun (Valentine's Day)

Explain that the class will concentrate on historical or national holidays. In addition, display a calendar and ask if there are any holidays during the current month. A time line could also be made of the national holidays during the year. The time line could include the name of the holiday, the date it is celebrated, pictures related to the holiday, and a short explanation.

At the minimum these holidays should be commemorated with a brief story followed by a creative activity such as writing a poem about the holiday. Focus on the achievement of the people associated with the holiday. Use the question, "What comes to your mind when you hear the word (name a holiday)?" Record the words and divide the class into pairs. Then each pair can put together a poem (it does not have to rhyme). The recorded words help the pairs to complete the task that might otherwise be too difficult. In many cases, each pair will be proud to read their very own poem to the class.

A thoughtful activity to honor Martin Luther King, Jr. Day is for students to interview elders about what life was like for them before the Civil Rights Movement (see interviews and oral history later in this chapter). This activity has almost brought tears to the eyes of students. Another challenging holiday activity is a comparison on how New Year is celebrated around the world. First, ask students whether their families have any traditions for this holiday. Then compare the traditions for Chinese New Year, Japanese New Year, and Rosh Hashanah, the Jewish New Year. What do they have in common? What are the differences? In the upper grades, students can also find out how older civilizations such as the Romans celebrated the New Year.

Historical Background of the Holidays   Children can understand the historical background of a holiday and how people lived at that time. Almost all holidays have some

TECHNOLOGY

geographic place associated with them. For example, a virtual field trip to Plymouth (http://pilgrims.net/plymouth) can illustrate the differences between how food was prepared in the 1620s and how food is prepared today. Similarly, you can use a virtual field trip to show how George Washington lived at Mount Vernon or Abraham Lincoln lived in Springfield, Illinois. You could also compare the transportation systems that President George Washington used with those President Abraham Lincoln used to go to the capital city to take the oath of office. Another alternative is to ask what hardships or difficulties individuals associated with given holidays faced, because they were often fighting for freedom and rights.

With the Pilgrims at Plymouth, attention needs to be given to American Indians such as Squanto, a Patuxet peacemaker.[7] As illustrated here in the example of the Pilgrims, different perspectives on the holiday should be welcomed since not all groups and individuals view the given holiday in the same way. Certainly King George III regarded Independence Day in a different light than the patriots, and American Indians do not regard Columbus Day as a celebration.

Other Holidays   In addition to the federal holidays already mentioned, classroom time may also be spent on such holidays as St. Patrick's Day, Mother's Day, Father's Day, the first day of Hanukkah, Kwanzaa, Mardi Gras, Buddha's birthday, and Ramadan. There may also be regional or state holidays that are celebrated, such as Cinco de Mayo or Chinese New Year. In addition, there are hundreds of local holidays and celebrations that often reflect the ethnic diversity of the United States. From Santa Barbara's Old Spanish Days to a Tulip Festival in Holland, Michigan, local communities celebrate many holidays. Remember, however, the guidelines for teaching of religion in the classroom (Chapter 9). If the holiday occurs during the summer when school is not in session for most children or on a Sunday, the holiday tends to be neglected. In addition, the collective U.S. memory of the importance of both heroes and events changes over the years. Labor Day, for example, is usually not given much attention compared to other school holidays.

Teachers should be aware that the religious holidays are a sensitive area in many communities and some administrators dread the month of December (more in Chapter 9). Increasingly, in the month of December, primary teachers are studying a variety of December holidays throughout the world. This is called *Multicultural Christmas*. This approach both increases the concept of what a holiday is, including festivals and feast days, and introduces students to the wide cultural diversity around the world. Some primary teachers may also include December holidays such as Hanukkah and Kwanzaa in the unit. It is now easier than ever to study any holiday since more resources are available on the Internet for students to explore how holidays are celebrated throughout the world.

In summary, the holiday curriculum has had many critics. However, primary children can increase both their historical and civic understanding by studying holidays. Encouraging critical thinking about holidays with different interpretations and going beyond simple explanations can help students focus on the values behind the holiday.

Primary History Standards

When the states prepared their standards, they wanted history to be taught to primary students. The intent is that history content in the primary grades be alive and centered on people,

---

[7]Remember when possible to give the names of the American Indian nations to help students realize that not all American Indians are alike.

Small Group Work **5.2**

Your Reaction?

Realizing that you are only seeing the history standards and not the standards for geography, economics, and civics, what do you think about Arizona's history standards for kindergarten and the primary grades? Have they listed the major concepts or big ideas? Are the standards realistic and can most children achieve the standards? How do they compare to your state's standards at these grade levels? ●

not events or dates. The focus is on the students' personal histories, the histories of their own families, and of people, both ordinary and extraordinary, who have lived in the students' own community, state, nation, and the world. It is suggested that stories, myths, legends, and biographies be used to study these histories. There is also an emphasis on historical skills such as understanding chronology and using primary sources even in the primary grades.

The typical state social studies standards for the primary grades list four core discipline standards in history, geography, economics, and civics. In addition, other social studies standards in skills and values are also normally listed. Technology skills are sometimes highlighted.

As just one example, see the Arizona Social Studies History Standards in Table 5.2. Arizona's standards were chosen because they appear to be typical of what is recommended for the primary grades and they also possess the virtue of brevity compared to some very detailed standards of other states. The numbers of the Arizona standards have been omitted.

Compared to the traditional social studies program, the Arizona history standards indicate the importance of time lines, historical research skills, and use of primary source materials along with an emphasis on individual action, character, and values. A wider range of U.S. heroes than has been taught in the past is outlined. Skills are also integrated with the content. In the unit plan "Historical Thinking Grade 1," we see how a teacher tries to meet these standards.

Theme

Other states may have one big theme or question for the whole year's social studies work. For the fourth grade, New York asked the following: Has the history of New York been one of progress for all? The inclusion of "for all" allows for different perspective taking as students look at explorers, the colonial period, the American Revolution, the Civil War, and the like. Using a theme question throughout the year can give a sense of unity to the year's work. A theme question also invites teachers to ask themselves what they want students to know and be able to do at the end of the year. This can be a helpful guide to planning. By following the theme question, the students can compare the different groups from various time periods.

Using comparisons moves questioning to a higher level of thinking. Remember to try to always use higher-level questions regardless of the topic or whether or not there is a theme question. Here are some examples: How were the local explorers (or settlers) alike? Different? In what ways have the early settlers affected our lives today? Was _____ a good citizen? Compare what other groups thought about him or her.

Table 5.2	Arizona's History Standards for Kindergarten and Grades 1–3, Approved in Year 2000

Kindergarten

- Describe how history is the story of events, people, and places in the past, with emphasis on:

  Tracing the history of individuals and families, and describing the way people lived in earlier days and how we live differently today

  The people and events honored in national holidays, including Thanksgiving, Presidents' Day, and Martin Luther King, Jr. Day

- Place familiar events in order of occurrence, with emphasis on:

  Identifying days of the week and months of the year

  Locating events on a calendar, including birthdays, holidays, and school events

Grades 1–3

Students know and are able to do all of the above and the following:

- Demonstrate the ability to place events in chronological sequence, with emphasis on:

  Using a time line to place in order important events in a student's life recognizing a sequence of events

  (Note: Historical research and analytical skills are to be learned and applied to the content standards for grades 1–3.)

- Describe everyday life in the past and recognize that some aspects change and others stay the same, with emphasis on:

  Using primary source materials, including photographs, artifacts, interviews, and documents to trace the history of a family from long ago

  The economies, symbols, customs, and oral traditions of an Indian community of Arizona, including the significance of the Eagle Feather, trade networks, decorative arts, housing, songs, and dances

  How past cultural exchanges influence present-day life, including food, art, shelter, and language

  (Note: Historical skills and analytical skills are to be learned and applied to the content standards for grades 1–3.)

- Use stories to describe past events, people, and places with emphasis on:

  Contributions from past events and cultures

  Examples of individual action, character, and values

  Descriptions of daily life in past time and different places, including the various roles of men, women, and children

- Describe the stories of important American heroes and their contributions to our society, with emphasis on:

  Those who secured our freedom, including George Washington, Benjamin Franklin, and Thomas Jefferson

  Those who fought for the rights and freedoms of others, including Chief Joseph, Chief Manuelito (Navajo, the Long Walk), Abraham Lincoln, Harriet Tubman, Martin Luther King, Jr., and Cesar Chavez

UNIT PLAN

Historical Thinking Grade 1

Arizona History Standards

Emphasis on time lines, sequence of events, examples of individual action, character, and values

Unit Goals

Place the events of a story, a day, or the school year in chronological order.

Listen to, read, and act out fables, myths, folktales, hero/heroine tales, biographies, and other stories from different cultures to answer the following: What happened? Who did it? Why did it happen? What was the consequence? How might things have ended if a character had behaved differently?

Use literacy links to reading, listening, speaking, and writing.

Day 1. Beginning the Unit

Objective: Students will use time lines to place important events in order.

1. Ask students, "What are some things that happen each day in our classroom?"
2. Read the book *My Day/Mi Dia* by Rebecca Emberly (Little, Brown & Co., 1993). The English/Spanish text describes activities in a child's daily routine. Record the text in sentence strips and have the students sequence the events of the day.
3. Take photographs of events that occur each day in class or ask students to draw pictures of three to five events that occur each day. Make time lines and post times for the events.
4. Assign homework (parent letter home) asking for significant events in their child's life to use in a time line. Earlier photographs encouraged.
5. A "Time Line of the Day" is then produced each day along with a monthly and, finally, yearly accumulation and evaluation of time lines. Use TimeLiner software for creating and printing time lines.

Day 2. Consequences

Objective: Students will understand the meaning of *consequences.*

1. Discuss with students and identify in real life the meanings of *problem, solution,* and *consequences.*
2. In pairs students brainstorm other problems they might face and list them on the following chart.

Problem/Solution/Consequences Chart

Event
Problem
Solution
Consequences
Alternative Solution
Alternative Consequences

UNIT PLAN continued   Historical Thinking Grade 1

Day 3. Interpret a Fable

   Objective: Students will interpret a fable in terms of story and value.

1. Read the classic story of "The Lion and the Mouse" from the textbook *I Know a Place* (Houghton Mifflin).
2. By asking questions, go through the sequence of event, problem, and so on.
3. Ask students what this story tells us (e.g., importance of friends, friends help each other, friends come in all sizes).
4. Brainstorm what lesson the lion learned.
5. Develop class moral for the story (e.g., everyone needs a friend).
6. Two students dramatize the story.
7. Students draw three pictures to show three events in the story, which they then paste in order on a strip of paper. Share with the class.
8. Students draw a picture of a time when they had a problem and a friend helped them.
9. Introduce *value.* Ask students what values are presented in the story and list the values in the story on the chart.

Story	Values

10. Introduce *fact* and *fiction.* Ask students if this is a true story. How do they know? Chart responses. Discuss characteristics of factual stories: names, dates, places, and actions that can be verified. List these student responses on a Fact/Fiction Chart. Divide into three parts: Story, Fact or Fiction, and Reasons.

Day 4. Developing the Topic

   Objective: Students will apply skills in interpreting a new story: (a) Identify a problem and solution by discussing events in story; (b) identify and chart values as they discuss stories; and (c) make time lines for characters.

1. Read the story *Paper Bag Princess* by Robert Munsch (Annick Press Ltd., 1980). A girl rescues her prince from a dragon and then decides he may not be as princely as she had first thought.
2. Ask students about the problem, solution, and consequences. What else could he or she do? Enter responses on Problem/Solution/Consequences Chart.
3. Ask students what values are presented in the story. Who has these values? List on the Story/Values Chart.
4. In pairs have students compare the characters of Ronald and Elizabeth on a Venn diagram.

UNIT PLAN continued   Historical Thinking Grade 1

5. Have students use three illustrations from the book and write a caption for each picture and place in sequential order.
6. Have students tell the story from the perspective of the dragon.
7. Discuss possible alternative endings and places in the book where such alternatives might occur. Use small groups for the activity.
8. Have a "hot seat" where one student is chosen to portray one character in the book and have the other students ask the character questions.

Day 5. Interpreting Stories

Objective: Students will apply skills to interpret another story.

1. Discuss what a hero or heroine is. Students discuss a story of a child who was a hero long ago in Holland. Locate Holland on the map and show canals.
2. Read the story "The Little Hero of Holland" from *The Children's Book of Virtues* edited by William Bennett.
3. Discuss the problem and what Peter did. Fill in class the Problem/Solution/Consequences Chart.
4. Discuss whether this story is fact or fiction. Introduce the term *legend*. Make an entry for the story on the Fact/Fiction Chart.
5. In cooperative pairs students discuss why Peter acted as he did. Ask students which values are presented in the story.
6. Use individual student clocks to demonstrate how long Peter had to stay in one position.
7. Pass out 9" × 12" sheets of construction paper in which a small hole has been made. Ask students to put the paper on a chair and kneel on the floor with their finger in the hole for 5 minutes. Discuss and chart responses.
8. Have students fill out the chart on Peter. I am . . . I hear . . . I see . . . I want . . . I say . . . I am. . . .

Next Days

Continue with other stories. Only a few are listed; you could substitute others.

Read *The Rough Face Girl* by Rafe Martin and David Shannon (Scholastic, 1992), an Algonquin Indian telling of the Cinderella story.

Read *The Story of Ruby Bridges* by Robert Coles (Scholastic, 1995). For months, six-year-old Ruby Bridges confronts the hostility of segregationists when she becomes the first African American girl to integrate Frantz Elementary School in New Orleans in 1960.

Culminating the Unit

Review each of the class charts and recall stories. Ask students to discuss, write (or dictate) new stories, and fill out the charts.

I am deeply indebted to Elizabeth Rickett, Montebello Unified School District, who explained this unit at the California Annual State Conference, February 19, 1998. This is a brief summary of a thirty-three-page unit that does not do justice to all the excellent ideas.

Small Group Work **5.3**

Controversial Issues for the First Grade?

Check how multicultural this unit is. Also notice that there is a discussion of a moral and controversial issue, segregation, in the Ruby Bridges story. The author of this unit also suggests the use of *The Lily Cupboard: A Story of the Holocaust* by Shulamith Levey Oppenheim (HarperCollins, 1992). This story tells of a young Jewish girl in German-occupied Holland who is forced to separate from her parents and hide with strangers in the country. It is a sensitive portrayal and powerful story of ordinary people who are heroes. Do you think controversial and sensitive issues should be brought up in the first grade? ●

Look carefully at this briefly sketched unit. Do you like it? Will students meet the state standards of historical thinking and have a better understanding of chronology? Do you like the values emphasis on how actions have consequences and there can be other alternatives? Are there many opportunities for assessment built in throughout the unit?

Linking History and Trade Books to Students

Using Trade Books and Magazines

One strategy to bring history or any of the social sciences to life is the use of trade books. Almost everyone loves a story. Books can bring past events into the lives of students. Books are usually more people-centered than text material and can give fresh insight into the ways of life in our culture—past and present—as well as cultures of other places and times.

The following skills can be emphasized in using historical fiction:

1. **Historical content**—learn about historical events from the novel
2. **Historical insight**—make observations and inferences to see beyond obvious facts
3. **Historical accuracy**—decide whether information being read is accurate
4. **Relevancy**—connect a historical matter in the novel with people and events today
5. **Literature skills**—characterization, theme, plot

Children are most familiar with storybooks. The narrative text structure is the easiest written format for children to understand since the emphasis is on characters and plot. Historical fiction combines the high interest of characters and plot by reconstructing the period in which the book is set, usually by describing the personal decisions of the characters. Historical fiction can invoke the powerful reality of events long ago; it often can serve as a springboard for examining diverse perspectives such as American Indians and frontier families or peasants versus feudal lords.

Historical fiction and biographies are especially powerful. Stories can combine historical incidents with emotion and conflict. Kieran Egan suggested that, for students up to the age of seven, stories with clear conflicts between good and evil or fear and security are best.[8] Students from eight to thirteen are in the romantic stage and prefer to read about people who struggle courageously with real problems. Children want to know how Sojourner Truth felt in the face of great odds, for instance, and will often be interested in books depicting human suffering.

Where can teachers find good books for the social studies? Each spring in the May/June issue the NCSS journal *Social Education* publishes a list of notable children's trade books in the social studies field (www.ncss.org/resources/notable). These books are selected because they (1) are written for readers from kindergarten through the eighth grade, (2) emphasize human relations, (3) represent a diversity of groups and are sensitive to a broad range of cultural experiences, (4) present an original theme or a fresh slant on a traditional topic, (5) are easily readable and of high literary quality, and (6) have a pleasing format and, when appropriate, illustrations that enrich the text.

Consult your librarian to see what is available in your school library related to social studies. In addition, more state departments of education now have online lists of the books that are appropriate for each grade level for the social studies. The most useful lists are those that are annotated. From these sources and *Social Education,* indicate to your librarian/media center your preferences for future orders. Check to make sure that there is a good match between your class and what is recommended for your grade level.

There are also history magazines for young people. The most popular is *Cobblestone,* which focuses on U.S. history and includes articles on entertainers such as Annie Oakley and the Wild West; explorers such as Robert E. Peary, who went to the North Pole; leaders such as Joseph, chief of the Nez Perce, and so on. *Cobblestone* is found in many public libraries and the back issues may be of interest to teachers.[9] Cobblestone Publishing also publishes other children's magazines that may be useful: *Calliope* features world history, *Dig* covers archaeology, *Footsteps* features African American heritage, and *Faces* covers world cultures and multicultural studies. They also have *Teaching with Primary Sources,* a helpful series which includes historical documents combined with teacher-developed classroom activities.

The number of good books is always increasing. Who would not be excited by a book on the Salem Witch Trials, such as *Priscilla Foster: The Story of a Salem Girl* by Dorothy and Thomas Hoobler (Silver Burdett Press, 1997)? Or consider *Passage to Freedom: The Sugihara Story* by Ken Mochizuki (Lee & Low Books, 1997), a true story of a Japanese consul to Lithuania who risked his job and his family's safety to provide visas to Jewish refugees during World War II, saving thousands of lives during the Holocaust. The Sugihara book raises the issue of what is a "good" person. Sugihara disobeyed the orders of the Japanese government when he issued the visas to the Jewish people.

Are there any problems in using historical fiction? First, children generally accept the accuracy of the information presented in textbooks. They tend to have the same response to historical fiction. Students need to distinguish fact from fiction as well as be able to identify the author's interpretation of historical figures and events. It is necessary for children to check with at least one other source, such as an encyclopedia, to see if it agrees with the accuracy and interpretation in the historical fiction. Sometimes children can compare one trade book with another trade book if it is on the same topic. Second,

---

[8]Kieran Egan, "What Children Know Best," *Social Education,* 43, no. 2 (February 1979): 130–139.

[9]Published by Cobblestone Publishing, Inc., 30 Grove Street, Suite C, Peterborough, NH 03458; telephone (800) 821–0115; e-mail custsvc@cobblestone.mv.com and www.cobblestonepub.com.

unfortunately, students read with high interest the characters and plot but too often do not really get the meaning of the historical background. For example, they read historical fiction about the Revolutionary War but do not know why General Washington and his army were suffering at Valley Forge.

This illustrates the need to make assessments on what social studies understandings children are actually making from their reading. This might include activities such as making time lines both from events in the trade book and a general background time line. Mapping the places in the book with a comparison of where actual historical events were occurring can be helpful. Character response journals can require the reader to record the actions of the main character and what historical events were happening at the same time.

Another teacher decision is how historical fiction will be shared with the students. Sometimes a teacher chooses to read the text aloud. Same-book literature circles can have small group discussions on an open-ended question after reading every few days, or there can be whole class instruction on the same book.

Books Used for a History Theme

Often it is appropriate to use a series of books that fit under a common theme instead of using books that are unrelated to each other. This is illustrated in the unit plan "How Things Change." Notice that in this unit on change, an essential history concept, the teacher is reading aloud to the primary-grade children. Prepare for the read-aloud experience by reading the book to yourself before reading it aloud to the class so you can read fluently with lots of expression in your voice. Being familiar with the book also allows you to maintain eye contact with the class while reading aloud. In addition, do not read aloud too long—between ten and twenty minutes is appropriate for most classes. Furthermore, break up your reading by asking children to answer questions or predict. Also break whenever you note student confusion. Observe that after the read-aloud portion of the lesson in "How Things Change" there was a related activity to reinforce the concept of change. Or the theme could be urbanism, using trade books such as Jeannie Baker's *Home* (Greenwillow Books, 2004) where a young girl see changes in an urban environment or Susan Goodman's *On This Spot: An Expedition Back through Time* (Greenwillow Books, 2004) on how Manhattan developed.

Using Biographies

Biographies are a special form of historical writing. Biography is a genre that tells the life history of a real person. Biographies can foster both historical understandings and skills as they can be a hook to a time period. Books about people such as anthropologist Margaret Mead; Thomas Gallaudet, a pioneer in the education of the deaf; Rosa Parks, who was instrumental in fighting segregation; and Molly Brown, a survivor of the doomed ship *Titanic,* are always popular. Help students by using the following categories for reporting on their biographies:

- Key events/dates
- Obstacles faced
- Key accomplishments

UNIT PLAN

How Things Change

Sequence

Lesson 1: Read aloud *The Little House.* Find instances of change in the story. After students understand the story's feelings about change, assign activity to create paper house puppets and write how the Little House would feel about these changes. Share student products.

Lesson 2: Display eight pictures from portfolio, *The Changing Countryside,* around room. Explain that pictures show same land area over twenty years. Students view pictures silently, then do cooperative group work to list ten changes they note. Share findings with class. Call attention to details of pictures.

Lesson 3: Read aloud *I Go with My Family to Grandma's.* Students compare transportation in the 1900s with that of today. Discuss how families still visit as continuity. Use last page to discuss how family photos are a record of change. Share own family photos that show changes in dress, toys, cars, houses.

Lesson 4: Students bring and share family pictures, clippings, or belongings that demonstrate changes in their lives.

Lesson 5: Read aloud *Bayberry Bluff,* eliciting ideas as to why Bayberry Bluff is changing. Encourage students to predict what will happen next. Discuss why people came: Vacation? Farming? Fishing? Making movies? Mining?

Lesson 6: Students view pictures from *The Changing City.* Ask questions about what has changed and why changes occurred. For example, widening street indicates growth, more traffic, and protection from fire; the new businesses and freeway alter community character and purpose. Ask what things remain the same in all pictures.

Lesson 7: Share the picture book *New Providence,* emphasizing how community strives to restore and preserve landmarks and structures. Student pairs choose something in own community worth saving. Discuss why it would be important to save as pairs share choices. Ask how preservation is good for a community. Compare and contrast the effects of change in *New Providence* and *The Changing City.*

Lesson 8: Students make up stories and pictures depicting how a place changed and stayed the same over time. Must include reasons for change in stories. Share with class. Discuss why changes were good or bad.

Lesson 9: For a global education perspective, use the free materials of *Read to Feed,* a program of Heifer International (www.readtofeed.org) and The Center for Teaching International Relations (www.du.edu/ctir). For example, use the book *Beatrice's Goat* about a young girl of Uganda whose life was changed by the gift of a goat.

Closure: Read aloud *The Sky Was Blue.* Ask students what has been learned about change and continuity.

Bridging: Read *The House on Maple Street* as a prompt for next unit on studying local geography, indigenous peoples, early settlers, and community development.

Assessment

Students react by writing two changes in *The Little House.*

Students in a group note visual change from pictures.

UNIT PLAN continued   How Things Change

Students share changes in personal history.

Students select and give reasons for place in own community worthy of preservation.

Students create pictures depicting change and explain reasons for them.

Resources

Burton, Virginia Lee. *The Little House.* Boston: Houghton Mifflin, 1942.

Lent, Blair. *Bayberry Bluff.* Boston: Houghton Mifflin, 1987.

Levinson, Riki. *I Go with My Family to Grandma's.* Illustrated by Diane Goode. New York: E. P. Dutton, 1986.

McBrier, Page and Lori Lohstoeter (illustrator). *Beatrice's Goat.* New York: Atheneum, 2001.

Muller, Jorg. *The Changing City.* New York: Atheneum, 1977. This portfolio consists of eight full-color, foldout pictures done by Swiss artist Jorg Muller.

————. *The Changing Countryside.* New York: Atheneum, 1977. A companion portfolio to the preceding title.

Pryor, Bonnie. *The House on Maple Street.* Illustrated by Beth Peck. New York: William Morrow, 1987.

von Tscharner, Renata, and Ronald Lee Fleming. *New Providence: A Changing Cityscape.* San Diego, CA: Harcourt Brace Jovanovich, 1987.

Zolotow, Charlotte. *The Sky Was Blue.* Illustrated by Garth Williams. New York: Harper and Row, 1963.

Source: California Council for the Social Studies Annual Conference.

Teachers looking at many state standards are often amazed at the sheer number of historical figures that their students are expected to learn. In many states the list from kindergarten to grade 5 can include over eighty names ranging from Abigail Adams to Roger Williams. One solution is for each child in the class to be responsible for one biography from the state's list as well as additions by the teacher's choice.

For ease in student choice, biographies can be grouped into different categories. For U.S. history the categories could be Explorers and Pioneers, People of the American Revolution, American Indians, and Humanitarians. Other possible categories could be Presidents, Scientists and Inventors, and Artists, Writers, and Entertainers. A student who may be unfamiliar with many of the names of historical figures at least has a clue when choosing a key person about the general occupation or lifestyle of the historical figure. In general, most of the historical figures named in state lists are considered outstanding figures, if not heroes or heroines. Individuals considered to be traitors like Benedict Arnold are not usually cited on the state lists that students are required to know. In some classes, reading the biography takes place during class time. In other classes, the reading is an independent study project in which the parent's signature is required to validate the reading of the book and how the book will be reported.

Table 5.3	Biography Report Template

Box 1	Name of person
	Picture of person [Use a primary source here.]
	By [your name]
Box 2	Born [where and the date]
	Died [how and the date]
Box 3	Family information
	[Include information about husband or wife, children, parents, etc.]
Box 4	What the person is *famous* or most known for
Box 5	List of *accomplishments* and important *dates* in the person's life [You can include pictures and drawings in the boxes to add more detail.]

Note: I am indebted to Dr. Priscilla Porter's Paper "People Who Make a Difference: Using Biographies in the Elementary Classroom," Presented at the 43rd Annual Conference of the California Council for the Social Studies, March 5, 2004, for this table plus other ideas on the use of biographies.

To have students avoid copying directly from the text, design a format or an **advanced organizer** that requires the student to summarize the data. For a second grader, a foldable with separate sheets of paper to be filled out can be useful. See Table 5.3 as an example. A rubric or scoring guide listing ten possible points for each of the five boxes can be given ahead of time to the children. In addition, for a mechanics category, ten possible points each could be given for spelling, grammar, punctuation, and neatness, if desired.

TECHNOLOGY

Technology also can help in the actual writing process. One useful website is www.ReadWriteThink.org, sponsored by the National Council for Teachers of English (NCTE) and IRA (International Reading Association). There you can find the biopoem form (line 2: write four words that describe the character; line 4: name three objects the character loves or cares for, etc.) The Inspiration software can create a concept web about a person's life (see concept mapping in Chapter 3).

How can students present their information about a historical figure to the rest of the class? The **living museum** format is very successful. Each student, often dressed with an appropriate hat or costume, memorizes a speech to be recited in the first person.

My name is (the name of the historical figure). I was born in _____ on _____.

I died on _____. I am famous for (details) . . .

Parents and other classes are often invited for the presentation. It is a good idea to have a rehearsal the day before the presentation so all students will be prepared.

Other formats for presentation of the biography could include the following:

- Label on a map the important places in your historical figure's life
- Create a time line with several significant events in your historical figure's life
- Write a resume for the historical figure
- Write a poem about your historical figure

- Write several newspaper articles about important events in your historical figure's life
- Write a conversation about your historical person between two people showing different perspectives about the person

Note all these formats avoid the dull written book reports that frequently turn students off.

Doing History or Being a Historian

*W*ill any of your units give students a hands-on experience of dealing with a historical problem, gathering data, and then reflecting on it? This approach has the potential of teaching valuable skills such as testing the data for their credibility and authenticity. Students can learn to differentiate between primary and secondary sources and pose relevant questions they encounter in a variety of primary sources: oral histories, letters, diaries, artifacts, photographs, maps, works of art, and architecture.

National History Day

Over 700,000 students each year participate in National History Day (www.nhd.org). Each year a theme is chosen and students can respond in a variety of formats to present their historical investigations. These might include a written paper, exhibits, performances, and documentaries. Typically students under the direction of their teacher start working on their topic in the fall and are able to enter the competitions held in the spring at local, state, and national levels. Students can choose to participate as an individual or be part of a group of up to five students.

Projects have ranged from students interviewing Holocaust survivors and heroes as well as using primary and secondary sources to find out more about individuals, institutions, and sites in their local community. Having served as a judge on the local level, I have been amazed at the high quality of historical analysis and interpretations made by participating students. It would appear that motivated students can "do" history. Of course, it should be noted that many teachers whose students participate in National History Day have received professional development by the National History Day organization and are more familiar with primary sources available to help their students.

Save Our History

The History Channel also has a project called "Save Our History" with the emphasis on local history, including preserving historic places, many under the custodianship of the National Park Service (see http://nps.gov/learn and www.cr.nps.gov for lesson plans). The National Park Service's National Register of Historic Places also has virtual field trips about many parts of the United States. In the category of preserving our nation's neighborhoods, buildings, homes, and sites, helpful hands-on activities are given. Along with their guide are free monthly American history lesson plans available by registering at www.saveourhistory.com.

Oral History

Students enjoy exploring the past through the collection of **oral histories.** Oral history is a living person's recollections about his or her past about events they have *personally* experienced. It is a historical inquiry that historians are increasingly using, especially with groups such as immigrants who may not leave traditional records. Historians obtain oral data not only from famous or powerful people but also from members of a given community such as an Indian pueblo. Oral histories can be obtained from Holocaust survivors, from individuals of an ethnic background, or from people who observed or participated in a specific activity such as a strike or a protest march. These kinds of firsthand accounts can fascinate children. Oral history is not dramatic play or role-playing the part of someone else.

Oral Histories on Grandparents' Lives at School Compared to Today's Class   Iris Lee has the following third-grade history standard to meet:

Classroom Episode
Looking in Classrooms: Designing a Questionnaire

*M*s. Iris Lee has introduced her students to the topic of interviewing their grandparents or a similarly aged adult about their experiences when they went to school in the first grade. Ms. Lee decided that asking about the whole elementary experience from kindergarten through eighth grade was too broad. But what grade level should be chosen? Kindergarten was a possibility but perhaps not all the grandparents actually attended kindergarten at that time. Grandparents who were immigrants might not be willing to tell that they had not graduated from elementary school but everyone probably had some school experience at the first grade. The children like the topic but feel a little uncertain about how to ask questions of their grandparents.

Ms. Lee: Our grandparents come from many backgrounds. What do we need to know about their first-grade school experience?

Manuel: Where the school was. My grandmother went to school in Mexico.

Ms. Lee: Good, we need to know where the school was located. What do you think Manuel's grandmother's school looked like?

Emma: I think it's small. Maybe one room. Schools out in the country are not big.

Manuel: She went to school in Guadalajara. That's a big city!

(Other children add comments about the various sizes of schools and how different they look.)

Ms. Lee: We know that some schools are located in big cities and others in the countryside. How do you think your grandparents got to school?

Ethan: They walked a mile in the snow. *(Class laughs.)*

Ms. Lee: Who told you that they walked in the snow?

Ethan: My grandfather is always telling us how hard it was for them when he was a boy. No school buses and that now we kids have tons of toys.

Ms. Lee: How our grandparents got to school is a good question. Is there anything else we need to know about our grandparents going to school?

Grace: Their report cards. Did they get good grades?

Ms. Lee: Should we ask our grandparents about their report cards and grades?

Elizabeth: I am not sure. What if they got bad grades?

After continued comments, the students agreed on a set of questions for their interviews. They decided not to include questions on report cards and grades.

Describe everyday life in the past and recognize that some aspects change and others stay the same, with emphasis on using primary source materials.

Initially the thought of using primary source materials overwhelms Ms. Lee. The reading level of her third-grade class covers a very wide range so she hesitates to rely too much on written documents. That would invite problems. She remembers, however, how successful the fourth-grade class was in using interviews for their family history/ancestors project. Everyone from parents to the principal raved about the results. Maybe her third graders could interview grandparents if the topic were familiar enough. Bonding with grandparents would be a great idea. Many schools now have a "Grandparents Day." What topic does every single student in my room know about? They all certainly know about going to school. Maybe comparing the schools now and with the schools that grandparents attended would pay off in terms of both learning and high interest. If the students do not have a grandparent available, an elder from about the same age group could be substituted.

Another alternative is for cooperative groups to formulate questions to ask their grandparents and then review all the questions. The problem here is probably the number of repeat questions or similar questions. However, the cooperative group experience does have a higher involvement for a greater number of students.

Ms. Lee was wise to narrow the topic to what life was like in a first-grade elementary school for grandparents. Asking students to question people about their whole lives is too involved.

Let us look at the grandparent respondents to get clues to the likely data. There will be a wide range of ages for these respondents. These data will be obtained by adding six years to the birth dates, considering six to be the average age when children start first grade. Grandparents or elders could be from around 50 to 75 years of age which means that the years covering their first-grade experience extend also over the same time period. It was decided by the teacher that the bonding experience with grandparents was worth more than the convenience of just asking children to interview adults from ages 60 to 70, a more narrow age

---

Background Information for Grandparents/ Elders School Interview

Respondent's Name_____

Age of Respondent_____

How old when in first grade?_____

Interviewer's Name_____

Questions:

1. Where was your first-grade school located? (name city, country if necessary)
2. How did you get to school? (walk, bus, car, etc.)
3. What did your school look like? On the outside? In the classroom?
4. About how many students were in your first-grade class?
5. What did you learn at school?
6. What did you have for lunch?

range. The teacher also decided to send a "Dear Parent" letter home explaining the assignment and the reasons for giving it. You may consider giving the principal the letter before it is sent home in case the principal wants to make any changes.

Notice that other questions could have been asked, such as what technology was used in the classroom or what the grandparents enjoyed the most in the first grade. Whether the respondents attended segregated classrooms is another question that could be asked. The Brown decision was in 1954 and many of the grandparents were in elementary school before this date. The children are not likely to ask questions about segregation or desegregation unless they are familiar with the 1954 Supreme Court decision and segregated schools. This points out the need for students to have a time line of important events that were occurring during the childhood of their respondents. In addition, it indicates that a teacher may want to provide background so children will ask more specific and relevant questions.

After the class has designed their questions, which should be as clear as possible, each child should receive a printed copy of the questions with space to write the answers. A form with the questions and spaces provided for answers is very helpful to most students. They then can take notes directly on the form. This means that you need to determine whether students will take notes or tape the interview. This may depend on what equipment you have available. Taping also requires the permission of the respondent. If students take notes, tell them that they cannot expect to take down every word. They will need to listen carefully and try to get the main ideas.

Practicing and modeling interviews in the classroom helps to reduce anxiety about interviewing. Many students will rigidly ask only the questions on their list, ignoring any possibilities of interchange that might arise during the interview. You can encourage them in the practice sessions to move beyond the interview questions while still insisting that they gather the required data. It is also clear from the class discussion that a few of the children will interview their grandparent by phone and will not be able to see the nonverbal clues of the respondent. With the availability of cameras, with permission the student can also ask to take a photo of the respondent along with the written responses. Again, stress to students that they should always be polite and courteous during the interview. The respondents, their grandparents, need to be thanked for giving their time. Another good idea is to later write a note thanking the grandparents and maybe giving the results of the class's oral history project.

Analysis of the Data

Usually a deadline has to be established by which all questionnaires are due. In this case, the children have to hand in two questionnaires: one from one grandparent (or equivalent elder) and one about their own experience in the first grade. Then comes the process of looking at what the data mean. Some of the questions have elicited objective data. For example, the children, perhaps with the aid of a handheld computer, can count how many of their respondents and the class itself walked to school, how many took a school bus, and the like. They can also find the average number of students in the class and the average age of the respondents. As for location, they may be able to count the number who went to school in their own state and the like. A class could chart the location by placing red dots on a globe or map for the location of the first grade schools. However, other categories are broad, such as lunches and what the schools looked like. These may be put into categories like food categories. There could be a discussion on who provides lunch and where lunch was or is eaten in school. Or they could make a list of which schools were urban, suburban, or rural. If they wish, they could list the types of classroom furniture.

Children have to weigh the information provided in the oral histories. Did the respondent, for example, stretch the truth? Did he or she *really* walk a mile in the snow every day during the winter? Have the respondents, both grandparents and children, painted a rosy picture of the school's appearance? By compiling all oral histories that the class has gathered and comparing them, children should be able to determine those areas on which most respondents agree. If there is a local historical society, its members may be able to confirm or disagree with some parts of the material your class has collected. The local library as well as your school system itself may have photos and yearbooks about how life was in the schools.

A **graphic organizer** could also be used to display the data (Figure 5.2). More columns can be added. When the children see the data, they can compare and contrast the information. Furthermore, the use of a Venn Diagram can be helpful. The left circle could be the students' schools and the right circle the grandparents' schools. In the area of overlap are the similarities between the schools now and the grandparents' schools.

As a result of this experience, Ms. Lee's class can have a valuable picture of what life in school was like in an earlier time period—*history*—and they will have acquired it through active participation in the process of historical research. In this case, students used individual interviews. However, **group interviews** can occur when students ask questions of a guest speaker.

Oral histories can also be found on the Internet. The American Memory Project of the Library of Congress (http://memory.loc.gov/ammem/amhome.html) is the premier site making oral history available to students. Most of the interviews in the oral history archives, however, are in a written format (transcriptions) such as the WPA Slave Narratives compiled from 1936 to 1938 from the memory of ex-slaves still living at that time. Photographs are available. Students can explore social history by reading the interviews of people in the oral history collections. Checking the reading level before embarking on a particular interview for your students is necessary. Sometimes just a quotation from a source will be enough for students instead of trying to read the whole source.

Family History   The same kind of active participation can be achieved through creating family histories. Many teachers use units on immigration, urban life, or other topics that actually depend on students' family histories for part of their content. Data from student family histories in effect are used to support or disprove generalizations.

Encourage students to make their own histories. When and where were they born? Have they seen their birth certificates? What do other family members remember about them as they were growing up? What do they remember about themselves? Are there photographs to analyze? What about written reports? Report cards? Certificates? Have these historical documents been saved along with "artifacts" such as baby shoes? Students can

Figure 5.2   Comparison of Our Class and Grandparents' Schools

	Transportation	Appearance	Subjects taught	Lunch food
Our Class				
Grandparents				

make grade-by-grade time lines and the whole class can correlate them with historical events for each year. High interest will be generated if you ask students to describe the most important event in their lives and why it was important.

Usually, your job in creating family histories is to structure the necessary data. Do you want to record birth dates and addresses of parents and other family members? The various jobs held by all family members, including grandparents? Use prepared worksheets showing the information to be gathered, such as family trees with blanks to be filled in. Determine what data you need and then structure a way to report the data. This helps students complete their tasks and makes analysis of the data simpler.

Do not make family trees a painful experience for students. Some students and parents become upset when they feel they must choose between charting the biological lineage or an adoptive one. Instead, it is probably best to allow options such as including whoever is important to the students instead of demanding that they fill out the blanks for a mother or father who may not be there. Or give students more freedom in telling their personal histories by using essays, family orchards (more than just trees), or by notifying the home in advance, asking parents if the assignment of a family tree presents a difficulty.

Or use just one family member. Ask students to make a connection between one family member and United States history. At once students will respond that their family members are not important people; were just housewives or recent immigrants. Give them hints—note if any family member served in the armed forces and where he or she served, how family members' jobs relate to history, or if any member received social security payments, or were disabled. This exercise may increase the perception that women as well as all individuals are also part of history.

Investigating Puzzling Problems

Younger children could investigate the Rosa Parks "myth." Did she refuse to give up her seat on the bus because she was tired or because she was tired of African Americans being treated unfairly? Third graders read several different books on Rosa Parks to answer this question and were exposed to multiple perspectives.[10] In the same issue of *Social Studies and the Young Learner* referenced in the footnote is "The Mystery of Sam Smiley," in which students play the role of detectives to try to explain Sam's disappearance. In the course of the investigation they create a time line to trace events of Sam's final day and make inferences, look at gaps, and ask further questions, taking the role of historians.

On Your Own **5.2**

Worth the Work?

Go back to the state standard that initiated the oral history project. In what ways did the oral history school project meet the state standards? Any disadvantages to this approach? ●

Studying Local History

Sometimes tied with the unit on studying family history, third-grade children study the local community as historians. Let us look at the appropriate standards/objectives for this type of unit. A teacher might only choose one standard depending on the time available.

[10]Hilary Landorf and Ethan Lowenstein, "The Rosa Parks 'Myth': A Third Grade Historical Investigation," *Social Studies and the Young Learner* 16, no. 3 (January/February 2004): 5–9.

- Identify the culture of the American Indians native to the area
- Find out how the community got its name
- Identify the key individuals and groups who came to the local area
- Trace how institutions developed in the community

Students will have to find facts to answer the standards. A challenge is that most of the sources for local history will not be available at your school library or the Internet. This means that students will have to leave the classrooms for information. In other words, this is a project that the students will have to do as an independent study. Informing parents and guardians is necessary so they know what is expected for their child to be able to finish his or her project. Here are possible sources that students can examine:

Local Sources
- Local library's published account of the city and county
- Local diaries, letters, and genealogies
- Local library's photos, posters, and other media of the city and county
- Local newspapers (e.g., old issues on microfilm/microfiche)
- Local history museum or historical societies
- Business and organizations' records or catalogs
- Local maps and telephone directories
- Longtime residents of the community
- Church records
- Cemetery records
- Death records, wills, and inventories

City and County Records
- Local government records (e.g., at the city hall or online)
- City or county offices, particularly the city clerk or county clerk

State and Federal Records
- Federal census records (e.g., U.S. Federal Records Centers, Genealogical Society of Utah)
- National Archives, including Presidential libraries[11]
- U.S. Geological Survey for maps
- Military records

These sources sound daunting and can easily dishearten and discourage students unless they are given help to succeed. Before students are sent out to the community, discussions probing what students already know about key people and events in the community are essential to establish a common groundwork about the local community. The first step usually includes a time line of the local community, often with major events of U.S. history written above the local time line. Did the Civil War or World War II shape the community? When did transportation systems such as the railroad or an airport come into the community? When were roads paved or freeways constructed? Then try to motivate students by asking

---

[11]For all National Archives research facilities across the nation, presidential libraries, and state archives see *Social Education* 67, no. 7 (2003): 397–400.

them to play the role of detectives to find out particular answers to questions. Read many of the trade books that discuss the fictional or real development of a community.

Before asking how the community got its name, ask students how they got their own first or middle names. An enlarged local map also can lead to a discussion and research on how the names of streets, parks, schools, or buildings in your community were named. How many are named after national figures such as Washington or Kennedy? How many refer to geographic locations or features such as Oak Road, Mountain View, Pine Avenue? How many are names of local historical people? Has the community changed the names of streets or places to reflect changes in what groups now live in the community?

Usually individual students or a pair are assigned to find information about a particular historical person, event, or organization in the community. Here the teacher's general background on the local community has big payoffs. Do not ask children to find out about natural disasters (fires, floods, earthquakes, hurricanes, tornadoes, and the like) unless you know that a natural disaster has occurred in the past. Some promising possibilities for research include tracing the founding of institutions in your community. Consider the many religious institutions, educational institutions (colleges or trade schools), civic groups (the chamber of commerce or clubs), local newspapers, and businesses. To answer questions on the history and impact of the institution, students often will have to interview the present individuals who now are in charge of the particular institution.

For conducting interviews, students should prepare a list of questions to be asked. This list should be approved by the teacher before the time of the interview. Make sure that there is a definite appointment time set up if the students are going to interview someone. This will avoid the disappointment of a respondent being unavailable. Remember that there actually may not be enough room for a whole class to visit some facilities and visits are best done by a pair. Ideally a parent should also be present since safety issues must always be in the minds of teachers. Some students can do a biographical sketch on individual local people, showing their contributions or impact by interviewing and using other sources (see previous section on biographies).

Historical Objects

In addition to learning from oral histories and family and community histories, students can gain insight from seeing **historical objects.** Some teachers start each unit by showing a historical artifact such as a flag or having a hands-on activity. Like the Biography Living Museum project discussed earlier in this chapter, teachers can create a Museum of Family Artifacts. Each student brings from home an artifact (may be an object or a photo) and writes a description of it. Then students explain their family artifacts.[12] Cemeteries, especially the old, historical ones, can be useful in helping students understand the community's roots. Cemeteries can either be an individual project or a whole class experience. If a cemetery is nearby, you and your whole class can walk to it. Provide guidelines about the information the students should gather. A worksheet can be useful. Look at the headstones and monuments of the oldest graves. Ask students to list the name, gender, age, and occupation, if it is given, of the person buried in each grave you look at. Have a designated student write down interesting inscriptions from the headstones. Students may be surprised to note that many more infants and children died in the past than do today. This observation may lead to a discussion of mortality rates and the reasons for changes in them.

---

[12]Judith Y. Singer and Alan J. Singer, "Creating a Museum of Family Artifacts," *Social Studies and the Young Learner* 17, no. 1 (September/October 2004): 5–10.

Other appropriate activities include a walk by a pair of students with a parent through an older section of your community or a field trip to view historical buildings. Students can find out when particular homes or buildings were erected. What is the architectural style of the house or building? What materials were used for the house or building? How were these buildings used in the past and how are they used today? Often larger buildings have gone through many changes in ownership and use. A former residence may now house a business.

A third-grade class studying the community used computer skills when they created a database of historical places and markers in their community. These included historic buildings, the oldest homes, and other items of historic interest. If this does not already exist, any community would appreciate this publication as a guide for community members and visitors to use in visiting historic sites. Another class investigated the forms of transportation used in their community about 100 years ago, including foot, animals, steamboats, and early automobiles. They compared the older forms of transportation with the present-day forms of transportation such as modern automobiles and airplanes.

TECHNOLOGY

Museums

Museums are filled with artifacts and history. If your class is not able to visit a local museum, check if the museum will send out a box of artifacts on loan to you. Or, in some cases, volunteers at the museums may be willing to visit your classroom. Museums also may have published material that is of interest to you. To find a museum either by topic or area, use http://museumspot.com.

Have a Dinner Party Project

Students at the end of a unit ranging from ancient history to the present, including such periods as the Renaissance or the Civil Rights period, can design a pretend dinner party. Often this is a small group project. Here are some of the factors that they can consider.

- Invite a certain number of guests.
- Write a brief biography stating why each guest is important.
- Design on paper an appropriate dinner table or area to eat.
- Write a seating chart for the guests and explain the placement.
- Write a menu of the food and drink that will be served.
- Write some likely dinner conversations.

Fortunately there are no dishes to wash for this high-interest project. In a few cases, classes have actually put on a party with costumes and food.

Thought must be given to assessment both during the unit and for the final projects. Will the class make a local history scrapbook showing the contributions of members of the class? Will the historical biographies be presented to the class? Or maybe a tourist brochure advertising the historical features of the community could be produced. After checking what is available on the Internet, perhaps you would decide that a website would be an appropriate vehicle for designing student work. These concluding activities can really show what students have learned. Visual art presentations may also be in order, such as 2-D (flat) or 3-D (parts of which stick out or stand alone) collages showing how the community looked long ago. A podcast may also be made.

TECHNOLOGY

The Promise of the Internet: Primary and Secondary Sources

TECHNOLOGY

Typically we think of **primary sources** as the written documents created by those who participated in or witnessed the events of the past. However, they can also include films, photographs, drawings, artifacts, and other items. The free "Our Documents" (www .ourdocuments.gov) is an easily available resource from the National Archives that contains 100 milestone documents from U.S. history. The documents include the familiar Declaration of Independence as well as other milestones in U.S. history covering the time period from 1776 to the Voting Rights Act of 1965. Thomas Edison's electric lamp patent and the canceled check for the purchase of Alaska are among the interesting items found here. A teacher sourcebook includes an annotated time line, key themes, guidelines to primary sources, and lesson plans.

When should primary sources be used in the elementary grades? More students are using primary sources for their research topics (dramatic performances, exhibits, documentaries, and research papers) when they participate in **History Day** (www.nhd.org). If students are not participating in the district, state, and national levels for National History Day, the first criterion for selection of a primary source is that it should have high immediate interest for students. For young children this may be a photo or artifact. Normally, this also means that students need the historical context to make sense of the primary source. The value of using primary sources is that it can give a sense of what really has happened to people and offers multiple perspectives of an event or issue. Students can question the accuracy of the document. Keep in mind that reading a written document can cause difficulties for students. Often it is best to only use a sentence or two of the document to analyze. Or with such documents as the Declaration of Independence, students can write the meaning of the document in their own words.

The superb Library of Congress (www.loc.gov) has millions of historical items, including films, manuscripts, prints, photography, maps, and sound recordings. The three major areas within the Library's website are **American Memory** (http://memory.loc.gov) with collections of America's heritage; **Exhibitions** (www.loc.gov/exhibits) showing digital versions of exhibits; and **Global Gateways** (http://international.loc.gov/intdlhome.html) multimedia collections focusing on the Western Hemisphere. A teacher uses search tools to tap these enormous resources. Probably most helpful for the American Memory Collections is "The Learning Page" (www.loc.gov/learn) where you can search for lesson plans, features, or activities or "Today in History Archive" for primary sources.

Consider using computers to ease the reading hurdle, bring history to life, and yet still allow the use of primary sources. Most of the other software on primary sources is produced for the upper grades. This is also true of the many commercial kits, such as those on American Indians, which contain lesson plans, a resource CD, and photographs and primary sources such as posters, charts, letters, telegrams, cartoons, and maps.

Debate the Sources

Helpful for the upper grades are the commercial products that have already assembled several conflicting documents about a historical period such as Shogun Japan or the Vietnam War. They often include visual features and raise questions such as "Was John Brown a Hero?" This allows for multiple perspectives and interpretations of an event. However, Calisphere (www.calisphere.universityofcalifornia.edu), like many other state websites, has thousands of primary source images and documents organized for teachers with source analysis worksheets, lesson plans, and other resource links. With these resources, teachers can have students compare various interpretations or perspectives from the primary sources, the social studies textbook, and historical fiction trade books to discuss what might account for different interpretations of an historical event. This may make students engage in critical thinking as they question where information comes from.

Primary sources can be used in a variety of ways. Based on primary and secondary sources, students can also put a historical person on trial, such as Caesar or Emperor Hirohito of Japan. This is similar to the hero or villain exercise found in Chapter 4 but involves the whole class. The pro group can cite evidence of the person's accomplishments while the anti side focuses on the negatives. Students play the roles of witnesses who can include family members, friends, government officials, or political and military figures. Or depending on the format of the primary source, students can write by answering a letter or commenting on a diary or cartoon. A small group can brainstorm responses to how a problem mentioned in the source may be solved.

Especially helpful for sixth- and seventh-grade teachers are artifacts and artwork when studying topics such as ancient civilizations in China or India. World-famous art museums can be accessed using the Internet; for instance, the Getty (www.getty.edu/education) offers lesson plans (K–12) and the Metropolitan Museum of Art (www.metmuseum.org/collections) displays virtual collections of interesting coins, photographs, jewelry, pottery, religious objects, and architecture, as well as outstanding artwork. Examples of valuable units that can be enriched by museum websites are women artists, arts of India, and American Indian artifacts. Websites such as the British Museum Compass (www.thebritishmuseum.ac.uk/compass) have objects featured such as the Rosetta Stone and the horsemen from the frieze of the Parthenon. Smaller museums may also be helpful, especially if you do not have to sort through thousands of images. The most comprehensive website is the Art History Index of Arts (http://wwar.com/artists). This site has images for 22,000 artists and over 200,000 museum images.

Thus, a combination of primary and secondary sources could add zest to help students learn history. To emphasize, look at the guidelines for using primary sources:

- Is the primary document related to the unit or curriculum?
- Does the primary document have relevance or interest for your students?
- What is usable in the document? Should it be cut?
- Can students take the role of historians to examine the document?

Try to use sources to get students thinking and not just as a way to motivate and engage students.

Artifacts

As you can see from the examples of using oral history and state and community histories, students can learn to use primary and secondary sources even in the elementary school. The nonprinted primary source materials like artifacts and photos can be especially interesting to students. For example, students can examine manual tools from the past such as a meat grinder or a nonelectric iron for pressing clothing. School yearbooks are also interesting (have students note changes in clothing, hairstyles, uniforms of athletic teams and the marching band, and so on).

Students can look at an artifact (real or digital) and describe the material from which it was made. Then ask questions on the uses of the artifact and what it tells us about the technology of the time and the life of the people who made and used it. Is there a similar item used today? Or use the Twenty Questions format asking students to guess the object you are thinking about or have hidden.

Photos

For photos, the following guide can be used so students can analyze photos carefully:

1. I see . . .
2. The photo suggests to me . . .
3. I wonder if . . .

Examining photos should also lead to a consideration of bias since most children do not even think about this when examining photos. Were the factory workers wearing clean clothing? Was that realistic for the time period? These and other questions by both teacher and students should be encouraged.

Learning About Time and Chronology

You already know from the Arizona state standards, other state standards, and the sample unit on "Historical Thinking Grade 1" that one of the essential standards/objectives in teaching history is to help children develop a sense of time and chronology. We all operate in a time–space dimension and constantly view social phenomena in a time–space orientation. We describe events this way: "On January 24, 2004, Opportunity Rover landed on Mars" or "Yesterday I attended the meeting of the local teachers' organization at Washington School." Time and space are interrelated as shown by the two previous sentences. For our purpose, however, let us consider them separately—first time and chronology and then space in Chapter 6 on geography.

How do children acquire the concept of *time?* Most children gradually recognize that events fall into patterns. From their home life, children learn that typically there is a time to get up, to eat, to play, and to sleep. Through the use of language and experience, they begin to distinguish among past, present, and future. In the Western model of time, the present is now, and it becomes past almost as soon as we think about it. The future is what will happen. *Yesterday* and *tomorrow* are early and important concepts.

A more mature time sense, **chronology,** allows us to move away from personal experience and to extend our understanding of time backward and forward. Dates become orientation points, and events fall into chronological order. We start to visualize how events a hundred or even a million years ago are related to the present. This perspective obviously involves more than simply memorizing dates. We begin to understand the concepts of cause and effect and of continuity. Individuals change, families change, social institutions change, nations change; the whole world changes. Most changes occur gradually; a child grows older, and the dynamics of her or his family shift a little each year.

You know that when you are enjoying yourself, time seems to pass quickly. On the other hand, when you are waiting in the post office line or for a medical appointment, time seems to go slowly. We as adults know that these are *subjective* conceptions of time. However, children do not necessarily understand that the differences they experience in time are an illusion. They do not comprehend the uniform motion or velocity of a clock. They believe that the clock works more quickly or slowly depending on how they experience the time. Some children have reported that school time really seems to drag.

To make time *objective,* we organize units of time by a calendar. There are three distinct types of astronomical calendars. The one with which we are most familiar is the *solar* Gregorian calendar, which is used in the United States and also serves as an international standard for civil use. There are also *lunar* calendars, such as the Islamic calendar, and *lunisolar* calendars of which the Hebrew and Chinese calendars are examples. The importance of calendars is that they give shape to the passing of time by endowing certain days with special significance. They are signposts that give meaning to our lives. The calendar marks our birthdays, the holidays we celebrate, our appointments, and our work and vacation schedules. Being able to use a calendar and telling time are essential to functioning in our society.

This section on time and chronology is organized in the order that material is usually taught in the primary grades and then in the upper grades, as shown in the following list.

Learn meaning of day, week, month, year	K–third grade
Use calendar to find dates	K–third grade
Understand today, yesterday, tomorrow	K–third grade
Distinguish between A.M. and P.M.	K–third grade
Learn to tell time by the clock	K–third grade
Understand time lines	First–sixth grades
Learn to translate dates into centuries	Middle school grades
Comprehend the Christian system of chronology—A.D. and B.C.	Middle school grades

However, there are no firm rules about when to introduce time and chronology. In addition, teachers often must reteach to maintain some of these skills.

The 1994 National Center for History in the Schools (see pages 146–147) went beyond these recommendations on what students should be able to do to demonstrate chronological thinking. Examples of student achievement included the following:

In Grades K–2

On listening to or reading historical stories, myths, and narratives, students should be able to reconstruct the basic organization of the narrative: its beginning, middle, and end.

In creating historical narratives of their own, students should be able to establish a chronology for the story, providing a beginning, middle, and end.

In Grades 3–4

Students should be able to group historical events for broadly defined eras in the history of their local community and state.

Students should be able to construct time lines of significant historical developments in their community and state.

In Grades 5–6

Students should be able to construct multiple-tier time lines (important social, economic, and political developments).

Students should be able to interpret data presented in time lines.

The New York State Social Studies Framework asked the following for elementary-level students:

Create personal and family time lines to distinguish near and distant past and identify family origins.

Interpret simple time lines by recognizing correct chronological order of major events such as the Native American settlement of North America, Columbus's voyage of 1492, the American Revolution, and the writing of the Constitution.

Almost all children eventually learn to tell objective time through the use of clocks, calendars, and time-zone maps in their mathematics and science work. Their social studies classes provide the addition of the *cultural* aspect of time. Students learn the distinction between B.C. and A.D. and the meaning of the terms *decade, century,* and *millennium.* Teachers frequently use terms such as *ancient times, the Dark Ages, the colonial period, prehistoric time, several centuries ago,* and *the beginnings of modern times.* We need to make sure all students know what these terms mean.

Time Lines

Like all abstract concepts, time must be personalized and related to a child's experience if it is to be understood. One way to organize and understand time is through a *time line,* one of the simplest ways to organize historical information. Here is how it is done:

1. Draw a line based on a consistent scale of your choosing; each inch might equal ten years, one year, or a hundred years, depending on what information you wish to include. You may also use a program like TimeLiner, software for creating time lines (from Tom Snyder Productions).
2. Write in significant events at the appropriate places. A time line reads from left to right, with earlier events on the left and more recent ones on the right, so children are using a reading convention like that of English with which they are already familiar.

In the primary grades you can also make time lines for a week or longer. Put up the days of the week. Then have children draw pictures or symbols for what happened during the week such as special programs or holidays. Be careful not to have so much clutter that the concept of time is not obvious.

Students can also make time lines of their own lives or those of their families, noting important dates such as marriages, births of children, and graduations. Personal time lines are a good way for students to start the year. Ask them to bring favorite pictures of events in their lives to class and insert these at appropriate places on their own time line. Have students write about why events were significant in their lives. Time lines also can be made for a grandmother's life, a fictional character, a community, events in a story, or happenings on a given school day. Many teachers post several time lines around their classrooms and ask their students to add the dates of the events they study. Symbols (such as a train for the completion of the transcontinental railroad) make the meaning of the dates clearer.

Continue to introduce more and more complex time lines to students throughout the year. Vary the format by moving the earlier events to the top of the page and the more recent ones to the bottom, as shown in Figure 5.3.

Ask your students to identify the year in which frozen orange juice was introduced. Then ask them how many years ago that was, but make sure that they are not simply calculating dates from the time line. Use time line exercises to introduce critical thinking about the data shown. For example, can students hypothesize from looking at the American foods time line what kinds of new foods might be introduced in the coming years? Also, you might ask them to talk about the impact that nationally available frozen orange juice has had on our society in terms of family roles or its impact on the orange industry or on our relationship with Brazil, the world's largest exporter of oranges.

Time lines are excellent aids in teaching American history or the history of specific states, as the periods involved in American history lend themselves to detailed time lines. A time line covering 200 years—or even more than 300 years, beginning in 1620 with the landing of the Pilgrims—enables you to include specifics about transportation, communication,

---

Figure 5.3　　Time Line for American Foods

1900		
	1902	Pepsi-Cola Company is founded.
	1904	Hot dogs are introduced at St. Louis World's Fair.
1910		
1920		
1930	1930	Sliced bread is introduced.
1940		
	1945	Frozen orange juice is introduced.
	1948	McDonald's hamburgers are introduced.
1950		
	1956	Colonel Harlan Sanders franchises his method of frying chicken.
1960		

and the development of industry as well as important dates in political history. Ask students to find or draw pictures of citizens in typical dress for each century or half-century, and paste them to the appropriate parts of the time line. Many students can calculate how many years ago the Pilgrims landed but have no real understanding of what life was like then or how long ago it was relative to the Civil War or the invention of the airplane. Why, they may ask, was setting out for the New World so frightening? After all, we now travel back and forth to and from Europe all the time. A time line can help them understand.

After using simple time lines, students may be more ready to tackle concepts such as *century*. A new century begins every one hundred years. In the year 2001, a new century began. Provide your students with a Western history chronology by centuries, such as the following:

Historical Events Classified by Century

1700	American Revolution
	French Revolution
1800	Industrial Revolution spreads
1900	World Wars I and II
	Computers
	Space exploration
2000	

Ask students to place specific events within the centuries. You can give them a random list of dates, including times such as 1776 (Thomas Jefferson writes the Declaration of Independence) or 1861 (U.S. Civil War begins) or 1911 (Mexican Revolution). Don't use the dates of an individual's life, since these often overlap century boundaries. Now ask students what events happened in each century. In upper grades, you might ask whether two historical figures might have talked to each other. Students should get a sense that James Madison could (and did) talk to Thomas Jefferson but could not have spoken to Woodrow Wilson or Franklin Roosevelt.

When they understand centuries, students may be ready to tackle the difficult concept of A.D. and B.C. in the Gregorian (Christian) calendar and the contemporary secular designation for these same dates, B.C.E. (Before the Common Era) and C.E. (in the Common Era). Students may also see these abbreviations written as AD, BC, BCE, and CE without periods or space between the letters. They may see AD put before the year, as in AD 1492. In addition, students might encounter the use of B.P. (before the present) rather than B.C. (before Christ) when they study the beginnings of early society. B.P. is used by archaeologists and paleontologists when referring to dates earlier than 1000 B.C. The P is usually defined at 1950 A.D. The reason for this is that the techniques used to date ancient objects and fossils are based on analyzing substances found in those objects today. These scientists feel that they risk introducing errors if they try to conform to B.C. terminology.

On Your Own **5.3**

Time Confusion

Do you recall any confusion you had in your youth about time concepts? Do you think that elementary teachers should use terms such as *19th century* and *20th century* while teaching? Or do you think it is better to say that in the 1800s the railroad was invented or in the 1900s the airplane was invented? ●

Summary

*D*espite controversies, more time of the elementary social studies program, including primary grades, will be spent teaching history. Historical understandings and historical thinking skills can be taught in creative ways by using oral history, drama, family history, community or local history, children's trade books and magazines, biographies, historical objects, photos, and primary and secondary sources. Using these varied approaches can result in increased interest in and valuing of history. The Internet with its many resources can help make history alive.

Suggested Readings and Websites

Bradley Commission on History in Schools. *Building a History Curriculum: Guidelines for Teaching History in Schools.* Washington, DC: Educational Excellence Network, 1988.

Suggestions of historians for teaching history.

Brophy, Jere, and Bruce A. VanSledright. *Teaching and Learning History in Elementary Schools.* New York: Teachers College Press, 1997.

The authors synthesize the most current research on children's historical learning and thinking.

Cheney, Lynne V., and Albert Shanker. "Mutual Suspicions." *The New Republic* 212, no. 6 (February 6, 1995): 4.

Critics of the 1994 history standards.

Edinger, Monica. *Seeking History: Teaching with Primary Sources in Grades 4–6.* Westport, CT: Heinemann, 2000.

Ideas on how to use primary sources.

Haas, Mary E., and Margaret A. Laughlin, eds. *Meeting the Standards: Social Studies Readings for K–6 Educators.* National Council for the Social Studies, 1997.

For the history standards, seven articles ranging from using customized photographs to the value of children's homes and neighborhoods. For the geography standards, seven articles ranging from environmental education to creating an outdoor learning laboratory, and for the economics standards, another seven articles ranging from the cupcake factory to little tykes become big tycoons. The best single source of journal articles for help in meeting the standards.

Hickey, Gail. *Bringing History Home: Local and Family History Projects for Grades K–6.* Boston: Allyn & Bacon, 1999.

History projects for elementary students.

Jorgensen, Karen L. *History Workshop: Reconstructing the Past with Elementary Students.* Portsmouth, NH: Heinemann, 1993.

Children create historical meaning as they interact with others.

Lamme, Linda Leonard. "Stories from Our Past: Making History Come Alive for Children." *Social Education* (March 1994): 159–164.

Uses familiar, quality children's trade books to demonstrate how to lead young children to discover links between the books and their own lives.

Levstik, Linda S., and Keith C. Barton. *Doing History: Investigating with Children in Elementary and Middle School,* 3rd ed. Mahwah, NJ: Lawrence Erlbaum, 2005.

Case studies of children engaging in authentic historical investigations.

Nash, Gary B., and Ross E. Dunn. "History Standards and Culture Wars." *Social Education* 59, no. 1 (1995): 57.

Codirector and coordinating editor for the world history standards answer critics.

National Center for History in the Schools. *National Standards for History: Basic Edition.* Los Angeles: University of California, 1996.

Revised report on history standards.

Parker, Walter C. *Renewal in the Social Studies.* Washington, DC: Association for Supervision and Curriculum Development, 1991.

Outlines directions in curriculum development and the need for it.

Provenzo, Eugene, Jr., and Asterie Baker Provenzo. *Pursuing the Past: Oral History, Photographs, Family History, Cemeteries.* Menlo Park, CA: Addison-Wesley, 1984.

Good for past oral history.

Ravitch, Diane, and Chester Finn, Jr. *What Do Our 17-Year-Olds Know? A Report on the First National Assessment of History and Literature.* New York: Harper and Row, 1987.

A critical report on the poor achievement of American students in history.

VanSledright, Bruce. *In Search of America's Past: Learning to Read History in Elementary School.* New York: Teachers College Press, 2002.

One helpful aspect of this book is how the author taught a fifth-grade class historical thinking.

Winston, Linda. *Keepsakes: Using Family Stories in Elementary Classrooms.* Westport, CT: Heinemann, 1997.

Each chapter describes how family stories can enhance curriculum.

Websites

American Memory
memory.loc.gov

Over 7 million digital items.

America's Story from America's Library
www.americaslibrary.gov

Target audience is the sixth-grade student. However, children as young as the second grade would enjoy using the site with a parent's or teacher's help.

Busy Teacher's Web site
www.ceismc.gatech.edu/busyt

Suggestions for K–12 history.

Colonial Williamsburg
www.history.org

Life in colonial times with a virtual tour of Colonial Williamsburg.

History Matters
http://historymatters.gmu.edu

Online course for high school students with resources helpful for teachers.

HistoryWired
historywired.si.edu/index.htm

Backstage tour of over 450 objects at the National Museum of American History.

Lesson Plans and Resources for Social Studies Teachers
www.csun.edu/~hcedu013

Lesson plans and resources for social studies teachers.

Library of Congress Online—Getting Started
http://memory.loc.gov/learn/start/index.html

Orientation for users of the Learning Page and the American Memory collections.

National Archives Digital Classroom
www.archives.gov/digital_classroom

One of the areas of the National Archives and Records Administration.

SIRIS (Smithsonian Institute Research Information System)
http://www.siris.si.edu

From the Smithsonian, excellent primary sources including photos and art.

Teaching with Historic Places
www.cr.nps.gov/nr/twhp

National Park interpreters have lesson plans by location, theme, and time period.

Note: Use websites of local government agencies, such as your city hall, to gain information about your local government.

PEARSON myeducationlab
Where the Classroom Comes to Life

VIDEO HOMEWORK EXERCISE

Debate

Go to MyEducationLab, select the topic **History**, and watch the video entitled "Debate."

In this video, fifth-grade students prepare for a debate on U.S. expansion in the early 1900s by giving different points of view on having a dress code.

CHAPTER 6

Teaching Geography

In this chapter we discuss the teaching of geography, a key discipline of the social studies. Special emphasis is placed on strategies and materials that help students interpret geography.

- Are Students and Adults Literate in Geography?
- Beyond State Capitals: Making Geography Engaging
- Teaching Map and Globe Skills

What makes a field trip successful?

Are Students and Adults Literate in Geography?

Importance of Geography

$\mathcal{S}$ince we all occupy space at every given moment, it is easy to forget the influence of geography on our daily lives. Perhaps we only become conscious about space when we feel crowded in an elevator or on public transportation. We then perceive an invasion of "our" space and wish we were in the wide open spaces without fences. A sudden realization of geography and maps may also occur when we move out of our traditional routines. We need better directions on how to get to a new place: a friend's house, the school district office, or a new pizza parlor. Furthermore, we forget that world geography is frequently featured on TV news reports and in the newspapers. Check how often the daily news has a geography focus. You often hear of a "conflict at . . ." or a "natural disaster at. . . ." One recommendation is for families to watch the news with a globe or atlas handy so children (and adults) know where the news is taking place. The world is increasingly global. Terrorism, global climate change, and air pollution show that we must often look beyond our national borders to solve problems. This means adults need geographic literacy along with positive attitudes toward basic geographic concepts and skills.

Geography is a field of study to help us understand people, places, and environment, and how they affect each other. Geographers ask questions about the interaction of humans and their environment. Geographers look at the world in terms of space or location. Whereas history has the time dimension, geography has the space dimension. All social phenomena exist in both time and space.

There is always a spatial content to local, national, and global issues as reported in the media. These issues are interrelated. What happens halfway around the world can affect other people and other nations. One cynic said it takes wars to make U.S. citizens learn some geography. In addition to wars however, present-day problems ranging from global epidemics to outsourcing all have a geographic dimension.

Geography Standards

Responding to the criticism that most people in the United States were poorly educated in geography, the Geography Education Standards Project published its eighteen national K–12 geography standards. These standards outline what students should know and be able to do in geography. In addition, their publication *Geography for Life: National Geography Standards 1994* emphasized the value and importance of geography for all citizens throughout their lives.[1] The groups involved in developing these standards were the American Geographical Society, Association of American Geographers, National Council for Geographic Education, and the National Geographic Society. These eighteen standards were then organized into six clusters as shown in Table 6.1 (www.nationalgeographic .com/education/xpeditions/standards/matric.html).

These geography standards reflected the changes that have occurred in geography and map making. Geographers are now concentrating more of their research on the interaction of people and environment. In fact, some geographers think of their discipline now as being environmental studies. They examine the rapid human transformation of the globe as it

---

[1]Geography Education Standards Project, *Geography for Life: National Geography Standards 1994* (Washington, DC: National Geographic Society, 1994).

Table 6.1	The Geographically Informed Person Knows and Understands . . .

1. The world in spatial terms (location)
2. Places and regions (particular places and the interpretations of regions)
3. Physical systems (processes that shape and change the Earth)
4. Human systems (people)
5. Environment and society (interaction of both)
6. Uses of geography

Source: Geography for Life: National Geography Standard, 1994.

increasingly is becoming more urban. As the physical environment has changed, air and water pollution, as well as solid waste and hazardous materials management, have become serious problems. Cartography is being transformed by dramatic technological innovations as maps are prepared directly from mosaics of satellite photography.

In 2000 and 2001, the National Geographic Society outlined the scope and sequence of geography education in *Path toward World Literacy: A Scope and Sequence in Geographic Education K–12* and *Path toward World Literacy: A Standards-Based Guide to K–12 Geography*.[2] Their guides followed what was typically taught on the elementary school level and emphasized the following:

- K–1   Personal/local geography
- 2–3   Local/state geography
- 4–5   State/U.S. geography
- 6–8   U.S./world geography

Sample learning exercises are given for each standard for the various grade levels. See the lesson plan "Geography Grades 2–3," which examines the environment and society standard. Note carefully that this lesson plan on environment is so broad that it could be used at all grade levels and also in science classes. There is a close relationship between environmental studies and science.

HNOLOGY

The National Geographic Society (www.nationalgeographic.com) has established its EDNet (www.ngsednet.org) as a one-stop online hub for education resources, discussion, news, and their monthly e-mail newsletter. In addition, My Wonderful World (www.mywonderfulworld.org) has geographic activities and resources. Also you may wish to contact your state/regional Geography Alliance for further information and resources. For geography for primary grades with a high visual content, try National Geographic Kids site (http://nationalgeographic.com/portal/site/Kids) for geography games, activities, videos, and stories. Sorted out for all grade levels, National Geographic Xpeditions (www.nationalgeographic.com/xpeditions/lessons) is excellent.

---

[2]National Geographic Society, *Path toward World Literacy: A Scope and Sequence in Geographic Education K–12* (Washington, DC: National Geographic Society, 2000); National Geographic Society, *Path toward World Literacy: A Standards-Based Guide to K–12 Geography* (Washington, DC, National Geographic Society, 2001).

LESSON PLAN

Geography Grades 2–3

Content Focus: Physical Environment Influences Human Activities

Objective: Describe the ways in which people depend on the physical environment.

Activities

- Make a list of things that people need, want, and obtain from the physical environment (e.g., food, clean air, water, and mineral resources) and identify those that are obtained from the physical environment in the students' community, region, state, and from other countries.
- Write a paragraph comparing how people in the local community and people elsewhere depend on the physical environment.

Content Focus: Environmental Issues (e.g., Solid Waste, Water Quality)

Objective: Assess the impact of human activities on the physical environment.

Activity

- Identify examples in the local community of ways in which the physical environment is stressed by human activities.

Source: Path toward World Literacy: A Standards-Based Guide to K–12 Geography, pp. 13–14.

State Standards

Almost every state has developed, and in many cases has revised, its geography standards that were first published in the 1990s. Some of the states retained more of the following geography "five themes" from 1984 than the 1994 standards of the National Geographic Society.

- **Location** (position on earth's surface)
- **Place** (physical and human characteristics)
- **Human/environment interaction** (relationships within places)
- **Movement** (humans interacting on earth)
- **Regions** (how they form and change)

There is some overlap between the two sets of standards (see for example the lesson plan "Using Standards to Teach Regions"). States found the 1994 standards with their emphasis on physical geography to be more complex. In general, borrowing from the 1994 and the older 1984 geography standards, the state standards in geography emphasized location and maps in the primary grades. In addition, how people interact and modify their environment was stressed at all grade levels. Then, in the fourth grade, the physical and human features of the given state and how people have interacted with the natural environment in the state's growth was given attention. The same pattern of interaction of environment and people

LESSON PLAN

Using Standards to Teach Regions

The regions of the United States have been a traditional geography topic for the fourth grade. Let us briefly explore how the geography standards can provide help in teaching this topic. The United States is typically divided into six regions—Northeast, Southeast, Midwest, Southwest, Rocky Mountains, and Pacific—classifications that can be used in the classroom.

Start this unit or lesson with any region of the United States other than the students' own region. Ask if they have lived or visited in the region. What images do they have of the region? What do they want to find out more about in this particular region?

Give each student a blank outline map of the United States and ask them to identify this one region on their maps. You can then present data about the region—using videos, textbooks, pictures, trade books, and so on. Have students make inferences from these materials by asking questions: Could this scene take place elsewhere in the United States? What appear to be the distinctive physical and human characteristics of the region? Have them sketch the major landforms and states of the region on their blank maps and then ask them to list evidence of what people have done to change and modify the physical environment. You can conclude by asking students to compare their original images of the region with what they now know. Was there misinformation before?

You could repeat this exercise for another region. Students can work individually or in groups.

then shifted to the regions of the United States and other places in the world. At all times students were to interpret maps and use other geographic tools.

Concepts

What commonly used concepts are embedded into the five geography themes? Let us look at Table 6.2. Notice that many of the concepts listed such as needs and wants could easily be found in a list of concepts from economics or other social sciences. Yet needs and wants

Table 6.2   Concepts Related to the Five Themes of Geography

Location	Place	Relationships	Movement	Region
Map	Topography	Ecology	Migration	Urban
Globe	Climate	Environment	Transportation	Rural
Distance	Population	Technology	Needs	Community
Absolute—streets, latitude, longitude	Human elements—who lives there	Pollution—how do we affect the environment	Wants—why we move	Land usage—what makes the area unique

are important in explaining the movement of people. Because geography is concerned with the interaction of humans and their environment, geography, along with specific unique concepts like *map* and *globe,* also is related to the content taught in history and the other social sciences. This connection allows geography to be integrated into the social studies curriculum.

Locating Geography in the K–8 Curriculum

Geography as a separate subject has almost completely disappeared from the elementary and middle school. Furthermore, most teachers themselves have had few or no courses in geography. Being practical, this means that the geography standards will have to be integrated across the curriculum, especially with history, in grades 4 through 8. In effect, geography has a supporting role to history. This approach can make for a rich history but may not do full justice to the unique perspective of geographers.

Almost everyone says that you really cannot teach good history without geography. Typically, this is interpreted as looking at maps to understand "where" historical events occurred. This is a good start and is always necessary. Examining the significance of the numerous maps found in the students' textbooks reminds everyone not to just pass over maps.

Geography is extremely important in understanding the history of the United States as well as other parts of the world. Geography does make a difference. Thus, the typical fifth-grade social studies U.S. history curriculum has the following geographic influences: the encounter of native populations, explorers, and conquerors with the physical geography and resources of North America; the location and boundaries of the colonial period; the geographic aspects of the Revolutionary War; regional differences; and geographic influences on the early Industrial Revolution. These are just a few of the content areas in which geography could be easily incorporated in the teaching of U.S. history. It is also important that geography, with a contemporary focus, be used when there are discussions of environmental problems ranging from oil spills to natural disasters. Typically, however, in the sixth grade attention to geographic features in the development of ancient civilizations is noted and then more or less ignored for the rest of the units in the sixth and seventh grades.

Yet a geographic background and concepts are necessary to understand the history of different groups at different time periods. For example, the three great American civilizations—the Mayan, the Aztec, and the Incan—each occupied a vastly different environmental setting. The Mayans first occupied the lowland tropical forests of the Yucatan Peninsula before shifting to a drier climate in the north and the highlands of the interior. The Aztec was centered in the Valley of Mexico, 30 to 40 miles wide and about 8,000 feet above sea level and their empire supported millions of people. The Incan civilization was centered on high intermontane valleys (high plains) with the capital city Cuzco at an elevation of 11,000 feet. The people of each of these three civilizations with different environments were successful in organizing their economies, trade, and development of urban societies.

The K–4 social studies curriculum easily lends itself to geography inclusion as children move along the expanding horizon curriculum from self, family, communities, cities, and states. The children's lives are rooted in a particular place that has distinctive human and physical characteristics. Their physical environment is being shaped by human activities in their community as well as afar. Thus, geography can fit in naturally in social studies curriculum in grades K through 4.

Using Multiple Geography Standards

Although each state standard is typically listed separately, it is often possible to combine geography standards as shown in the example of South Africa.

Using Multiple Standards

1. *The World in Spatial Terms.* What images or mental maps do you have of South Africa? Where is South Africa located? Is it closer to Brazil or India?
2. *Places and Regions.* What are the physical characteristics of South Africa? How is South Africa different from or similar to your community?
3. *Physical Systems.* What are the different climates of South Africa? How has mining changed the physical environment of South Africa?
4. *Human Systems.* Where do most people live in South Africa? How do people earn their living in South Africa?
5. *Environment and Society.* How have the people of South Africa changed their environment? What are South Africa's nonrenewable resources?
6. *The Uses of Geography.* How is South Africa changing? Do you think South Africa will have more conflicts or fewer conflicts with its neighbors?

You might ask: Where are map skills? A later section in this chapter provides more detail on teaching the interpretation and making of maps. But note that a critical concern about how geography is taught is that too often *only* map skills are stressed rather than all the major six elements of Table 6.1. Geographers ask three important questions:

- Where is it?
- Why is it there?
- What are the consequences of its being there?

Students may learn the topography of their state or nation but pay little attention to how that topography has been modified or how people have adapted to natural settings. In studying Brazil, for instance, students often learn that Brazil has a large forest area and that its major cities are located on the coast but not that Brasilia, its capital, was carved from a high plateau once thought uninhabitable, or that the migration of Japanese immigrants to Brazil has changed the character of the nation.

A second criticism of how geography is taught is that thinking skills are underemphasized and low-level memorization is overemphasized. Geographers strongly emphasize geography skills to try to correct this weakness. It is, thus, no longer enough to ask students where the Nile River is; they should also know the consequences of its being where it is and its connections to other parts of the world. Rather than having students simply locate cities on a map, have them find common elements about the locations. They may be surprised to note that some 90 percent of all major cities are located near waterways. For those that are not, such as Madrid or Phoenix, ask students to hypothesize *why* not. Do politics and technology influence the location of cities? Are newer cities more or less likely to be located near waterways? Why? Also, rather than having students learn only about the climate of their own region, have them compare it with other climates. How does climate influence the way we live? The way we dress?

NAEP 2001 Geography Results

Some optimism about geographic literacy was shown by NAEP's geography results. The average scores of fourth and eighth grade students improved in 2001 compared to those in 1994 when the first standards were published. In particular, lower-performing students made noticeable gains. However, the gap, indicated in both 1994 and 2001, continued between male students' higher scores and female students' lower scores. In addition, the gap between achievement of whites and Asian/Pacific Islanders compared to Hispanics and African Americans remained.[3]

You may be interested in how geography was tested by NAEP. In Figure 6.1, we see a sample fourth-grade question assessing students' understanding of how geography plays a role in conflict between nations. Only about one-third of fourth graders marked the correct response. Apparently many students did not see or understand that oil resources on the map were divided between two nations, A and D. Why do you think this question was difficult? Is the map too cluttered for fourth graders? Too much information on a map can hinder understanding.

[3]A. R. Weiss, A. D. Lutkus, B. S. Hildebrant, and M. S. Johnson, *The Nation's Report Card: Geography, 2001* (Washington, DC: U.S. Department of Education, Office of Research and Improvement, National Center for Education Statistics, NCES 2002–484, 2002).

Figure 6.1   Sample Geography Question

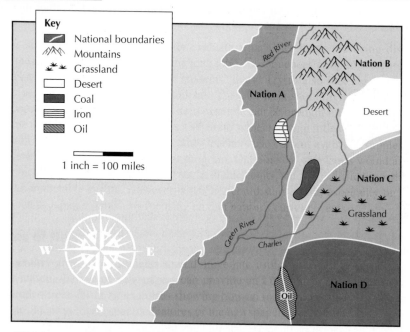

Which two nations are most likely to have a conflict over mineral resources?

(A) Nation A and Nation B   (B) Nation C and Nation D

(C) Nation A and Nation D   (D) Nation A and Nation C

In two response-type questions, fourth graders were asked the following after being shown a map outlining all of the states and provinces of the United States and Canada. Canada was included because some students took the test in Alaska. The states and provinces were outlined but none of the names were labeled.

Write down the name of the state or district where you live.

I live in _____.

Directly on the map, draw an "X" on the state or district where you live.

About two-thirds, 66 percent, of all fourth graders were able both to name the state they lived in and to identify it correctly on a blank map. One wonders about the other one-third who could not respond accurately to these two questions. It is true that students in Rhode Island or Washington, DC, had a more difficult time in responding simply because of the small size of their state or district. However, because most fourth graders are studying their states or regions, they could be expected to could locate their own states. Or is this not an authentic question? How often do we as adults actually use a blank outline map? Almost every map we use labels the states and Washington, DC. This illustrates the difficulties in interpreting or evaluating geography test results.

2006 National Geographic Literacy Study

Let us examine what young American adults age 18 to 24 knew about geographic concepts and information. You may be in this age group and the results may reflect what your peer group knows about geography. The 2006 National Geographic study concluded from the survey that far too many young adults in the United States are unprepared for an increasingly global future.

Headlines about this particular survey announced that 63 percent of young adults could not find Iraq on a map of the Middle East, although there has been daily media coverage since the U.S. invasion in March 2003. With regard to the Middle East, six in ten could not find Saudi Arabia on the map and 75 percent either Iran or Israel. On a map of Asia, 88 percent of young adults could not find Afghanistan and many did not know that Sudan and Rwanda are in Africa. In fact, 20 percent placed Sudan in Asia and 10 percent put it in Europe. Perhaps because it is a large nation, 69 percent of young adult Americans could find China on a map. However, they had a number of misconceptions about China—its population, language, and believing that China, not the United States, is the world's largest exporter in dollar value.

Similar to the fourth graders, one method used for assessing geographic knowledge was for the young adults to match names of nations with corresponding locations on blank outline maps—three international and one of the continental United States. Again, there are limitations to using this artificial format since we seldom encounter maps without the names of countries or important places. There also might be bias in the interpretations of the results since the National Geographic Society certainly wants more attention devoted to improving geographic education.

The good news was that over 66 percent of the young adult respondents were able to effectively use a map when told they would need to evacuate in advance of an oncoming hurricane. A majority can say on which continents different countries are located and where significant natural landmarks are found as well as recalling timely facts. Among the factors correlated with better performance were higher education, getting news online,

| **Figure 6.2** | Geographic Online Quizzes for Students |

My Wonderful World
www.mywonderfulworld.org
Organized by The National Geographic Society and sponsored by educational organizations, this site has online quizzes and games along with information for parents, teachers, and students.

National Geographic Society
www.nationalgeographic.com/geobee
Has both lower- and higher-level questions on geography. New questions each day.

Houghton Mifflin Geonet
www.eduplace.com/geonet
Students can choose to take the quiz on the United States or the world map as well as select the question category. The categories test student knowledge of a variety of geographic knowledge.

Funbrain
www.funbrain.com/where
Emphasis only on the basic skill of location. Students pick maps (Africa, Asia, etc.) and difficulty level such as capitals of states or nations.

Test Your Geography Knowledge
www.lizardpoint.com/fun/quiz
Emphasis on basic skill of location. Students choose a map.

On Your Own **6.1**

Teaching Your Geography State Standards

Look at your state's geography standards. How much attention do you think you will give to teaching geography? Do you think you will need help in teaching geography? ●

using two media sources rather than one, being male, and having experience with international travel.

However, on the whole, the National Geographic Study presents a dismal picture about young American adults' geographic knowledge. You can go online to take the test yourself (www.nationalgeographic.com/roper 2006) or to get a copy of the full report. Your brighter students could also take the test and actually might feel smug when they compare their scores to other young adults. To help your student practice location skills as well as higher level skills, you may want to use the various online quizzes (Figure 6.2, Geographic Online Quizzes for students).

Beyond State Capitals: Making Geography Engaging

Can we really move geography away from factual memorization of the state capitals? True, students should know the names and locations of their own state capitals. But how often do adults need to know the state capital of North Dakota or Illinois? When necessary, how to find the state capital on the map is an important skill. A more engaging activity for the fourth-grade students studying their state history is to find out why their state chose its state capital. In many cases, cities like New York City, Chicago, Los Angeles, Dallas, and the like are now far more powerful than the official capitals in those states. What geographic factors influenced the early decision on where to locate the state capital? What geographic factors have contributed to the formation of the larger cities in these states?

Start with the Students

Although there is no single best way to teach either geography or history, try to design learning experiences built on your students' own background. Yet it is important to stress the major concepts or elements of geography in the process. Sometimes the misconceptions that students have can be jumping off points for geography. Questions such as "Can we take a drive to Europe?"; "Can we drive this afternoon to Disneyland?" (located 1,000 miles away); "Will global warming make our neighborhood a desert next year?" can introduce opportunities for teaching geography.

Where Born: Human Migration   Ask your students to name or to find out where they were born. Plot the locations on a map. Using the concept of **migration,** check if any of the students have moved from a different community, state, or nation since they were born. Chart the results. Ask and list the reasons for the move. What form of transportation was used to move to the present community? You may use the accompanying chart.

My Family's Migration to _____

Date Arrived	From	Reasons for Migration

Conduct a class discussion explaining the push–pull factors that promote migration. *Push factors* are those that help convince people to leave an area whereas *pull factors* are those that attract people to a new area. For example, push factors may include a lack of jobs in the current community and pull factors may include the availability of jobs and educational opportunities or the prospects for a higher standard of living.

Ask students how they felt about moving. What were the good things about it? What were things that they did not like?

School's Location: Land Usage and Place   Tell your students that **land usage** refers to the way land is being used, including housing (single-family housing and apartment buildings), commercial/industrial, government service, agriculture, and public use. Take a tour around the school and its associated grounds. Locate, identify, and list the spatial features (playground, office, cafeteria, and so on) on a prepared base map. Ask students what

LESSON PLAN

Theme of Place

Standard: Identify the characteristics of your school and neighborhood.

Geography Activities Related to Your School

1. Where is your school located? (street intersections, relation to other places)
2. Make your school's map orientated toward the north.
3. Describe the human elements of your school. Who is there? Ages? Ethnic/racial groups?
4. Is your school's student population growing? Declining? Remaining about the same? Name some effects of the current size of the student population.
5. Should any features of the school be changed? How could this be accomplished?

Geography Activities Related to the Local Neighborhood around the School

1. List three attractive features of your school's neighborhood.
2. What kind of buildings are around the school?
3. Is transportation convenient to your school?
4. Describe the people of your local neighborhood around the school. Ethnic/racial groups? Languages spoken?
5. Do a neighborhood survey to find out if the neighbors have any complaints about the school.
6. Compare the living conditions in your local neighborhood with cultures that have already been studied such as ancient China, medieval Japan, or Philadelphia during the Constitutional Convention.

symbols should be used to identify and mark the special features of the school. See the lesson plan on "Theme of Place."

Ask why the school is located where it is. How much space is needed for your school? Why is a school not normally erected in the central business section? Compare the amount of space necessary for a school to that of an average home in the neighborhood. Was the school built before parents drove their child to school or before there was school bus transportation? Are there presently difficulties as students arrive and depart from school? Do teachers, the school staff, and visitors have adequate parking spaces? Are there temporary portables on the school grounds? What does this suggest about the needs of the school grounds? One extension to this study of location is the study of transportation systems that are available for going to school as well as other places. Check on what the physical environment of the land was before the school was built. What did it look like? Summarize on a chart the factors to consider in the location of the school.

TECHNOLOGY

Another extension to this study is to map the local neighborhood. Make a large map (an old shower curtain sometimes works well or an overhead transparency may be used) showing the school and the location of the children's homes. Another alternative is to enlarge an existing map with a photocopier. Remember that an existing map may have too much clutter. Just copying the main streets may give enough detail yet not be overwhelming. If you are concerned about student privacy or think students might be embarrassed

Table 6.3	What Can You Find in the Mall

(Use tally marks to count)

bakery	grocery store
bank	library
bookstore	movie theater
church	park
coffee shop	police station
doctor or dentist	restaurant
fire station	school (any type, including yoga, art instruction, etc.)
florist	veterinarian
gas station	video rental

Optional: furniture, lawyer, clothing, shoes, real estate agency, post office, or others

After your tally, what were you surprised to find?

What was missing?

about where they live, mark just the school's boundaries. Then mark locations for imaginary families and ask which of these would have to walk the farthest and what routes they would use. Another alternative includes using three-dimensional figures of precut house shapes for students to lay out their homes' locations on a large local map. Students may also use Google Maps (http://maps.google.com), and type in their home or school address. Students then can see how their home fits into the larger world. From one's address, you can also get directions to another place.

Neighborhood Services: Land Usage, Location, Human/Environmental Interaction
Why is the police station located where it is? What stores are on Main Street or in the shopping mall? Using geographic concepts such as location, place, and human/environment interaction, have students investigate and map the local shopping center, Main Street, or neighborhood, classifying the types of stores and shops there (Table 6.3). Note the presence of infrastructure elements such as streets, sidewalks, streetlights, and the like. Make a map of the area.

Students can also map the interior of a supermarket, indicating aisles, major food categories, and other sections. A "Supermarket Rubric" that can be used is shown in Table 6.4. After making a map of the layout of the supermarket, students can discuss why certain items are located where they are. Is it just for the convenience of the buyers? What areas of the store are most likely to be used by customers? An extension for this activity is to compare the layout of the local supermarket with a "big box" store that also sells groceries and other similar items. Students can also do a "Find the Ethnicities through the Food Aisles." This investigation may help to identify what different ethnic groups live in the community as well as the increasing number of "new" foods that are appearing in American diets due to more global imports.

Students can investigate the many items in the supermarket that come from other parts of the world or states and plot information about them on a map. They may take just one or

Table 6.4	Supermarket Rubric

The supermarket includes:

- produce, dairy, frozen food, bread, canned goods, and other sections
- checkout area
- loading dock or delivery area
- cold storage areas
- meat processing/packaging area
- manager's office
- restroom
- grocery cart area
- parking lot, including handicapped parking
- bakery, deli, flowers, other optional areas
- paper goods

two categories such as fruits and vegetables. Why are more fresh fruits now available during the winter season? How limited would your diet be if the only foods available were grown and processed in your own state? Or should your food be locally grown? Using a radius of 150 miles, what foods would be available? Not available? A web site called http://eatlocalchallenge.com uses a stricter "100-mile diet."

Candy Bars to Pizza Toppings: Where Do They Come From?   Many classes have investigated where the ingredients of many popular foods come from. Using a candy bar as an example, students look at the ingredients listed on the paper wrapper. Often small groups then take on the task of locating where one ingredient is grown, how it is transported, and how the product is ultimately manufactured. Students can post on maps where the ingredients (beans, sugar, etc.) come from with different colors, using, for example, brown sticky notes for cocoa beans. Students can also check about the history of a particular ingredient such as sugar or other sweeteners.

Or various pizza toppings could be a topic, including how cheese is made. Students can also make tables showing the workers involved in the process and the necessary capital (factories, equipment, computers, and so on) needed to produce the final product or goods. Besides food, students can also investigate what is needed to make a clothing item or even a small item such as a pencil or chewing gum.

Trade Books

Trade books can take your class to faraway places—to distant continents with elephants or rainforests. Books can vividly tell about other cultural perspectives. Some classics are Heidi in Switzerland, Ping in China, and Madeline in France; make sure to remind students that these particular stories were written many years ago and changes have occurred in these countries. Some books also show the perspective of a mouse, a bird, or an armadillo as the animals move around. As you read to your class or as students read books, opportunities for examining geographic concepts often arise. Try asking geography questions.

Where did the story take place? How did the environment in the story affect people? How did people affect the environment (buildings and the like)?

Other trade books such as *Me on the Map* by Joan Sweeney (Crown Publishers, 1996) focus on geography concepts. Here a young child creates a drawing of her bedroom and then moves on to her home, street, state, country, and the planet. Young children may enjoy making a "My Map Book." This can include space for a drawing/map of My House and a place for them to write their address (My Street). For My City, My State, My Country, and My Continent, the teacher can supply an outline map for each child's map book.

Controversial Issues

Beyond memorization of facts, a definite plus for geography is that its knowledge and tools can help citizens in deciding public issues. For example, floods and fires are regularly reported in the media. Often there are photos of government officials like the governor or even the president visiting the disaster area to comfort those who suffered loss. After the disaster, the individuals who have experienced losses usually want to move back to their old homes as soon as possible. One question is whether people should be allowed to move back to a disaster area where there is a high probability of another flood or where the local fire department cannot easily get to isolated exurbs, canyons, or rural areas. Geographic information of the area certainly can help in making these decisions.

Another issue is the problem of water. There is grave concern that some parts of the United States may face a shortage of fresh water in the future. Given projections of increased population, the supply of water may not be adequate in future years. Drought may become more common. Options range from doing more to clean up the pollution of water to denying water for irrigation to crops like rice and cotton. These crops could be grown in other parts of the country or other nations. Geographic factors need to be included in considering the potential water shortage.

The overuse of unique popular areas such as Yosemite National Park, known for its granite peaks and majestic views, is another issue to consider. Each year 3.5 million people visit Yosemite and cause excessive traffic jams in some areas. Yosemite now violates a federal smog standard. Some of the pollution comes from outside the park. Should there be restrictions on day use and should visitors be required to park at central parking lots outside the boundaries of the park? Then the visitors would be bused into the park with hybrid shuttles. These and other controversial issues involve geography and are worthwhile for students to investigate.

Discussions on controversial issues can be organized by having students discuss and research all the arguments in favor of the proposal, the pros, and all the arguments against the proposal, the cons, and place them in two columns. Examples could be "Should our community have a new shopping mall?" or "Should our state remove or destroy some dams?" The class then can examine the likely consequences of either decision both in the short term or the long term.

ECHNOLOGY

Numerous WebQuests (http://webquest.sdsu.edu), inquiry-oriented activities in which participants draw most of their information from the Internet, are available about controversial geography issues. Ecology WebQuests such as "Energy Quest," "Wetlands Under Attack," and "Landfill Controversy" are probably most common. In "Location, Location, Location!" students choose what city would be the best new location for a manufacturing plant. WebQuests on immigration are also popular. Make sure that the resource links are current, since many of these inquiry-type activities may have been designed a few years ago.

Value of Student Projects

A **student project** requires a student task and a resulting product. It usually takes at least a week to complete, and several skills like reading and writing are often needed to complete the project in a satisfactory manner. The assessment of the project may be an oral presentation, a PowerPoint presentation, a physical or art product, a written piece of work, or some combination such as a poster. More creative presentations might include a story rap, role playing, storytelling, a podcast, and making crossword puzzles.

TECHNOLOGY

   Multimedia projects using a variety of media might include digital moviemaking: collecting resources/research, creating storyboards and scripts, and constructing the movie. In order not to let the technology be the main focus for the students, it is helpful to have students first create the storyboards and scripts and then integrate the images, sound, text, video, and narration. Of course, a rubric outlining expectations is helpful so students understand how they will be evaluated. For example, will all projects require three or more references even if it is an oral presentation? In making a film, what has been left out? If well done, successful projects can produce a growth in geographic knowledge and skills. However, teachers must constantly monitor student progress while working on the project, especially if it is the first time that students have worked on such a project. Like all assessments students need feedback on how well they met the standard/objective of the project.

Teacher Decisions on Projects

Projects can be done individually, in pairs, or a small group. The work for a project can mainly be done during classroom time or it can be assigned to be done mostly outside of class. Often a class will have one project each semester or year. Especially if projects are done outside of class, teachers need to carefully monitor student progress. Many students have difficulty working independently when the due date is far off, but working independently is an important skill needed both in school and later life.

Geography Topics for Student Projects   Geography as a subject lends itself to student projects. Another teacher decision is whether students can choose their own topic for their projects. Usually motivation is higher if students can have a choice. As an example, using the Five Themes of Geography, a class could choose to do projects on what will be the future in their community (or region or nation) in ten, twenty, or fifty years from now. With the concern about global climate change, more information is now available on this futuristic topic. Students could choose among the subtopics such as population, transportation, climate, food, housing, jobs and occupations, recreation, government, media, pollution, immigration, schools, and the like. Some of these subtopics could further be divided such as specific forms of media. Focusing on the present rather than the future, classes have played the role of town planners doing group projects on some of the same topics listed above. More specifically students could choose such topics such as Traffic Control or Land Use and Zoning. The aftermath of such group projects is designing plans for improvement of the community with presentations to the town council, making it more of an action research project.

TECHNOLOGY

   Another broad topic for projects is Africa with an emphasis on environmental and geographic origins of cultures and the issues affecting different African cultures. Other continents also could be chosen. In some cases, online mentoring programs can allow students to ask experts for help. Sometimes this is called **e-mentoring.** Usually the experts are scientists, scholars, and other professionals who respond by e-mail to the students.

Environmental Issues Pollution and energy problems both in the United States and worldwide have also been receiving more attention for student projects, particularly what is happening as China increases its production of coal, a leading source of acid rain and air pollution, and its effect on the rest of the world. Sometimes these projects are tied into a science connection since environmental issues overlap with science.

Human/Environmental Interaction Teachers have also used topics like mountains or rivers to relate geography to culture. For example, five rivers—the Ganges, Indus, Mekong, Huang He (Yellow) and Chang (Yangtze) all originate in the Himalayas. Or the Amazon River could be chosen. Yet there are vastly different cultures and ways of life among people living along each river system. For their projects, different students can choose different areas of a given river system to show the relationships between the physical environment of the river and the way of life of people living in the area.

Immigration Immigration of one's own family or a specific ethnic/racial group has always been a popular topic for individual projects (see the earlier section on migration). Students pick a country that they descended from or that they find interesting. Students research the locations, landforms, and climates in their country of origin (or interest) and their effect on the social, political, and economic development of that particular country. With a geography focus, whole-group activities such as placing red dots on a map showing where immigrants came from are worthwhile. In addition, the migration patterns of grandparents, parents, and students within the United States are emphasized rather than seeing their family's immigration story within the greater historical immigration patterns, as would be done with a more historical focus.

For certain topics, online projects or **online communities** allow students to participate in collaborative learning with students both in the United States and around the world. Besides matching classes as e-pals (the old pen pal now using e-mail), the ePALS Classroom Exchange

(www.epals.com) also offers links to online projects. The Global Classroom Project (www.sofweb .vic.edu/au/gc/ projcurr) has projects promoting global education for all grade levels. The potential for exchanging and analyzing information spanning different places can be exciting for students. By choosing certain items such as newspapers and photos from their local scene, the whole class can compare the geographic, economic, and cultural aspects of their communities. As a class receives information from the other class, they can write thank you notes and send additional information such as local postcards. Remember that your district may want each parent to sign a consent form for their child to participate in the pen pal project.

Small Group Work **6.1**

Your Experiences with Social Studies Projects

Do you recall any social studies projects you did while in elementary or middle school? Was the project a challenge that made you use higher-level thinking skills? ●

Teaching Map and Globe Skills

Maps, like graphs and charts, are specialized ways of presenting information. However, too frequently maps remain a mystery to some adults. They have not benefited much from their experiences in elementary school learning map skills. Map and globe skills are often taught for

On Your Own **6.2**

Map Skills and Textbooks

Check the map skills program in an elementary textbook series. If attention is being given in textbooks to map skills, why do you think so many children and adults have trouble using maps? ●

TECHNOLOGY

a few weeks at the beginning of the year, isolated from the rest of the social studies program. This practice has been encouraged by publishers, many of whom have traditionally started textbooks with a concentration of *map skills* in the first unit. That situation has changed. More publishers now provide a well-thought-out sequence of map skills in their elementary social studies series. In fact, of all the skills of the social studies—listening, small group work, problem solving, and so on—map skills are probably receiving the most attention from textbook authors. In addition, of all the areas of elementary social studies, more computer software programs have been designed for teaching geography and map skills than for any other area. Popular geography programs are GeoBee (National Geographic Society), Geography Search (Tom Snyder Productions), My First Amazing World Explorer (DK Interactive Learning), Where in the World is Carmen Sandiego (The Learning Co.), and World Discovery Deluxe (McGraw-Hill Children's Publishing/Great Wave Software).

Ability Levels

Although geography and map skills have been taught for generations, the research in this area is still inconclusive, especially regarding the appropriate time to introduce students to specific skills. In other words, although charts on scope and sequence may state that children in grades 4 to 6 should use scale and compute distances or compare maps and make inferences, we are not really certain that all children are cognitively ready at these grade levels to learn map skills. Research has shown, however, that when teachers are well prepared and materials are carefully sequenced, most elementary students can indeed learn the basics of map literacy.

In teaching map-reading skills, you need to be aware of the differing levels of ability among your students. Map reading may be too difficult for some students, especially if the maps contain too much data. Research exists that girls at the elementary level might not perform as well as boys in map-reading skills and geography. You should be aware of your own teaching methods and make sure that you give girls at least as much time and attention in reading maps as you give boys.

Field Trips

If there is one "magic" guideline in teaching map skills, it is to make the concept concrete. Relate what you are teaching to student experiences. Students in the primary grades, especially after exposure to globes, should be provided direct contact with landscape features. Every town has a landscape that includes some of the geographic, geologic, and cultural features that students find symbolized on maps. But simply taking students outside for a walk is not necessarily productive. To make effective use of outdoor time, you need to plan activities before and after the trip, as well as planning the trip itself. If you do not plan carefully, you run the risk that students will think your walk is simply free time outside the classroom. Before the trip, line up any equipment you wish to take, such as cameras.

First, know what you want to achieve. This means visiting ahead of time the sites your class will see and identifying the major features; it also means communicating the purpose of your trip to your students.

TECHNOLOGY

There are administrative considerations to any field trip, even a short walk to local sites. Make sure you inform your principal so that issues of legal liability and safety can be checked. To avoid trespassing, ask property owners for permission, even in the case of an apparently abandoned cemetery. For longer trips, your school will certainly have a policy about permission slips and number of chaperons. Given the cost of a bus for field trips, most teachers now investigate the possibilities of using virtual field trips. The number of virtual field trips on the Internet is increasing and offers many opportunities to "visit" interesting sites.

During the trip, try to focus students' attention and help them understand concepts such as *swamp* and *treeline* and how these are related to symbols on a map. Symbols for cultural features (buildings, ruins, canals, dams, or even battle sites) must be explained; show students how the buildings they are seeing appear on maps. Finally, water and weather features are sometimes observable: dry salt lakes, tide pools, channels, coral reefs, ponds, warm and cold currents, and prevailing winds. You may want to have students take pictures or fill out worksheets. Anything students can touch (e.g., rubbing their hands against rock formations, dipping fingers into ponds) will make the trip more memorable.

Finally, plan posttrip activities and use the experience in future classroom activities. Ask students their impressions and observations; review your major objectives with them. Continue to discuss the field trip as a reference in future lessons. Students can make three-dimensional maps of the area they visited. Tabletop maps, clay or sandbox constructions, and paper maps on the floor can also help students demonstrate graphically what they have seen. You might want to have them use blocks or boxes to show miniature buildings, schools, or neighborhoods. The more effectively children can use their experiences, the better they are able to understand the basic ideas and concepts of any field.

Especially for disadvantaged groups, a field trip to the local community college can be both promising and interesting. Almost all parents want their children to go to college but some may be unfamiliar about what is offered locally. Students may be excited in seeing what local college students are really like as compared to media portrayals. Typically, the community college has many buildings with maps posted, so that students can see if they can find certain buildings. Where is the science building? The gym? Often the community college also may have a museum or a planetarium.

Local and Beyond the Local

In learning map and globe skills, primary-grade children begin with a realization that their local area is only a tiny part of the whole world and move to a broader conception of the world. Use students' trips to help them become more careful observers, as emphasized in the tips on having successful field trips. It is easy to pass through an environment without appreciating or noticing much about it, but all children can develop skills in observing cultural and physical features through short walks, field trips, and trips with their families. Learning to observe is especially important in the primary grades.

Because of the limitations of the local area, media—videos, Internet, and television programs—are usually needed to supplement students' understanding. But the importance of the local environment should never be forgotten at the elementary-grade level. Frequently, teachers concentrate on a national commercial textbook and ignore what is right outside the windows of their classrooms. Given a map worksheet with directions on it, students can usually determine locations of key items. But many of these same students do not know the directions in their own community. Ideally, children should learn the cardinal directions (north, south, east, and west) by the position of the sun (or shadow). Outdoor exercises can be most helpful when they are introduced about the third grade.

TECHNOLOGY

We also recommend classroom signs or maps indicating north, south, east, and west. But what if you aren't sure where north is? This is not at all unusual. Many people drive freeways without any sense of direction; highway signs indicating east or west exit points mean little to them. Children who get perfect scores on map exercises in the classroom cannot walk or ride their bikes to a specific location using local maps because they cannot orient themselves to where they are. If you are not sure, ask a reliable individual, such as a police officer, or use a compass. Whenever you take students outside on walks or on field trips in a bus, indicate in what general direction you are all going. Using a compass can often be fun; let students pass it around. Just as students now often know more about computers than their teachers, students sometimes have better senses of direction than their teachers. Identify these potentially helpful students as soon as possible. Often they are children who score extremely high on nonverbal and spatial areas of intelligence tests.

Local maps as well as other areas also can be secured from the Internet using sites such as Mapquest, Google Earth or Google Maps, and TerraFly. Try online mapping. For example, go to the website www.earth.google.com and download Google Earth. Type the name of your city or town and state in the "Fly To" boxes. You can make adjustments with the zoom feature for more detail and put in such locations as schools and parks. More sophisticated than paper maps is for children to use **GPS units** (global positioning system) that can create a map as you walk and can indicate your place on the earth's surface. GPS units serve millions of users ranging from hikers to airline pilots. This number will multiply quickly as receivers are placed in cellular phones and automobiles. Furthermore, the newer GPS units are expected to have more coverage and accuracy. Teachers have played "hide and seek" using GPS units and geocaches for students to find. Usually students are taught first how to use the GPS units and then the teacher provides the coordinates and clues for small groups to find the cache. Parent volunteers have often been invited to help out for this activity.

TECHNOLOGY

In addition, software is available on a geographic information system (GIS). These GISs are used extensively by government agencies, utilities, industries, and real estate and travel agencies as they analyze data. A GIS allows for more complex tools for location-based information and mapmaking that can support inquiry learning. Unfortunately, it does take a teacher time to learn how to use this software. Louisiana is using GISs in K–12 classrooms related to the topic of disaster preparedness.

Even without sophisticated equipment to make your own maps, you can acquire maps from many sources. Typically, your local chamber of commerce is a good source for local maps and your state tourism office will send you free maps of your state. One problem with these maps is they often contain too much detail and may be confusing for many students. However, getting a set of maps for each pair of students in your class is a good idea.

Some teachers laminate the local maps so that they can last longer. Then students can use water soluble pens to mark various routes on the map. The teacher, after explaining (or reteaching) about the map's legend, index, and symbolic representations, asks each pair to mark various routes. You can activate prior knowledge by asking what local or state trips students have made lately and use these for the map routes from one place to another. For accuracy, you can ask pairs to compare their routes with another pair. Discuss which routes were difficult. Why?

The U.S. Geological Survey offers their own topographic maps for a modest fee. Satellite photographs from different sources are available at cost. In addition, going online, you can obtain maps from many organizations and nations. The websites of textbook publishers offer free maps to all, not just those who have purchased their textbooks (see for example the Houghton Mifflin or Scott Foresman sites, www.eduplace.com/ss/ssmaps/index.html and www.scottforesman.com/educators/index.html).

Teachers should not forget to use the maps found in children's literature as characters move from one place to another. If there are not maps, some fictional characters such as Harry Potter go on journeys that children can map out as they read. Students gain meaning from reading if they understand better the geography of the novel.

Specific Map Skills

Along with labeling and identifying aspects of the local environment, map teaching involves systematic, step-by-step presentation of a series of questions to help a student learn specific skills.

1. Locate places on a map and globe.
    a. Identify continents by shape.
    b. Identify hemispheres.
2. Orient a map and note directions.
    a. Find compass points.
    b. Use scale and compute distances.
3. Interpret maps and symbols.
    a. Use a map key.
    b. Visualize what the map symbols mean.
4. Compare maps and make inferences.

Each one of these skills may have to be explicitly taught. Although brighter students will absorb the concepts without much direct teaching, many others will need as much assistance as you are able to give. Working in pairs may be helpful for many students when they are doing activities or worksheets on map skills; it also makes these activities more fun. Because there is often a sense of accomplishment in completing a map exercise, students frequently report that they like geography and map work at the elementary level.

What can be done specifically to teach these map skills? You can show students silhouettes of the continents such as the ones in Figure 6.3. Ask them to label the continents. Once you are confident that students really know the shapes of the continents, move on to identifying hemispheres and locating continents within them. Typically, students see maps only of the Western and Eastern Hemispheres. Occasionally, they are shown maps of the Northern Hemisphere but very rarely the Southern Hemisphere (see Figure 6.4).

Yet it is important to be able to recognize continents from different perspectives. In effect, this is what happens to astronauts. Try to show your students maps that were produced in other nations. Maps printed in Germany or Britain, for example, have the prime meridian in the absolute center of the map. World maps made in China or Japan show those nations

Figure 6.3 Silhouettes of Continents

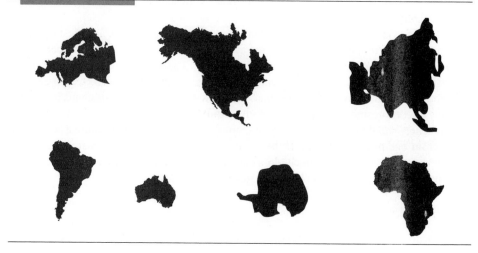

Figure 6.4 Maps of the Hemispheres

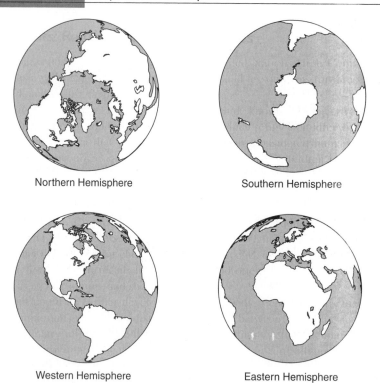

Northern Hemisphere

Southern Hemisphere

Western Hemisphere

Eastern Hemisphere

Source: "Teacher's Resource Binder-Level 3," *Communities Large and Small* (Lexington, MA: D. C. Heath, 1985). Reprinted with permission.

in the center with the American continents squeezed into the right-hand edge. (Good sources for these maps are the offices of consuls of different nations.) At first, students may say that something is wrong with these maps. This is a good lesson to show that people have different perspectives on what the world looks like.

The issue of perspective is important. Young children need to be shown that an object looks different if you view it from the top or from the foot of a mountain. In classrooms, a toy doll can be put on top of a miniature mountain and children can be asked to imagine they are seeing through the doll's eyes. Ask the children what they would see if the position of the doll changes. This is similar to exercises asking students to draw their own desks or their shoes as seen from an overhead position. Often students put in heels or other features that they really could not see from above.

As with chronology, specific map skills have to be taught and retaught, both as separate lessons or exercises and as integrated parts of other subjects. You cannot assume that students will transfer the learning of one map skill to another type of map skill or the use of map skills to real life without your help.

Almost every expert in the field has stressed the importance of introducing the globe to primary students and of explaining that globes are small models of the world. Some primary teachers bring in a model car to illustrate what they mean by a model so that students will not get confused and think that the world is the size of the globe shown in the classroom. Globes, and especially those with only water and continental land masses indicated, can help students visualize continents, a sphere, a hemisphere, and the equator. Furthermore, correlation with the science and math programs can help provide students with a general understanding of the rotation of the earth and seasonal changes. Photographs of the earth taken from outer space are also helpful in giving a new perspective on how the earth looks.

Understanding a Variety of Maps

Flat maps are usually introduced in the intermediate grades, when students learn about scale, geographic grids, and the use of color and symbols in maps. Each skill must be taught and retaught separately. Students should become aware of the following ideas: (1) A map is flat and cannot show true roundness; (2) all flat maps have some distortion (although the technical reasons for different map distortions need not be explained); (3) the legend or key explains what each symbol means; and (4) the scale of the map controls the degree to which we can generalize.

You can have students do a map analysis worksheet (see the lesson idea on map analysis). Emphasize the information that a particular map provides. Intermediate-level students can be exposed to different kinds of maps: Students need to learn to interpret a temperature map, a time-zone map, a telephone area code map, an historical map (of the Roman Empire, for example, where the boundaries and names of regions are different from what they are today), and a political map (of the United States, for instance, showing the number of members each state has in the House of Representatives).

Intermediate students must also learn how to locate places on a map. Most maps use a letter-number index to give the location of smaller cities or streets. Each student should have his or her own map with which to practice finding different places by using such indexes. Some teachers like to start this activity with small groups, but you must take care that each student learns the appropriate skill and that one student does not do all the work for the whole group.

LESSON IDEA

Map Analysis Worksheet or Teacher's Questions

1. What type of map? (Political, weather, satellite, etc.)
2. What three things does this map tell about?

   A.

   B.

   C.

3. What information does the map add to the textbook's account of this event?

An activity that is fun as well as instructive is comparing maps of Pangaea. Have students look carefully at a world map (top, Figure 6.5), especially the Atlantic coast of Africa. Tell students to think of the continents as pieces in a jigsaw puzzle. Where would Africa fit? This relationship among the continents was first noticed in 1912 by Alfred Wegener, a German scientist. He proposed the *continental drift theory,* that continents had moved and drifted from one large land mass, which he called Pangaea (center, Figure 6.5). Research has upheld Wegener's basic idea, although scientists have made some changes in his theory. The bottom map (Figure 6.5) shows how present-day scientists think the earth looked more than 200 million years ago. Ask students what differences they see among the three maps. Then ask them to explain a bumper sticker on a car reading "Reunite Pangaea!" and why the bumper sticker is really a joke. Students who want to learn more about continental drift can be advised to read about plate tectonics in encyclopedias online and other sources.

Mapmaking

Notice that we have been emphasizing map-*reading* skills. Map*making* (or making one's own charts, cartoon drawings, etc.) is more difficult than simply reading or interpreting a map or table. Making maps requires visualization abilities. Mapmaking is the supreme test of map understanding. With proper instruction, however, most students enjoy map production.

TECHNOLOGY

The steps in making a map are somewhat similar to steps in making charts and graphs. They usually include (1) collecting or observing data, (2) organizing or simplifying data, (3) planning the map (chart) in terms of scale, and (4) drafting or drawing the map or chart. Of course, computer programs can help students in making charts. Computer programs can eliminate a lot of the drudgery associated with steps 2, 3, and 4. One of the advantages of making maps (or charts) is that students can present what they have learned, especially local data, in a simplified format.

Primary children can make maps. Some teachers start with making a map of their own classroom. Children have to be told that they are looking down from the ceiling as they place desks and other room equipment in the classroom map. After this, children can be asked to make a map of their own bedroom or a room that they wish could be theirs. This activity can be expanded to include a map of their house or a house they would like. Finally a map of the local streets can be made, showing where the children's homes are located. As mentioned previously, some teachers have used old shower curtains as the material for the local street

| Figure 6.5 | Changes in the Continents |

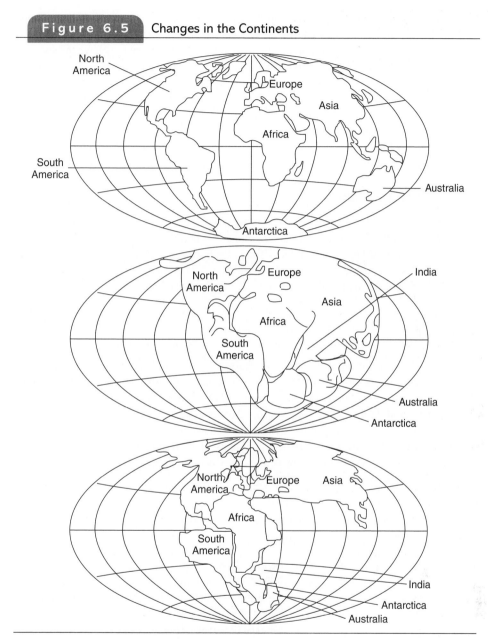

Source: Adapted from A. Hallam, "Alfred Wegener and the Hypothesis of Continental Drift," *Scientific American.*

map. The advantage of the shower curtain is its large size, making the streets visible in the back of the room. Note in all of these examples that the maps were local and personalized for the class. Usually, students must be taught each separate stage before they can draw the map.

Because of the time involved and the visual skills needed to make maps, many teachers ask students to place data on already assembled globes and maps. Unbreakable globes and wall maps that can be marked with crayons and washed off are especially useful. Even inexpensive outline maps (frequently found in teachers' guides for map exercises for students) that have a minimum amount of information on them can be used to real advantage.

TECHNOLOGY

Mapmaking has been revolutionized by technology. Your library may have the specialized software for atlases that will find a map after you type in the name of a place or country. There are maps with animated markers that show particular places. There is a street atlas of all the streets, roads, and highways in the United States with different levels of enlargement. In other words, with these tools it is easier than ever before to locate places with the use of an atlas. With these maps may come pictures, tables, charts of comparison data and articles, and Internet links. Never before have teachers and students had access to as many maps as they now do, but students still need some background to interpret a map.

Summary on Map Skills

We hope that the teaching of map skills will move beyond the rote-memory format that in the past has been typical of many map skills programs. We should try to teach students that maps and globes are designed to help us think. Maps in textbooks as well as globes should be used throughout the year and not just during a September unit. This way geography knowledge and skills will truly be used appropriately, helping all students to be geographically literate.

Summary

To aid students in becoming geographically literate, states have produced standards for geography. Geography is more than map skills, although map skills are essential. Geography can easily be implemented into the typical primary curriculum but should not be limited to rote memorization. In the upper grades where history is the core social studies subject, geography has to be integrated specifically into the units. Trade books, observations, real-life experiences, videos, controversial issues, field trips, skits, dramatic reenactments, simulations, and investigations are but a few of the many active learning strategies that can promote the knowledge and skills of geography.

Suggested Readings and Websites

Geography for Life: National Geography Standards 1994. Washington, DC: National Geographic Society, 1994.

Report on the geography standards.

Websites

Geocaching
www.geocaching.com/articles

Resources to use geocaching.

Indigenous Geography
www.indigenousgeography.si.edu

The Smithsonian's National Museum of the American Indian has this bilingual website (Spanish) for educators about the Native communities across the Western Hemisphere.

National Atlas
http://nationalatlas.gov

Maps of North America for downloading and a program to make your own maps

National Geographic Society
www.nationalgeographic.com

The national geography standards; atlas, publications, and so on.

National Geographic Xpeditions
www.nationalgeographic.com/xpeditions

The home of National Geography Standards with lesson plans sorted by standard and grade level plus activities and maps.

RESEARCH ARTICLE READING EXERCISE

How Global Is the Curriculum?

Go to MyEducationLab, select the topic **Geography,** and read the research article entitled "How Global is the Curriculum?" by A. F. Smith.

Smith's article is a call for global education that will help prepare students to become "globally literate citizens." Global education involves disciplinary knowledge such as history, language, and cultures of the world, but in all of this is the ability to think about the world geographically. This article provides several guidelines for integrating global/international and geographic studies into the curriculum. It also provides several guidelines for studying the world by exploring global challenges, culture and areas of the world, and global connections.

Complete the homework questions that accompany the article. You may print your work or have it transmitted to your professor as necessary.

CHAPTER 7

Teaching Economics

*I*n this chapter, we discuss the teaching of economics, a key discipline in the social studies. Emphasis in this chapter is placed on strategies and materials that help students understand economics. Students can apply economic reasoning to make choices so that they can be intelligent consumers, savers, investors, members of the workforce, and citizens participating in a global economy. Even for elementary students, more attention is now being given to financial literacy or personal finance.

- Economic Standards
- Strategies for Teaching Economics
- Financial Literacy or Personal Finance

What might these children learn about economics?

Economic Standards

Growing Importance of Economics

Economics is the study of people making choices in the allocation of scarce resources. **Economy literacy** is defined as the ability to identify, analyze, and evaluate the consequences of individual economic decisions and public policy. Economic education can help students to make decisions about their economic lives and their futures. Economic literacy includes knowledge of the market economy, the national economy, and the international economy as well as the skills of applying knowledge and reasoning.

From your daily experiences, you know how important economics is in your life. You probably are making economic decisions every day. Do I stop to buy coffee today? If I buy a new pair of sandals, what will be my credit card balance? Should I spend money repairing my old car or hope that with a teaching position I will be able to afford a new car? We all have learned that we cannot have everything we want and have to make economic decisions. Sometimes we also realize that we have not made good economic decisions. The pants shrink in the wash and the interest rate on the student loan rate is too high. When we get gas for our car, we become aware that international decisions like those of OPEC also influence our lives. In the back of our minds is also the realization that some part of our income also goes to pay for the services of the local, state, and federal governments. Thus, economic issues affect our lives as workers, consumers, and citizens.

Technologies are also changing our financial world along with the growing global economy. The world is becoming more financially complex. Just think of all the "new" ways to pay bills—debit cards, online payments, electronic check conversion, and direct deposit. It is also essential that populations that have not benefited from our financial system know about financial products (IRAs, mortgages, mutual funds, and the like), services (credit card companies), and financial information providers (banks, financial advisers, financial newsletters) to avoid making devastating financial decisions.

Let us clarify the organization of this chapter and some terms in economic education. This chapter discusses first the national economic standards. However, the academic economic standards developed in 1997 did not directly focus on financial literacy or personal finance for students. For that reason, there is a separate section on financial literacy because of its growing importance. On the individual level, **financial literacy** is now more strongly advocated to prevent young people from making poor economic decisions. The terms **financial literacy, personal finance,** or **financial education** are often used interchangeably. The goal is that financial literacy in the early grades can establish the basis for wise savings and spending habits that will help students throughout their lives. Critics believe that too many American children are caught in the idea that their self-worth is connected with what they own and that they absolutely "need" to obtain certain items. A few children and teenagers believe "I (or my parents for me) should be able to buy anything I want." Therefore, what was formerly called the consumer education approach now is more tied into economic principles such that each economic decision involves costs. *Financial literacy, financial planning,* and *personal finance* are replacing the old term *consumer education.* Sometimes you also will see the term *consumer literacy.*

National Economics Standards

How knowledgeable are citizens about economics? In a 2005 test developed by the National Council on Economic Education (NCEE) covering the 20 economic content standards plus additional concepts related to personal finance, adults received an average grade of 70 and the students' average score was much lower, 53. Men scored higher than women and whites higher than African Americans and Hispanics. Although progress has been made over the years, the majority of high school students still do not understand basic concepts in economics.[1] To increase economic literacy, NCEE has issued twenty content standards and related benchmarks.[2] Their website (www.ncee.net) shows these standards. Note that all twenty concepts concentrate on economics, not personal finance. However, since 2003 more states have mandated increasing personal finance education for all students and NCEE also now emphasizes this part of economic education.

Along with these standards, the council has a wide range of excellent practical curriculum materials. Each standard has a set of benchmarks, divided into achievement levels for grades 4, 8, and 12. These benchmarks give samples of what students can do to demonstrate their understanding of economics. One helpful feature is that the economic benchmarks are tied to specific lessons and curriculum materials available from NCEE's catalog. A CD-rom is available for purchase with over 1,200 lessons by grade level, concept, Voluntary National Content Standards in Economics, or your state economics standards (www.ncee.net).

The National Council on Economic Education, like the Geography Alliance, has state centers on economic education in almost every state. Their workshops and courses help support teachers in teaching economics. NCEE also has many other fine publications on the teaching of economics and personal finance as well as hundreds of economic lesson plans available online.

Economic Principles

To help overcome some of the confusing and abstract ideas about economics, experts in the field with NCEE introduced the following simplified list of economic principles.

1. People *choose.*
2. People's choices involve *costs.*
3. People respond to *incentives* in predictable ways.
4. People create *economic systems* that influence individual choices and incentives.
5. People gain when they *trade* voluntarily.
6. People's choices have consequences that lie in the *future.*

Your state may have a longer list of economic principles. These could include the following:

1. Government economic policies have both benefits and costs.
2. Monetary and fiscal policies influence the economy.
3. People make better decisions when they weigh the present as well as future benefits and costs of alternatives.

[1]National Council on Economic Education, *What American Teens & Adults Know About Economics* (New York: National Council on Economic Education, 2005).

[2]National Council on Economic Education, *Voluntary National Content Standards in Economics* (New York: National Council on Economic Education, 1997).

4. People's skills influence their income.
5. Markets work best when competition, incentives, information, and property rights exist.

Economic Concepts

Along with the economic principles listed above, a challenge in teaching economics is the sheer number of important economic and related concepts that eventually all students should understand. For example, NCEE Standard 1 defines the concept *scarcity.*

Scarcity   Productive resources are limited. Therefore, people cannot have all the goods and services they want; as a result, they must choose some things and give up others.

But this definition is followed by twenty related concepts: *choice, consumers, goods, human resources, opportunity costs,* and the like. You can easily understand why NCEE's excellent website with its five hundred free lessons (EconEdLink, www.econedlink.org/lessons) is popular. Although the vast majority of these lessons are for grades 9 through 12, there are still many lessons designed for grades K–2, 3–5, and 6–8. For example, these K–2 lessons are tied to literature such as "Costs and Benefits of 'The Three Little Pigs',," "Country Mouse Makes a Decision!" and "The Right Job for 'The Tortoise and the Hare.'" Interesting lessons tied to the Hawaiian units (Chapter 2) for grades 3 to 5 are "Hawaiian Economics: From the Mountain to the Sea" and "Hawaiian Economics: Barter for Fish and Poi." These lessons describe the land division system of ancient Hawaii and the barter system needed to exchange goods and services without the use of money. Tied in with United States history is "Lewis and Clark Barter with Native Americans." Lewis and Clark could not take all of the goods necessary for their long exploration, so they took with them items most useful in bartering with Indians. It would have been impossible to buy anything from the Indians with cash or money. Lewis and Clark could not have survived without exchanging something of value with the Indians. Students from grades 3 through 8 might also enjoy "The Productive Blues (Jeans)." Mathematics also can be integrated into the economics lessons at all grade levels.

Example of an NCEE Content Standard   After examining the basic economic principles, you can see how one of NCEE's twenty economic standards on incentives flows from the basic economic principles.

Content Standard 4, On the Role of Incentives
Students will understand that:
People respond predictably to positive and negative incentives.

Students will be able to use this knowledge to:
Identify incentives that affect people's behavior and explain how incentives affect their own behavior.

*At the completion of **grade 4,** students will know that:*

Rewards are positive incentives that make people better off.

Penalties are negative incentives that make people worse off.

Both positive and negative incentives affect people's choices and behavior.

People's views of rewards and penalties differ because people have different values.

Let us look at teaching this standard. Economics learning need not be just a memorization of important concepts. Examples of the standard should tie into students' lives. Personal examples can lead to more difficult global issues. What incentives can be used to reduce crime? Terrorism?

Starting from their personal experience, it is easy for children to understand that advertisers use incentives to try to encourage people to buy more of their products and that wages persuade people, including their parents and relatives, to work. But discussion of this standard can also be brought closer to home. What penalties or negative incentives are used by parents to discourage inappropriate behavior at home? What incentives are used in the classroom to reward positive classroom behavior? What does the public library do to encourage its patrons to return books on time? A discussion of these questions may also indicate that not all incentives work the same way for all children or adults. As you can see from this one economic standard, NCEE has outlined an important concept and given enough detail on how it can be taught in the classroom without being a dull sterile exercise. Economics does not have to be a dismal science.

State Standards

Since NCEE's economics standards were not published until 1997, many states used older economics standards as they set about making their own. Like geography, economics is seldom taught as a separate course in the elementary school. The development of state standards for economics was a definite improvement in many states since they outlined how economics should be taught at every grade level. In the past, economics was often not very visible in the elementary curriculum. Allowing the high school to teach economics was the common view.

Similar to geography, the economics standards for the primary grades focus on self, families, school, and community. Also like geography, economics fits easily into the primary curriculum pattern. Primary students were already studying about community helpers (different kinds of jobs) and how we get to school (transportation systems). In the past, however, these activities were typically not described in economic terms such as the division of labor. Note how interwoven geography and economics are. A good unit could be "Expanding Children's Geographic and Economic World." The main objective of the unit would be for students to understand the geography and economics of their neighborhood or community. Children would learn about economic activities such as producing goods, providing services, buying and selling, as well as geographic elements of the neighborhood.

However, where history was predominant from the fourth to the eighth grade, the economic concepts had to fit into the content of the historical periods the students were studying. Teaching economics in middle school then was more of a challenge than teaching it in the primary grades. However, comparing work roles today with those of other periods of time is always a possibility.

Rationale for Teaching Economics

The rationale for teaching economics is that it will help students make better decisions in our modern global economy. Advocates of economics also stress the value of the skill of **economic reasoning** (*problem solving* or *strategic thinking*) as applied to making decisions. Here are the stages of economic reasoning:

1. Identify the question or problem
2. List the alternatives
3. Identify the advantages and disadvantages of each alternative
4. Choose the best alternative
5. Reevaluate the consequences of the decision

Different Economic Interpretations Incite Controversy

All agree that economists, like historians and geographers, hold different views or interpretations about various economic topics and recommendations for what the government should do. In addition, different economists focus on different areas of economics. A labor economist probably has a different perspective than an international/trade economist. Research continues to change economics. A recent trend is that behavior economists believe that individuals do not always behave in a rational manner. For example, if investors in the stock market regard a company as "good," they are reluctant to sell even when the stock goes down. Economists are also investigating such questions as whether happiness relates to income. Furthermore, individuals have to make decisions based on inadequate information. Given the wide range of perspectives of economists, some economists want greater emphasis placed on scarcity, the influence of incentives, and economic reasoning.

Economic policy decisions address political issues. Governments, like individuals, cannot have everything they want. Budgets must be approved by legislators with different interests. Frequently budget cuts must be made. The distinction between facts and values in economics is critical in evaluating policy proposals. Students should be prompted to look for points of view and opinions when using free materials such as videos and publications from business, labor, or other groups. The controversial nature of economics should lead students to engage in thinking critically. How much money should be allocated for space exploration or cancer research? What are other alternative ways to spend government funds? What are the advantages or disadvantages to each alternative? This is the process of economic reasoning.

Economic choices also involve **values.** As you observe your class, you may feel that your students spend too much money on clothing and electronic toys. Your values may be different from theirs. This may make you think that a lesson or two on advertising or making choices (opportunity costs) on how you spend your time is in order. Again, your values influence what topics you think are important to teach and for your students to learn.

Children and Economics

What do children know about economics? Children learn from an early age that they cannot have all of the toys and games that they want. As they grow older, they become more aware of the importance of money and credit cards as they go shopping with their parents or guardians. However, children are often confused about transactions that they do not directly see. There is evidence that young children have many misconceptions about money and the economic world. For example, Brophy and Alleman interviewed primary children and reported that most of the children understood that people have to pay for shelter and most people prefer homes to apartments. However, most children had difficulty understanding why some people prefer apartment rental to home ownership. Some confused apartments with hotels and most were vague about what is involved in renting apartments. Only a few understood most people get a mortgage loan to allow them to buy a home when they have not accumulated the full purchase price. The students possessed only limited and spotty knowledge of the economics of housing, an area that applied directly to their lives.[3]

An issue of privacy arises about making students more aware of the costs of their housing. Is it an invasion of privacy to have primary children ask their parents if they rent or own their home? Some parents would welcome the opportunity to make their child more realistic about the expenses the family faces. Others might not think this was a good idea. If students filled out a form without their name on it asking if their family rented or owned their house, would this address concerns about privacy?

Small Group Work 7.1

Should We Be Teaching about Mortgages?

How valuable do you think it is for primary students to learn more about the expenses associated with where they live? The amount of money spent by their family on gas, electric, water, phone, and cable bills? ●

Brophy and Alleman also interviewed primary grade students for their knowledge and thinking about food production and the origins of common foods. These foods included applesauce, cheese, bread, and meat in hamburger. Students were asked where the meat came from and what the process of making the hamburger patty was. Additional questions were why a restaurant meal costs more than the same meal eaten at home, and why many fewer farmers per capita are needed today than in the past.[4] The primary students had several misconceptions and little awareness of economic, geographic, and historical factors. Again, as indicated by testing and assessment surveys, by the time they are teenagers, students still have a lot of misconceptions about economics.

Strategies for Teaching Economics

Teaching about Costs and Benefits at the Primary Level

*L*et us look more closely at Arizona's Standard 2 on *scarcity, resources,* and *costs and benefits* for the primary grades (Table 7.1). Here are some suggestions for students to write about or discuss. First, find out how many have pets, what kind of pets they have, and the costs associated with a pet. Some may forget that caring for pets usually requires purchasing special food for them and taking them to the vet. Then go through these examples.

---

[3]Jere Brophy and Janet Alleman, "Primary-Grade Students' Knowledge and Thinking About the Economics of Meeting Families' Shelter Needs." Paper presented at the 1999 annual meeting of the National Council for the Social Studies, Orlando, Florida.

[4]Jere Brophy and Janet Alleman, "Primary-Grade Students' Knowledge and Thinking about Food Production and the Origins of Common Foods," *Theory and Research in Social Education* 31, no. 2 (2003): 9–49.

Table 7.1	Arizona's Economics Standards for Grades 1–3, Approved in the Year 2000

1. Describe how scarcity affects students' daily lives, with emphasis on:
    1. The opportunity cost of a choice
    2. Natural resources, human resources, and capital resources, and how they are used to produce goods and services
    3. The costs and benefits of personal spending and saving choices
2. Describe the characteristics of production and exchange in an economy, with emphasis on:
    1. The use of money and barter in the exchange of goods and services
    2. Why some things are made locally, some elsewhere in the United States, and some in other countries
    3. The work that people do to manufacture, transport, and market goods and services
    4. The interdependence of consumers and producers of goods and services

I. Pets
   A. Costs of buying and caring for a pet
   B. Benefits of buying and caring for a pet

Ask the children to tell you on Monday what they did on the last weekend or other weekends.

II. Use of their own time on a Saturday afternoon
   A. Costs and benefits of earning money selling lemonade, raking leaves, and so on
   B. Costs and benefits of riding bikes with friends
   C. Costs and benefits of going shopping for groceries with parent
   D. Costs and benefits of helping with housework

If you do not wish to ask directly if your students get allowances or earn money, or the amounts they receive, use characters in stories. What do you think Jack in "Jack in the Beanstalk" should do with his money? How about finding the "pot of gold?" What would you do if given a large sum of money?

III. Use of their own money
   A. Costs and benefits of saving all or part of their money
   B. Costs and benefits of spending all or part of their money

After doing a few of these exercises, most students will better understand the importance of making decisions that provide the greatest satisfaction for them. For example, a child must make a choice of what item to buy for his or her mother on Mother's Day. Given the amount of money available, if the child buys cut flowers from the local supermarket, then he or she cannot buy a small plant. One choice eliminates other possibilities. Or a child must make a decision at a fast-food outlet on what to order. A parent will normally not allow a child to order every single item on the menu. To make these decisions, a child must weigh the costs with the benefits. For example, what are the opportunity costs of sleeping late on Saturday morning? Being late to school? Choosing snacks? In most cases, choices involve doing a little more or a little less of something. Few choices are all-or-nothing decisions.

Songs also can be sung to illustrate economics concepts.

"Oh, Give Me a Choice"[5]
(Tune: "Home on the Range")

Oh, give me a choice,	Opportunity cost!
Oh, a difficult choice,	It's the thing you give up when
And I'll think about what I could use,	You choose.
I'll have to decide,	It's the price that is paid
With my eyes open wide,	When a choice must be made
What I'll give up and what I will choose.	It's the thing that I surely will lose.

Teaching about Production and Exchange in the Primary Grades

As a teacher you may want to do more to get your students to meet the second economics standard (i.e., understand characteristics of *production* and *exchange* in an economy). How might this be done in a way that can build on your children's experiences? Appropriate economics books, teaching strategies, and resources for classroom use are available from the National Council on Economic Education.[6] Another way is to take a specific food item and see how it is produced and finally arrives at the table. Good choices might be pizza, cereals, tostadas, pita bread, noodles, biscuits, pancakes, spaghetti, pretzels, and orange juice. You could also investigate other items, such as how teddy bears or books are made in a factory or how subways are built. For each food product, make flowcharts with the class showing the sequence of events in planting, growing, harvesting, processing the crop into a food product, packaging the product, distributing (transporting), and selling the food product at a market.

An example of available trade books is *Bananas—From Manolo to Margie* by George Ancona (Clarion Books, Houghton Mifflin, New York, 1982), a story that follows a crop of bananas from a plantation in Honduras to the breakfast table of a child in the United States. Along the way the bananas are handled by many workers and carried by different forms of transportation. Both economics and geography objectives can be stressed, such as having students trace the route of the bananas, finding out why Central America is an ideal place for growing bananas, and making a list of the workers necessary for us to get bananas to eat.

Another popular choice is pancakes, partly because of the wide variety of related books available.

Pancake Books

Little Bear's Pancake Party by Janice Brustlein

Pancakes, Pancakes! by Eric Carle

---

[5]Teaching Strategies K–2, Economics America.

[6]National Council on Economic Education, 1140 Avenue of the Americas, New York, New York 10036. Phone 212-730-7007; www.economicsamerica.org.

Pancake Boy by Lorinda Cauley

Miss Mable's Table by Deborah Chandra

Pancakes for Breakfast by Tomie dePaola

Critters of the Night-Mummy Pancakes by Mercer Mayer

Curious George Makes Pancakes by Margaret Rey, H. A. Rey

Journey Cake, HO! by Ruth Sawyer

Pancakes and Pies: A Russian Folk Tale by Carole Tate

Although each book has value and students may enjoy the antics of good-hearted but mistake-prone Curious George in his attempt to make pancakes, some books lend themselves better to exploring the economics concepts. *Pancakes, Pancakes!* is a beautifully illustrated book about Jack, who wakes up hungry for an enormous pancake for breakfast. But before he can enjoy his pancake, he must get flour from the miller, an egg from the black hen, milk from the spotted cow, and butter churned from fresh cream. The book provides a step-by-step guide to making a pancake from scratch and introduces all of the people and their special work that are essential parts of its preparation, showing the ways in which we are interdependent in our world. After the teacher reads the book aloud, students could make a sequence chart of the steps described on how to make pancakes long ago. Headings could include: Ingredient, Source, Who or What Involved, and Trade. Ask how Jack gathered the ingredients. Who helped? How did they get "paid"? What was exchanged in "payment"?

Then display a box of Bisquick and its recipe for pancakes—today's version of the story—or use a recipe from a cookbook. Students can also compare the cost of making a product from scratch or purchasing it. Make a class chart about making pancakes today using the same headings as earlier. Compare the two charts—then and now! How are they alike and how are they different? Why is transportation so important for our pancake breakfast today? Review the economics concept of trade as an exchange of goods and services. Discuss money and what we know about it. How do we get it? What work do our parents do to earn it? Do we earn money? How? How do we use our money? How does money substitute for swapping items or working to pay off a debt?[7] Using flowcharts, show transportation, marketing, and workers needed to get food to the table. Notice that this unit about pancakes also helps develop historical thinking about now and long ago.

Depending on your class, more lessons could be developed on facts about wheat, a staple food item throughout many cultures, and where it is found. If your state grows wheat or produces dairy products or eggs, write to your state for free materials from such organizations as the Dairy Council of California or the California Wheat Commission. Wheat could be a springboard to teaching about the basic needs, structures, and functions of plants. You could bring in a variety of flour samples or wheat stalks from the dried flower sections of your local stores. You may refer to the food pyramid and the placement of grains on the chart. Or you could discuss basic health measures for handling food and hand washing. You could read more books on how pancakes are made and eaten around the world. All of these are interesting activities, but in the process don't forget that your purpose is to teach economics concepts. Sometimes the main objective can get lost.

[7]Idea based on Julie Hume, Orange County Department of Education, presentation entitled "Literature Line-Up, A Standards-Based Approach" at the California Annual State Social Studies Conference, February 2000.

Table 7.2	Making Pancakes	
Ingredients	**Utensils**	**Steps for Making Pancakes**

Then comes the fun part—a cooking experience of a pancake party. Have your students in small groups fill out the chart headings in Table 7.2, Making Pancakes. Always inform other school personnel, including administration, food service, maintenance, and parent volunteers, about an upcoming cooking experience. Encourage their assistance in any available capacity, such as obtaining supplies. Organize the logistics of the cooking activity with stations, groups, and adult helpers. Make sure that the atmosphere for both making and eating the pancakes is pleasant. Some classes have had a pancake party for others than themselves: another class, parents in the evening, or for mothers before Mother's Day. For these occasions, the children have often made thinner pancakes like crepes so that fruit like strawberries can be rolled into the crepe to serve to guests. Children learn that varying the amount of liquid in pancakes makes a thicker or thinner pancake and that tastes vary on what is the best type of pancake. Students also learn that, when serving guests, as a cultural preference we want our pancakes and other food servings to look as attractive as possible.

If making pancakes is not suitable, teachers can use the old favorite of making butter. Buy whipping cream at the store and pour it into a clear pint-sized jar with a tight-fitting lid. Have students take turns shaking it until it turns into butter. Serve on crackers, or serve the butter along with the pancakes.

Teachers also have reported success with a Gingerbread Man curriculum, using the folktale as a starting point and ending up making gingerbread men and gingerbread cookies. Students learn about the resources needed to produce gingerbread products, the opportunity cost of choosing one cookie decoration over another, and the goods and services produced in the community. They can try a division of labor with one child or a small group of children putting just the eyes on the gingerbread man versus doing all of the decorations. What are the advantages and disadvantages of having a division of labor? If they sell their products, they become aware of earning income, prices, and their productivity.

These examples of economic activities show the value of concrete experiences and examples. Too often young children have inaccurate ideas about the economic world. They think that buying things in stores is a ritual, not an exchange involving profit. They do not see that work and income are connected. Try to make learning about economics meaningful and memorable for children by focusing on children's own real-world experiences, thereby correcting economic misconceptions. There is also a treasury of children's literature to help meet the economics standards.

Small Group Work **7.2**

How Did You Learn about Economic Concepts?

Do you recall how you learned economic concepts? Were they explicitly taught in school? Informally at home? Did you learn from experience, sometimes a negative experience? Do you think the school should do a better job of teaching economic concepts? ●

General Methods for Economics in the Fourth to Eighth Grades

Field trips and resource people can help students understand local businesses. Some teachers have students make and sell some product of their own, such as school t-shirts, cookies, or holiday gifts. Students have operated in-school bookstores. In a few classes, instead of pooling the money in an activities fund (the usual procedure), the school sets up individual accounts for each student, reflecting how much money each has raised. Then students can withdraw money out of their accounts for school activities. Some students have more, some less, and others nothing at all. Do you like this idea of individual accounts? What lesson does it probably teach students?

TECHNOLOGY

Getting up-to-date information on economic topics such as the current population of the United States or any other country, unemployment rates, and inflation rates is now made easier by the Internet. Researching these data on the Internet often gives good experience to students on how to interpret data, tables, and graphs. Students, however, need to evaluate the purpose and reliability of the website. Is the site maintained by an insurance company? Is it promoting sales in the stock market?

Teachers can also directly teach from an economics standard such as "Different methods can be used to allocate goods and services." This could be used to examine how different cultures at different times have allocated *goods and services*. Moving to the present, what method of allocation should be used to give patients a new heart or a lung? How should seats on a bus or use of the classroom computers be allocated? Closer to home, how are household tasks distributed in students' homes?

All of these general methods are used to teach economics in the upper grades. Let us now examine more specifically teaching economics in history units.

History as the Background for Economics

In studying history, the common core experience in the upper elementary grades, there are numerous examples of the important role of economics in history. Students can gain a better understanding of history by using both basic economic reasoning and examining economics concepts. Starting in the fourth grade, most students begin to learn about the economic history of their state. What attracted people into the state (colony/territory) at the time being studied? What were the natural resources of the state and how did people change the environment over centuries?

Many fifth-grade topics lend themselves to teaching economics, starting with how property rights were regarded among North American Indians—they used both public ownership and private property. Markets played a key role in both the early explorations and settlement by Europeans. The beaver trade attracted the French to the New World. At first what would become the thirteen British colonies did not look promising. They did not have the rich gold and silver of the Spanish colonies. However, with the important exception of the slaves, the colonists in time had a higher living standard than British citizens in the home country. Students could study what makes economies grow by looking at the thirteen colonies.

To understand the causes of the American Revolution, the *benefit–cost analysis* can be applied as well as the concepts of *choice, trade-offs, opportunity costs, incentives, property rights,* and *economic conflict*. A study of the economic problems under the Articles of Confederation can indicate how it contributed to the formation of the U.S. Constitution. In a similar manner, the impact of inventions, such as the barbed wire used in fences, the telephone, the steamboat, the cotton gin, McCormick reaper, and eventually the computer, can show how technology affects the economy.

The sixth and seventh grades illustrate the relationship between economics, politics, culture, and geography as students study many cultures throughout time. Examples are the development of agriculture that permitted the rise of cities, the Roman Empire's fostering of economic growth through the use of currency and trade routes, and the development of feudalism. The eighth grade can explore the economy at the time of the Constitution, the development of the capitalist economy, economic incentives for westward expansion, economic conflicts behind the wars of the period, economic differences between Jefferson and Hamilton, and the Industrial Revolution. Case studies could examine why cotton was king or Andrew Jackson's fight against the Second Bank of the United States. They could look carefully whether free land under the Homestead Act was really a good deal and whether people like Rockefeller and Carnegie were robber barons or outstanding entrepreneurs. Unless such promising topics are used, it is likely that the economic standards will be neglected.

If specific attention is not devoted to the role of economics, most students are only vaguely aware of its importance. It passes over their heads. How can economics be pulled out and spotlighted when history is the main topic? Let us look at several strategies to accomplish this goal.

Using Literature

Using literature to promote economic literacy is a little more difficult as the novels become more complex and longer. For example, *Uncle Jed's Barbershop* by Margaret King Mitchell with illustrations by James Ransome (Scholastic, New York, 1994) can illustrate economic concepts such as *opportunity cost* and *production* for students from grades 2 through 5. This book, the winner of many awards, tells the story of Sarah Jean, whose Uncle Jed sacrificed his dream in order to help others. Uncle Jed is the only black barber in the county and wants to own his own barbershop. Only after many setbacks, including giving up his savings for Sarah Jean's operation and the Great Depression of the 1930s, is Uncle Jed finally able to open his own barbershop (see the unit plan).

Uncle Jed's Barbership has only forty pages, and it is relatively easy to identify economic concepts like opportunity costs. However, let us look at literature books used in the seventh grades, such as *Of Nightingales That Weep* by Katherine Paterson (HarperCollins, 1989). Set in feudal 12th-century Japan, Takiko, the daughter of a samurai who dies in battle, accepts a position at the imperial Japanese court where her beauty and nightingale voice are appreciated. As a civil war breaks out between the two feuding clans, Takiko is forced to choose between loyalty and her love for a young warrior, an enemy spy. Takiko has to make many decisions (opportunity costs), but probably most useful for teaching economics using this book is NCEE's Standard 3: Allocation of Goods and Services. *Of Nightingales That Weep* describes through the lives of the characters and plot how feudalism in Japan was used to allocate goods and services. Related concepts for Standard 3 are *economic systems, supply,* and *traditional economy.*

In a similar manner Standard 3 on allocation of goods and services can be used with many historical novels and stories set at different times and cultures. For example, the Newbery classic *Adam of the Road* by Elizabeth Gray Vining (Aladdin Press, 1943) is set in

UNIT PLAN

Using Literature to Teach Economics: Uncle Jed's Barbershop

Objectives

Students will identify instances of opportunity cost and production from reading *Uncle Jed's Barbershop.*

Students will identify the human/environment interaction in the story.

Activities

1. Depending on the number of copies, the teacher or students read the book. Teacher may give some background of the story. Some students will read the book in pairs, other individually, and the like.
2. In small groups, students discuss something they always wanted. Did they do anything to earn it?
3. List the opportunity costs in making decisions for the following characters. Which decisions were difficult?
   Uncle Jed
   Sarah Jean's father
   People who could not pay for haircuts
4. Using the table, compare your home/community environment with the description in *Uncle Jed's Barbershop.*

Comparison of Book and Our Community

Category	Uncle Jed's Community	Our Community
Housing		
Property Ownership		
Prejudice		
Banks		
Stores		
Transportation		
Communication		

Assessments

1. In small groups, students discuss what choices they made on how they spent their time last evening. What did they give up and what did they gain?
2. Informal observations of small groups and written work on opportunity costs and comparisons.

medieval England, where a young eleven-year-old boy, Adam Quartermayne, whose mother is dead, is accidentally separated from his father, a minstrel. On the road he encounters a variety of different people and many adventures until their happy reunion. Along with

Standard 3, this book could be used to focus further on economic concepts by investigating occupations in the Middle Ages and in particular, what it was like to be a European minstrel and the types of musical instruments that were used. Or students could write a resume applying for a job, in that time period listing the skills and qualifications they have, such as a merchant or an artist. By going into depth on economic material, teachers can avoid encouraging students or parents to go online to pay for guides on well-known historical fiction books. These guides offer analysis of significant themes and characters, as well as the historical context and social concerns in the work to help students who have not actually read the book. Asking students to support their work by citing evidence from the original book plus additional research helps to encourage the actual reading of the book.

Case Studies

Case studies are collections of data about a *single* individual, a single social unit such as a business, a particular event (a strike), a decision (Supreme Court on affirmative action), or a given issue. Case studies can appeal to human interests since they often involve conflict between two or more parties. One economic example of case studies might examine the tobacco industry. After studying this industry, students could become more media aware after learning how marketing is used to exploit "self-concept problems" in young people and create a favorable image of smoking. They can also examine the costs of smoking to the individual and to society.

The price of gasoline is another economic case study where the following three NCEE standards could be used:

Standard 1: Scarcity

Standard 7: Markets-Price and Quantity Determination

Standard 8: Role of Price in Market System

There are also many additional economic concepts such as *demand, production, profit, supply,* and *taxes* appropriate for this case study.

TECHNOLOGY

Initial activities could start with a discussion on why the price of gasoline has gone up in the past few years. The teacher can ask why this price increase is a problem. Resources from the Internet and the library can be found for the Organization of Petroleum Exporting Countries (OPEC), the U.S. Department of Energy, various global oil companies, economists, environmental groups, and consumer groups. The following questions can be used as a guideline:

1. What is the demand for oil? What is the supply for oil?
2. How much have oil prices increased since 2007?
3. What is the breakdown of costs (crude oil, taxes, refining, marketing, etc.) for gasoline?
4. How much do oil companies make on a gallon of gas?
5. What is the cost effectiveness of alternative fuels?
6. Can you make any policy recommendations as a result of this case study on gasoline prices?

Or the case study could involve just one large global oil company. Again, it is easy to see the value of the Internet where recent data and statistics can be found. In addition, the correlation with environmental topics can be stressed.

Skits, Dramatic Reenactments, and Simulations

Skits   Divide the class into small groups with each group responsible for writing a skit about one of the following explorers: Christopher Columbus, Bartholomeu Diaz, Vasco da Gama, and Ferdinand Magellan. You could also use an event like the Fall of Constantinople in 1453. Provide a list of economic terms on the chalkboard or on a worksheet: *benefits and costs, incentives, opportunity cost, competition,* and the like. Go over the meaning of each of the economic terms. You can ask students to make a pictograph, a simple illustration, to express the essence of each economic term. Use the following directions:

1. Each group is to write a skit using economic terms about their explorer looking for a cheaper way to get valuable spices to Europe. When giving the skit, the economic words are to be emphasized verbally.
2. Each group will also identify the route taken by the explorer.
3. At the end of the skit, the narrator asks the class to mark down what is happening to the price of the spices. It is assumed that the population and consumption of spices are increasing.

Dramatic Reenactment or Dramatic Play   Besides writing skits produced by either the teacher or students, dramatic play that reenacts historic economic decisions is worthwhile. Have two students play the roles of Jefferson and Hamilton as they discuss the merits of a national bank for the new nation. Remember that the views should be accurate. Or Henry Clay and Andrew Jackson could discuss whether improvements such as roads should be the responsibility of the national government. Inventors such as Steven Fulton, Samuel F. B. Morse, or advocates of a new transportation/communication system or technology could ask for money for their inventions or projects. Moving away from historical figures, students could take the roles of the traditional shoemaker and a new manufacturer of shoes. Or students can reenact the Great Migration of African Americans out of the rural Southern United States from 1914 to 1950. What were the push and pull factors that individual African Americans had to consider?

U.S. historical figures making economic decisions may be easier to find in the fifth- and eighth-grade curriculum but it is also possible in the sixth and seventh grades. Sixth- and seventh-grade students could role-play between the Chinese emperor and a court official about building the Great Wall of China. The roles of ruler and court official could portray the economic consequences of building large projects such as pyramids or irrigation systems in ancient times. Migrating people could discuss the incentives that caused them to leave their homelands. Medieval city officials could converse about wanting a charter for their city from the ruler in charge of the land.

To ensure that the dramatic play is successful, it is necessary that the participants really understand the point of view that they are to role-play. It is also best to allow the participants to practice outside of the classroom for a few minutes. If possible, try to critique these efforts before they are presented to the class to catch any inaccuracies. If this is not possible, after the dramatic play, you can ask if the play was accurate in all respects. Then any misinformation can be clarified. You may find that some of your more verbal students really like dramatic play and that the rest of the class will remember the economic concepts better when dramatic play is used. Remember to focus on the economic concepts underlining the dramatic play.

LESSON PLAN

The Price of Spices

The focus is on what is happening to the price of spices. Students learn that when Constantinople fell to the Ottomans in 1453, the desirable spice trade was cut. As a result, **the supply of spices decreased. Incentives** to find a new source of spices increased. Here are examples of what students could produce.

First group Act 1 Scene 1, in the castle of Isabella and Ferdinand in 1492

Isabella: So, Chris, what about this trip you want to take? Follow the Portuguese, right down the coast of Africa and then on to get the spices and gold. If we can find a way to get to Calicut by sea, we will all be in the money.

Columbus: Well, my royal lady, the spices and gold are right, but the direction is wrong. I want to sail west.

Isabella: OK. I will talk to my bankers and those who owe us money. You better come back with some hot stuff, or the **opportunity cost** will have been much too high. You know that **every choice has a cost**, don't you? There are plenty of other things that my husband and I could do with the money.

Ferdinand: You know that the government policies have both **benefits** and **costs**. Our **monetary and fiscal policies** influence the economy.

Scene 2. Columbus returns to the Court

Columbus: I brought back some natives.

Isabella: Nice, nice, very interesting. Where are the spices and gold?

Narrator: As a result of Columbus' voyage, what happened to spice prices in Europe? Why?

Act 2 Scene 1, in the Court of King Manuel; the king is speaking to Vasco da Gama

King Manuel: Now go down the coast of Africa, sail around the Cape, up the east coast of Africa, and across the Indian Ocean and get those spices. There are many **benefits** if you succeed.

Vasco: I will do as you command.

Scene 2. Vasco has returned to court after his successful voyage to India

King Manuel: So, how was the trip?

Vasco: It was great. We had to kill quite a few people along the way, but we got what we wanted—lots of spices.

King Manuel: Now we won't have to depend on those Venetians anymore. After all, markets work best with **competition**. Great job.

L E S S O N   P L A N   continued   The Price of Spices

Narrator: What will happen to the price of spices now?

Continue with scenes with other explorers. Always ask what is happening to the price of spices in Europe and why. Assessment at the end will include going over the responses of the students to what was happening to the price of the spices after each exploration.

Source: I am indebted for this idea to an article by Jim Charkins, "Voyage of Discovery," *Social Studies Review* (Vol. 43. Fall/Winter, 2003), 38–45.

Simulations   Students can learn about economic concepts through computer simulations, such as those demonstrating the old, familiar selling of lemonade or other products. Or they can be decision makers like a ruler making economic decisions for his people. See especially the "Decisions, Decisions" series from Tom Snyder Productions where students pretend to be leaders dealing with a food crisis and a growing rebellion. The popular SimCity (Maxis) simulations also engage in many economic decisions. The various stock market simulations are usually used at the high school level. However, students playing these games often do not really realize they are making economic decisions.

TECHNOLOGY

Use Video Games? Are You Kidding?   Many of your students spend more time playing in the digital worlds than with any other media such as television or watching films. Video games have wide visual appeal. Although critics may decry the violence and misogyny in some video games, obviously children and adults enjoy the interaction environment in gaming or simulations. In some cases, a parent and a child or two children play together or even become part of a larger group of players. As a shock to some parents and teachers, some games actually may promote thinking. Games may also make school more engaging for students.

Along with video games that are designed for entertainment, increasingly there are more serious video games being produced that corporations, the military, and nonprofits use to express their values or ideologies. Yet the designers of games have to use models to depict reality and also have to simplify reality. For example, the different versions of *Civilization* are based on a geographical and materialistic goods theory about civilizations. Students, however, may not be aware of the hidden curriculum—that is, what has been left out. Games may focus the players on what the game designers believe is important in the world and give less attention to achievements in art, architecture, literature, and philosophy in world history.

It appears that in the coming years, there will be more use of video games in the classroom. Video games have the potential to be a powerful learning experience for the participants. Students can immerse themselves into complex situations in which they learn by their mistakes and see other perspectives. The video games portray models of economic, political, and social organizations and how to interact in such environments. The disadvantage is the amount of time it takes to play the game.

With the increased complexity of video games, economics appears to be a very promising area for new video games that could be used in the schools, as students can play the
roles of consumers, entrepreneurs, and citizens looking at economic policy decisions.
However, this means that both teachers and students must become more alert to recognize
the bias, values, and ideology presented in the video games. For example, what perspectives does the game present about the environment? According to the video game, can you
trust government officials, organizations, or fellow citizens? Should you be loyal to your
family and friends?

Noncomputer Simulations   The most popular noncomputer economic simulation is
Marilyn Kourilsky's *Mini-Society*.[8] This simulation begins with the teacher introducing
some item of scarcity—a shortage of desirable games or colored markers. After a discussion, the class often decides to start a money system so students can pay for what they want.
This may lead to the creation of different jobs and students making items to sell or selling
their services—how to dance or how to shoot a basketball. In many successful Mini-Society
enactments, students have gone home to discuss with their parents how to earn money.
Then from these ideas, selling insurance for a rainy day (when students are paid) are introduced or banks are started to charge interest for loans and to give interest for deposits. Each
classroom's implementation of *Mini-Society* is different. Debriefing is essential to exploit
the economic knowledge that is used by participants in the society. This simulation can last
for many weeks with about 45 minutes devoted each day to *Mini-Society*.

More simple is one paragraph statements on decision making and incentives that face
everyday characters:

> I, Hans Schmidt, am a Hessian soldier hired by the British to fight against the
> American colonists during the Revolutionary War. George III sent his agents into
> Europe to rent soldiers. My ruler of Hesse-Cassel rents out his trained army for
> money. My ruler was greedy for the money but we in the army had no choice. I
> look around at the countryside in Pennsylvania and notice a lot of large prosper-
> ous farms compared to the small plots of land German farmers have at home.
> Some of the farm families also speak German although some of the Germans are
> Amish and Mennonite, different religions than mine. The children here are
> healthy and there are large families. Life here is better. Should I desert? I like my
> fellow soldiers. We have trained together and have been through good and bad
> times. But being in the army I risk life and limb. If I try to desert and am caught,
> the penalty would be very severe flogging.
>
> What are Hans's alternatives?
> What do you think Hans should do?
> What role does opportunity cost play in your decision?

Other characters and situations could also be used. For example, should you become an indentured servant or a patriot during the Revolutionary War? Should you go west to Kentucky

---

[8]Marilyn L. Kourilsky, *Mini-Society: Experiencing Real-World Economics in the Elementary School Classroom*
(Menlo Park, CA: Addison-Wesley, 1983). The author years ago was in charge of a workshop of thirty teachers
who implemented *Mini-Society*. Many of these teachers were extremely successful in their efforts. I have not seen
much of this type of activity recently, probably because of the amount of time needed for this project.

(or California or any other place)? As a slave in Virginia, should you run away and join the British army where you will be free? For world history, you could be an Irish family in 1847 during the famine. You could be a single person in present-day Mexico thinking about entering the United States by crossing the desert. In designing these cases, make sure that there are both good and poor consequences for the decisions and use a diversity of individuals—slave and free, girls and boys, and the like. These examples illustrate the economic reasoning process that students should be able to apply to many situations, especially with the attention given to the costs and benefits of every alternative.

Small Group Work **7.3**

Economic Reasoning

Were you taught the process or method of economic reasoning? Do most children or adults consider the alternatives in making a decision? Could some of the strategies described in this section help students to do economic reasoning? ●

Financial Literacy or Personal Finance

Importance

The media are constantly sending the message that far too many Americans are getting into debt by the misuse of credit cards, leading to an increasing number of bankruptcies, and do not save enough, especially for retirement. Many families live from one paycheck to the next. Given these problems, it follows that elementary and middle school students should be learning more about how to manage their own financial affairs. It is not too early to start since children are already consumers. They are already spending their own or their parents' money. Children are constantly influencing decisions on what to buy or how to spend their own time and that of their families. They may go shopping a few times each week, an activity more common than some activities like going to church or participating in after-school group activities.

Peer pressure is a real phenomenon and many students want to copy what the more popular students do, have, and wear. More and more ten-year-olds and older have cell phones, computers, video iPods, and MP3 players. The increasing popularity of electronic equipment is unlikely to abate. In higher-income schools, lost and found departments are overflowing since lost clothing and other articles are quickly replaced by parents. It appears that parents go to great lengths to satisfy their children. Critics would call these kids "pampered."

In addition, for a variety of reasons, many parents do not talk to their children about the household finances other than to occasionally say "You can't have that." In some cases the reason for the silence is that parents do not want their children to become too worried about the family's income and expenses, especially if the family budget is tight. As a result, many children are not learning about financial literacy from their parents/guardians. In some cases what they are learning from their parents is confused. Hence, only in school will these children learn about financial literacy.

Talking about Money Is a Sensitive Area

Teachers are aware of the neighborhood in which their students are living. The school also has data on the number of families living in poverty. However, one must be careful not to stereotype. For example, although most immigrant families have lower incomes compared to the average American family, it is possible that an immigrant child's parent is a professional and that the family has chosen to live in a neighborhood with many residents from their native country. In most classes, there may be a range in the economic status of the children in the class. Some are better off financially compared to their classmates while others are poorer.

Some adults are reluctant to be open and talk about their personal finances. Talking about money can be emotional. Therefore, teachers rightly should be concerned about invasion of privacy and not have parents perceiving that the teacher is meddling into a sensitive area. Communication to the parents of the goals of financial literacy is essential. This issue harks back to the previous discussion on whether children should be asked by their teacher if their families own their house or they are tenants. It might not be a good idea to have an open discussion on if or how much money each child receives as an allowance. If the teacher feels this information is important, there should be an anonymous survey with the teacher reviewing the data so that other children do not recognize the handwriting of some of their classmates.

The problem is that to be effective on teaching financial literacy or personal finance, it should ideally focus on the students' own financial decisions and not be too abstract or distant from their lives, such as teaching about the Federal Reserve system. There are areas that are close to a child's financial experiences and these can be pursued. An important consideration is that the activities associated with financial literacy be as active and engaging as possible and not textbook driven. In general, the standards/objectives is for students to identify the importance of money, the banking system, savings, and earning money.

Advertisement Activities

Why So Much Advertising?   Children and adults are exposed to numerous ads and commercials during a day. There is no escaping from them. Ads are so numerous that in one sense, we ignore the sheer number of them although subconsciously we may remember them. Furthermore, ads and commercials are more likely to increase in number as businesses believe that this is the best way to tell consumers about their goods and services. Since there is no avoiding ads, the objective of the unit plan on advertising is for students to identify both obvious and more subtle forms of advertisements in their everyday lives. With awareness comes the ability to look critically at ads. Note that this is similar to teaching about controversial issues. The student must distinguish between fact and opinion.

TECHNOLOGY

Television Commercials   Television is now the main source of news and information as well as entertainment. Therefore, it is not surprising that advertisers heavily use this medium. To help students be more aware of the appeal of commercials, you may wish to videotape some for the class to view. This also allows replay for student evaluation.

- Ask students to keep a record of how often in a week they watch television. Ask them to list their favorite programs and tell why they like them. What alternative activities or other choices did they give up by watching TV?
- For three of the programs that they watch, list the number of commercials in a given time period. For five commercials, answer the following.
  a. What benefit would you get by buying this good or service?
  b. Did the ad feature a famous person? An expert? Average people?

UNIT PLAN

Identification of Ads

Objectives
Students will identify the pervasiveness of ads in their everyday life.
Students will identify both the obvious and more subtle forms of advertisements.

Activities
1. Have children search for as many examples of advertisements as they see during a given week. If you think there are too many advertisements, limit the time to one day or even to hours after school. Or you could limit the number of advertisements to a given number such as five or ten. Ask students to try to find ads in unusual places. If possible, have them bring in the newspapers, catalogs, and fliers. You may want to make a bulletin board for these materials. For ads on billboards and public buses, have them describe the visual component and what the advertisement said. Students may forget some categories such as store signs and displays as well the packaging of products, or a shopping bag with a store logo.
2. Data Analysis
    a. Calculate the number of ads students were exposed in one week, or the time period covered.
    b. List and count where the ads were placed (newspapers, on packaging of food)
    c. List ads found in school (logos on backpacks, T-shirts, brand names on food)
3. Discussion
    What would happen if businesses did not advertise? Why do businesses advertise goods and services? What do you see as the future trends in advertisements?
4. Investigate the historical development of mass advertising and how it was tied into the growth of mass production.

Assessments
1. Have students take a certain number of their ads and answer the following.
    a. Words used to describe the good or service
    b. Price of good or service
    c. Audience for ad
    d. Appeal of the ad
    e. Older students check to see if there is any deceptive advertising. Is only factual information given? Exaggeration?
2. Make a mock ad under the assumption that there are no laws or government agencies concerned with deceptive advertising. Then make the same ad with no deceptive advertising.

c. Did you like the commercial? What helped to make it attractive? (Hints: humor, music, color, different from other commercials)

An alternative is to use ads on the Internet, but tell students not to use the pop-ups.

Money

There are a lot of emotions attached to money. Most kids want more money but have many misconceptions about it. Adults may associate money with power and have certain feelings toward it. If either a child or adult is given money as a gift and told to buy anything they would like, she or he is most likely to spend the money rather than to save it. Gift money does not have the same value to people as earned money. Often the emotions associated with money can interfere with wise decisions on how to spend or save money.

In the primary grades, most math programs teach how to count the money used in the United States. Primary children learn to recognize American coins and bills. Often by using play money, they learn how to make change. These learning experiences are necessary to function in our society. But even as children have had concrete experiences in paying for their lunches, smart cards are being introduced in schools for that purpose. This trend makes it harder for children to understand the economic meaning of money and its importance. They may not realize that money makes it easier to trade, borrow, save, invest, and compare the value of goods and services. The relevant NCEE standard is Standard 11: Role of Money.

Learning Experiences with Money   **Money** is anything that people accept as the final payment for goods and services. But money has not always looked like it does today. In the past, beads, shells, cattle, feathers, and salt are but a few forms that have been used as money. Showing pictures of these items, ask students what would be the advantages or disadvantages of using any of these forms of money. It becomes quite obvious that it is easier to use metal coins, paper bills, and bank checks than the older forms of money. Money needs to be portable and not too heavy or inconvenient to carry. Money also should be durable. True, paper bills do eventually wear out, but they can give years of service before they are replaced. In addition, money should be divisible. If you have a ten dollar bill and your purchase was less than ten dollars, you need to be able to get change. It is hard to divide a cow or a feather.

For outstanding photos of older American currency, go to the website of the Federal Reserve Bank of San Francisco for their Showcase of Bills by historical periods (www.frbsf.org/currency). See Pocahontas and other scenes of the westward expansion of the United States commemorated in American currency. Especially if you have students who have traveled outside of the United States or are from immigrant families, ask what currency was used in their countries. What currency would you use if you wanted to visit Turkey, China, New Zealand, or Mexico? Show examples of different currencies.

Discuss the following questions. What if you wanted some food but there was not an available money system? What would you do? In the past, a *barter system* has been used to exchange goods and services. Reread previous trade books to students (see earlier sections of this chapter) in which barter was used or the example of Lewis and Clark's expedition using barter with the Indians. What are the negatives of a barter system? A plus for a money system is that it allows you to make comparisons. Sandals cost so many dollars but boots cost more. A money system also encourages specialization of occupations. Everyone does not have to grow their own food or make their own clothes. Instead, certain people do these jobs while others can be artists or carpenters. People can save money and not worry if the older forms of money will decay, break, or become lame.

Is money the most important feature of our economy? Remember that money is just a convenient way of buying goods and services. How helpful would money be in the following situations?

- A backpack filled with American bills in a distant jungle when you are hungry
- In the fable, King Midas getting thirsty while turning everything to gold
- Getting along better with a sibling

All of these activities can help students better understand the concept of money and its importance.

Using Literature   In their reading, students are constantly encountering characters involved in the economic system. In many cases, the characters and their families are facing money or financial problems. Identify what economic roles the characters play in the novel: workers, consumers, citizens, savers, and the like. What did the characters do to solve their financial problems? Work, emigrate to the United States, or some other solution?

Banking

Banks are an important institution in our country and the world. According to NCEE Standard 10: Role of Economic Institutions, banks, labor unions, corporations, legal systems, and non-for-profit organizations are examples of important institutions that have evolved in market economies to help individuals and groups accomplish their goals. Yet banks are a source of confusion for many children. They cannot understand why some people can write checks and get money or why some people use ATM machines to get money from the machine. To many children, the bank is not an impressive building with a guard standing by but a small space in the local supermarket where one or two people seem to be clerks. For children to better understand banks and their importance, try the following activities.

Activities: Where Is a Safe Place?   Tell students to presume that each student has $100, and they do not need to use this money for a while. What should you do with it? You do not want to carry that much money around in your pocket or backpack. It's all right to carry enough money to pay for lunch or a snack, but $100 is just too much to carry around school. It also does not make sense to have it visible around the house. You probably should not leave it any place where it can be seen so that anyone can take it. You could hide it. What would be a good place? An old joke is that people have hidden money under the mattress and in cookie jars. There are probably other good hiding places such as under a lamp or in a book. Any negatives to doing this? You have to remember where you hid the money and that no one disturbs the hiding place—fire, cleaning the house, and the like.

To avoid losing or having the money stolen, more people have decided that a safer place to deposit money is a bank. Not only is this a convenient solution in terms of safety, but the bank will pay *interest* for every dollar you keep in a savings account. Interest is usually expressed as a percentage such as 5 percent. When you need this money, you can *withdraw* your money.

The bank may pay you 5 percent interest per year but they do not just keep most of your money in the bank. Most of your deposit will be used for making *loans* to other customers of the bank. These customers will pay a higher interest rate, let us say 8 percent or 10 percent so that the bank will make a profit. For riskier loans, there will be a higher rate of interest charged. To write checks, a person needs enough money in the bank to cover or pay the amount of the check. To further reinforce these concepts, teachers may want to use NCEE's lesson on "What Happens When a Bank Makes a Loan."

Simulation of a Bank   *Mini-Society* and other simulations of banks have been very successful using pretend or play money. First, some students volunteer to have certain jobs in the classroom's bank. Tellers are instructed on how to open accounts (or you can automatically enroll everyone in the class with a set amount of money), and to accept deposit and withdrawal slips. A bank manager is the person who makes loans. If you wish, you could have a guard, though they are now found only in large urban banks. However, students may have seen security cameras in banks to reduce the possibility of a robbery. For keeping track of the balance after additions (deposits) and subtractions (withdrawals), students can use calculators, which are very convenient to compute interest. Other teachers have used a simple simulation where one student in front of the class is a bank manager and another student asks for a loan. Both calculate what the interest will be for a year.

Field Trip   A visit to a bank can be a good learning experience if students already know the basic functions of the bank. It may even be more worthwhile for disadvantaged groups who have not been inside of a bank as opposed to middle class students whose parents may have already taken them. However, it is possible that the middle class students have not gained much from this bank experience.

Most banks want students to eventually be their customers and usually are eager to explain the functions of the bank. However, just seeing people sitting behind desks and customers in line may not be worth the time or effort, especially if the explanation from the bank personnel is not concrete and goes over students' heads. Filling out deposit and withdrawal slips and being given receipts should be demonstrated by a bank personnel. If possible, seeing the safety deposit boxes may be a first-time experience for children. Another alternative is to visit a credit union instead of a bank.

Earning Money

Students face the problem of whether they can afford to buy a new scooter or a pair of shoes. Scarcity and limited resources are always a problem. Earning money may be a way for a young person to buy what she or he wants. Some young people earn money by doing chores at home but other young people may get an allowance without having to do chores. If skilled enough, young people can earn money by doing chores for neighbors ranging from raking lawns to watching pets and picking up newspapers while families are gone on vacation. With more parents working, babysitting has been a popular activity to earn money. Students may be amused by reading *Lunch Money* by Andrew Clements in which a young boy named Greg has been earning money since he was little. However, students need their parents' permission to start working for someone else. Some parents may not want their children to work too many hours if their schoolwork or their own chores are neglected. There are also child labor laws to prevent children and youth from working where they might be injured or harmed.

Some students are sensitive to having what is not in fashion and looks "old." So these young people earn money by selling their toys, clothes, and electronics that they have outgrown or no longer want or use. This may be at a family garage sale. Other young people are actually selling iPods, cell phones and the like on Craigslist, the free online bulletin board. Sales may not be limited to the Internet but can occur in the school hallways or local sidewalks. Young people do have to be careful and need an adult with them in transporting goods to a stranger.

More formal experience to earn money can be facilitated by various organizations like Junior Achievement (www.ja.org/programs). Junior Achievement's K–12 programs also cover personal finance, work preparation, and economics. There may be a Junior Achievement club organized in the school for entrepreneurship. Other local community organizations provide free assistance with their business personnel to help guide students to make goods or give services.

But they warn the students: there is a risk of business failure!

Earning Money for a Charitable Project   Sometimes a class will decide to earn money for a charitable project. Students perceive a need and are interested in helping others, often children living far away who need assistance. Fund-raising is a major time commitment and needs to be carefully planned.

- *Goal:* What is the target amount and how will the money be used?
- *Schedule:* What is the best date for the event? Calendar conflicts?
- *Type:* What product or service will be sold? Sometimes this involves a festival or bazaar. Students may decide to sell food. They have to research rental fees for popcorn or snow cone machines. In addition, students have to decide how much to charge to make a profit selling these treats. Or they may organize a raffle with gifts from local businesses.
- *Who Is in Charge?* In these activities, students can take responsibility for earning money for a worthwhile purpose. Fortunately, in most cases, students are successful in raising money and feel a sense of satisfaction in their achievement. They also may learn something about economics and the usefulness of math.

Spending Money

Spending money for most young people is easy to do. There are lots of things and services—fast food, lunches at the school cafeteria, clothing, movies, CDs—to buy. Impulse buying may quickly deplete their money. To reduce impulse buying, everyone has to ask if they really *need* the item and if they really *want* it. Frequently many people do not slow down to ask these questions. They do not save their money. *Saving* is setting aside money for the future and not spending it now on goods and services.

Students' quick decisions may not always promote what they really want and need. Longer-term saving goals may include a pet, skateboard, video game player, or the like. Often money is spent at once on many lower-priced items, and the larger goal of purchasing a more expensive item in the future never happens, since there are no savings. Saving for the future means giving up buying things today. In most cases, students have not opened a savings accounts at a bank with a parent as a custodian. With their money not safely stored away from home, their available money is quickly spent as soon as it is received, resulting in no savings.

Consumer education has now moved away from the moralistic approach of finding the best buy for a can of pineapple. With more awareness of using economic principles such as opportunity costs, students still can gain by finding out how their money was really spent. For simplicity, they could track for a week how many snacks they are buying. Older students can benefit by having a budget, a statement of how much money is earned and spent over a period of time. This means jotting down what they earn or receive and what they spend. Students are often surprised to see how much they are actually spending. Websites exist that give information on creating a budget as well as other financial areas. Knowing how much you are spending in general categories such as clothing may be the first step in making better spending decisions. Remember the privacy concerns if you have students make a budget.

Sometimes students are not aware of actually how much they are spending for a given item. For example, looking at clothing at a department store, students often are faced with the problem of how much a pair of jeans really costs. The ticket attached to the blue jeans has the original price of $55.99. But there is a sign showing a discount of 15 percent and another sign on top of the rack stating that if you buy the item this weekend, there is another 30 percent discount. "Discount will be taken at the desk." In some stores, there are scanners to show you the price you will actually pay. Uncertain about the price, young people take the blue jeans to the cashier to ring up the bill. When they actually see the amount, they are often afraid to back down and admit they do not want the item. In most cases, students need to round off and make an estimate of what the item will cost. If not, they can go to the clerk and say that they are uncertain what the item costs and to please scan for the price. Then you can make a decision before starting the process of the sale.

Teachers may benefit by using some of the free lesson plans of the National Council for Economic Education (NCEE). The Learning, Earning and Investing series (lei.ncee.net) has free online lessons for fourth- and fifth-grade classes showing the benefits and strategies for long-term investing success. You may have noticed that NCEE has many website addresses. All will work. In addition, many of the websites funded by for-profit organizations are using lessons from NCEE such as ECONnections (www.e-connections.org) and The Mint (www.themint.org).

World of Work

All students will eventually need to have the knowledge and skills to be able to earn a living. Formerly, there was an emphasis on career education in the schools. Now with jobs changing so quickly, it would not be wise for teachers to stress "what do you want to be when you grow up." Today's rapid changes in jobs suggest that everyone has to be prepared to make many work and career changes. Students need a flexible attitude toward change as well as the capacity to readily acquire new knowledge and skills to compete in an increasingly global market.

Students are now encouraged to see their futures as participants in the economy. In effect, students need to see themselves as workers in their school, whose jobs are to develop their human capital. There is a connection between what is stressed in school and the outside world. Working cooperatively as a team, being dependable, and being responsible are all qualities that are required in a work situation. With these values and skills, students can participate in the economy of the future.

Students need to learn that they are *human capital* and that they already have some skills. There are trade books that teach about human capital. Mary Skillings Prigger's *Aunt*

Minnie McGranahan (Clarion Books, 1999) tells how resourceful Aunt Minnie must be when she inherits nine orphaned nephews and nieces. Or Marie Bradby's *More Than Anything Else* (Orchard Books, 1995) tells about a nine-year-old boy who wants to learn to read but has to work with his father and brother in the salt mines of West Virginia.

Students can be made aware of the working world by field trips to hospitals, stores, offices, or factories. These places can illustrate the division of labor necessary in our society as well as the variety of jobs. Do not visit a factory or business that is too complex or abstract for your students. Generally, visiting an office or computer center is not as useful as visiting a place that makes a single product such as soft drinks or candy. Students can also "tour" several manufacturing sites on the Internet. However, students should realize that manufacturing jobs are declining and that they are more likely to be in the service industry as adults.

Small Group Work **7.4**

Our Emphases?

Financial Literacy or Personal Finance

Do you think you should spend more time on personal finance? Do you think personal finance is a problem for the children or youth you are likely to teach? ●

Summary

*T*eaching economic education is becoming more important in our global society. Students need to apply economic reasoning both to choices they make as citizens as well as their own personal finance. Incorporating economic topics into history is well worthwhile. In addition, activities moving away from the textbook such as literature, case studies, investigations, projects, field trips, skits, simulations, video games, and dramatic play can make economics more meaningful for students. More attention is now being given to personal finance with topics such as money, advertisements, banking, earning money, and spending money.

Suggested Readings and Websites

National Council on Economic Education. *The Great Economic Mysteries Book: A Guide to Teaching Economic Reasoning Grades 4–8.* New York: National Council on Economic Education, 2003.

Students solve seventeen engaging mysteries by applying an economic way of thinking.

Websites

EconEdLink

www.econedlink.org

Online lesson plans plus other economic data.

Foundation for Teaching Economics Lessons

http://fte.org

Online lesson plans.

Marco Polo by WorldCom, Inc.

http://marcopolo.worldcom.com

Good for both economics and geography.

The National Council on Economic Education

www.economicsamerica.org

The best and most comprehensive site for economics lessons and resources. See also the many websites for this organization mentioned in the chapter.

VIDEO HOMEWORK EXERCISE

Teaching Vocabulary

Go to MyEducationLab, select the topic **Economics**, and watch the video entitled "Teaching Vocabulary."

In this video, a middle school learning coordinator uses various techniques to facilitate the learning of the new and challenging vocabulary of economics.

CHAPTER 8

Teaching Civic Education

In this chapter we view civic education or citizenship education from a broad perspective. Civic education is defined and examined moving outward from the classroom, the school, the community, and finally the global community.

- Different Meaning of Citizenship
- Civic Education
- Classroom Civic Education
- Instruction in Civic Education
- Current Events/Current Affairs Programs
- Teaching Controversial Issues
- Linking Schoolwide Citizenship to the Community
- Teaching Global Education

recycle

PLASTIC

PAPER

What civic education is being promoted here?

Different Meaning of Citizenship

More and more the term **civic education** is being used instead of **citizenship education,** particularly in the listing of state standards. However, the term *citizenship education* is often still used to describe a student's behavior or *global citizenship* is used, for example, on a report card. In addition, the term *democratic citizenship* is often used.

At a general level, almost all individuals and groups espouse civic education and democracy but vary on their definition of civic education and what a good citizen does. Therefore, there are a wide variety of educational approaches for civic education and democracy. As described in Chapter 1, Westheimer and Kahne[1] outlined three current main conceptions of a "good citizen":

- Personally responsible citizen
- Participatory citizen
- Justice-oriented citizen

How do these three concepts translate into teaching civic education? The personally responsible citizen aligns more with the character education approach, with a focus on personal qualities. According to this approach, personally responsible citizens show honesty, integrity, respect, and compassion. These citizens pay taxes, obey laws, vote, and work hard in the community. They pick up litter, give blood, recycle, and stay out of debt. Personally responsible citizens help those in need by contributing to food or clothing drives to help those less fortunate. They may also help in volunteer programs.

The participatory citizen is an active member who participates in the civic affairs and social life of the community at the local, state, and national levels. To do this, the citizen needs both knowledge and skills. Participatory citizens *know* how the government and other institutions such as churches and community-based organizations work. *Skills* are needed for citizens to be able to participate in meetings and take part in community-based efforts. The ideal is an informed and engaged citizen. Many of the state standards as well as the National Council for the Social Studies advocate this approach.

Lastly, the justice-oriented citizen critically assesses social, political, and economic structures and then takes social action to redress injustice. By critically studying problems such as poverty and searching for root causes, students look to what social and political action should be taken. This is more like the social reformer approach, judging that inequality must be examined. The concept of the justice-oriented citizen is the least commonly found in the schools.

You also may encounter other terms such as *transnational* or *cosmopolitan citizenship,* reflecting increased global awareness. Less likely seen are such terms as *civic republican citizenship, liberal citizenship, feminist citizenship,* and *reconstructionist citizenship.*

NAEP Civics Results

According to the 2006 NAEP's Report Card, what do students know about civics? Civic knowledge improved for younger fourth-grade students, but eighth and twelfth graders' scores were relatively unchanged since 1998. Most of the improvement at grade 4 was

---

[1]Joel Westheimer and Joseph Kahne, "Educating the 'Good' Citizen: The Politics of School-Based Civic Education Programs." Paper delivered at the 2002 Annual Meeting of the American Political Association, Boston, MA, 2002.

among lower-performing students. At grade 4, the performance gap narrowed for Hispanic students compared to white students. On the whole, about two out of three American students at grades 4, 8, and 12 have at least a basic knowledge of civics. At grade 4, 73 percent scored at or above basic knowledge.

Here are some particulars from the NAEP Civic Report Card.

Fourth Graders
- 75 percent knew that only citizens can vote in the United States
- 47 percent identified the role of the Supreme Court
- 14 percent recognized that defendants have a right to a lawyer

Eighth Graders
- 80 percent identified a notice for jury duty
- 63 percent determined an instance of abuse of power
- 28 percent explained the historical purpose of the Declaration of Independence
- 15 percent interpreted a phrase from the Gettysburg Address

Just to make sure the question on the Declaration of Independence is clear, the first paragraph was included ("We hold these truths to be self-evident" including the phrase "Right of the People to alter or to abolish it") and then students were asked the following multiple-choice question:

The Declaration of Independence was written to

a. appeal to other countries for help in fighting Great Britain
b. convince Great Britain to repeal the Stamp Act
c. make laws for a new form of government
d. explain why the colonies were breaking away from Great Britain (correct answer)

One wonders why such a small percentage of eighth-grade students marked the correct response. It would appear that too many students are clueless about this important primary source document, and civic education needs to be improved.

In reality, classroom practices on civic education can be a bit fuzzy. Is the service learning experience designed to critically assess nursing homes or is it really closer to volunteer service? The three different concepts of civic education do produce a variance in what teachers do and what students learn.

Civic Education

Improvement? Civic Mission of Schools

Many organizations and foundations want to improve civic education in the schools. Among their concerns is the number of young people who do not vote and who are disengaged from civic and political institutions. In addition, some young people are not informed or do not understand how to participate fully in our democratic society. On the positive side, more young people believe in helping others through community service and volunteering.

What can be done about these problems? The schools are one answer. Fostering and developing civic understandings, skills, values, and participation have always been important goals for the schools. Schools reach almost all children and young people. Thus, the schools have been designated to foster the necessary civic knowledge, skills, values, and commitments to become good citizens. However, family, religious institutions, political parties, and the media also influence students' civic education.

A major national initiative to renew and restore civic education was proposed in the Carnegie Corporation & Circle report titled *The Civic Mission of Schools.*[2] Making use of the best available research, this report recommends the following six promising approaches to improve civic education.

1. Classroom instruction in government, history, law, and democracy
2. Discussion of current events
3. Service learning linked for formal curriculum and classroom instruction
4. Extracurricular activities, particularly student government and journalism
5. Student voice in school governance
6. Student simulations of democratic processes and procedures (voting, mock trials, legislative deliberation, diplomacy)

All these six approaches are covered in this chapter.

As a starting point for implementing the Civic Mission of Schools, have students brainstorm what makes an effective citizen. Students may give you insights on what kinds of things go on in the school, both in and out of class, that promote or discourage effective citizenship. Using these six promising approaches, teachers and administrators have identified weaknesses as well as bright spots in their civic education programs and have initiated changes. Looking beyond your own school, check if your state has an active campaign for Civic Mission of Schools.

Teaching Patriotism

After the terrorist attacks on America at the World Trade Center towers in New York City and the Pentagon in Washington, DC, on September, 11, 2001 (often called 9/11), there was a great outpouring of patriotic feelings from many people, including children and young people. Along with sharing a love of their country, almost everyone in the United States agrees that democracy is the best form of government. Furthermore, we cannot take its survival for granted. Each new generation has to be socialized to support the democratic values and traits necessary for our society to function. Almost everyone also agrees that rote memorization of patriotic songs and slogans is not sufficient.

Patriotism, a devotional feeling toward our country and our way of life, our democratic values and a republican government, is an abstract concept. Therefore it lends itself to symbols like the flag and the Pledge of Allegiance. Flags are displayed and patriotic songs sung everywhere from ball games to memorial rites. Given its emotional underpinnings, it is no surprise that patriotism is controversial when it comes to the daily activities of the nation's

[2]Carnegie Corp. of New York and the Center for Information and Research on Civic Learning and Engagement (CIRCLE), *The Civic Mission of Schools* (New York: Carnegie Corporation of New York & CIRCLE, College Park, MD, 2003). Available online at www.civicmissionofschools.org

schoolchildren. Should there be a flag in every classroom? Should a student be suspended for wearing a t-shirt with an upside-down American flag? Individuals and groups disagree on what should be done to teach patriotism in public schools.

Both conservatives and liberals assert that it is not enough just to have positive patriotic feelings about our nation. To oversimplify, conservatives tend more toward the personally responsible citizen approach but also want all students to have a strong knowledge of our nation's history and constitutional heritage. Liberals, on the other hand, are wary of efforts that could encourage unthinking obedience to authority. A more radical group espouses the third position of a justice-oriented citizen. The issue comes down to what type of socialization should be encouraged since political socialization is not neutral. A key difference between the groups is whether a market-based economy is an essential element of democracy. Tension on the teaching of patriotism is likely to remain because of these differences. You will note that many of the arguments made by conservatives and liberals are the same that were presented in the "history wars" (see Chapter 5). But regardless of the perspective one takes, patriotism calls for responsibility and acting to honor our ideals. It requires civic engagement and participation that may require time and effort.

Small Group Work **8.1**

Your Choice

Which of the three citizenship approaches is the closest to your values? What do you think is the best way to teach patriotism? Why? Which approach do you think is most similar to the one espoused by the community in which you expect to teach? ●

Classroom Civic Education

Looking at the classroom, civic education may sound abstract compared to teaching about the American Revolution or opportunity costs. First, look at the following three goals for all our students to become effective citizens.

1. Citizens are informed and thoughtful and have a knowledge of our system of government with its underlying values, rights, and responsibilities.
2. Citizens gain skills and have the commitment to participate in their communities.
3. Citizens develop democratic and civic dispositions to participate in civic affairs. This goal includes having concern for the rights of others, having tolerance and respect for others, and believing in the capacity to make a difference.

You will recall that the main goal of history, geography, and economics is also civic education. Civic education is the very heart of social studies. These three main civic goals aim to equip students with both an adequate background and thinking skills. Then a student can at a minimum be an informed citizen who votes and participates in the community, two commonly agreed-on goals for adult citizens. In addition, we readily realize that civic education does not just take place during the time in class devoted to social studies. Civic education takes place all day long in the classroom, as well as in other school venues such as the playground and the lunch room.

Rules and School Governance

Children and young people need special guidance in citizenship skills. They are learning to deal with authority in their lives. Their parents, teachers, older siblings, school-yard aides, and older peers give them orders and rules to follow. Unless you highlight the need for rules and order, children and young people may believe that authority depends on who has the most power and size. Give examples of power (bullies) and authority (government officials) and have children distinguish between the two.

For primary children, discuss why we have specific rules in the classroom and the school. At all grade levels, students can help create classroom rules for the purpose of maintaining order and establishing an environment for learning to occur. Most classrooms have a broad general rule that everyone has the right to be respected. What happens when this rule and other rules are not followed? Who is responsible for enforcing the rules?

Making rules and practicing the use of authority open children's understanding of justice and fairness. For example, this can be done by having classroom rules that stress fairness in determining when a student can use a computer or participate in other popular activities. In addition, roles and responsibilities like doing room maintenance or being a class officer can be rotated throughout the year so each student participates in both leadership and following roles.

These activities can move students to consider other figures of authority, ranging from firefighters to the president. What rules are necessary in the community, state, and nation? What authority do elected officials and public servants have? What rules do they follow? What happens if they do not follow the rules?

Discuss the meaning and purpose of laws such as speed limits, stop lights, wearing seatbelts, and going to school. Fables can instruct too. Leo Lionni's *It's Mine* (Dragonfly, 1996) tells about three quarrelsome frogs, Arnold Lobel's *Fables* (HarperCollins, 1980) are humorous contemporary fables about responsibility and citizenship, and the old classic *Aesop's Fables* can illustrate the need to cooperate along with other important lessons.

Once the reasons for the rules are clarified, you can play the devil's advocate to help children reason through decisions. For example, should the traffic patrol guard who lets them cross the street ever be disobeyed? What if the patrol guard is laughing and joking and has not checked the traffic? If an insect lands on another child's back, can you break the classroom rule by swatting the insect and the child? In what circumstances could you break the school rule about tardiness?

Students also can learn that rules and laws change or that new ones are needed to fit current situations. What role will students have in changing the rules of the classroom? Of the school? Hopefully the student council is seen as more than a popularity contest for students to win elections or raise money by selling candy or magazines. For older students clubs also can offer opportunities for decision making. Although teachers and administrators have the final authority in a school, students should be given as many opportunities as possible to learn how to make decisions and see their consequences. There is always the need to evaluate the reasonableness and effectiveness of given laws of the classroom, community, and nation.

A Caring Classroom

What really is more important than the specific roles and responsibilities of students is the atmosphere or the climate that gets established in the classroom. How often have you walked into a classroom and "felt" that it was a friendly place? In the same school in another classroom the ambience may be totally different. One teacher may appear to promote a positive classroom climate where learning occurs while another may not. The atmosphere or classroom climate may seem poor when there is frequent disruptive behavior that wears down teacher morale, depresses students' academic and social outcomes, and creates parental dissatisfaction.

We all want classrooms in which caring and learning prevail. Building caring classroom communities takes considerable effort on the part of both the teacher and the students, and it does not come automatically. An important first step, done with both informal and planned opportunities, is for children to feel that they are among friends. How did you feel when you entered a new class in September and did not know one soul in the room? We need to help students to get to know and respect one another and, thus, create a safe classroom environment that fosters learning and citizenship goals.

Classroom and Town Meetings   Classrooms and town meetings can give students a voice in school governance. They are another essential strategy for modeling decision making. Decisions about real choices must be the agenda.

Whatever the issue, the meetings should have the following criteria:

1. A signal for wanting to speak
2. A discussion leader (teacher for earlier grades)
3. A discussion of the choices that examines good and bad possible results of each choice
4. The possibility of seeking more information before voting
5. A way of voting secretly so that each child votes according to his or her own feeling
6. A way of following through to see that the vote is honored

Look for these criteria in the classroom episode. As you read, think about the payoffs for the citizenship skills children can gain from classroom time spent this way.

There is a moral to this episode. As a teacher, you should not allow class decision making unless you honor the class's results. Note that Mr. Sanchez did have some power as he directed the discussion. For example, it is common that teachers do not list on the board ideas that they do not think relevant or appropriate. Furthermore, Mr. Sanchez should not have been surprised that his class did not vote for the "Getting Out the Vote Campaign." Both children and adults like to see concrete results from a service project. Service or community projects such as packing food and canned goods into boxes and clean-up campaigns are popular because you see the immediate results. In contrast, the "Getting Out the Vote Campaign," although fundamental for our political process, appears vague and abstract to children. Mr. Sanchez wisely followed the class decision because he knew if service learning is coerced, the activity may lose value in the minds of the students.

Small Group Work **8.2**

Class Cooperative Planning

What were the advantages of having the class decide the service learning choice? Disadvantages? Would you have allowed the class to decide on the type of service learning activity? ●

Other teachers have used the town meeting format. Often there is a mayor and this job rotates so that every student gets a chance for this job. The mayor along with the teacher writes an agenda for the town meeting. Any student can submit a proposal for discussion but the issue has to be written and given to the mayor before the meeting. At the town meeting the class discusses the issue and may vote to resolve the issue. Sometimes committees are formed to find out more information or to see that the new rule is enforced. If the issue affects more than one classroom, students can write to the Student Council or, if there is a school newspaper, a letter to the editor.

Settling Disagreements and Conflicts

The second part of learning ways to live together goes beyond organizing students to having them assume classroom responsibilities for certain procedures and activities. Disagreements and conflicts between individuals and groups will arise no matter how imaginative and

Classroom Episode
Looking in Classrooms: Classroom Decision Making

Mr. Sanchez's fifth-grade class is discussing what type of service learning they want to do. Mr. Sanchez would like his class to work on a "Get Out the Vote Campaign." The community in which the students live has a lower than average voter participation rate and he feels that the schools should reach out to the community.

Mr. Sanchez: What places do you think would make a good service activity for our class?

Anna: I think we should help the Sunshine Nursing Home. I've been there and there is nothing for the old people to do. It's close to our school.

Mr. Sanchez: That is a good idea. I will put that on the board as a possibility.

Delores: I don't want to go to a nursing home. It smells.

Elijah: I think we should plant trees. My uncle says you can get some free small ones from the county.

Mr. Sanchez: That is another good idea. Let's consider planting trees too. (But does not put the suggestion on the board.)

Mia: I like the idea of planting trees. It's good for the environment. You are supposed to plant trees.

Mr. Sanchez: Does everyone agree about the suggestion of planting trees? (Several students nod their heads. Puts the suggestion on the board.)

Maya: Planting trees is hard work. Where will we get the spades and shovels? How are we going to water and take care of the trees once they are planted?

Mr. Sanchez: Those are good points. We can't take on too big of a project. How about "Getting Out the Vote Campaign" as a project? As we talked before, we should help the community.

Adeline: My family does not like politics.

Children add more comments.

Postscript

After putting all the suggestions on the chalkboard, the class voted with a secret ballot to plant trees as their service project.

Table 8.1	Strategies for Resolving Conflict

Between Individuals	Class Meetings
1. Both individuals stop, cool off.	1. Leader asks whether anyone has a problem group needs to discuss.
2. Both take turns talking about what is wrong.	
3. Both listen to each other without interrupting.	2. When problem is volunteered, leader asks show of hands for agreement to hold meeting on problem mentioned.
4. Each one tries to tell what he or she needs.	
5. They brainstorm possible solutions.	3. Leader asks group to define what the problem issue is.
6. They choose solution both like.	
7. They plan how to put solution into action.	4. Group lists ways problem can be solved.
8. They "go" for plan by writing it out.	5. Group evaluates and chooses solution.

thorough the system for making classrooms and playgrounds run smoothly. One suggestion is to ask students to write letters when they acted in ways contrary to the teacher's expectations, such as a disruptive disagreement with another student. This technique provides a cooling down period and also gives more time to the teacher to react. From the letter(s) the teacher can see what was important to the student and it gives an opportunity for the students to develop reasoning and writing skills.

Two additional strategies for helping students learn how to work through these incidents complete the well-rounded plan for citizenship development. One is conflict resolution, which engages individuals involved in a dispute in finding a mutually acceptable alternative. The second is the class meeting, which leads the whole class to work out a solution to a generally felt problem.[3] See Table 8.1 for conflict resolution strategies.

In using conflict resolution or mediation, it is first necessary to realize that not all conflicts can be resolved by this technique. Some individuals do not want to or cannot easily change or give up what they feel is important. It is easier to resolve conflicts that are based on misunderstandings than to resolve conflicts over beliefs and values. The conflict resolution process requires a mediator or person trained in the steps in conflict resolution: opening, listening, creating options, and planning to solve the problem.

To implement a peer-mediation program or conflict resolution program requires the support of the administration and the selection of students and staff who are trained as mediators.[4] Peer mediators should be chosen from a cross section of the school community and be willing to learn, have good verbal skills, and have the respect of their peers. In many schools, peer mediators are assigned to work in pairs. This gives mediators a degree of support needed to conduct their "Peace Patrol" during out-of-class time as they try to stop conflict between two individuals before it escalates. The mediators try to be nonjudgmental and impartial. Schools have reported great benefits on all grade levels when conflicts are able to be resolved. Sometimes this is called "Peace Education."

Let us look at the following example. Sharif and Bernie are brought before peer mediation because of a conflict that ended when Bernie bopped Sharif on the head with a cafeteria

[3]William Glasser, *Schools without Failure* (New York: Harper and Row, 1969).

[4]Conflict resolution is commonly a component of districtwide programs for reducing violence in schools.

tray. Two versions are presented. "He ate my cookie!" "He gave it to me and then wanted it back but I'd already eaten it!" After many questions by the mediators, both Sharif and Bernie shake hands and agree that things could have been done differently. A successful outcome, or a win-win situation.

If your school does not have a peer conflict resolution team, the teacher can take this role. Here are the steps to follow, which are similar to peer mediation.

1. Identify the problem without blame.
2. Brainstorm alternatives together.
3. Agree on a solution.
4. Evaluate the result.

The teacher, however, cannot be an impartial mediator after going through the preceding steps. For example, a school rule could have been broken and the consequences for such behavior are already spelled out. In addition, as said before, this process is not a cure-all for some individual children. However, one successful antiviolence program for young children required that *all* the parents of children in the program be trained in management, discipline, and supervision. Teachers learned how to better manage inappropriate behavior. Volunteer playground monitors learned how to supervise more effectively and reward behavior during unstructured lunch and recess periods. At the end of the program, it was found that even the most initially aggressive children were virtually indistinguishable from the average child in behavior. The important key was to influence all parts of a child's world and to include the entire population rather than selected "problem" students within that group.[5] In other words, it may take a whole village to educate a child.

An increasingly common problem as children become older is an increase in verbal aggression like insults and taunts. Many students report being made fun of for their dress, their religion, racial/ethnic group, their language, intellectual ability, shyness, weight, socioeconomic status, or for being perceived as different. These examples show the face of bullying. **Bullying** is defined as persistent teasing, name-calling, or social exclusion. It may also include physical acts, although it is more likely to include threats of violence rather than violence per se. Unfortunately, too often teasing and bullying are part of daily life for students. Research has found that boys initiate most of the teasing and bullying incidents, but both boys and girls are the recipients. However, boys are more likely to respond physically, whereas girls are more likely to respond verbally to incidents initiated against them. The prime area of bullying behavior is the playground where play is unstructured and competitive games can be a problem. Usually teachers and other adults do not intervene in these incidents, often because they are not aware and they are easily overlooked. Typically the "victim" does not report the problem to the teacher or principal. Furthermore, the other students, the bystanders, often do not speak out either. Also ignored are bullying tactics of girls—organized shunning, whispering, spreading negative rumors, and mocking targeted students. Students typically serve as passive bystanders to bullying. However, students can examine strategies to stick up for their peers who are bullied.

If there are problems on the playground, students can discuss in a class meeting the value of noncompetitive games in the playground. Dodgeball has been banned in some school playgrounds. For example, new games of "tag" are available in which the players are never

---

[5]Henry Tama, "Targeting the Adults in Young Kids' Lives Helps Halt Aggression," *USA Today* (April 24, 2000): 1D.

permanently "out." Either their roles change or they can be released back into the game by other players. Many students, especially those not well coordinated in physical ability, might like to try out some of the noncompetitive games, and it could reduce bullying incidents. However, although all students should be encouraged in physical activity, no students should be made to do an activity at free time recess and lunch if they are uncomfortable about it.

Cyberbullying

As students get older, you might want to try an anonymous survey about Internet safety. Include some of the following statements and ask that students mark if the statement is true for them, even it is true only once.

TECHNOLOGY

- I have pretended to be someone else online.
- I have been cyberbullied.
- I have been a cyberbully.
- I have given personal information out on the Internet.

Often teachers have been surprised by what their students are doing on the Internet.

Small Group Work **8.3**

Bullying
Do you recall any incident of bullying when you were a child? Was anything done to stop the bullying? ●

Instruction in Civic Education

Standards for Civic Education

Knowledge about the key concepts of government is essential for citizens to participate in our society. Formal instruction in civics or government has been part of the elementary public school program for well over a century. The goal in civics and government programs is to produce informed, responsible participation by competent citizens committed to the values and principles of the American democratic system. What standards should be used to see if students understand our political systems and the roles of citizens?

The Center for Civic Education issued in 1994 *National Standards for Civics and Government,* a K–12 curriculum, including specific standards for K–4 and for grades 5 to 8.[6]

The five organizing questions for K–4 are as follows:

1. What is government and what should it do?
2. What are the basic values and principles of American democracy?
3. How does the government established by the Constitution embody the purposes, values, and principles of American democracy?
4. What is the relationship of the United States to other nations and to world affairs?
5. What are the roles of the citizen in American democracy?

---

[6]Published by the Center for Civic Education, 5146 Douglas Fir Road, Calabasas, CA 91302-1467; telephone (800) 350-4223, www.civiced.org

The organizing questions for grades 5 to 8 are these:

1. What are civic life, politics, and government?
2. What are the foundations of the American political system?
3. How does the government established by the Constitution embody the purposes, values, and principles of American democracy?
4. What is the relationship of the United States to other nations and to world affairs?
5. What are the roles of the citizen in American democracy?

Few would disagree with these standards. How to assess completion of the standards is more of a problem. Ideally in civic assessment, written responses, oral discourse, group discussion, and portfolio presentations should be included along with more traditional achievement test items.

Formal Instruction

Formal instruction in U.S. government, history, and democracy helps to increase civic knowledge. This knowledge can lead students to engage in future adult participation in the political process. However, if instruction is just rote learning about the structure of government, it can actually alienate students from participation in politics. Civic education also has to be expanded at all grade levels and impart the skills and knowledge necessary for young people to become active participants in their communities. Like geography and economics, it can be integrated at every grade level.

Typically in the primary grades civic education includes content on rules and laws, good citizenship, and American ideals and values. By the fourth grade the emphasis is on local, state, and federal governments. Fifth-grade content is on colonial self-government, religious freedom, the Declaration of Independence, and the development of states' constitutions and the Constitution of the United States. Grades six and seven concentrate on the historical development of laws and various forms of government, the foundation of English political institutions, and the rise of democratic ideals. Eighth grade includes the foundation of America's political system and the development of democracy.

Strategies

Again, as in the teaching of history, geography, and economics, the local community can be an important resource in civic education. Look at the possibilities of just law-related agencies for field trips or guest speakers invited from the following agencies: the local police, the state police, and the Federal Bureau of Investigation; the local, state, and federal courts; the offices of the public defender and the public prosecutor; and the various people and facilities connected with corrections such as probation officers, work camps, and detention halls for juveniles. In addition, lawyers are always a good resource.

Thus, the use of field experiences and guest speakers can enliven civic education. Speakers reflect current views. As always, using these resources effectively requires planning and helping students to observe and to ask good questions. Debriefing students and summarizing the experience are always worthwhile in assessing what students have learned.

As noted as a promising practice by the report of the Civic Mission of Schools, try to use mock trials or simulations of town meetings or court hearings. Conduct a court hearing of a crime in Babylon, ancient Greece, the Roman Empire, or the Middle Ages or simulate a Salem witchcraft trial or the Zenger trial concerning freedom of the press. Compare historic trials with trials today. Do a "You Are There" on Shay's Rebellion, an abolitionist debate, or a rally for women's rights. Role-play authority situations: a police officer and a child who has broken the law against biking in a park, a city council deciding on whether dogs must be on leashes at all times or what local rules on skateboarding should be. Role playing also can include conflicts between students' responsibilities at home and school.

Even young children can actively participate. Obtain a mini-mock trial from such organizations as the Constitutional Rights Foundation (www.crf-usa.org) on the case of the *People v. A. Wolf* (the big bad wolf). As a witness in his defense, Granny Wolf explains why her grandson is a nice boy. The class (jury) then deliberates to decide if A. Wolf is guilty or not of murder and the attempted murder of Mr. Little Pig Three. The verdict is then announced and either A. Wolf is found guilty or not guilty. In addition, before the trial, teachers can use a simulation where students take the roles of attorneys, judge, and prospective jurors to learn about the jury selection process. Roles for prospective jurors are based on traditional fairy tales and legends. In addition, students can draw political cartoons. All of these engaging activities offer promise to increase civic understanding and skill.

Many organizations such as the Center for Civic Education (www.civic.org), the prime organization for civic education, can be helpful. Their programs such as "We, the People" and "Project Citizen" have been successfully implemented in many classes with a positive impact on civic knowledge, skills, and students' tolerance. It is estimated that over 80,000 teachers have received training by the Center for Civic Education and more than twenty-six million students have participated in their programs. The center provides participating teachers in "We, the People" with student textbooks and suggested learning activities that culminate in a simulated congressional hearing. For grades 5 through 9 "Project Citizen" identifies a community problem or need under the jurisdiction of some public government agency. The students then research the problem, discuss its possible solutions, and take steps to effect a solution. Teachers who choose to attend the professional training are self-selective and want the opportunities to learn which might explain the positive results of these programs. Surveys show that the student alumni are more likely than are their peers to vote, pay attention to public affairs, or participate in politics.

An example from the Center for Civic Education on responsibilities as well as rights show approaches to encouraging civic education:

Freedom of Expression
Suppose you attend a meeting of students in your school. The group is supposed to suggest rules for the playground. You have the right to speak and give your suggestions. What responsibilities should you have in the way you speak and in what you say? List and explain these responsibilities.

Freedom of Religion
Suppose you believe in a particular religion. You attend a church or temple in your community. List and explain what responsibilities you should have in the way you practice your religious beliefs.

The Right to be Treated Fairly by Your Government
Suppose someone has accused you of doing something wrong in your school or community. What responsibilities should that person have toward you? List and explain those responsibilities.

Two other helpful organizations among the many for elementary and middle school teachers are the PBS Kids Democracy Project (www.pbs.org/democracy/kids) and The Center for Youth as Resources (www.cyar.org).

A Mandate to Teach about the U.S. Constitution

In 2005, Congress mandated that all schools that receive federal monies must "hold an educational program pertaining to the United States Constitution on September 17 of each year." If September 17th falls over the weekend, educators can schedule their programs either the week before or the week after. This law reflects the grave concern about the quality of the history and civics courses taught in the public school. To meet this requirement, schools have focused on lessons for all grade levels and in some cases, school and communitywide events.

Numerous methods and tons of resources are available for teachers who normally do not teach the Constitution as part of their curriculum. As mentioned before on the simulation *People v. A. Wolf,* The Constitutional Rights Foundation (www.crf-usa.org) has sample free lessons from grades 3 to 12 as well as other materials. The Bill of Rights Institute (www.billofrightsinstitute.org) also has free lessons along with other publications. A Bill of Rights lesson that can be done in one period has many real applications to students' lives. Students first in pairs can think whether or not they have a right to do something. Give a list of cases such as a mother who refuses to send her children to public school because of her religious beliefs, the principal who searches student lockers and backpacks, students who direct negative verbal put-downs against other students, and the like. Then discuss in a whole group using specific amendments whether their activities are protected. Or small groups could take the role of students, small business owners, parents, and the like and cite which of the amendments is most important for them. The groups then report back to the whole class. Primary documents like the U.S. Constitution are not just limited to teaching history. Similar lessons could also be used on December 15, Bill of Rights Day.

Activities involving more one class have ranged from everyone, including teachers, wearing red, white, and blue to assemblies where the Preamble is recited by the whole group. If not explained at the assembly, teachers can ask the following questions.

- Should the goals stated in the Preamble be reordered to reflect modern priorities?
- What are the main functions of government? A good government?
- As a republic, how do citizens bring forth demands and how is our government held to account?

Or every student in the whole school on an index card or larger piece of paper can express themselves about the meaning of the Constitution. These are then put together in a mural or mosaic by classrooms and students view other classrooms' work. Students have also illustrated their interpretation of terms in the Preamble such as "perfect union," "establish justice," and the like. In some cases, community members explain how the Constitution plays a role in their lives. So if planned ahead of time, this mandated requirement can be made into a worthwhile experience for students.

Current Events/Current Affairs Programs

$\mathcal{A}$s recommended by the report of the Civic Mission of Schools, current local, national, and international issues and events need to be discussed in the classroom. What is the role of current events or current affairs programs in the elementary school? Part of the rationale for such programs is the assumption that all citizens must eventually be aware of current issues in order to vote and make intelligent decisions. One of the purposes of teaching current events, then, is to begin arousing student interest in what is happening in the world.

In your own classroom, current events can be the glue that binds all other social studies elements together. A newspaper article about an earthquake in Indonesia can bring together history (have there been earthquakes there before?), geography (where is Indonesia and what region did the earthquake affect?), economics (what will be the long-term economic damage to the people who have lost their homes?), and political science (how will the government respond?). Frequently, current events can be related to whatever unit you are studying, or, in reverse, you might ask students to look for newspaper articles about the country or period you are studying. It makes sense, if you are studying China, to have your students be aware of what is happening today in China.

Current affairs programs are not limited just to the upper grades. Primary students can also be encouraged to become interested in current events. However, as reading and viewing abilities become more developed, older students are more likely to have the skills necessary to find and locate information about current events. Because current events programs serve multiple purposes, different teachers use different formats for them, as the following cases illustrate:

1. Barbara Carpenter, a fourth-grade teacher, has a current events period every day after lunch. Students are encouraged to bring in newspaper articles that are of interest to them to share with the class. There are no specific criteria for what should be brought in, so the items range from what is happening in the Middle East to local crime reports. There is only coincidental correlation between current events time and what is happening in the social studies program.

2. Maria Gomez, a fifth-grade teacher, has current events every Friday. On Thursday, she usually goes online to one of the school publishers like Scholastic to find a free high-interest article to download for her students. She makes copies and distributes the written news item. Because she considers her class interests, including many who do not have newspapers and magazines in their homes, Ms. Gomez thinks her students enjoy reading and discussing the news item. If there were more money for her class, Ms. Gomez would subscribe to a service such as NewsCurrents, (www.newscurrents.com), weekly current events discussion programs written on three levels for grades 3 to 12. If you are a subscriber, each week you receive a new issue on DVD or online, including images. There is also a teacher's guide to lead current events discussions.

3. Sam Bronski, a sixth-grade teacher, has current events every Thursday. At that time he uses the previous day's local newspapers, which are delivered to the school free of charge. Mr. Bronski never forgets to have current events day on Thursday because the stack of newspapers becomes a nuisance if they are not removed. His last social studies class of the day gets to keep the newspapers. Sometimes Mr. Bronski finds that certain sections (e.g., the sports section) disappear before the last period of the day. Throughout the year

Mr. Bronski has explained the different sections of the newspapers to the students. To be certain that they read more than just the comics, Mr. Bronski prepares a few questions for each student to answer during the current events class period. He thinks the students enjoy having and reading the adult newspapers.

4. Andrew Oleson, a seventh-grade teacher, coordinates the current events program with the unit he is teaching. When the class is studying Russia, only items from newspapers or magazines that pertain to Russia can be brought to the class to be reported on. The items then are put on the designated bulletin board under the heading "Russia." Students get extra credit for the news items they bring as their class reports. Current events teaching occurs only within the regular social studies period.

5. Ann Bronstein, an eighth-grade teacher, has current events every Friday. At the beginning of the year, five categories are chosen: international news, national news, state news, local news, and sports. The category of sports is a concession to students' high interest. At the beginning of each week, five students are given one of the preceding topics, which they report on in class on Friday. All students eventually have a turn, and every five weeks a new cycle is started. The students use the format of a television show, with each specialist reporting on his or her category. Students are encouraged to make use of magazines such as *Time* or *Newsweek*. Students are motivated to illustrate or use the chalkboard in their reports as they each receive a grade based on content *and* delivery. Some use PowerPoint presentations. In a few cases where there is a multimedia and computer course, students have prepared a five-minute news show that is broadcast to the appropriate classrooms.

Relate Current Events to Students' Lives

Teachers and students should constantly evaluate what news items are being discussed. Why is the event important? What are the long term consequences or options regarding the item? What does this mean in terms of students' lives? Try to also link the current event with the personal experiences of the students. These criteria should reduce time spent on less important news items. Or the news item example can be brought into a larger picture.

Some teachers use current events as a separate subject having little or accidental correlation with the social studies program; other teachers use current events to supplement or reinforce what is going on in the regular program. Only in very rare cases would a teacher use current events as the basis for actual social studies units, since it is difficult to plan units around unpredictable events. However, a teacher could start a unit, especially on a given nation such as Japan or Israel, by focusing on that nation's current events.

Sources of News

Ideally, as they grow older, students should move into using adult sources of information. For this reason, the use of newspapers can provide an opportunity for learning valuable skills. Students can profit by exercises showing how an index such as "Today's Contents" or "Inside" helps to locate specific features of the newspapers. Reading headlines is important, and it is especially helpful if your community has two local newspapers so that students can compare the headlines of the two newspapers on a given day. Occasionally, bringing in a well-regarded national newspaper such as the *New York Times* or the *Los Angeles Times* is helpful; compare them with local newspapers. Bringing in foreign newspapers as well as specialized newspapers such as the *Wall Street Journal* can also help students see the wide variety of newspapers available. Constantly encourage students to evaluate news sources in print and on the Web. Can you believe it or not? Is there bias in the news? Middle grade students can examine how other nations also interpret the same event. Newspapers Online (www.newspapers.com) and other websites give access to hundreds of online newspapers across the world as well as the United States.

Distinguishing between an editorial and a news story is another important skill. Give students a news item that is accurate, fair, and objective and an editorial on the same topic. Ask them which article wants action to be taken; which article best describes what is happening; which articles tells the writer's feelings.

An increasing number of people depend on television and the Internet as their sources of news. It is likely that more of today's teachers will tape parts of current news programs on their VCRs to show to their students. CNN Student News is a daily commercial-free, cost-free new program that is available for teachers to record while accessing daily curriculum materials, video clips, and other links.

TECHNOLOGY

The top news stories of the day are also easily accessible on the Internet. Major magazines and newspapers also have their own websites. Here are some starting points:

ABC News: www.abcnews.go.com

The Associated Press: www.apalert.com

BBC News: http://news.bbc.co.uk

CNN Interactive: www.cnn.com

NewsLink: www.newslink.org

Newsweek: http://school.newsweek.com

The Paper Boy: www.thepaperboy.com

PBS: www.pbs.org

USA Today: www.usatoday.com

U.S. News and World Report: www.usnews.com/usnews/home.htm

The WashingtonPost: www.washingtonpost.com

World Press: www.worldpress.org

These websites are especially designed for elementary-age students:

CNN Student News: http://learning.turner.com

Time for Kids: www.timeforkids.com

CBC4Kids: http://cbc4kids.ca

Scholastic News Zone: http://teacher.scholastic.com/scholasticnews

Pencil News www.studentnewsnet.com

These websites are good for political cartoons and media.

C-SPAN Classroom: www.c-spanclassroom.org/SearchVideo

Newsweek: www.newsweekeducation.com/extras/2001cartoons.php

New York Times: www.nytimes.com/pages/cartoons

In addition, the *New York Times* Learning Network (www.nytimes.com/learning) has a free daily current events mini-lesson for many grades levels. The lesson Plan search allows teachers to search the *New York Times* Learning Network's archive of hundreds of lesson plans free of charge.

Current events may be related to the teaching of controversial issues, as many aspects of current events at the local, state, national, and international levels are controversial. Here again, teachers must decide what role they will take in teaching controversial events. Having access to a wide variety of information sources such as newspapers and magazines will help students see the emotional impact of a division of opinion on a given issue as well as the differences in viewpoints. Many teachers encourage students to bring news items for a bulletin board. If this is done, students should change the news items frequently.

On Your Own **8.1**

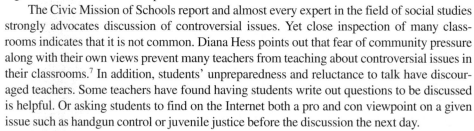

Keeping Up with the News

Do you keep up with current events? Many college or university students are so busy that they cannot find the time to keep up with the news. How important do you think it is to keep informed and up-to-date on what is going on? ●

Teaching Controversial Issues

TECHNOLOGY

As students become older, they become better able to discuss controversial issues, of which there is no shortage in our society; economics and government policy, for example, have always provoked differences among citizens. Drugs, AIDS, and abortion generate strongly held views among citizens. What should be done to improve the economic well-being of our nation? There is certainly a wide divergence of opinion among citizens as well as between groups such as business and labor. What should be our policy on terrorism? Again, a wide difference of opinion exists.

The Civic Mission of Schools report and almost every expert in the field of social studies strongly advocates discussion of controversial issues. Yet close inspection of many classrooms indicates that it is not common. Diana Hess points out that fear of community pressure along with their own views prevent many teachers from teaching about controversial issues in their classrooms.[7] In addition, students' unpreparedness and reluctance to talk have discouraged teachers. Some teachers have found having students write out questions to be discussed is helpful. Or asking students to find on the Internet both a pro and con viewpoint on a given issue such as handgun control or juvenile justice before the discussion the next day.

Are there any topics that teachers should avoid? The Holocaust and genocide are probably not appropriate for young children, especially graphic images. These are both sensitive topics and should be postponed until children are at least in middle school. Frequently these topics are used to promote tolerance and to link moral choices to today's issues. The best known education organization for teaching about the Holocaust is Facing History and Ourselves (www.facing.org) with publications, units and lessons plans, and online modules. In addition, teachers are urged to not just emphasize the numbers of lives lost, to avoid simulations, and to place the Holocaust and genocide in a historical context.

[7]Diana E. Hess, "How Do Teachers' Political Views Influence Teaching about Controversial Issues?" *Social Education* 69, no. 1, (January/February, 2005), 47–48.

Among social studies educators, there is much debate over what role teachers should assume in the teaching of controversial issues. Teachers' methods have been criticized in their communities. There have been court cases in which the question of academic freedom to discuss controversial issues for both teachers and students has been considered. In general, the courts have ruled that teachers can discuss these controversial issues if they are appropriate to the academic subject area and follow the districts' guidelines. This means that a math teacher would probably not be protected by the courts if he or she discussed abortion during a math class.

Teachers' Roles

Here are four typical cases involving teacher attitudes to presenting controversial issues:

1. Gloria Young does not discuss any topics that she thinks are controversial in her fourth-grade class. She believes that the classroom must be a neutral place and does not like it when students argue and bicker among themselves. Ms. Young thinks it is best to shield students from unpleasant topics that may upset them. She believes children have a greater sense of security if they can think that all is well in their community and that they should not be unduly concerned about local or world events. Ms. Young also thinks that her principal appreciates her not posing a problem for parents who might be upset to learn that controversial issues are being discussed in the classroom.

2. In the next room, teaching the fifth grade, is Carol Taylor. She is a civil rights advocate and a feminist and has a deep commitment to educating students on the injustices that women and other minority groups have suffered in the past. In her teaching of U.S. history she emphasizes how these minority groups were unfairly treated.

Ms. Taylor believes she knows the right position on controversial issues that come up in the classroom and made it clear to the parents at an October open house how she feels. She argues that all U.S. citizens should have equal rights. Unlike Ms. Young, Ms. Taylor does not ignore controversial issues and actually welcomes their inclusion, especially as they relate to her teaching of U.S. history. Ms. Taylor is constantly bringing up questions on how the budgets of governmental units should be changed, with more emphasis on job retraining and antidiscrimination efforts.

If a student with a different viewpoint suggests another idea, Ms. Taylor calmly ignores it and proceeds to present her point of view. She thinks that students hear and learn more in the media about accepting the status quo than making changes to improve the position of women, African Americans, and other groups. She feels her job is to free her students from these "false" ideas.

3. Marianne Ash teaches seventh grade in the same school. She believes that controversial issues should be discussed in the classroom. However, she also believes that she should be neutral and downplay her own views on certain issues. Even when students ask her how she will vote on a certain issue or what she thinks about a policy, Ms. Ash does not think it is appropriate for students to know. She is afraid that some students might accept her position without considering it carefully or that a few students who are not fond of her might immediately take the opposite position.

Ms. Ash encourages her students to present a variety of viewpoints on a given controversial issue. She tries to guide the discussion toward who will benefit within a given issue (e.g., pollution) and who will be the losers. Ms. Ash believes that with rational discussion students can clarify their own positions after hearing a variety of viewpoints.

4. Nicholas Baker is a teacher in the eighth grade in the same school. Like Ms. Taylor and Ms. Ash, Mr. Baker believes that controversial issues should be discussed in the classroom. But unlike Ms. Ash, Mr. Baker gives his own point of view on issues. He tells students how he will vote on certain issues. On his car is a bumper sticker indicating his viewpoint on ecology. In his classroom, Mr. Baker thinks he should be a model of a politically active citizen. He tells the students about the organizations he belongs to that have a political focus. In the classroom, Mr. Baker brings in a variety of speakers with different points of view. He also uses a combination of other methods such as library research and group discussions to help students clarify how they feel on a given controversial issue.

Small Group Work **8.4**

Viewpoints on Controversial Issues

Which position do you think is the best of the four previously described for the teaching of controversial issues? Which one would you like to model? Give your reasons for your position to your group. ●

Possible Problems

As you can see, there are many opinions on the proper role of an elementary teacher in teaching about controversial issues. But in the previous four cases, there is another person whom we may have overlooked. That person is Dr. Jane Menshi, the principal of the school. She keeps hoping that the school district will issue some guidelines on the teaching of controversial events and the role of academic freedom for teachers and students. She knows that her teachers are handling controversial issues in many different ways. She has received a few complaints from parents about Ms. Taylor's strong position but was able to tell them that at least Ms. Taylor is open about her principles. If the parents want to bring up additional facts to teach their own children what they think is right, they should do so. Dr. Menshi always points out to parents that the research on political socialization indicates that parents and the family are the most important factors in influencing what children believe about political issues. Dr. Menshi's discussions with parents have satisfied them and no parent has complained to a higher administrator.

Dr. Menshi, however, is a little concerned about the social actions that Mr. Baker wants to take. Mr. Baker believes that students need the experience of working in their community. He wants students to help support the local political candidates of their choice. The students would attend meetings of these political candidates and do tasks such as handing out political literature for the candidates. No student would be forced to do this community action, but students who want an A in the class probably realize that Mr. Baker is apt to look with favor on those who participate actively in community affairs. Mr. Baker even suggested to Dr. Menshi that students help in the political campaigns of school board members. What would the board members think of that? Dr. Menshi was very worried about this but did not know what she should do. What do you think would be the best position for the principal to take with regard to outside political action on the part of the eighth graders in her school? Can your class role-play some of the alternatives?

In looking over the four teachers' positions on teaching controversial issues, you can see that each has its advantages and disadvantages. The four positions move along a continuum from the teacher who does nothing about controversial events to the teacher who would like students to take social action in the community. Social studies experts themselves disagree on the proper position for teaching controversial events, but most of them would not support Ms. Young's total avoidance of controversial issues in the classroom. This is simply an unrealistic position in an age in which students are bombarded by the media with news of their community, nation, and the world. Children are aware of problems and controversial issues outside the classroom, and sheltering them from these real problems, especially as they are growing older, does not make sense. To become effective citizens, students need to be able to make judgments on issues. Furthermore, even if Ms. Young does not realize it, she is teaching values. Her stance as a person unconcerned about controversial issues is probably not a good model of what a teacher should be.

Ms. Taylor is trying to get students to accept certain positions. In effect, this is a form of indoctrination. Viewpoints different from hers are not given much attention. In this case Ms. Taylor is supporting a liberal position; however, advocates of indoctrination can range from Marxists to conservatives, all of whom believe it is their duty to pass on their particular ideology. These true believers are really authoritarian teachers with regard to the teaching of their own value systems. They are not giving students the opportunity to hear other points of view.

The advantages of Ms. Ash's position are that students are exposed to a wide variety of viewpoints on a given issue, and Ms. Ash uses a variety of methods with which students can study the issue. Mr. Baker's position is similar to that of Ms. Ash, except that Mr. Baker gives his own position on issues. He makes his positions clear to the class.

Is this good? At least students know what Mr. Baker believes. In many cases, students are perceptive enough to guess where teachers such as Ms. Ash stand by reading verbal and nonverbal clues. For example, without realizing it, teachers often do not write on the board the ideas suggested by students who disagree with the teacher's viewpoint.

In effect, Ms. Ash and teachers like her want to play the role of a nonpartisan referee. This position probably receives the most support in teaching controversial issues. It is also a noncontroversial point of view with the community, which normally does not object if the teacher plays this role. Advocates of social action such as Mr. Baker are likely to find themselves being attacked for pushing young "impressionable" students into political action. This is especially true when the action involves local issues. In some cases, however, teachers have been rewarded with praise and publicity, especially if the social action takes the form of doing something popular such as cleaning up the local beach or getting out the vote.

All experts believe that teachers should deal with controversy on current local, national, and international issues. Students also should be free to express different perspectives. If, however, teachers disclose their personal positions, they are open to accusations of one-sidedness. This was illustrated in 2003 when the United States launched military action against Iraq. Many teachers faced the issue of what role they should play in discussing this controversial issue. Teachers had both pro- and antiwar sentiments. This was an especially sensitive issue when children of military personnel felt that they were harassed by antiwar comments from teachers.

From lower court decisions, there are limits on free speech for teachers in their classrooms. In particular, a teacher has no constitutional right to say anything in the classroom that conflicts with the principal/school district's policy. If teachers are told not to teach a certain topic such as creationism, or to keep their opinions to themselves, they can risk dismissal for not following district guidelines. However, outside of the classroom, teachers, like all citizens, have the protection of free speech. The safest procedure is the "fair and balanced" rule of diverse opinions.

The proper role of the teacher in teaching controversial events is not likely to be settled in the near future since it is basically a values issue. Topics such as abortion are highly sensitive in many communities. Students may feel offended by certain topics and are likely to complain to their parents. Teachers can be accused of being insensitive or biased. Court cases on the rights of teachers and students continue to define the limits of academic freedom and free speech. Policy statements by local districts on the teaching of controversial events are helpful, as these statements generally support academic freedom. The National Council for the Social Studies has issued a position paper on academic freedom and the social studies teacher, which treats explicitly the teaching of controversial issues.[8] The guidelines outline the rights and responsibilities of teachers, the selection of educational materials, and visiting speakers. These guidelines also encourage teachers to introduce controversial issues in their teaching. School guidelines are also needed for student use of the Internet. Many schools have both students and their parents sign statements that they understand the rules for using the Internet. All parties involved—students, teachers, administrators, and the community—need to know the guidelines that the school is using in the teaching of controversial events.

TECHNOLOGY

Rules for Students

Students also need to be aware of the rules for discussion and abide by them. All students should be encouraged to participate in any discussion, including of controversial issues. However, while every student should feel comfortable to bring up her or his viewpoint, there should not be any name-calling or put-downs for anyone's expressed views. This may occur when someone advocates a more contrary opinion. Instead, all students need to listen carefully to others and not interrupt a classmate who is speaking, even if it is not a popular viewpoint. By asking for reasons for opinions, the whole class benefits from a wider range of viewpoints about a controversial issue.

Values in the Classroom for Civic Education

Besides conflict management, classroom meetings, and classroom citizenship, some parents and curriculum planners are calling for more direct education in the teaching of values. For example, the national civics standards call for content standards in "Fundamental Values and Principles" of American democracy. These **values** of American democracy are as follows:

- Individual rights to life, liberty, property, and the pursuit of happiness
- The public or common good
- Justice
- Equality of opportunity
- Diversity
- Truth
- Patriotism

How can you help citizenship development by teaching these values? From Chapter 1, we have discussed several values approaches. Let us examine more carefully the "Analysis

[8]National Council for the Social Studies, "Academic Freedom and the Social Studies Teacher: NCSS Position Statement," *Social Education* 55 (January 1991): 13–15.

Approach" in which students use logical thinking to decide values issues primarily by rational class discussion and gathering resources from a variety of sources.

Values Analysis Strategy

1. Identify the problem.
2. Clarify the values question(s).
3. Gather and evaluate the facts about the problem.
4. Suggest several solutions to the problem and the good and bad consequences of each solution. Older students can examine the short-term and possible long-term consequences.
5. Decide among the solutions proposed.

Let us see how the values analysis strategy could be used in the classroom episode "Spiders and the Assistant Principal." Ms. Torres could take the opportunity to discuss this values issue with the whole class following the outline of the values analysis strategy. If she does not, the class will see modeled a passive role on the part of an adult and wonder if justice, private property, and the common good are really respected. The problem can be identified easily. What should be done with the black widow spider? The values question is more complex. There are the values of the teacher, Ms. Torres, the values of the assistant principal who wants the school environment to be safe, and the values of the children who like the opportunity of looking at the black widow spider.

Is there further evidence needed to make a decision on this issue? Looking at the wording and authority of the rule about destroying dangerous animals is essential. How serious

---

Classroom Episode
Spiders and the Assistant Principal

Ms. Torres was considered the "nature lover" at her school. If an insect was in her room, the children watched it for a while, caught it, and released it outside.

One day a black widow spider was found by a child in another classroom.

The child's teacher called Ms. Torres who caught the spider in a jar for everyone to see. She taped the lid on tightly and spent time with classes discussing spiders, black widow spiders, and what it means to be venomous. She decided this was a great learning opportunity. She planned to keep the spider for only a few days and then release it in a field away from the school. Everyone in the school heard about the spider and wanted to see it.

But on the next day the assistant principal told Ms. Torres she needed to take the spider away. They had called an exterminator to destroy the spider because school policy insisted that any animal that could be dangerous to the children must be destroyed. What should Ms. Torres do?

Source: Carole Basile and Cameron White, "Tad Poles and Tough Questions," *Social Studies and the Young Learner* 12, no. 2 (November–December 1999): 17–20. The scenario is condensed.

would it be if the black widow actually bit a young student? Is the black widow an endangered species? Does killing the black widow have any effect on the rest of the environment? Is having the black widow in a classroom such an "attractive nuisance" that a child or children might be attempted to play with it?

Then students and the teacher could suggest solutions to the problem. One solution is to disobey the rule and release the spider. What would be the consequences then to Ms. Torres? Another is to move the decision making up another level to the principal or even higher or enlist the aid of parents to speak up on this issue. Ms. Torres and her students then could marshall facts to show why the spider should not be killed. Or the assistant principal could explain her concerns about safety to the class. There are different possible consequences for each solution.

This values analysis case study shows that often there is not a clearly "right" answer, partly because of the differences in values of some of the participants. Nevertheless, how problems are handled in the classroom is a valuable experience for students and illustrates how lofty and abstract values such as the right to life (even for a spider), liberty, and the pursuit of happiness are played out on given issues. It also shows that events are shaped, in part, by people who make decisions about what should happen in a certain situation. Human choices make a difference and not being engaged in policy issues allows others to make the decisions.

Instruction about the justice system is a necessary complement to direct experiences that schools can provide young citizens. To round out their instruction in being citizens, children need to consider their roles as citizens of the world.

Citizenship in School

Student voice in school governance can help civic skills and democratic dispositions. Most schools have student councils. Other schools are using a system of "commissioners." A few students are elected to office but other students apply for jobs such as to run the Thanksgiving food drive. Qualifications for commissioners may include a short interview, writing an essay on why they want the job, or having appropriate teacher recommendations. The commissioner system usually results in a wider cross section of the student body participating. School student councils usually help a few students gain active citizenship skills. Those students who are confident enough to run for office and lucky enough to get elected will gain leadership practice. Typically, these students meet with an administrator and bring messages about schoolwide functions back to their classrooms. Children in such groups gain experience by participating in meetings and presenting messages to their classmates; in some schools, they vote on issues at the meetings. The rationale for having a student council is that learning by doing promotes growth in active citizenship. The issue is how to extend the benefits of student council participation to more than one individual student from each class. For example, one school created three branches of student government: a legislative branch, a judicial branch, and an executive branch. This dramatically increased both the number of students involved and the interest of students. The students had their own bill of rights, which was often used in cases that came before the court.

Beyond classroom responsibilities, some schools organize schoolwide positions and announce them in want ads. These positions include street and building traffic patrol, school lunch helpers, checkers for distribution and collection of noontime and recess equipment, librarian helpers, media center technicians, office helpers, playground cleanup patrol, and student council officers. These positions are mostly for middle graders. Students are not elected to these places but rotate through them periodically. Children apply for their positions by signing up for interviews. Teachers in charge of each job category check to make sure children understand the responsibilities involved. Children not selected for the first six weeks usually get a chance to serve during the second six-week period.

By giving their time and talents, children are contributing to making their school a place they own and can make better. Children can learn cooperative skills and see the benefit of working for a common cause when they participate in schoolwide campaigns. Fund raising and cleanup drives are common to most schools. Class and individual awards for accomplishment help children recognize the value of their achievements and have pride in group effort.

Encouraging the expression of opinions about school events is a positive technique for building a sense of civic efficacy among students. Classrooms can reserve a bulletin board with the heading "Citizenship: Success and Needs." Children can be encouraged to draw or write on the board about acts or situations they wish to compliment or ones they wish to improve by offering suggestions. Periodically, during sharing time, these contributions should be commented on and then removed to make room for new additions. Extending this idea is an effective strategy for focusing attention beyond individual classrooms. Directing students' attention to needed improvements in the school or local community can lead students to find out who is responsible for such things as repainting the traffic crosswalk or replacing the worn playground equipment. Students can write a class letter to comment on the needed change. Teachers and classes have been amazed to learn that such letters are read at school board and city council meetings.

We should not underestimate what students can do. Joel Blanco and two other students delivered a stack of letters from their classmates asking the Berkeley city council in California to clean up a creek at their elementary school. The students also sent a delegation to lobby the council and produced a video about the contamination. The creek had been off-limits because it was contaminated with bacteria. The mayor of the city came to the school and answered questions from a student panel. The mayor reported that the city had paid $120,000 to identify and block several sources of likely contamination. The city engineers spent about 200 hours on the problem and public maintenance crews spent another 140 hours while public health staff worked many hours. Students were thrilled by the response of city officials and were looking forward to the day when the creek would be open to students for science projects.[9]

Linking Schoolwide Citizenship to the Community

Service Learning or Community Participation

$\mathcal{P}$roviding children access to the community outside of the school is an important element in the development of citizenship. Traditionally, elementary classes have learned about community helpers in ways that most often did little to involve the children in active citizenship. But this is changing by the increasing popularity in the schools of promoting service learning or community service. This movement reflects the grave concern that more has to be done to teach youth to participate in a democratic society. The declining adult voting turnout is often cited as a reason for the schools to counter the current apathy and cynicism

[9]"Students' Real-Life Civics Lesson Pays Off—City Cleans Creek near Their School" [Patrick Hoge], *San Francisco Chronicle* (March 31, 2004): B5, C2.

about government and political leaders. In addition, it is felt that volunteers are needed if national problems are to be addressed and young people are at a stage of their lives when attitudes are still being formed. Thus, volunteer service is seen as a tool for teachers to build both interest in social studies and to interact with the community.

Service learning is the integration of community service with academic learning. This means that students doing volunteer work need to do something in the classroom such as discussing their experience or giving an oral report. In service learning, students are to gain knowledge about their community, use skills such as acquiring information and evaluating it, and develop a sense of effectiveness in the community. In contrast, **community service** is giving back to the local community and is associated with charity and altruism. The purpose is to help those in need. Focusing on helping others is not necessarily tied into what is going on in a particular school course or topic. A visit by a class to a local nursing home might be an example of community service. The students may have prepared holiday decorations, visited in their Halloween costumes, or distributed Valentine candy. Often these one-shot activities, although very worthy, have little connection with the social studies program. However, one second-grade class "adopted" a nearby nursing home for a full year. Along with frequent visits, the students also communicated by e-mail with the residents because many nursing home residents now have access to the Internet. In practice it is often hard to distinguish between service learning and community participation, as when a class cleans up a public area such as a park.

For example, students may define a community problem—making it a safer neighborhood, helping the hungry, helping the elderly who are homebound, or protecting the environment—and follow up the class consensus by searching out community agencies that will be willing to work with the students to represent a bona fide program or institution in the community. These efforts have encompassed a wide variety of agencies. One school planted a garden to grow vegetables that were then sold on Saturdays at the local farmer's market; the money they made was donated to a soup kitchen where they were too young to work. This garden project went on during the summer even when school was out of session. Beautification and art projects also have been popular along with ecology projects. In doing these projects, students need to keep records of their hours and activities, maintain ongoing debriefing and planning sessions under teacher leadership, and reflect on what they are learning.

A difficulty with implementing service learning is the transportation problem. Unless children are able to walk to the agency's site, usually service learning or community participation is limited unless parent volunteers are willing to drive. Teachers also need to be careful that they are not forcing students into service activities that students do not want to do.

Even when the difficulties in the implementation of service learning or community participation are overcome, service learning or community service is not a panacea for improving citizenship. However, classes using it have reported high satisfaction and a sense of accomplishment among students, both of which are important in promoting citizenship in the community. Service learning can improve academic achievement, meet real community needs, promote seeing the problem as an issue, and improve self-esteem of the students.

Small Group Work **8.5**

Links to the Community

What, if any, community service have you participated in? What individuals or groups organized the community service? What do you think are the problems and promises of community or service learning in the classroom? ●

Implementing Service Learning

Let us assume that you want to implement a meaningful service learning program. You believe that service learning can do good things for those giving as well as those receiving the services. Your goals are to provide volunteer service and aid students to become aware of and address community needs. Your first decision is how much *time* should be spent on a project. Will it be forty-five minutes every Friday for six weeks? Remember that a few hours of service learning probably will not have much of an effect. Related to this time question is whether students will spend time after school on the project. In addition, do you plan for the whole class to engage in one project or could different groups have a different service project?

The second decision is who will choose the type of service learning. You, the teacher? Or will you give students several projects to choose from? If you just ask for suggestions, usually students are limited in their responses. However, to help them you could have various speakers talk to your class about local needs to give them more ideas of what they could do.

Besides time for the project, are there any money or supplies needed for the project? Commonly a fund raiser is necessary for certain projects. You cannot do landscaping unless you have plants and some gardening equipment. You might obtain funding from an interested organization or the PTA, but these economic constraints need to be considered. Here are some possible suggestions for you and your class for service learning projects. In addition, excellent suggestions can be obtained from The Constitutional Rights Foundation (www.crf-usa.org), a prime leader in service learning. Other help is available from the Corporation for National and Community Service (www.nationalservice.org).

Ecology Projects
- Renovate a nature trail
- Create bird habitats
- Participate in weed abatement
- Add interpretive signs to a hiking trail
- Create gardens
- Increase community awareness of recycling
- Hold a teach-in about recycling; write letters for the school or local newspaper

In-School Projects
- Tutor younger children
- Garden/landscape
- Procure more books for the library
- Educate about or otherwise increase school safety
- Make posters advertising a project or honoring a group
- Create art space for students to post their thoughts and feelings about an event

Senior Citizens
- Become pen pals or exchange e-mail with seniors
- Record oral histories from seniors
- Produce a video for seniors
- Visit and communicate with a senior one to one

Government

- Help with neighborhood maintenance (identify roads, sidewalks, and playgrounds that need improvement)
- Help solve traffic problems around school and elsewhere
- Make and display posters reminding people to vote
- Remove graffiti, clean up parks
- Visit a public agency and make a video for other classes
- Have a teach-in on health (diabetes, high blood pressure, and obesity)

You can see the wide range of possibilities. You may want to scale down the choices to about three if the class is to make the decision. Remember that they are more likely to buy into the project if they have been involved with the decision making. If the class is more or less divided between two choices, think about allowing more than one service activity to be implemented.

Students may need some instruction on how to proceed. How do they introduce themselves as tutors to younger children? What are they to say to the nursing home administrator or the residents of the nursing home? Role playing and telling students what to expect is essential for the project's success. Guidelines of the requirements need to be explained carefully and also in a written format. Permission slips to parents explaining your educational goals also may be necessary.

While students are doing the project, they should be writing journals about their reactions to the project. Reflection, discussion, and debriefing after the project are essential for checking what the students have gained from the service learning experience. It also helps to put the project in context within the larger society. Ask a what-if question. For example, "What would happen if most people did/did not [insert a specific activity]?" Otherwise, the service learning will be a temporary involvement and will not really shape citizens who understand their civic responsibilities. Link service learning to the formal curriculum as much as possible. For example, examine what local government is doing. In that way, service learning can be a good strategy to help civic education. In addition, the principal will welcome all possible links to the community to help both the school and the community.

Teaching Global Education

First let us clarify some definitions. One is the distinction or difference between **global education** and **multicultural education.** Global education emphasizes the cultures and people of *other* lands whereas multiculturalism deals with racial and ethnic diversity *within* the United States. For other experts, global education examines global equity and multicultural education addresses national equity in the United States. This distinction is often not clear in the minds of students when students in a global education unit think the focus is going to be on American Indians or Asian Americans. Some students think global education means economics, probably as a result of thinking of globalization. Others think multicultural means culture, so studying the Masai in Africa is multicultural education. However, both fields have shared purposes to increase students' civic understanding and participation in national and global citizenship. International studies is often used at the university level and refers to an in-depth study of a specific area or region of the world. For K through 12, *global education* is increasingly the term that is used. More recently the terms *cosmopolitan* or *transnational* are being cited, referring to being at home in all parts of the world and not confined to national boundaries. It implies the ability to look at the multiple perspectives of many people.

Global education is also often confused with **globalization.** The World Bank defined globalization as "the growing integration of economies and societies around the world." Globalization is driven by international trade and investment and is aided by improved information technology. Globalization is not new but at the present it is rapidly transforming the whole planet with increased world trade. Globalization is not confined just to physical goods; money, information, and communications quickly flow from one part of the world to another. This stream of activity also includes cultural items such as movies, music, books, fads, and dress styles.

Globalization is deeply controversial with active resistance by some groups. If students are studying globalization, there are many publications and websites stating the pros and cons on this issue. Some Americans fear the increase in their own nation of non-U.S. companies, stores, and products as well as the loss of jobs. On the other hand, other nations feel that they are being "Americanized" with media, McDonald's, and Starbucks. Almost everyone is concerned about environmental problems and the violent conflicts in the world.

Advocates of global education see the following as important topics for students:[10]

- More understanding of world cultures
- Teaching world history
- Connecting the United States to the world
- Teaching global issues
- Teaching current events from a global perspective

Other advocates stress teaching the following:

- Seeing the *interconnectedness* of the many systems to which we belong (family and local community linked to international issues)
- Understanding the importance of *context* (study of geography, history, culture, and economics of a problem)
- Awareness of the variety of *perspectives*
- Working to manage and resolve *conflict*

From this list you can see how global education is to be infused and made part of everything that goes under the name of social studies. History, geography, economics, and civics should all contribute to preparing today's children and youth for tomorrow's future world. Fortunately, textbooks increasingly show a more global education focus. Geography texts have case studies on individual nations and groups. U.S. history texts emphasize more that the United States has always been globally connected to other nations and that to understand the contemporary role of the United States in world affairs it is necessary to know the historical background. World history has now moved beyond being just Western Civilization. However, this does mean that more does not need to be done to infuse all of the academic social science disciplines with a global perspective. Global education typically focuses on the four major areas or issues as shown in Table 8.2.

---

[10]Merry M. Merryfield and Angene Wilson, *Social Studies and the World: Teaching Global Perspectives,* Bulletin 103 (Silver Springs, MD: National Council for the Social Studies, 2005).

Table 8.2	Problem Themes in Global Education

Peace and Security	**Environment/Ecological Problems**
War and terrorism	Pollution of air and water
	Depletion of rain forests
National/International Development	**Human Rights**
Hunger and poverty	Refugees, political and religious
Population growth	Persecution
Natural resources, oil	

Instruction that incorporates a global perspective on peace, environmental problems, international development, and human rights is a challenge. Teachers must make choices on how much harsh reality should be portrayed to children. The main question for all teachers to face is: Should children be shown reality or be shielded from it? Each teacher makes his or her own decision about this question and perhaps there is no single answer, only a balance. Yet from the media children are often aware of the problems.

Teachers are also divided on how to teach about different cultures. Do they support a policy of tolerance toward all cultures? In other words, should they be nonjudgmental about norms and practices in other cultures which their own culture considers "bad"? This is not an easy question.

Human Rights: Refugees and Gender Issues

Let us look at a possible unit on refugees. The United Nations High Commissioner for Refugees has a website (www.unhcr.ch) with units and lesson plans for three age groups, 9–11, 12–14, and 15–18, on this topic.

The unit objectives for "Refugee Children" include knowledge objectives such as understanding the abnormal and trying conditions in which refugee children live and endure and introducing the idea that people's basic needs are considered human rights. Other objectives are to encourage *empathy* and *respect* for refugee children in the world. The content may be a case history of Jacob, a Sudanese refugee child who fled Sudan without his family and had to walk across thousands of miles of barren land to the safety of a refugee camp in Kenya. Another case study could be Sybella Wilkes, *One Day We Had to Run!* (London, Evans Brothers, 1994). After listening to or reading the case studies, students explore in pairs the wants, needs, and basic human rights of children. They can better understand that no one likes or chooses to be a refugee. Being a refugee means more than just being a "foreigner." It means living in exile and often depending on others for basic needs such as food, clothing, and shelter.

This unit could be further developed by reading the rich children's literature about American immigrants. Usually a distinction is made between voluntary and involuntary migrants. Voluntary migrants are those who have willingly left their homelands, usually with expectations of improving their standard of living. There are still groups coming to the United States that meet the definition of refugees—persons who fear being persecuted for reasons of race, religion, nationality, membership in a particular social group, or political opinion, and who are outside of their country. There are also internally displaced people.

LESSON PLAN

Population and Feeding the World

Objectives: Students will develop an improved mental map of the population characteristics of major regions of the world.

Students will suggest ways to respond to the issues of hunger and population.

Materials: Signs for the six regions; slips of paper naming a region for each student; food such as chocolate kisses with 1 kiss = $500. Do not use candy such as a chocolate bar that can be divided easily.

Procedures

1. Tell students to imagine a global village. If the world were a village of 100, this is the number that would come from each world region. You could have students try to guess about the data for each category before showing the data on either the board or a handout.

Global Village

Regions	Percentage of World Population	Students in Class of Twenty	Per Capita GNP	Population Growth
North America	5%	1	$28,230	Highest of industrial nations due to immigration
Latin America	9%	2	$3,880	Above average
Africa	13%	3	$670	Highest, with women averaging six children
Europe including Russia	12%	2	$13,420	Lowest
Asia excluding China	40%	8	$2,910	Above average
China	21%	4	$750	Above average

Source: Population Reference Bureau. For over thirty years, the Population Reference Bureau has updated the data for this simulation. Data are also available on energy consumption, waste, and safe drinking water and could be included if more time were available.

2. Randomly distribute to your twenty students slips of paper showing to which of the six regions they are assigned. If you have more then twenty, you can put the extra students into a committee from the United Nations. Or calculate the correct distribution for the class. Students go to their assigned

(continued)

LESSON PLAN continued   Population and Feeding the World

regions. Each group will select an ambassador to orally give the data about his or her region to the whole class. The ambassador also identifies the space on the world map.

3. What does per capita GNP mean? (Total value of all goods and services produced in a region divided by the population of the region.) Stress the diversity within a region such as Japan in Asia and Eastern Europe and Russia in the Europe region.

4. Show the candy. Each piece represents $500. Distribute the appropriate number of pieces of candy to each group. Make it very visible. Say: "Will the ambassadors hold up their candy for all to see?"

5. Each group discusses the following questions.
   - How does your group feel about the distribution?
   - Which regions can give a piece of candy to every member in their group? Which regions do not have enough? Is this a problem?
   - If someone wanted to share, what region would he or she give the candy to? Why?
   - Is there anything your group can do about this situation?

6. After groups have discussed their answers to these questions, call on each group to share the information with the whole class.

7. Ask questions about the population. Explain that though China has a one child policy it is still increasing its population. Note that some of these questions are very controversial.

8. Discussion of policy issues with groups responding as representative of that region.
   - Should foreign aid be given to countries that have not yet come to terms with their "population problems"?
   - Do donor countries have the right to link food aid to certain policies?
   - Should rich countries reduce their food consumption? How could this be done?

9. After the final debriefing of the simulation with special emphasis on "how they felt," have students summarize what they have learned.

Extensions

1. Find individual data on nations such as Japan, Sweden, Swaziland (lowest life span on earth).
2. Each group makes a poster for their ambassador to present to the United Nations and other groups.

Evaluations

1. Teacher observations during the simulation.
2. On paper, ask students to rank in order the highest to the lowest region on population and GNP. Write if there is linkage of population to GNP.

When people flee destruction yet stay within their own country, they become internally displaced people. If they cross the border to another country, they become refugees. Internally displaced people do not qualify for aid from international organizations but are dependent on aid available from their own country, often a country with few resources to help.

Children need information and experiences that help them understand their relationship with all children of the planet. The goal in learning about refugees, global hunger, poverty, and ecological disasters is not to cause guilt feelings about the lifestyle possible in the United States. Rather, children need to see how global problems will affect them. It raises the question of what should be done to promote equity and fairness within and among nations. It is not enough to provide children with information about global problems. You must also show them avenues to personal efficacy in relation to these problems as part of the instructional sequence. However, children cannot be expected to solve the worldwide problems of millions of refugees. They may, however, see some connections to the refugee and immigrant experiences that apply to their own communities in terms of stereotypes and prejudice. Children can make small and meaningful differences in their own schools and communities. The UN website also has many helpful lessons on such topics as "Water as a Human Right." Educating girls in developing countries has big payoffs with added health benefits as well as reduced poverty as educated girls command higher wages and increase agricultural productivity.

A further example is for students to investigate slavery and human trafficking in the world today. Students may not be aware that slavery occurs today and not just in the past. Ask students to brainstorm their thoughts associated with the term *slavery*. Most will refer only to slavery in America and perhaps a few to slavery in ancient civilizations. Students can use websites such as the Coalition to Abolish Slavery and Trafficking, Amnesty International, and the Anti-Slavery Portal (www.iAbolish.com) to find more about this topic. Students should be aware of the perspectives of these groups as committed strongly to ending slavery. They then can write letters to the editor or inform others about this problem.

Environment/Ecological Problems

Global citizenship is a complex, contradictory, and often controversial idea. The ecological principles of balance and relatedness present endless opportunities for value analysis in this era of global citizenship, asking us to focus on the bumper sticker slogan "Think globally; act locally." It is easy for children, and adults, to thrill to the warm, protective sentiments of faraway campaigns to preserve environments and protect species as presented in films and the media. But students also should be aware of the balance between protecting the environment and meeting human needs. For example, valuable forests are being cut down (deforestation) on the justification of meeting human needs. Bringing these feelings to bear on issues closer to home is crucial for helping children see the complexity and interrelatedness of defending the earth. Every region is replete with "acting locally" environmental issues; see the following list.

Sampler of Ecological Conflicts

Hazardous waste dump sites versus acquiring attention and funds for removal

Logging economies versus endangered species

Species overpopulation leading to environmental degradation versus animal rights

Ranchers and sheep herders versus survival of predators such as wolves

Fishing industry (overfishing) versus protecting and limiting the resource

Housing development versus protection of green space or wetlands

Domestic animal birth control versus animal and individual owner rights

Species extinction and ozone depletion versus airborne pollutants and pesticide- and herbicide-bearing agricultural water runoff

When teachers involve their students in local environmental issues by organizing learning about these issues through observation, sampling, and other scientific processes, they are exhibiting the most responsible kind of global citizenship education. Long-term teacher and school involvement with a specific site can reap not only the rewards of student enthusiasm and learning but also a school role in community improvement. Global citizenship truly begins at home. "Where Does Your Trash or Garbage Go?" could be a topic to be explored.

Collaborative Projects Using the Internet

TECHNOLOGY

To help students gain a global perspective, several organizations have set up websites to help students and teachers engage in interactive collaborative learning. One of the oldest organizations is Global Schoolnet (globalschoolnet.org) where your students can join in many projects. Examples for younger students are to share information about the plants, animals and nonliving objects found in their schoolyard environment with others students around the country and the world. Or with a more science flavor, students will collect water samples from their local rivers, lakes, or pond and access the quality of their local water. iEarn (www.iearn.org) is probably the largest nonprofit global network with many projects such as youth worldwide designing kites with personal and group images of their dreams. Global Nomads Group (www.gng.org) tries to foster dialogue and understanding among the world's youth, including in their blog. Students report how "They See the World" and compare photos and discuss them. Many of these organizations encourage students to reach a wider audience for their work using a variety of media outlets such as a project on the history of regional music.

More controversial are action projects. But remember that unless students take some action, especially after learning about dismal conditions, students can gain the feeling that nothing can be done. It is also recommended that students choose the issues that they are most interested in. Students may want to research child labor. Data published by the World Bank (www.worldbank.org) and the World Affairs Council (www.world-affairs.org/GlobalClassroom) are available. Our image of child labor is that of children hitting rocks with a hammer and "Kids for Sale." We may even think of child soldiers. But of the estimated over 200 million working children under the age of 14, most are helping in their family farm or business. Students can research and support evidence for the following questions:

- What is child labor?
- Does child labor have long-term costs in education and health?
- After examining the origin of certain clothing, should there be boycotts or bans on the clothing? Would the child laborers want this?

Students at the end of an analysis of a global issue can design a collage or brief video to inform and influence others, including their fellow students in other classes. They can write letters to political leaders or participate in local groups concerned about the issue.

The United Nations Cyberschoolbus (www.un.org/cyberschoolbus) has many curriculum units on issues such as Human Rights, Peace Curriculum, Poverty, Health, and Women's Rights where the lesson "To Be Born a Girl" can be found. In addition, this website has information on different nations, publications, quizzes and games. Activities are often suggested for students to take some actions such as giving a pledge to help

LESSON PLAN

To Be Born a Girl

Have students read the following case study, then do the following activities.

"My name is Maya. I am fourteen years old and live in a poor peasant family. No one was happy that I was a girl. When I was still very little, I learned to help my mother and elder sisters. I swept the floor, washed clothes, and carried water and firewood. I could not play when I had to work.

"I was very happy when I was allowed to go to school. I made new friends there and learned to read and write. But when I reached the fourth grade, my parents stopped my education. My father said there was no money to pay the fees. Also, I was needed at home to help my mother and the others. If I were a boy, my parents would have let me complete school. My elder brother finished school and now works in an office in the capital. Two of my younger brothers go to school. Maybe they, too, will finish."

1. What important right does Maya *not* have?
2. The statistics taken from United Nations' reports and other reports on illiterate adults (two-thirds of whom are women) and on the years of education offered to males and females in certain nations or in the United States. Check the gender and ethnic/racial distribution in the professions such as medicine and law.
3. Bringing the case study to the local school level, survey the class on what students want to be. Are there gender differences?
4. Survey the class anonymously with only a check for gender by asking students how important education is: very important, important, somewhat important, or unimportant. Are there any gender differences?

Source: Adapted from United Nations CyberSchoolBus (www.un.org.cyberschoolbus)

the campaign to plan one billion trees or help a community in gain access to safe drinking water.

This and the following websites represent advocacy groups promoting their own policies and plans. As one example, students can examine the origins of their clothing and the conditions under which the clothing was produced. Please remember that many of the websites represent advocacy groups promoting their own policies and plans.

American Forum for Global Education, www.globaled.org

Amnesty International USA, www.amnesty.org

Children First, www.childrenfirst.org

Children's Labor, www.CRY.org

UNICEF, www.unicef.org

World Resources Institute Environment Education Project, www.wri.org/wri/_enved

Before inviting guest speakers into our classrooms, another check we as teachers must make is to review our responsibilities toward citizenship education. Are we providing

Small Group Work 8.6

Reflections on Your Perspectives

What events or people helped you learn about cultures and religions other than your own? You may want to consider travel, friends, work experiences, moving, and the like. ●

the children with an opportunity to consider data from a variety of opinions about the issue we are studying? Do we ask them to question the opinions and data they hear and gather? We need to explain these responsibilities to guest speakers invited to present their perspective on the problem. We should always aim for balance and use multiple sources for information.

Summary

To summarize our exploration of citizenship education, we need to recall that it is the major historical goal of public education in our country. In this chapter, we have suggested concrete, direct experiencing of decision making in the classroom and conflict management. Students need instruction in civic education. Moving out into the school with student councils and then further into the community with community or service learning broadens the citizenship perspective. Finally, global education looks beyond our nation. In global education, we have stressed the dictum of thinking globally and acting locally by examining environmental problems and the like. The key to internalizing the citizen role, for most elementary students, is active, personalized involvement.

Suggested Readings and Websites

Banks, James A., ed. *Diversity and Citizenship Education: Global Perspectives.* San Francisco: Jossey-Bass, 2004.

Conference proceedings of programs and practices of citizenship and diversity from twelve nations.

Dinwiddie, Sue A. "The Saga of Sally, Sammy and the Red Pen: Facilitating Children's Social Problem Solving." *Young Children* 49 (July 1994): 13–19.

Detailed presentation of social problem solving with young children that, with other articles in same issue, amply illustrates the connection between building a culture of responsibility in school and preparing children for citizenship in an expressive, not repressive, society.

Fine, Esther Sokolov, Ann Lacy, and Joan Baer. *Children as Peacemakers.* Portsmouth, NH: Heinemann, 1995.

Teachers of downtown alternative school in Toronto relate development of peacemaking program that changed tone of the school.

Fountain, Susan. *Education for Development: A Teacher's Resource for Global Learning.* Portsmouth, NH: Heinemann, 1995.

Classroom guidelines for helping students explore global issues—violence, hunger, prejudice, environmental abuses—in a positive, empowering way that links local to global issues.

Girard, Kathryn, and Susan J. Koch. *Conflict Resolution in the Schools: A Manual for Educators.* San Francisco, CA: Jossey-Bass Publishers, 1996.

Book sponsored by the National Institute for Dispute Resolution and the former National Association for Mediation in Education gives advice to educators planning conflict resolution programs in their schools.

Isaac, Katherine. *Civics for Democracy: A Journey for Teachers and Students.* Minneapolis: Free Spirit Publishing, 1993.

Book-length discussion of necessity for linking goals of citizenship development with action in larger community, recounting broad range of actual school-based programs.

Lewis, Barbara A. *Kids with Courage: True Stories about Young People Making a Difference.* Minneapolis: Free Spirit Publishing, 1992.

Stimulating annotation of citizenship efforts that may begin in school but extend far beyond and return to change student lives and visions.

Miller, F. Gene, and Michael G. Jacobson. "Teaching for Global Mindedness." *Social Education* (March–April 1994): 4–6.

Argues that a global view is an extension of multicultural perspectives.

National Council for the Social Studies. *Mission Statement.* Washington, 1992.

Official statement by content area professional organization of centrality of citizenship to this subject and totality of schooling.

Nelson, Jane, Lynn Lott, H. Stephen Glenn. *Positive Discipline in the Classroom.* Rocklin, CA: Prima Publishing, 1993.

Details year-long program for positive approach based on class meetings and cooperative problem solving.

Noddings, Nel, ed. *Educating Citizens for Global Awareness.* New York: Teachers College Press, 2005.

Articles on what global citizenship means and how it should shape the curriculum in K–12 classrooms.

Parker, Walter C. "Assessing Citizenship." *Educational Leadership* 48 (November 1990): 17–22.

Argues centrality of citizenship in curriculum and presents ways to organize for assessing citizenship.

Parker, Walter C. *Teaching Democracy: Unity and Diversity in Public Life* (New York: Teachers College Press, 2003).

Attempts to yoke multicultural education to democratic citizenship education. Believes strongly in the value of deliberation.

Websites

The American Promise
www.farmers.com/FarmComm/AmericanPromise

Organization endorsed by NCSS promoting civic education.

Ben's Guide to U.S. Government for Kids
www.bensguide.gpo.gov

Official government information about the three branches of U.S. government

The Center for Civic Education
www.civiced.org

Civics standards, curriculum guides, and programs.

Human Rights 101
www.thirteen.org/edonline/hr101

Insights on tolerance, racism, women's rights, refugees, and religious freedom. Helpful to teachers and teenagers. Available videos can also be useful.

National Service-Learning Clearinghouse
www.servicelearning.org

Database on service learning literature, programs, events, trainers, and organizations.

Peace Corp
peacecorps.gov.wws

Peace Corp volunteers write about their experiences along with lesson plans.

PEARSON
myeducationlab
Where the Classroom Comes to Life

VIDEO HOMEWORK EXERCISE

Conflict Resolution

Go to MyEducationLab, select the topic **Character Education**, and watch the video entitled "Conflict Resolution."

The video illustrates how conflict management, as discussed in this chapter, can work out on the playground.

CHAPTER 9

Helping All Our Diverse Students

In this chapter, we focus on helping all our students in the diverse classroom to learn social studies. We must ensure that our social studies curriculum, as well as all school experiences, include each student so that he or she is prepared to participate in our democratic society.

- Growing Diversity
- Gender
- Multicultural Education

- Teaching Religion
- Exceptionalities
- Differentiated Instruction

What are students learning about culture and diversity?

Growing Diversity

Definitions

You probably have had a diversity or a multicultural course as an undergraduate. Multicultural education probably also is being stressed in all of your education courses. As you remember, multicultural education started with the Civil Rights Era and initially focused on race and ethnic groups *within* the United States. In addition, from your many courses, you know that **multicultural education** has many definitions. Bennett[1] gives the following four dimensions to her definition of multicultural education:

Movement toward equity or equity pedagogy (positive classroom climate, and so on)

Curriculum reform; seeing the curriculum through multiple perspectives

Multicultural competence; being conscious of your own as well as other cultural perspectives

Teaching toward social justice; combating prejudice and discrimination

Essentially the term *multicultural education* can include the themes of cultural pluralism, the concept that all students can learn, the incorporation of multiple perspectives into the curriculum, and the idea that social change is necessary and desirable.

Multicultural education, in contrast with global education, also gives more attention to *racism.* Racism is attaching nonphysical characteristics, often negative, to physical characteristics. It is the extreme end of prejudice. Racism can be defined as individual, structural, political, economical, and social forces that serve to discriminate against disadvantaged people of color on the basis of their race. An *ethnic group* is a group of people who identify with one another or are identified by others as being different. This difference may take a number of forms—racial, cultural, linguistic, economic, religious, political—and may not be fixed. However, realize that defining yourself or a student as Mexican American is a one-dimensional category. We are all members of several groups such as the following: age or peer group, exceptionality, gender, area we live in (urban, suburban, rural) and region, religion, socioeconomic level, race/ethnic or national origin, U.S. citizen, global citizen. Some of these identifications are more important to us than others. This is also true of the students in our classroom.

In recent years, the term **diversity** has become more popular. *Diversity,* a broader term than *ethnicity,* includes gender, sexual orientation, physical and mental differences, religion, and socioeconomic status. The term *diversity* arose partly because multicultural education was perceived as mainly stressing race and ethnic groups in the United States. Feminists and other groups in society felt that they were being neglected. Now, however, newer definitions of multicultural education have incorporated more elements of diversity. In fact, the more recent definitions of multicultural education include global perspectives because both global education and multicultural education include respect for human rights for all people, an acceptance of cultural diversity, and the need to combat racism, sexism, and other problems. Still multicultural education concentrates more on race/ethnic groups within the United States and global education gives more coverage to people outside of the United States as well as global issues.

[1]Christine I. Bennett, *Comprehensive Multicultural Education Theory and Practice,* 5th ed. (Boston: Allyn and Bacon, 2003), 14.

One challenge of diversity in education comes as predominantly white female elementary school teachers face classrooms with a changing demographic profile. The National Education Association (NEA) in 2004 estimated that 9 percent of elementary teachers are male (an all-time low), and that teachers of color make up 16 percent of the teaching population. A later NEA survey in 2005–2006 indicated that the number of male teachers hit a record forty-year low as fewer men are entering teaching.

A second challenge is the achievement gap in history, geography, and civic education (see Chapters 5, 6, and 8) between nonminority whites and Asians compared to Hispanics and African Americans. Students need a good education to become successful workers and citizens. Therefore, all of our students must be held to high standards to be able to participate in the mainstream culture.

Changing School Population

As you are well aware, our nation's public schools are becoming more diverse as more racial or ethnic minority students enroll. This is primarily due to the growth in Hispanic enrollment. Hispanic students made up 19 percent of public school enrollment in 2004 and will probably continue to grow. In 2004, minority public school students have exceeded white enrollment in the West (Alaska, Arizona, California, Colorado, Hawaii, Idaho, Montana, Nevada, New Mexico, Oregon, Utah, Washington, and Wyoming). Note that the term "minority" is a useful shorthand term although in the previously named states, the total minority students are actually a majority.

In 2006, around 55 million students were enrolled in U.S. schools, the highest number in our history. Millions of both native-born and foreign-born children are enrolling in schools. The challenge is to educate all of the children of today's school more successfully and to eliminate the "academic achievement gaps" that presently exist for some minority groups. However, one should be careful not to stereotype any group. There are successful academic students in every group.

This means that many beginning teachers will be in classroom environments different from what they experienced when they were in elementary school. You may not desire to teach in urban schools but the suburbs also have changing demographics. There are now more English language learners (ELLs) whose needs must be met (see Chapter 10 on Literacy). All teachers have concerns about classroom management. Even the best of experienced teachers have nightmares about not being prepared and having classes that are out of control. They get anxious before the first day of school in the fall. We may each love kids but also have fears that "the kids will test me." How to interact with parents and guardians is also a worry. All of these factors illustrate the importance of learning about diversity as applied to social studies, the curriculum area where the content is people, now and long ago. It is also the area that includes fostering civic responsibilities and dispositions toward democratic values.

Know Your Class

After you compare your perspectives with others in your class, you probably noticed many

Small Group Work **9.1**

Know Yourself

First, about you. Think about your own culture. What groups do you identify with? What was your neighborhood like? What were the parental expectations for you? Thinking about these questions allows you to recognize your own perspective or values. Compare your perspective with others in your group. ●

similarities as well as differences. Probably most of your group came from families that encouraged higher education. Many of you may have lived in the suburbs. But even with these similarities, there are probably wide differences in values, religion, interests, political identification, and the like. Each of us is a complex, changing, multifaceted individual. This is also true of every student. Even what looks like a homogenous class really has a wide range of differences in abilities, interests, and backgrounds. Be careful not to stereotype a group—there is both unity and diversity within a group. For example, Asian Americans or any other ethnic/racial group masks incredible diversity. Each child is special and not a carbon copy of a group.

Getting to know your class is the first step. Try to find out as much information as possible about the specific cultures represented by your students. Even if it is only an encyclopedia article about Samoans, background information is useful. Then talk with parents and guardians. What do they see as the strengths of their child? What are their hopes for their child? What is the family's background? For example, are both parents from Mexico but their eldest daughter is in nurses training at the community college? How long has the family lived in their neighborhood? Does the family regard you as an authority figure who knows what is best for their child? This background is important since the socialization of children may influence how they learn best. You can also build a better relationship with your students if you know more about them and their families.

But remember that your class is also interested in learning as much as possible about you. This raises the question of how much of your personal life you think should be told to the class. Students are curious. They may want to know if you are married, if you have a boyfriend or girlfriend, or if you have children. They may learn which car is yours as you come and go from school. They may ask where you live. Younger children may have identified you as only belonging in a classroom. They may be surprised, for example, to see you shopping.

On Your Own **9.1**

Personal Life?

How much information about yourself do you think is appropriate for your class to know? ●

Learning about Yourself

Students need to realize they, like their teachers, are complex, cultural, changing human beings. One example to help them understand this is an exercise called "Who Am I."

Teachers and students respond to the topics and share with the class. These exercises can also help the classroom climate and help make students feel emotionally safe so they can share their thoughts. Often students initially react negatively, both emotionally and cognitively, when they hear about cultural differences and customs that are strange to them. For example, hearing that some Japanese Americans may like to eat seaweed or raw fish may make some students uncomfortable. They do not see that others could consider some of their own customs to be equally odd and distasteful.

Small Group Work **9.2**

What Would You Do?

Ms. Mercer, a white woman, taps on the classroom door and introduces herself, asking permission to give her daughter Julie the lunch she forgot. Julie is a curly-haired African American child. From the doorway, you announce, "Julie, your mother is here." On seeing Ms. Mercer, Connor calls out to Julie, "Julie, are you adopted?" How would you respond to this situation? ●

LESSON IDEA

Who Am I?

Objectives: Students will identify their interests and background.

Students will identify the groups they belong to.

Students will recognize that individuals in a group vary widely from each other.

Interests and Background Activity

Here are some items you could ask your class to tell to a partner or small group or to write down. You could do a few items over several days.

- Favorite food or foods (limit to three)
- Best holiday in the year
- Parents' hopes
- Family sayings
- Favorite toy/game

- Language(s) spoken at home
- How they describe themselves
- Favorite TV program
- Favorite story
- A pet they would like to have

Students could share their responses in pairs, first with their partners and then with the whole class. Try to encourage the idea that not everyone has to have the same favorite TV program or favorite foods. Students may draw pictures of one category such as their favorite foods.

Group Identification Activity

Explain to the class that they probably belong to at least two groups: a family and a class at school. You could also say this information would be interesting since we are studying the family (or the community, state, United States, or a world culture). Remember that data about children's families may be a sensitive area. Children may have caregivers who are single, are older relatives, are not biologically related, or are in same-sex relationships. Remember to keep parents or guardians informed by letters sent home or by e-mail.

Use the following examples but try not to give too many examples. Many children will identify their ethnic/racial background as an essential part of who they are. Others whose families are promoting acculturation to mainstream American culture may not. Some are "cultural straddlers" moving between the home and school environment. In addition, more children now see themselves as having a multiracial background. Ask the class to think of what they do after school or on Saturday and Sunday. This may suggest some groups to them. Older children may write that they are citizens of a state, the United States, and the world. Religion identification may be important to some children.

I am a member of the _____ family.

I am the sister (brother) to _____.

I am a member of the _____ class at school.

I am _____.

I am _____.

Have students share their responses first in pairs and then later with the whole class. An extension for this activity could be for each child to list qualities that make him or her special. Or have students make an "I Am" poem about themselves.

Gender

$\mathscr{L}$et us first examine the research on gender and its influence on learning. The data are based on test scores and questionnaires examining interests.

Academic Differences

In the fourth grade, scores indicate only minor gender differences for a range of school subjects. The gender differences are smaller than most people realize. Females have slightly higher scores in writing, language use, and reading in the fourth grade. From the fourth to eighth grades, females significantly increase their performance advantage over males in writing and language usage. From the eighth to twelfth grades boys increase their performance advantage over females in math concepts, geopolitical subjects, and natural science. Geopolitical subjects include economics, history, and geography. Females have substantially closed the math and science gap over the past thirty years, especially white females, although a difference remains. The fairly large gap between the higher female writing skills and the lower skills of males has not yet closed. In all subjects, there is more of a spread of male scores. This means that there are more males among the very highest scores and also more males among the very lowest scores.[2]

On average, females make higher grades than males in all major subjects. Female grades exceed males' grades the most in English, followed by smaller differences in social studies, science, and math. Grades may include a constellation of desirable characteristics that are valuable in both school and in work such as persistence, doing required work, homework, class participation, and the like. Both test scores and grades are helpful indicators of future success both in school and the working world. Informal evidence indicates that girls work harder in schools. Boys are not working as hard, saying it is not important. Girls are exploring nontraditional fields such as law, but most continue to go into more traditional female careers. Peer pressure and media exposure continue to affect both girls' and boys' choices and opportunities in the occupational world, tending to reinforce the traditional patterns.

Notice that by the twelfth grade males are ahead in what we would call the social studies. Males on the average also have a greater interest in social studies, both the traditional content found in social studies textbooks and in the news. Females tend to like more creative and visual materials. Teachers should always be mindful to look at each student as a unique individual and not stereotype anyone because of gender or other characteristics. Furthermore, there are basic social studies knowledge and skills that are essential for both females and males to have in order to participate in our democratic society.

Females

By the 1990s there was great popular concern expressed about the miseducation of girls and women. In general, books and research presented the view that the schools were structured to ensure advantages for males and to shortchange females. Female students, it was reported, received far less attention from their teachers and were not asked higher-level questions. Male students were given more help in answering questions by teachers prompting

---

[2]Nancy S. Cole, "The ETS Gender Study: How Females and Males Perform in Educational Settings" (Princeton, NJ: Educational Testing Service, 1997).

them. Girls were called on less. In literature, both girls and boys visualized heroes as males who exhibited male characteristics such as being strong and aggressive.

Teachers, it was reported, did not encourage girls in science, math, and computers (male-dominated professions). Computer knowledge and skills are vital for today's job market but the software appeals more to males. Girls, it is said, are socialized to be nice whereas boys are socialized to get what they want. Girls are praised for neatness rather than assertiveness or creativity in school. Finally, too frequently females encountered bullying and sexual harassment, with some research reporting very high incidence of harassment. Schools were apathetic on sexual harassment. As a result, girls suffered tremendous psychological damage with lower self-esteem (eating disorders, depression, etc.) and educational neglect.

To correct the gender balance in the social studies, there were calls to increase women's history in the curriculum. This need can be easily illustrated by asking students in small groups to brainstorm the names of women in history. Count how few are given. In turn, list the males the groups remember in history and count the number of responses. With this contrast, making women more visible in history becomes a priority. Women portrayed in textbooks too often have material in sidebars unrelated to the main history. Progress has been made in making women more visible in social studies textbooks and curriculum compared to the past, but more can be done. The National Women's History Project (www.nwhp.org) offers ideas for lessons and activities.

Advocates of women's history do not want just an add-on approach of including women as "famous firsts" to the narrative of men in power in war, politics, and the economy. One suggestion is to examine women's work and families, now and in the past. This means for each time period, both in the United States as well as other cultures, more attention is given to what women were doing and men and women's relationship within the family. Additional thought also should be given to how women participated in social movements ranging from the abolitionist movement to peace movements today. For projects, make sure that some topics appeal to a variety of students and not just military battles and heroes. Library resources should also be examined such as the number of biographies on male subjects and female subjects.

In teaching content and skills, teachers should be aware of how they interact and respond to girls. Girls should be called on as often as boys. Good ideas should be praised and rewarded with girls also being told that they are good thinkers or problem solvers. Check also if some gifted girls are hiding their true ability for fear of being labeled as "smart." Feedback should always be given so students, both male and female, know how to improve in learning content and skills.

However, it is not just teacher–student interactions that need to be observed. Girls in the class are interacting with the boys. Girls have looked at how teachers spend their time and attention and come to the conclusion that boys need more help. In small groups, therefore, many times girls will actually do the work for boys. This may result in girls working harder and boys having greater freedom. This may also interfere with boys developing greater self-discipline and focus in their learning. Be aware of what is happening in small groups and identify if there are "freeloaders," usually boys but also girls.

On Your Own **9.2**

Still Sexist?

Looking over your school experiences (from kindergarten through higher education) did you encounter or observe sexism at school? Do most teachers give the same attention to the misbehavior of girls and boys? ●

The Boy Crisis—Fact or Myth?

By the late 1990s, gender was no longer just a girls' or women's issue. Books and the popular media reported that now boys were disadvantaged in school, especially the early elementary years. Boys were behind in writing and reading. Males outnumbered females in suspensions, expulsions, dropout rates, special education placement, and diagnoses of attention deficit disorder. In addition, it was pointed out that boys have real problems: depression, drug use, teen sex, academic failure, and violence. Furthermore, now more women enter college than men. It was reported that when teachers focused on the contributions of women, it was a loss for boys. The schools therefore, according to those advocating more attention toward boys, were not meeting boys' needs. The schools appeared to only want quiet and conforming boys.

In general, many teachers often like girls more since girls tend to cooperate better with the teacher. Boys tend to misbehave more often and are more disruptive than girls. The result is more teacher–student interactions and more negative interactions with boys than girls. Boys receive lower ratings on classroom behavior. Although boys are over-represented in disciplinary actions, many boys do not seem to see this as a fair consequence for misbehavior. However, typically a minority of male students dominate the teacher interaction, namely those with behavior problems or "star students." Besides the students' behavior, the teacher's gender and race can also shape teacher–student interactions. In addition, primary children are accustomed to obeying adults and they typically follow this path with their teachers. However, as students become older, they typically test adult authority with each grade level, making classroom authority more problematic.

Part of the gender problem is that the societal norms for the roles of both men and women are changing, confusing, and complicated. Everyday life, including in the schools, appears to be changing faster than before. In addition, there is no single, universal definition of masculinity to which all cultures subscribe or aspire to. Different social groups living in the United States create their own versions of masculinity with differences in race, ethnicity, and social class. In other words, there are several forms of masculinity in our society. It varies across time and place. However, mainstream males have higher status.

An important question is which boys are disadvantaged in the schools. Not *all* boys are disadvantaged. Examine the NAEP achievement results in history, geography, and civics. On the average, white and Asian-American middle class males are achieving in schools. Boys who are already disadvantaged by race, class, religion, learning disabilities, and sexual orientation are the ones in need of more attention in the schools.

If there is a boy crisis, it is among inner-city and rural boys. Being poor and male is a disadvantage in terms of schooling. The "boy crisis" is concentrated on poor males. In addition, because boys are concentrated at both the extremes of gifted and low academic performance, you do see more boys at the poorest levels of school performance. Often boys of color and of lower social class wind up at the bottom of school performance with more likelihood of being referred to special educational services and more likely to be retained and not promoted.

For example, the gap in graduation rates for U.S. high schools is small for Asian Americans with only 3 percent more girls receiving a diploma. For white girls, the gap favoring girls over boys is 5 percent. However, the gender gap favoring girls is 9 percent for Hispanics and 11 percent for African Americans. But even with these statistics, remember that boys have wide variance in skills and abilities. Not all boys fit the stereotype of being troublemakers in classrooms—unable to focus or sit still, unwilling to work or read and usually bored.

What Can Be Done for Boys?

First, there is no simple solution that can "quick fix" boys, nor do all boys need to be fixed. One size does not fit all. Look at the particular boys in the class who need help. Try to get them engaged in some activities. You may need to have student inventories on what topics are of interest to them and how they learn best. Give choices. As long as trade books cover a general theme such as the Civil War, allow topics such as war and weapons.

There is evidence that it is not academic capacity but work habits and conduct that may be interfering with some boys' learning. This means adopting a proactive stance toward classroom management. Give explicit instruction on classroom policies and procedures and why they are necessary. Provide examples of what is expected for every child to do their best. Weak reading comprehension can be attacked by using engaging booklists.

Teachers cannot change the child's family or the neighborhood although there is some evidence that boys have more difficulty than girls in a single-parent family. But in some cases, teachers can help low-achieving students cope by creating areas of calm and safety. Sometimes physical movement including recess, exercise, and relaxation techniques can be helpful when interwoven during the school day. Draw on dramatic talents, use of manipulatives, and engage students in music and art as forums for learning.

Remember that most students drop out of high school because they become disengaged from school. The highest at-risk population for not graduating from high school are young African American males. However, this process of disengagement starts years before the actual high school dropout takes place. The early grades are essential to help boys stay connected to school, learning, and educational achievement. It is even more important for boys stay in school now, because the labor market now seeks workers with more schooling. It does become a crisis if too many young males cannot become employed.

Boys' disadvantages are short-term. Males, on the average, continue to get higher paying jobs after schooling is completed. Males also have more power in society as indicated by their large majority role in high positions in government and large corporations. Although girls have measured higher in verbal skills, school grades, and other achievement areas, these advantages, especially verbal, have not translated into women's dominance in higher education fields such as English literature, law, or philosophy in major universities. Women are now earning a growing percentage of college degrees. Males still earn the majority of the doctorates although the proportion of women who receive doctorates has increased dramatically in the past thirty years. Science and mathematics participation by women still needs to increase. This means that both girls and boys must experience schools as welcoming, safe, supportive, and accessible for educational opportunities.

Small Group Work 9.3

Do Boys Need More Attention?

Based on your observations, how do most teachers interact with boys? Should more attention be given to boys? Is it fair to the girls? ●

Name-Calling

Teaching Tolerance (www.teachingtolerance.org), a free and useful magazine for teachers, surveyed teachers asking the following question: How often do you hear these types of comments from your students?

LESSON IDEA

Are Girls and Boys Treated Equally in Schools?

Federal and state laws mandate equal access to education. In small groups discuss the following questions:

1. Do female and male students have equal opportunities to participate and get called on in class? Why or why not?
2. Do female and male students equally participate in small group work? Are girls working harder?
3. Are female and male students treated equally in terms of grading? Why or why not?
4. Are female and male students subject to the same amount of discipline and treated equally when they are disciplined? Why or why not?
5. Do female and male students have equal opportunities to participate in sports and are facilities and equipment adequate for both? Why or why not?
6. Are there any other ways in which one gender is discriminated against or treated unfairly?

After discussion, debrief by asking if there were any significant differences in the responses of female or male students to the items. Then based on the discussion, do you think gender equity has been achieved in education?

Source: Modified from the Constitutional Rights Foundation's "Bill of Rights in Action," Spring, 2004.

Racist

Sexist

Anti-gay/lesbian

Biased against a religion

For students nationwide, the highest category of name-calling was sexist, followed by homophobic comments, then racist, and the lowest was directed toward religious groups. Many have heard the term *gay* frequently used on school playgrounds and other unsupervised areas of the school. Some elementary students insult other students with the terms *gay* or *fag*. These are usually interpreted by younger children as meaning stupid, as in "Are you gay or something?" Or "That's so gay." The word *gay* is here used as an all-purpose term for something stupid, silly, or dumb. It is possible that a given student may not know the origin of the term *gay*. However, a school does have the duty to protect students from harassment.

Often name-calling, telling demeaning jokes, and bullying go hand in hand. In one study, 47 percent of sixth graders have said they were bullied at least once in the course of just five school days. Insults on students' identity, who they are, are occurring in unsupervised informal hallways and play areas. Teachers and administrators may not recognize the negative influences on students' identity. Although students may not suffer physical blows, the psychological impact can be devastating to those students who are targeted. This may result in their being sick more often, missed school, lower grades, and depression. This type of harassment can reach its peak in middle school.

Besides the four categories of name-calling (racist, sexist, anti-gay/lesbian and biased against religion), increasingly heavier and overweight youngsters are called names by their peer group because of their size. As the public has become more alarmed about the obesity crisis, schools have given more attention to what food is available at school and what the school is doing for the nutritional, exercise, and health needs of students, especially overweight students. Weighing children and talking about obesity makes everyone aware of who in the classroom is overweight. Although every teacher wants to establish a trust relationship with every student, teachers should try especially hard to establish good relationships with heavier students so that they will be more likely to tell you about name-calling and being the butt of jokes. Supporting all students regardless of their size, ethnicity/race, gender, and ability is the goal.

Like women's history advocates, another issue is how the rights of gays, lesbians, bisexuals, and transgender individuals should be treated and what their place in history should be. Gay rights battlefields have spread to public schools on three issues: whether classrooms are an appropriate place to explore the issues of homosexuality, whether schools should allow extracurricular clubs and activities for gays, and whether textbooks should acknowledge homosexual relationships. In general, there has been only a slight increase in attention to lesbian/gay material in the social studies. More attention by the school has been given to preventing harm to gay and lesbian students.

All agree that if a student comes to you citing an incident of name-calling, bullying, and sexual harassment, you cannot ignore the incident. The school must afford every single student a safe environment. If you do nothing, the victim feels powerless to stop further abuse. In addition, the school may face serious legal lawsuits for not correcting unacceptable behavior. Either you or the principal must conduct an investigation. You must be fair. Were there any witnesses? The school should have a written policy that is clearly stated on name-calling, bullying, and sexual harassment. This policy should be widely communicated to everyone and enforced. Clear consequences should follow misbehavior. The procedures to come forward with complaints without fear of retaliation should be known to all. Teachers should also not allow slurs or intentional hurtful remarks in class.

Usually the first response by a principal is punishment of the abuser. However, if a student is corrected for name-calling, harassment, and bullying, it may mean that he or she learns only that it is not acceptable to behave in that manner at school. It may just drive the behavior underground to be used outside the school. Ideally, the student needs to learn that everyone has a right to an education and name-calling, harassment, and bullying are harmful both in a school setting and elsewhere. Everyone must realize they do not have to like every person, but they must respect the rights of every individual.

Cyberbullying

TECHNOLOGY

Bullies now have a new turf, the Internet. Nationwide many teens have been victims of taunts and threats via social network websites such as MySpace and Facebook, instant messages, and text messages from cell phones. These teens have often been devastated by nasty bullying, most often sexual and antigay harassment. Most of this form of bullying occurs off campus on home computers. The school, nevertheless, does need to check if the bullying is happening on their campus even if initially it was started off campus.

Most Internet providers address complaints about inappropriate behavior by their users. Parents/guardians also need to be informed since many teenagers do not want adults to know about this bullying in fear that they will be cut off from the Internet. Meanwhile, legislators are considering what laws need to be put into place to protect young people from cyberbullying.

Students can learn that the best way to settle problems is through democratic decision making, not threats or violence. Name-calling, bullying, and sexual harassment can be brought up in class meetings without naming the students involved. Other possible solutions are having small groups brainstorm ways to cut down unacceptable behavior and examine why such negative behavior is occurring. Discuss gender and cultural inequities, especially those that are classroom related. Some teachers ask students to bring examples of name-calling and incidents to class to discuss how a person feels when he or she is hurt. Schoolwide assemblies or time set aside in each classroom for discussions of this misbehavior can help to educate all.

Elders

Respect for diversity often neglects the elderly or the aged. Although not usually mentioned in name-calling, this group also is likely to have negative stereotypes associated with being "old." As the number of elderly people in our society increases, it is essential for students to develop positive attitudes toward elders and also see how they themselves are getting older. At the primary-grade level, the elderly easily can be included in studying the family and discussing grandparents and other elders. Often this can be done by using literature portraying positive images toward the aging. Possible books for young children that are appropriate are *Supergrandpa* by D. M. Schwartz (HarperCollins, 1991), the familiar *Miss Rumphius* by B. Cooney (Puffin, 1985), and *The Wednesday Surprise* E. Bunting (Clarion Books, 1990). Biographies, especially of individuals who worked all of their lives for justice like Gandhi, or political leaders are appropriate for the upper grades.

It is especially important that students do not have the image of the elderly as all being frail and confined to nursing homes. The more publicized discussion of Alzheimer's also may contribute to the viewpoint that all the elderly are senile. Indeed, *My Little Grandmother Often Forgets* by Reeve Lindbergh and Kathryn Brown (Canderwick, 2007) may help children deal with Alzheimer's disease of a relative. However, a well-intentioned visit to a nursing home could contribute and reinforce negative ideas about the elderly. Other stereotypes are that the elderly always are grandparents, are all alike, and they depend on their children. Children should see that most of the elders are healthy and active. Interactions between the generations such as interviewing elders (See Chapter 5 on oral history) or being tutored by a volunteer senior should stress that most of the elderly are still active and live independent lives. This does not deny that children do get upset and concerned with the serious illness or loss of a grandparent or an elderly friend or relative.

Small Group Work **9.4**

What Should Be Done?

What do you think are the best ways to help children to stop name-calling, harassment, and bullying? ●

Multicultural Education

In our multicultural society, teachers from kindergarten to higher education need to develop a meaningful curriculum for all students to understand and respect the history and perspectives of many groups. Multicultural education is for all students. Diversity is a strength. Students need to get along with others and to respect others. At the same time,

TABLE 9.1 Curriculum Emphasis			
	Importance for Teachers (as Percentage)		
Curriculum Emphasis	Grade 2	Grade 5	Grade 8
Promoting the acceptance of cultural diversity	88	81	84
The Constitution and the U.S. system of government	69	88	96
Thinking critically about American institutions and American culture	70	77	86
Learning to interact socially with others	86	72	66
Injustice in the American system, with particular attention paid to race, gender, and class injustice	64	66	78
American historical heroes	69	70	64

Source: James S. Leming, Lucien Ellington, and Mark Schug, *Social Studies in Our Nation's Elementary and Middle Schools.* The Center for Survey Research and Analysis, 2006.

teachers also have to teach a common, mainstream American culture, rooted in the history of this nation. Therefore, in learning history, it is helpful for children to have the opportunity to understand the multiple viewpoints that different individuals and groups have had about events (see Chapter 5). Immigration units with multiple perspectives are a fine example of how students can learn both about their own heritage and major events in U.S. history.

Look at Table 9.1. Note that in the random sample of 1,000 elementary teachers, second-grade teachers believed that "acceptance of cultural diversity" and "learning to interact socially with others" ranked as the two most important curriculum emphases. By contrast, eighth-grade teachers thought teaching about the Constitution and the U.S. system of government was most important. However, at all three grade levels promoting cultural diversity was high.

However, teachers vary in how "multicultural" an educator they are prepared to be. There may be levels of diversity starting with the beginning level of concentrating on the "Five Fs" of teaching about diversity: food, fashion, fiestas, folklore, and famous people. Be careful in teaching about food and fashion that you do not reinforce common misconceptions. All Japanese Americans are not eating rice three times a day or dressing in kimonos for traditional Japanese holidays. The next stage is moving to a wider use of multicultural materials. And finally, the idea of social action is the third stage.

Multicultural education occurs in two ways. First is the formal instruction. Second is the classroom environment in which the content is being taught and learned. This is more the area of the hidden curriculum. Which students do teachers call on and what nonverbal messages do they send certain students? Does everyone receive equal attention? Praise and attention are often only given to the academically able. Those children who are not academically able are frequently not valued by the rest of the class. Too often then, these children feel that working hard will not be rewarded and so they do not even try to learn.

As mentioned previously in "Knowing Your Class," educate yourself. Seek out information from books, online sources, parents, and from people in the community to learn more about the norms and traditions of your students' cultural backgrounds. If teachers are able to tap into the cultures of their students, students will be better able to participate in learning. Teachers can better relate new information to the students' life experiences. Teachers can also incorporate different cultures into the curriculum. This is called culturally responsive curriculum.

Multicultural education like civic education is an all-year-round responsibility. Realize that one-shot too-brief lessons will not cause much change in your students. A lesson or two normally expands students' knowledge with facts and other information. But it probably has little or no effect on attitudes or behavior. Often media can be effective, such as film or video presentations that dramatize the unfairness of prejudice and the harm it causes. But films that are thinly veiled propaganda for a particular set of beliefs and values frequently meet with resistance. Students, especially as they grow older, resent being "preached to." On the other hand, cooperative learning can be a powerful tool to building positive interactions between diverse children.

Small Group Work **9.5**

Your Emphasis?

Looking at the six categories in Table 9.1, first by yourself rank from 1 to 6 what categories you think are most important. Then check your results with your small group. Would a different grade level change your choices? ●

Multicultural Teaching

Teachers also want to promote antibias attitudes in students. Usually this means that you first have to know what your students presently think about themselves and different races and ethnic groups. Your own observation of the interactions at lunch and recess as well as in class give clues about their attitudes and behavior. Do students initiate work and play activities across ethnic and racial lines? Have friendships developed across diverse groups? Exercises such as "Who I Am" may provide further insight about your class.

A more direct way to gather information is to ask students to create a visual representation of themselves, including their families, heritages, and interests. First discuss the different cultures in the classroom or school. Brainstorm how one could represent these cultures. Then for homework students can prepare either a poem or a collage that represents themselves. The following day, you can create a large Venn diagram and discuss the similarities and differences of students. If you wish, the Venn diagram could be pasted on blue paper and posted on a bulletin board. The various collages and poems could be pasted on red or white construction paper surrounding the blue Venn diagram indicating that, regardless of our differences, we all are U.S. citizens with shared beliefs.

In addition, students need to understand the meaning of such important social studies concepts as *prejudice* and *stereotypes*. *Prejudice* is making a decision about a person or group of people without all of the information. It is an attitude of a closed mind. See the sample unit plan "Understanding Prejudice." Vivid examples are given to illustrate the concept.

On Your Own **9.3**

More Unit Evaluation

What are the strengths of the unit plan "Understanding Prejudice"? From the lessons provided, do you see any weaknesses in this unit? What skills might a teacher need to make this unit work properly? ●

UNIT PLAN

Understanding Prejudice

The following excerpts are from a unit developed by the San Mateo, California, Elementary School District. The unit emphasizes the affective (emotional) domain. It is designed for the sixth grade and is intended to last almost four weeks. Notice the difficulties in writing objectives in the affective domain.

Unit Goals

Students will demonstrate an acceptance of human differences while engaged in activities in the classroom and in other situations.

Students will define prejudice and give examples.

Students will distinguish between dislike and prejudice.

Students will recognize stereotyping, including male and female roles.

Students will recognize prejudgment against persons with disabilities, either physical or mental.

Students will understand the physical differences of ethnic minorities.

Students will describe differences related to socioeconomic, religious, and emotional factors.

Lesson: The Stranger

Objective: Students will define prejudice and give examples of it.

Procedure: Ask a visitor to come to the room dressed entirely in paper bags. The visitor comes in and sits down with no introduction or other attention directed toward him or her. After the visitor has spent about fifteen minutes in the room, he or she leaves and a discussion follows.

Possible questions: What did you think about the stranger when he or she first came into the room? Who can tell us about the stranger? (Record answers since they may bring out fears and stereotypes.) How did you feel with a stranger in the room? Would someone tell us about a time when you were a stranger in a group of new people? How did you feel? What did you think of the other people? Why? How do you react to words such as *the homeless* and words describing other groups?

Lesson: Stereotyping

Objective: Students will be able to give an example of stereotyping.

Procedure: Review the meaning of prejudice. Ask the students how they think children learn prejudice. Then do the following:

Instruct the students to close their eyes and imagine a Native American. Have them draw their idea on paper. Show some of the pictures to the class. Next show them some pictures of Native Americans without feathers, war paint, and so on. Ask them where they learned about Native Americans.

Discuss with the students how they might expect a typical person of another race, nationality, and so on to look. Discuss why they might expect these things because of stereotypes. Ask if stereotypes are good to have. Ask if stereotypes can make us treat people unfairly.

Lesson: Stereotyped Attitudes

Objective: Students will recognize and give examples of stereotyping attitudes.

Procedure: Discuss with the class the opinion of some people that most children are terrible. Have them give examples of things they have heard people say about their age group.

Ask the students what they think about these things. Are they fair? Why? Why do some people feel that way? Do the children have reason to be upset?

Point out that ideas are formed by our experiences, but we should try not to group all people by the actions of a few. Ask students to write a description of a teacher. When they have finished, read the descriptions and explain that all teachers are not exactly alike simply because they are teachers.

Lesson: Letters to the Editor

Have cooperative groups write replies to the following letters written to a newspaper advice columnist.

Dear Mrs. Helpful,

I am a girl from Iran. I am worried that I cannot make friends in my new school in the United States. I feel that the kids in my fifth grade class think all Muslims kill people and are terrorists. They do not call me names but I am not included. I sit alone in the lunchroom. What can I do?

Yours truly,
Amal
P.S. My name means Hope. Please give me hope.

Dear Mrs. Helpful,

Being a boy from Sudan is hard. Some of the other boys call me names. They say: "This is America. Go home." What can I do to make them understand that my family as refugees cannot go back? There has been genocide in Sudan.

Yours truly,
Asir

After each group has read its responses, let students analyze each response in terms of solving the writer's problem.

Lesson: Counterstereotyping

Focus on sample individuals of a given racial/ethnic group who counter the popular stereotype. For example, Jewish athletes, African-American scholars, Hispanic executives. Or look at the positive characteristics of whole cultures such as the fact that the majority of Puerto Rican New Yorkers are gainfully employed.

Let us take as an example the concept *prejudice*. In small groups ask students first to write the word *prejudice* and draw a circle around it. Then students can brainstorm the characteristics for which people can be *prejudged*. Typically the list will include race, language, gender, physical disability, religion, sexual orientation, age group, national origin, weight, income, and the like. The small groups give their lists of characteristics and the class discusses the harm of prejudging individuals.

Stereotypes are ideas about a group that define members of the group without regard to their uniqueness as individuals. Ask each student to list one stereotype related to culture, race, ethnicity, age, gender, and ability, that he or she has heard from the media or other students. List each stereotype. For example: *All Asian American students are smart and get good grades.* Then discuss the impact of this stereotype:

- Creates unrealistic expectations
- Creates bad feelings between groups
- May neglect Asian American students having difficulty

FRIENDLY

Respect
Positive and open approval of others

Tolerance
Accepting people who are "different"

Prejudice
Hostile attitude

Discrimination
Excluding certain people

Scapegoating
Physical or verbal abuse

HOSTILE

Conclusion: "All" members of a group are not the same.

For younger children, the teacher could read and discuss books like *Oliver Button Is A Sissy* by Tomie dePaola (Harcourt Brace Jovanovich, 1979) or *Tough Boris* by Mem Fox (Voyager, 1998). Students could then make a list of what both boys and girls "can" do. They could discuss what heroes do and learn to recognize stereotypes. Or students could identify if characters in books such as *Little Red Riding Hood* display social responsibility. Other concepts besides *prejudice* (the thought) and *stereotyping* could include *discrimination* (the action), and *scapegoating,* physical or verbal abuse of people who are "different." Older children could give definitions of *hate crime* and *genocide*. As much as possible, use visuals like the one shown to create a common vocabulary.

Other Strategies for Teaching Multicultural Education

Using Trade Books   Just as in teaching almost every area of the social studies, using trade books for multicultural education is an excellent idea. Books can open the doors for promoting awareness of different individuals and groups, causing insight and multiple perspectives of the histories of various cultural groups and for facilitating consciousness of social issues. Books can remind us of the great diversity of the human family. Readers can be drawn into identifying with the characters' lives and their difficulties. Care, however, must be used in choosing the books, especially older books which could reinforce stereotypes. Even here, it is possible for the teacher to point out what individuals a generation or more ago thought about different groups. The number of quality books now available for teaching multicultural education is promising. Again, look at the lists of Notable Trade Books for Youth at the NCSS Web site (www.socialstudies.org) or in their journal *Social Education* for every

May/June issue. Notice that many books show girls in varied and courageous roles. Consider, for example, the following:

Atkins, J. *Aani and the Tree Huggers.* New York: Lee & Low, 1994.

Aani, an Indian village girl, inspires the women in her village to rally against the threat of possible destruction of the forests in her country. (Grades 3 through 6)

Cherry, L. *A River Ran Wild.* San Diego, CA: Harcourt Brace, 1992.

History of Nashua River Valley, New Hampshire and efforts to clean up the river. (Intermediate grades)

Chocolate, D. *The Piano Man.* New York: Walker & Co., 1998.

A young African American girl and her grandfather share their love of music. (Primary/intermediate grades)

Coles, R. *The Story of Ruby Bridges.* New York: Scholastic, 1995.

The first African American child to integrate an all-white school. Used in unit in Chapter 5. (Grades 1 to 6)

Dorros, A. *Abuela.* New York: Dutton, 1995.

A Hispanic grandmother who takes her granddaughter all around the city by bus and imagination. (Primary grades)

Fradin, J. B., and Fradin, D. B. *The Power of One: Daisy Bates and the Little Rock Nine.* New York: Clarion Books, 2004.

Mentor of the nine African-American students who integrated Central High School in Little Rock, 1957. Tireless civil rights activist. (Intermediate grades)

Freedman, R. *The Voice that Challenged a Nation: Marian Anderson and the Struggle for Equal Rights.* New York: Clarion Books, 2004.

Account of a great African American vocalist's career in the context of the history of civil rights. (Intermediate grades)

George, J. C. *Julie.* New York: HarperCollins, 1994.

A sequel to *Julie and the Wolves.* Julie returns to her father's Eskimo village, where she struggles to save the wolves and her way of life. (Intermediate grades)

Hopkinson, D. *Sweet Clara and the Freedom Quilt.* New York: Knopf, 1993.

Courageous young slave creates a map of the route to the North by stitching it as a pattern in a quilt. (Primary/intermediate grades)

Lester, J. *Black Cowboy, Wild Horses: A True Story.* New York: Dial, 1998.

Bob Lemmons, a former slave, was an outstanding cowboy. (Primary/intermediate grades)

Polacco, P. *Chicken Sunday.* New York: Scholastic Inc., 1992.

As a thank you gift for Miss Eula's wonderful Sunday chicken dinners, three children sell decorated eggs to earn money to purchase a hat for her. (Primary grades)

San Souci, R. D. *Fa Mulan: The Story of a Woman Warrior.* New York: Hyperion, 1998.

Young woman disguises herself as a man and joins the army to fight the Tartars. (Primary/intermediate grades)

Walter, M. P. *Alec's Primer.* Middlebury, VT: The Vermont Folklife Center, 2004.

Alec Turner, a young boy born into slavery, lives at a time when it was forbidden for slaves to read. Reading is the first step he takes for freedom. (Primary grades)

Books can portray cultural groups in a positive light. But it is not enough just to read the book to students or have them read the book by themselves. In many cases to really get the true benefit of the learning experience, background information is needed to appreciate the setting and the time period of the story. Discussion among students is normally essential. In addition, try as much as possible to move students into higher levels of thinking. Can students offer different solutions to the problem or issues raised in the story? What are the different perspectives shown in the story? Can they create a script for dramatic play of an interesting part of the story? Asking students to see if there are any parallels in the book to current issues brings the book up to the present.

Students can also write journals about how the main character is facing challenges. Some teachers like journal entries for every chapter. The three questions for the journal could be as follows: What did the main character do in this chapter? What did the main character learn? How does the main character feel? Some teachers limit the length of the entry so students do not try to write down the whole chapter. Others allow drawings to show what is happening to the main character. Using journal writing about a character helps comprehension and also helps students to see the perspective of the character.

Social Action

In school or in the wider community, are there contemporary problems of diversity? One issue is how different ethnic/racial groups of students seat themselves in the lunchroom or eating areas. *Teaching Tolerance* magazine reported that students see boundaries or fences the most in the cafeteria, classroom, bus, recreational activities, and after-school clubs. This might be a problem that the student council would like to consider. Steps suggested for looking at any problem are to first analyze the problem and discuss it with others. Then brainstorm possible solutions. Evaluate each option and select the best option. Since 2003, thousands of schools have participated in "mix it up" at lunch time. Among the solutions they used to break out of their homeroom rut was eating their lunches in different rooms, designated by birth months, or using random methods for seating at different tables.

Does the school not appear to be welcoming to all parents and guardians? Is this shown by poor attendance by certain groups at parent conferences and PTA meetings? Although some children might not see this as a problem to be corrected, teachers and the principal do want better communication with all parents. What action could be taken to encourage all parents to attend school functions?

Consider initiating a cookbook or a collection of oral histories from the many groups that are part of the community. Students and parents could create a mosaic or a multicultural display for the hallways. Or develop a partnership with another school whose student body composition is different than yours. More controversial, hold a debate on immigration policy within the class, school, or for the community. Or your class might want to make a mural showing the contributions of the various diverse groups in the community. Students working on the mural may develop a sense of collaboration and camaraderie. All of the arts offer possibilities beyond awareness of different cultures. Music, artwork, dance, and poetry can bring both enjoyment and appreciation of other cultures. Always try for a variety such as traditional as well as contemporary songs (or art, and the like) to reflect the complexity of the culture. Strive to have community participation both as an audience and partner. In many cases, these performances can send a message or support a social action.

Visiting the Broader Community and Its Celebrations   Sometimes in a given school there is not much "diversity." Talking with administrators, think about interdistrict partnerships or urban/suburban partnerships. This means exchange programs that have to be carefully planned. Typically like global class exchanges, students using the Internet share their ideas, write letters, make videos of their class, art products, and the like with another classroom. At the end of the year this may climax with visiting each other or an overnight adventure, especially with an environmental emphasis. Some cooperative classrooms have raised money for relief, investigated local history and cultural heritages, or other forms of active citizenship. Teachers have reported success in these programs but stress that just throwing kids together does not automatically build tolerance. Students need to be able to get along with their own classmates on their own playground before embarking on a cross-cultural experience.

Some teachers inform parents about community celebrations such as a Chinese New Year parade or an American Indian Pow-Wow. Often these events are held over the weekend and offer possibilities for seeing how other groups celebrate. Remember, however, without a little knowledge of the culture, a spectator may miss much of the meaning of the event. Providing some background information may help both adults and children learn more from the event.

Teaching Religion

Students do not come to school with their religious affiliations branded on their foreheads, although teachers may sometimes get clues from students' dress and discussions. Especially younger children may tell their teacher about their religious beliefs and activities. "I am making my First Holy Communion next Sunday." "I'm fasting now for Ramadan so I won't eat lunch." "Our children's choir gets to sing next Sunday." How should a teacher respond to these statements? In most cases, children want you to approve of their actions. Neutral statements such as "You must be looking forward to that" or "Your family must be proud of you" are appropriate. Frequently, such students' comments as those given here can be found in the same classroom, showing the religious diversity within classrooms. Remember that asking students directly about their religious beliefs may make them uncomfortable and should be avoided.

Teacher's Role

What is the teacher's role in teaching religion? The First Amendment Center[3] has the following four guidelines, which have also been endorsed by the National Education Association (NEA) and other groups.

1. Focus on studies *about* religion, not the practice or celebration of religious holidays.
2. Be academic, not devotional.

[3]Charles C. Haynes and Oliver Thomas, *Finding Common Ground: A Guide to Religious Liberty in Public Schools.* Download a free copy from www.freedom/forum.org or go the U.S. Department of Education guidelines on religious expression in public schools at www.ed.gov/inits/religion and www.teachingaboutreligion.org.

3. Strive for student awareness of religions, but do not press for student acceptance of any religion.
4. Expose students to a diversity of religious views, but do not impose any particular view.

Inclusion of religion is important in order for students to be properly educated about history. What can you teach? In U.S. history, the religious background of explorers (English, French, Spanish, Portuguese) and colonial settlers are essential to understanding their history. The missions established in the Southwest and California also deserve attention, as well as any group that came to the United States for religious freedom. There is a long tradition of religious ideas influencing politics in the United States. Religion played an important role in the abolitionist movement continuing to the 20th-century civil rights movement that was deeply rooted in southern African American churches. World history courses should teach about the origins and histories of the major religions found throughout the world. At a minimum, this includes Buddhism, Hinduism, Judaism, Islam, early Christianity, and the Protestant Reformation. When teaching about religion, set a tone for the classroom discussion that allows students to deal with religious diversity and nonreligion without being offensive or defensive about religion. Teachers must be neutral in teaching about religions and they also must be neutral about those who are nonreligious. Every individual in the school has First Amendment rights and some students or their teachers may reject religion. Their personal views on religion should be honored and respected since freedom of religion also means freedom not to practice a religion.

What should you be careful about in the teaching of religion? Avoid having students role-play a pilgrimage to Mecca (Hajj), or a similar simulation of religious ceremonies or beliefs. The rites and practices of religions must be respected and must not be reenacted in any manner. You can have a speaker talk about a particular religion if you follow your district's guidelines about guest speakers. However, make sure that the speaker knows what your purpose is. When teaching on your own religion, be careful to say what the adherents of the religion believe and not "I believe." Better to say "most Buddhists believe" or "according to Hebrew scriptures." If a parent asks a teacher to ensure that his or her child observes a special religious obligation such as not eating a certain type of food, the teacher should explain that it is *not* a teacher's responsibility to enforce religious practices.

Teachers should not use the classroom to proselytize or otherwise inject their own personal religious beliefs into the discussion. Do not allow a student to try to convert the class to his or her religious views. Teachers cannot pray in the presence of students during school hours. They can pray privately while in school. Teachers can teach about religious holidays but not *celebrate* them. This means that a Christmas party is off limits. Many schools have a classroom party before the winter vacation (not Christmas vacation) but call it something other than a Christmas party. All of these suggestions should contribute to making all students feel they belong in the classroom and are not outsiders.

Besides Christmas, Halloween in public schools is becoming increasingly controversial. This has become a religious issue since some believe that the holiday derives from and celebrates pagan superstition as well as glorifying occult and satanic forces. Most children, however, think Halloween is a fun holiday, which means that the school is caught in the middle. The administration in your school will probably give guidance on how Halloween is to be or not to be celebrated. To avoid offending students and parents with sensitivities about this holiday, as a teacher, go lightly on the witchcraft, ghost, or graveyard decorations and emphasize more the harvest or the transition from summer to winter. Older students could study the history of the holiday or certain aspects of the holiday, such as carving pumpkins.

Exceptionalities

The term *exceptionalities* refers to the characteristics that differentiate some children from the rest of their classmates. Children with exceptionalities are often divided into the gifted and those with disabilities. English language learners (ELLs) are not and should not be put into this category (see Chapter 10). Remember that to some extent everyone is both gifted and also challenged or has some disabilities. You should also be aware that the term *learning disabilities* is often overused, with more attention given to labeling and not enough given to helping the child.

The Gifted

Parents and others concerned with talented children and youth have expressed their frustration that the gifted are sorely neglected by the schools. Only a very small proportion of money goes to the gifted compared to the amounts that go to those with learning disabilities. What does *gifted* really mean? There is now a broader definition of *gifted*. Gifted children excel in general intellectual ability, performing or visual arts, creativity, and social skills and leadership. Most have IQ Scores between 130 and 155. A few above that range are truly gifted. Usually only between 2 to 5 percent of all students are considered gifted but in many states the number of students considered gifted has recently expanded.

The gifted, like all individuals, are not all alike. Some have a keen sense of humor and these students have at times distracted and frustrated some teachers with their comments. These students also may enjoy amusing the class with their jokes. Others have high ability but are not particularly creative. A few are both highly intelligent and highly creative. Some are focused on one subject area or discipline. Belying the image of a nonathletic, isolated gifted student with Harry Potter glasses, many of the gifted are well coordinated and have good social skills. What they may have in common is that they are frequently bored in the classroom.

Parents and others concerned with these talented children and youth have expressed frustration that the gifted are sorely neglected by the schools. Only a very small proportion of money goes to the gifted compared to the amounts going to those with learning disabilities, because schools concentrate resources on slower learners to get test scores up in reading and mathematics. Parents want a No Child Left Bored program for their gifted and talented students. In fact, parents have been up in arms when gifted children have been diagnosed as having psychological problems or a disorder. This can occur when gifted children have an intense curiosity, have problems getting along with their peer group, or have become impatient with teachers who often tell them to stop asking so many questions. If a gifted student knows more about a certain subject than the teacher, this can become a real problem.

In the social studies, it probably is best to use enrichment of the current year's social studies curriculum rather than to accelerate the gifted to the next year's work. Try to use pretests, either oral or written, to check what the gifted already know about the coming unit. You may be surprised how much they already know. This will offer an opportunity for going further in depth on topics that are interesting to the gifted student. Some teachers use **contracts** with gifted students outlining what they will do for the coming unit. Why contracts? Not all gifted students or those with high ability can easily work independently. Some of the gifted, like other students, need structure and clear directions. The contract, signed by the student, defines the objectives, identifies possible materials, and outlines how the work is to be evaluated. It also states the time period in which the contract/project is to be completed.

Unfortunately, pretests and contracts with the gifted are not often used. Since many gifted students are excellent readers, they are able to finish their social studies assignments rapidly and with comprehension. The teacher needs to decide what these students should be doing after they finish their work before the rest of their classmates. Avoid assigning dry research reports or twice as much average work. One solution has been for gifted students to help teach other students, either as a tutor or in small groups. The rationale is that explaining to another reinforces their own learning. Research has shown, however, that the gifted actually benefit in small groups of other gifted students. This suggests that at least part of the time, the gifted student should be placed with the other gifted students.

For social studies learning, the gifted are typically the ones that have the fewest difficulties reading and interpreting primary documents. Secure appropriate documents from the many excellent websites related to the unit (see Chapter 5). Try to have the gifted read additional interesting perspectives and report their work back to the rest of the class. Their reports could be in a creative format such as a cartoon or a news bulletin. In addition, doing challenging, problem-solving WebQuests already available from the Internet can be of interest, especially if students have a choice of which WebQuest to do. For WebQuests using the Internet, the teacher preparation has been reduced. However, this activity presumes that there are enough computers with Internet access in the class so that the gifted are not the only group that can use the computers. Visiting places where research or creative activities occur can also be stimulating. Sometimes a school volunteer can be recruited to be the guide to the facility. Such visits, which only involve one or two students, must be planned carefully in advance for maximum benefit.

The important thing is not to ignore gifted students. Surprisingly there are a few gifted students who actually drop out of high school, probably due to an accumulation of boring and poor experiences during their school years. If possible, always give the gifted choices on what to do. Some of the self-motivated will perform well above expectations. If nothing else, allow the gifted to read a variety of materials—paperbacks, magazines, encyclopedias, newspapers—when they finish their work. Have these resources available at all times. This is better than planning nothing for them to do.

Other Forms of Exceptionalities

The gifted are just one of six categories of exceptionalities. Classification and diagnosis are often difficult and subjective. The same child could be labeled as learning disabled in one school and not another. Only the medical model can clearly identify children with physical disabilities like cerebral palsy. Here are the other five categories of exceptionalities.

- Learning disabled (LD)
- Communication disabilities (delayed language development, stuttering, etc.)
- Mentally retarded (MR)
- Sensory, physical, and health impairments (epilepsy, hearing loss, etc.)
- Emotionally disturbed (ED)

Sometimes SWD, a general term for students with disabilities, is used.

About 14 percent of public school children, nearly seven million students ages 3 to 21, are in special education. About half have learning disabilities. The number of special education students has been slowly increasing. Many critics are questioning these numbers, especially for minority groups. The fastest growing areas are speech and language impairments, autism and traumatic brain injuries, and health impairments due to chronic and acute conditions such as asthma, epilepsy, and diabetes.

Who really belongs in special education? The diagnosis of learning disability often takes place around the fourth grade. Most of these are reading problems. Many believe that an early intervention instead of waiting until the fourth grade would help many struggling students to succeed in a regular classroom and to avoid the label of being a "special education student." If you think the parents of the gifted are frustrated, just talk to some parents of children with other exceptionalities about how they regard what is happening to their child in school.

In general, many "regular" inclusive classes welcome and help students with obvious physical disabilities, such as those in wheelchairs or with limited vision. However, these classes are often less likely to be as welcoming to low-achieving students. Yet the goal is that everyone in the class be regarded as being worthwhile. Prosocial behavior should be the norm. Having a good relationship with each child can be a model for building a climate of peer acceptance.

Suggestions for Teaching

Realize that not all of the following suggestions will work for each child, given the diversity of disabilities. However, **cooperative learning, peer tutoring,** or a **buddy** system are usually essentials for helping students with disabilities. Remember that students need factual information before they can discuss any topic adequately. In addition, note if noise and impulsive behavior interfere with working with others.

Collaborate on Individualized Education Programs (IEPs) Legal requirements mandate an IEP for each child with disabilities. In planning the goals and objectives for the year, social studies is too often neglected. The concentration is usually on reading and math. This means that students with IEPs get almost no exposure to social studies, yet one of the main goals of education is citizenship. This happens in both the inclusive classroom as well as specialized rooms. In planning the IEP, talk with the educational specialists, the parents, and the students about what can be done for social studies. Work with special education teachers to provide assistance with reading chapters, writing assignments, and completing social studies projects. Clarify social studies textbooks reading by previewing vocabulary, breaking down assignments into small segments, and summarizing the big ideas.

ECHNOLOGY

Use Technologies Technologies can be used to minimize vision, hearing, and mobility problems. Use technologies to support learning by the effective use of visualizations and sound. Check if a given student would benefit from having a computer or other equipment for herself or himself. If a student has a computer, worthwhile homework can be assigned to extend the learning beyond the school's walls. Use computers for frequent formative assessment to check how the student is progressing.

Strengths of the Child   Social studies instruction can be adapted to the individual needs of children with disabilities. The wisest solution is to look for the strengths of each child and build on these strengths. For example, it does not make much sense to give a nonverbal child a worksheet, but, unfortunately, this is a common experience. Find out as much as possible about each student. What is the student's comfort level for working with others? Does he or she have friends in the class? This background information is important in setting up **small group instruction** where the student can learn both content and social skills.

What does the student find interesting? How does the student learn best? Is it by visualization, listening, using the written word, or action? What is the motivation and persistence of the student for completing a task? Normally after reviewing these questions, the teacher must use a **variety of activities** and a **variety of teaching methods** to help this student and others to learn. Using the same lesson plan of reading and filling out a worksheet is not the answer.

Lesson Plans   Teachers have to decide the minimum basic knowledge and skills almost all students will need to learn from the unit.

- What is the basic idea that the students need to learn?
- What are the different ways to learn this idea?
- If reading is involved, can students use other tools and strategies to get the information?

Let us work through the details of the three planning steps. Think about other areas of enrichments that could be skipped by some students. Typically in social studies what is important is the mastery of the key concepts from the fields of history, geography, economics, or civics. Examples are concepts such as regions, opportunity costs, rules and laws, and the like. Consider how these concepts can be taught to ensure learning. Include real-life examples to clarify concepts and other new material. Just as for the gifted, pretests given orally can give you some ideas about how much students already know about the concept or topic. Sometimes there are surprises. Knowing the beginning point also reinforces the student's ability to see progress by the end of the unit.

TECHNOLOGY

To help all students to learn, use as much media and other multisensory devices as possible, including illustrations, charts, and graphics. Ideally, videos should be short. Use helpful technology. Often there is software available that helps with skills such as reading and writing. Software for social studies content for specific levels is not as common.

Consideration must also be given to what materials are needed to help students with disabilities. Social studies textbooks at the appropriate reading level are necessary. But do not be limited to just one textbook. Check if trade books, children's magazines, current event newspapers, and other materials are appropriate. The use of **advance organizers** (see Chapter 10 on graphic organizers) can help students organize the information found in these materials. Use charts, outlines, and webs to summarize information.

In addition, what modifications will be made in the regular lesson plan? One consideration is **time.** Some teachers allow more time for students to complete assignments. Yet allowing more time does not always mean that students will use it productively since some students have very short attention spans. In some cases, it is better to shorten the assignment and the time allocated to the work. Some students benefit more with two short, independent social studies sessions rather than one longer session.

This points to the need for **structure.** Many students, not just those with disabilities, need clear directions for what to do and how to do it. They have difficulty working independently. In many cases, this also means establishing definite and consistent rules and procedures for doing social studies activities. This includes clear instructions on deadlines. Often students are confused on what they are supposed to do. Clarify directions by providing them in oral and written forms. Have students rephrase or repeat back to you what they are to do. Encourage them to ask questions if they are unsure on the assignment. With regard to structure, one student may like a familiar routine for the social studies period while others like more novelty in learning.

Often **direct teaching** works best rather than students indirectly doing discovery learning. Be careful that the input session is not too long but make sure that checks for understanding and guided practice are included before the student works independently. Regardless of method, students need **feedback** on their mastery—the more immediate the better. In giving feedback, try to foster feelings of competence and worth and display their work. In addition, provide **frequent reviews** of the content and skills. Review briefly each day what has been done the previous day. Reinforce the benefits of learning the concept or skill as related to their lives so they see the learning as relevant. For assessment, use shorter tests or reading aloud the questions or even interviewing students about what they know. In summary, provide hope that their school lives can improve and that they are not just passing time in school.

Differentiated Instruction

Given the wide range of abilities in the average class, **differentiated instruction** has been promoted as one possible solution. In a differentiated classroom, the basic idea is that each child is taught according to his or her academic needs. That sounds easy. But how to implement it is more of a challenge. Students vary in abilities. Just think of the wide range of reading levels in a classroom. Contrast students' interests from ballet lessons to playing computer games. Students also differ in their learning styles (see Chapter 3). Toss in the criterion of appropriate and challenging work, and many teachers at this point are almost ready to give up. In differentiated instruction the teacher is mixing up groups throughout the day according to interest, abilities, or learning styles. However, *readiness,* rather than *abilities,* is the proper word to use with this approach. At times there can also be whole group instruction. See, for example, how it might be done in a fifth-grade social studies unit on the American Revolution.

The first step for teachers is to develop by inventories a thorough understanding of all their students. A key to successful differentiated instruction is teacher familiarity with the strengths and weaknesses of each student. Computer software on academic achievement with frequent formative assessment makes this task less burdensome for teachers. Inventories include each student's varying interests, talents, and reading levels. The easiest way to do differential instruction is by grouping students according to reading ability (readiness). For the unit shown, the teacher could have grouped the students by interest, for example, those interested in the battles of the American Revolution or the role of women during the

UNIT PLAN

The American Revolution

Objective

Students will identify several of the major events of the American Revolution.

Initiating Activity

Whole class views a video on the "American Revolution."

Activities

1. Students are grouped by reading ability into four groups to read trade books on the American Revolution. The top reading group reads the classic *Johnny Tremain* by Esther Forbes (Yearling/Random House). For average readers, popular are Scholastic's "Dear America" historical fiction series written in a diary format to record experiences in the daily lives of girls. Average readers could choose *The Winter of Red Snow: The Revolutionary War Diary of Abigail Jane Stewart, Valley Forge, Pennsylvania, 1777* by Kristina Gregory (Scholastic) or Kristina Gregory's other book *We Are Patriots: Hope's Revolutionary War Diary* (Scholastic). Both of these books center on Valley Forge. For boys, the "My Name is America" series (Scholastic) provides historical fiction in the format of journals. *The Journal of William Thomas Emerson A Revolutionary War Patriot—Boston, Massachusetts, 1774* by Barry Denenberg could be used. Lower-achieving readers read *The Boston Coffee Party* by Doreen Rappaport (Harper and Row) or *Sleds on Boston Common: A Story from the American Revolution* by Louise Borden (Margaret K. McElderry Books). There are wide differences in the number of pages as well as complexity in each trade book ranging from 63 to well over 200 pages. **Warning.** A well-written book about the Revolutionary War is *War Comes to Willy Freeman* by James Lincoln Collier and Christopher Collier. James Lincoln Collier is the author of the Newbery Award Book, *My Brother Sam Is Dead* (Four Winds Press), illustrating the conflicts caused by the Revolutionary War and probably more suited for strong readers. Willy Freeman is a free thirteen-year-old African American girl living during the Revolutionary War and in danger of being returned to slavery when her patriot father is killed by the British and her mother taken prisoner. The book illustrates both racism and sexism. However, parents have objected to the use of the word *n*— in the book. At the end of the text, the authors defend the use of the term and say that it would have been a "distortion of history to avoid its use entirely" (p. 178).

2. There may be different assignments for each group. Students at the end of each reading session mark down on a worksheet the number of the last page they have read. The teacher monitors what has been accomplished by glancing at these worksheets. Students may be assigned a given number of pages to read at home if they appear to be falling behind on their classroom reading.

Closure

At the end of each silent reading period, students in their small group discuss what is happening to the main character or characters. What political events are happening in the community? Why? An alternative would be to give different groups different discussion topics.

UNIT PLAN continued   The American Revolution

Day 2 On

Several days may be spent following the above lesson plan until students finish reading and discussing their trade books.

End of Unit

1. Discuss, write, dramatize, debate the content of each group's book.
2. Are there multiple perspectives shown in how different characters acted toward the historical events?

American Revolution. Regardless of what method is used to form the small groups, a wide variety of trade books with various reading levels on one historical topic is necessary. Trade books are easier to locate for certain historical periods, such as the American Revolution and the Civil War, than for other historical periods. Multiple resources are often necessary to do differentiated instruction well.

The teacher should observe how much time it is taking for each group to finish their trade books as well as if there are groups that are not working well together. There is a high probability that all groups will not finish at the same time and that some other activity will have to be available for the early completers. Use this "extra" time by having students write, practice dramatizing interesting parts of the book, or debate whether the characters should have made the decisions they made. Avoid the pitfall of having some groups just sitting around chatting and being off-task.

Realize that from this reading experience some students will learn a lot more about the major events in the American Revolution than other students. This points out the need for the teacher to give all students sufficient background. The use of time lines with the major events of the American Revolution marked is essential as students plot what was happening to their characters in the text, often focusing on one historical event. Students also gain by hearing what other groups are reading: what was happening to the Boston Common (the Sled book) or what a boycott was (the Coffee book) or how Johnny Tremain become a patriot.

Using Technology for Differentiated Instruction

HNOLOGY

If you and your school can afford it, KidBiz3000 is a Web-based program that differentiates reading instruction for grades 2 through 8 by providing students with a daily current events article written at their specific reading level. First students respond to a short prompt triggering students' prior knowledge. Then they read the article of the day with vocabulary and audio supports included. Assessment of comprehension and vocabulary check is next. Students receive immediate feedback based on their test performance. Then the students write a written response to a question and can participate in an online poll related to that day's article. There is also an ELL version where students read the articles in Spanish but complete the activities in English. Regardless of reading level, students can discuss the same content in small groups or with the teacher.

Also helpful is MY Access! to improve writing skills. This program frees teachers from the task of correcting the written work of students. A writing prompt is given through an online web portal and scaffold support can be used such as graphic organizers and checklists. Different prompts can be chosen for different students based on their writing ability. Students electronically submit their essay for scoring and receive immediate feedback.

Using videos can also engage and motivate the wide range of student abilities. More video clips are now available, often tied directly into the state standards. Normally all students benefit from a video. But be careful to preview the video to see how it fits in with your curriculum and tell students before what they are to look and listen to. Then follow through after the video to see what they have gained from the experience.

Disadvantages

Unless you are using a lot of technology and are getting assistance, the disadvantage of differentiated instruction is the workload it puts on teachers. Critics believe that one main lesson plan with modifications is the best approach and will avoid having the average teacher leave the profession because of overwork. In other words, according to this viewpoint, this approach can be done by outstanding teachers but is not for everyone. Perhaps this indicates that the implementation of a differentiated classroom should start gradually. Do one subject area first and then add a second. For this sample social studies lesson, a major task for the teacher is to find and have available enough trade books for the different groups.

Small Group Work **9.6**

Differentiated Classroom?

Have you observed a differentiated classroom? Is a differentiated classroom asking too much of a beginning teacher? ●

Another disadvantage to differentiated instruction is that research on this method is not yet available. It appears that in the communities where differentiated instruction has been adopted, more parents are pleased because it avoids labeling who is smart and who is not. However, critics believe that students at the extreme ends—the gifted and students with disabilities—have needs that are too far from the norm to be met in the average classroom.

Summary

Teaching diverse students means each child is taught according to his or her needs with appropriate and challenging work. Both girls and boys should be held to high standards in the social studies program and should be able to learn in a safe, friendly environment. Multicultural education occurs both indirectly in the classroom as well as in specific content areas. Teachers have to be careful in teaching religion. The gifted and other exceptionalities need adjustments in the curriculum to further their abilities. Differentiated instruction offers the promise of meeting the needs of all students. All students should enjoy social studies.

Suggested Readings and Websites

American-Arab Anti-Discrimination Committee. "Reaching the Teachers." 4201 Connecticut Avenue, N.W., Washington, DC 20008-1158, Suite 300; phone (800) 343-5540.

Resource and action guide addressing needs of Arab American students highlighting history, culture, and current events of the Arab world.

Banks, James A., and Cherry A. McGee Banks. *Multicultural Education: Issues and Perspectives,* 6th ed. San Francisco: Jossey-Bass, 2006.

James Bank is one of the most influential educators in multicultural education and author of many textbooks. This one focuses on pertinent issues in multicultural education.

Bolgatz, Jane. *Talking Race in the Classroom.* New York: Teachers College Press, 2005.

Resource to develop a culture of tolerance in schools.

Byrnes, Deborah A. "Teacher, They Called Me a!" *Prejudice and Discrimination in the Classroom.* New York: Anti-Defamation League of B'nai B'rith, 1987.

Practical definitions and activities for classroom teachers. The same source also offers a study guide for *A World of Difference* program and many more pertinent resources.

Cohn, Amy L., ed. *From Sea to Shining Sea.* New York: Scholastic, 1994.

Multicultural collection of stories and songs related to all periods of American history.

Coles, Robert. *The Spiritual Life of Children.* Boston: Houghton Mifflin, 1990.

Respected child psychologist explores children's feelings and thoughts about spiritual issues.

Cortes, Carlos E. *The Children Are Watching: How the Media Teach About Diversity.* New York: Teachers College Press, 2000.

Looks at the ways that media present diversity and what the schools and parents can do to address the implications of the media.

Derman-Sparks, Louise, and Patricia G. Ramsey. *What If All the Kids Are White?* New York: Teachers College Press, 2006

To help young white children resist message of racism.

Howard, Gary. *We Can't Teach What We Don't Know: White Teachers, Multiracial Schools,* 2nd ed. New York: Teacher's College Press, 2006.

Personal experiences of a multicultural educator over the past twenty years.

McCracken, Janet Brown. *Valuing Diversity: The Primary Years.* Washington, DC: National Council for the Education of Young Children, 1993.

Sourcebook for resources and activities beginning with preschool years.

Muse, Daphne, ed. *The New Press Guide to Multicultural Resources for Young Readers.* New York: The New Press, 1997.

Reviews over 1,000 multicultural books and related materials, organized by theme and reading level.

National Council for the Social Studies. "Guidelines on Multicultural Education." *Social Education* 56 (September 1992): 274–293.

Statement by professional association listing ways pluralism can be integrated in social studies.

Pang, Valerie. *Multicultural Education: A Caring Reflective Approach.* New York: McGraw-Hill, 2001.

Applies Ned Noddings's caring approach to multicultural education.

Schniedewind, Nancy, and Ellen Davidson. *Open Minds to Equality: A Sourcebook of Learning Activities to Affirm Diversity and Promote Equity,* 2nd ed. Boston: Allyn & Bacon, 1998.

Activities appropriate for upper elementary and middle school.

Teaching Tolerance. From the Southern Poverty Law Center. Free periodical for teachers, replete with multiculturally related teaching ideas and experiences. 400 Washington Avenue, Montgomery, AL 36104; fax (205) 264-6892.

Websites

American Anthropological Association
www.aaanet.org

Good articles explaining how race is not a scientifically valid biological category, but a socially constructed category.

Anti-Defamation League
www.adl.org

Provides educational resources and general information for combating hatred and prejudice.

The Asia Society's International Education
http://internationaled.org

Globalization and other topics.

The Council for Exceptional Children
www.cec.sped.org

Helps learners with disabilities and their parents.

National Association for Gifted Children

www.nagc.org

Nonprofit group that wants to improve the quality of education for the gifted.

Teaching Tolerance

www.teachingtolerance.org

Along with their free magazine, ask for their free kits such as *Rhinos and Raspberries: Tolerance Tales for the Early*

Grades that includes a hardcover book for teacher and whole-class use and two student sets of books for individual and group reading (www.teachingtolerance.org/resources)

United Nations

www.un.org

CyberSchoolBus link provides teaching resources, lesson plans, facts, and quizzes.

VIDEO HOMEWORK EXERCISE

Designing Multicultural Curriculum to Meet Education Standards

Go to MyEducationLab, select the topic **Multicultural Perspectives and Ethnic Studies,** and watch the video entitled "Designing Multicultural Curriculum to Meet Education Standards."

This video portrays two teachers planning around the theme "holidays around the world."

CHAPTER 10

Linking Social Studies and Literacy

Social studies and literacy are mutually dependent on each other because social studies learning cannot be divorced from literacy. Social studies can improve reading, writing, and critical thinking. This chapter explores ways to help students make better sense of social studies materials by improving their reading, listening, and writing skills.

- Linking Social Studies and Literacy
- Meeting the Needs of English Language Learners
- Reading
- Listening and Writing

Why is literacy important in social studies teaching?

Linking Social Studies and Literacy

Typical Social Studies Instructional Activities

$\mathcal{M}$ost administrators and experts recommend a student-centered form of instruction in schools. Moreover, most teachers say their teaching style is student-centered. But when you look at the teaching of social studies, the most common style is whole-class teacher presentations/discussion. Popular activities include reading the textbook, completing worksheets, and listening to the teacher lecture; these three activities increase from the fourth to the eighth grade.[1] Educational researchers spent thousands of hours in more than 2,500 first, third, and fifth-grade classrooms, tracking the same 1,000 children as they were promoted from the first grade. Researchers found that the fifth graders spent 91 percent of class time in their seats listening to a teacher or working alone. Only 7 percent of the time was spent working in small groups that can foster social skills and critical thinking. Findings were similar in the first and third grade. This was a discouraging report on the quality of students' learning experiences.[2]

Note how these social studies instructional activities are dependent on literacy (see Figure 10.1). Reading skills are essential for social studies learning. Positive correlations exist between reading skills of students and their social studies grades. Thus, a poor reader is often a poor social studies student. This indicates the importance of using social studies as a vehicle to improve reading, listening, speaking, and writing.

How to teach reading has been a long-standing debate between the **whole language approach** and the more traditional phonics transmission approach. Among its strategies, the whole language approach stresses children's responses to literature as opposed to their recall or comprehension of stories. In many cases, in implementing the whole language approach, social studies textbooks were deemphasized and replaced by nonfiction trade

[1]Anthony D. Lutkus, Andrew R. Weiss, Jay R. Campbell, John Mazzeo, and Stephen Lazer, *The NAEP 1998 Civics Report Card for the Nation* (Washington, DC: U.S. Department of Education, Office of Educational Research and Improvement. National Center for Education Statistics, NCES 2000–457, 1999).

[2]Roberta C. Pianta, Jay Belsky, Renate Houts, Fred Morrison, The National Institute of Child Health and Human Development Early Child Care Research Network, "Opportunities to Learn in America's Elementary Classrooms," *Science* 315, no. 5820 (March 30, 2007): 1795–1796.

Figure 10.1   Relationship of Social Studies to Literacy

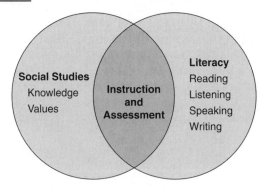

books. Thus, research in 1995 showed that 85 percent of the primary teachers and 45 percent of the intermediate teachers reported using children's literature at least once a week in social studies.

In teaching reading and social studies, often the debate focuses on two choices. Should instruction be *explicit,* with teachers leading students through predetermined lessons and activities? Or should instruction be *exploratory,* with teachers guiding students by responding to students' own questions and interests? Too frequently, this debate is framed as the traditional "teachers as knowledge transmitters" versus "teachers as facilitators," but it is best to think of these two approaches as complementary opportunities for teachers and not as an either/or. Students can benefit from both explicit, teacher-led activities and from exploratory, student-centered but teacher-facilitated activities. Knowledge and skills are essential for participation in social studies and this is often gained by explicit, direct teaching. In turn, decision making and problem solving are often best taught by a more exploratory approach. Both approaches are essential.

Both approaches also can strengthen reading. Social studies need not be put on the back burner. Look at the reading standards for your grade level. Most include such statements as "make inferences and draw conclusions supported by text evidence," "identify and explain various points of view," and the like. In teaching social studies, you are really "reading" teachers.

On Your Own **10.1**

Worksheets?

Why do you think many teachers use worksheets, a practice most experts recommend keeping to a minimum? ●

Meeting the Needs of English Language Learners

Growing Numbers

The United States continues to be enriched by immigrants from all over the world. The number of children who need extra help in learning English has increased in recent years. In 2006, it is estimated that one in ten students spoke only limited English with around 68% speaking Spanish. However, many schools have students who speak Chinese, Vietnamese, Russian, Arabic, and many other languages. Often, children speaking a non–Latin-based language have more difficulty learning English.

The terms to describe this group of students are varied. Currently, the most popular and positive term to describe a nonnative speaker who may need English language instruction is **English language learner** (ELL) or EL (English learner). ELLs are immigrants or children of immigrants. An older term is *Limited English Proficient* (LEP). This term has a negative connotation because it denotes limitations. You may also find another term, *English as a Second Language* (ESL), frequently used to describe this population. Other less frequently used terms such as *English Language development* (ELD) or the more generic *second language learners* are also encountered.

English language learners include a wide range of students with varied cultural and socioeconomic backgrounds. You may have a student in your class who has just arrived in the

United States. More likely, the ELLs in your classes will have had some exposure to learning English before being mainstreamed into your class. School districts and states have various policies to teach ELLs, including bilingual programs, English as a Second Language (ESL) programs, and dual language immersion programs. English immersion programs appear to be increasing over bilingual programs.

Yet our economic and civic well-being depends on an educated immigrant population. Immigrants will be more than one-fourth of the labor force over the next decades. Education can help ELLs to prepare for jobs, social life, and citizenship. Although many children succeed in learning English in school, some children are not fluent. Teachers report that lack of time and appropriate materials makes it difficult to teach ELLs.

Essential Skills

It is estimated that about 85 percent of the social studies that students learn comes from the written word, the text. Social studies is an academic subject with its own specialized vocabulary—Industrial Revolution, Puritan, hard-to-pronounce names, and the like—that puts demands on native speakers, let alone ELLs. History may appear abstract since it occurred long ago and does not have immediate relevance for some students. Concepts like implied powers of the Constitution and sovereignty cause further difficulties. Unlike math and science, social studies does not have many manipulatives and hands-on instructional materials. Literacy skills are more essential in the social studies than in many other content areas.

To read well, a primary goal, all ELLs need to develop the following skills:

- Word recognition (including phonics skills)
- Vocabulary
- Comprehension of texts (ability to identify the main ideas)
- Speech

English language learners need explicit instruction in phonics—how letters stand for sounds and how sounds combine into words. Some native speakers who are visual learners can thrive in reading even if their knowledge of phonics is limited. But almost all ELLs need systematic training to develop awareness in distinguishing and manipulating sounds in the English language. With this training, ELLs can then decode words on a page. To become proficient in decoding, ELLs need a lot of practice reading with frequent assessments to identify both what they know and in which areas more help is required.

ELLs must also close the gap in vocabulary since native speakers enter kindergarten knowing thousands of English words. ELLs may be limited to a few hundred. Unless this vocabulary gap is closed, it will increase each year of schooling. An adequate vocabulary is especially essential in the social studies so students can comprehend the text. ELLs also need to be taught strategies to make sense of texts. In addition, oral language skills are necessary for school success (and eventually adult success) for students to communicate what they have learned, ask questions, and discuss in small groups.

This is a tall order and does take time. Remember, however, that lack of English does not indicate lack of intelligence. In particular, there is often an initial silent stage in which the newcomer does not speak in the classroom, giving a false picture of the child's abilities. Consider the following steps teachers can take to improve social studies achievement of ELLs. Some of these suggestions also apply to struggling readers and those with disabilities.

First Step: Making ELLs (and Everyone Else) Welcome

We all learn better if we are not anxious and worried. You may have encountered frustration when you learned a second language. Think what was troublesome to you. Remembering all the vocabulary words you were learning? The verb tenses? It was probably easy to tune out and not concentrate on listening if too much of what you were hearing was beyond your comprehension. Often the words were going by too quickly. ELLs encounter these same difficulties. This can result in lower self-esteem and less motivation to learn English. But *motivation* is a key element for anyone learning a second (or third) language. For example, if the child's family actively encourages the acquisition of English, usually the child is more willing to learn English. This suggests having a conference with parents even if an interpreter is needed. Ask about the amount of formal education the student has had and if there were gaps in school attendance—information that is often not volunteered. Try to send home updates, weekly assignments, and class news. If possible, these communications should be in the ELLs' primary language.

ELLs are often learning a new culture as well as learning a second language. They have to learn the classroom expectations about learning and behaviors. Sometimes there is the potential for cultural conflict with other students, for example, concerning gender roles. Furthermore, the situation in their native land may not have been ideal, such as for refugees. In other cases, the students may not have wanted to leave their native homes. Their self-confidence and efficacy may be reduced as they make their ways into new situations. Thus, ELLs are often embarrassed if forced to read or report in front of the class or a small group. They also may be subject to being corrected publicly by other students. All these factors may impede the learning of English. In other cases, ELLs are ignored and segregated from the rest of the class. In such cases, teachers should place them in the middle or front of the room where they can be easily seen and interacted with. Try to encourage the rest of the class to interact with them. Participation with others provides access to more language and learning. In addition, give clear directions that in many cases must be communicated individually.

ELLs need to be welcomed into your classroom like all other students. Find out as much as possible about the background of the student. If the student attended school in her or his native land, what was the style of the typical teacher there? Was there an emphasis on the teacher as a giver of knowledge? How can the background of the student be incorporated into the social studies curriculum? Can the student's extracurricular interests be tapped? Can parents be involved to support what is done in school?

Getting Materials and Instructional Resources

Contact the school or district ELL specialists and ask whether they can obtain social studies materials that are appropriate for your students. English materials at a lower reading level are available that focus on the basics in government and U.S. history. An example is Globe Fearon's *The United States: Its Past, Purpose, and Promise* with a reported reading level at the third and fourth grades. In addition, most of the major publishers have their basic social studies textbooks available in Spanish for first through sixth grades. The Spanish editions are parallel to the content of the English textbooks. For an additional cost, publishers may also supply color transparencies, worksheets, and lesson plans to go with the textbook. More and more publishers now have supporting materials and ideas for teachers to meet English learners' needs.

At a minimum, a small bilingual dictionary is extremely helpful. A visual dictionary is very appropriate for ELLs at the beginning stages of learning English. As soon as possible ELLs should be encouraged to use the dictionary to look up words. The dictionary is useful for you to be able to communicate with the child. Use the Internet as much as possible. Ben's Guides (as in Ben Franklin) explains how the U.S. government works (http://bensguide .gpo.gov). This government site is a civics course by grade level: K–2, 3–5, 6–8, 9–12. The same topics, ranging from "Branches of Government" to "The Election Process" are covered, but at different levels of complexity.

Buddy or Peer Pairs and Assisted Reading

Frequently an ELL student, a limited disability student, or a struggling reader can be placed with a "buddy" or friend who is a more capable reader (see the classroom episode "Peer Teaching"). This is often a good commonsense solution, especially useful when a new student arrives. The ELL student can learn a lot both in language and social studies. The more advanced student practices the skills of having to explain, illustrate, and clarify language and ideas to another. The novice student is placed in a nonthreatening, friendly atmosphere that fosters a sense of belonging and self-esteem.

It is important to see that the task or assignment is one in which the pair can naturally support each other without the exchange being perceived as a hindrance to the more advanced student. For that reason and for giving opportunities for more friendships to develop, some teachers use a different buddy for different subject areas or many buddies for a given child in a given day. Nonetheless, in addition to supporting friendship, there must be individual accountability for both students. If possible, the novice student should be the one who reports back what has been accomplished.

Other Group Arrangements

Flexible grouping offers many opportunities for students with special needs in a social studies program. Cooperative learning produces more opportunities for content-related communication among students than a traditional, teacher-centered classroom environment. Cooperative learning can enhance academic learning, motivate students, and promote a positive climate. The following Kagan structures are helpful (more on Kagan structures in Chapter 3).

- *Timed Pair Share.* First one student talks for a specified time and the other listens, then they switch roles.
- *Interview.* Student is interviewed by classmate.
- *Mix-N-Match.* Students circulate in the room with cards, quizzing each other and then finding their match. A student who has the economic term "need" looks for someone with a picture of food, clothing, shelter, and the like.

These qualities make cooperative learning a particularly appropriate strategy for diverse learners. Let us examine the pluses and minuses of different group arrangements.

Classroom Episode
Peer Teaching

In the library, students from both the second and fifth grades are listening to Mrs. Anna Hamilton, a retired homemaker who was raised on a farm. She describes her life as a child during the summertime. She stresses the time it took to do her chores: pumping water from outside, washing dishes and clothing, preparing vegetables, canning food, weeding and tending the garden, picking fruit, and doing housework. Mrs. Hamilton also talks about the fun she had with her four siblings, going swimming, and going to town once a week on Saturday to see a movie.

After her discussion and answering questions, the fifth graders and second graders go to find their buddy. The assignment is for the second graders to dictate to their fifth-grade buddies what they would like and dislike if they had lived on a farm at the same time as Mrs. Hamilton. One pair is Janeula, a second grader, and Mia, a fifth grader.

Mia: *What were some of the things you would like the most about living on a farm long ago?*

Janeula: *Swimming. The horses, cows, the cats.*

Mia: *Were there any other things you would like?*

Janeula: *(softly) Don't know.*

Mia: *Did the family ever have any fun together?*

Janeula: *Going into town on Saturday.*

Mia: *Let me write that down. What did they do in town?*

Janeula: *She sometimes got to go to a movie. They liked that. No TV.*

Postscript

Janeula continues to recount what she has remembered about what the speaker said. When necessary, Mia prompts and gives hints to Janeula to recall more. List the skills that were used by each student. What are the advantages of peer tutoring? What would happen if Mia did not prompt? If Mia did not smile at the correct responses?

Homogeneous English Competency Groups

Although recognizing that all groups are heterogeneous in that all students bring different strengths to the classroom, sometimes a teacher may wish to reduce the amount of heterogeneity within a group by establishing groups that share approximately the same level of English proficiency. The essential point is that the teacher must carefully avoid the negative stereotype that may result when students are grouped together because some are smarter and, therefore, more valued than others.

The advantage of this arrangement is that different tasks and materials can be assigned to different groups. Although all students may be learning about the Trans-Mississippi West Movement, the reading level of materials for each group can vary as well as the amount of visual representation. There can be different levels of material with a similar theme. Or materials can be on different themes within a topic, such as one group looking at routes the pioneers used and another group examining the lives of pioneer women. The students in each group may record their consensus information as they learn about the Trans-Mississippi West Movement.

Later, their information will grow with information provided by the other groups. This can be done by classroom discussion in which students develop and refine their understanding of the subject by finding out, comparing, and evaluating other students' knowledge and ideas. It is essential when students read different materials or do different tasks that they get the impact of other groups to complete their understanding of the subject.

Same Language Groups with Varied English Competency

Sometimes a teacher has several students who speak the same language (e.g., Spanish) and these students typically have varied English literacy. At times it is effective to organize them in a group or groups of the same native language when the teacher wants students in the group to efficiently convey key concepts, instructions, or information to their peers who speak the same language. The teacher knows that students may use their native language to teach the concept of government when students are to list the goods and services not privately produced and to explain how these goods and services are paid for. In most cases, students in the same language group will discuss first in their mother tongues and then, working collaboratively in English, will present their work to the whole class.

The advantages of this group arrangement is that there is assistance from more capable peers; students' knowledge and understanding, regardless of language background, are used and validated, and it usually takes less teacher time than explaining the work to all students. The disadvantage is that students may label some students as "the Spanish kids" and not promote integration of the classroom. In addition, students may not want to be defined by their parents' language and may not appreciate being put into a special language group.

Jigsaw or Experts Groups

The jigsaw technique (see Chapter 3) in which each group becomes experts in a certain subject area can best be done successfully with a diverse group of learners only if the teacher supplies each group with a wide range of reading and visual materials, audio books, fiction and nonfiction literature, and other ways to acquire information. Relying on a section of the textbook with the range of reading being "all over the place" may be too difficult for many students. On the other hand, many activities connecting to students' own experience of the content will help them become experts in a certain area and teach other students.

Teachers know that language learning is a social activity involving discussing and thinking of ideas. Understandings and capacities grow and deepen through interactions with others. Students who regularly engage in buddy or peer tutoring (see the classroom episode) and cooperative learning are able to share ideas with each other and respond to one another's thoughts. This contributes to language learning.

Sheltered English or SDAIE Strategies

More teachers are using Specially Designed Academic Instruction in English (SDAIE) for their ELLs. Sometimes this is called sheltered English or sheltered instruction. The goal is for the teacher to communicate in English the social studies content and skills. This strategy only works with students who have gained some English fluency.

How can this be done? There are two basic elements: modified input and modified output. Important elements in this approach are for teachers to simplify their speech, use lots of nonverbal actions, and show the relevance or worth of what is being learned by giving concrete examples. Then students are provided with opportunities to practice what they have learned. This might include communicating effectively in a discussion with others or writing a paragraph about a given topic.

In other words, the teacher's lesson must clearly define both content and language objectives. Then the teacher moves students from the known to the new by relating the concept or material to the students' experience. In the primary grades these experiences might involve foods or shelter. In the upper grades they might involve geography or government. Key vocabulary is also identified. This requires teachers to check the text material for possible difficulties.

Modified Input

Simplified speech by teachers:

- Speak slowly
- Pause to allow comprehension to occur
- Ask a question, pause, call on a student, pause again, provide feedback
- Enunciate clearly
- Use no slang or idioms
- Limit vocabulary and sentence structure
- Repeat key points and summarize

Nonverbal actions by teachers:

- Use clear body language
- Extensively use visuals, illustrations, prints, magazines, objects, realia, and the like
- Utilize semantic maps, diagrams, graphic organizers, and the like
- Write directions on the board as well as speak them

Try for as many opportunities for *interaction* and discussion between both teacher and students and among students as possible. This includes giving sufficient wait time for students to respond to questions.

Modified Output

ELLs demonstrate their learning:

- Ask questions
- Orally retell or summarize the content
- Group activities to practice the social studies content
- Perform dramatic play or role-play
- After teacher elicits suggestions for a paragraph, write paragraph
- After teacher shows how to write a paragraph with main idea and supporting detail, write paragraph

Try to review the key vocabulary and key content concepts at the end of each lesson. This includes feedback and often informal assessment. In addition, some teachers use *daily sentence writing* for their whole class. In this activity, choose one of the important vocabulary words. Have each student write three separate sentences, not a paragraph, using the vocabulary word. Then use peer editing to check on the sentences to find ways to improve. Finally, have students read one sentence from each group. Students love to hear the variety in the sentences.

Although methods may vary in using sheltered English, more commonly a direct teaching approach is used.

Speech

Most English learners lag behind in oral language skills that are essential for success both now in reading and later adult life. ELLs need many opportunities for academic conversation, not just informal conversation. The many buddy and small-group experiences already described can encourage a broad academic vocabulary and understanding in social studies. Students need to use the specialized social studies vocabulary in context. Every day each student, not just ELLs, should have the opportunity to talk and write informally.

After talking in a small group, ELLs and all students need practice in **summarizing.** In a summary, the key ideas and main points are stated. What often happens if you ask students to summarize? They copy complete sentences and write too much. Other students get stuck and write little or nothing. To summarize actually is a higher level of thinking.

To teach students to summarize, frequently model how you do it. First try only a small piece of the text for students to summarize. Tell them to use the newspaper format to identify who, what, when, where, and why.

Students often have to summarize what was accomplished in their small group. What is most important for the rest of the class to know? Help students to look at their KWL formats (Chapter 2), concepts maps, graphic organizers, charts, and notes to organize what they are going to say. Then they can use the following guide.

Summarize
- The main point is ...
- The key people or events were ...
- The time and place were ...

They may want to practice it first before their small group before talking to the whole class.

Machine Translation Software and Media

TECHNOLOGY

Free online machine translation software such as Mendez iTranslator allows teachers to paste English text such as lessons and tests into a box and, with the push of the mouse button, have the text translated. There are some adjustments to be made. While the machine translations are not always perfectly accurate, they are an improvement over the limited language facility that most teachers have with their ELLs' languages. This is especially true when you have non–Latin-based languages in the classroom. If bilingual staff are available, they can occasionally look over the translations, but most teachers are wholly dependent on the software to do the job of translation.

Better yet is some of the translation software that is commercially available. For example, Easy Translator 4 translates English Web pages into other languages. In addition, this software allows teachers to save the original English word processing documents with the format intact. Teachers now can build up a set of support social studies materials on their grade level that can be used in future years for their ELLs. Students are pleased when they see material translated into their own language. The use of translated materials can help students learn both social studies content as well as English because most teachers have their students write their responses in English to avoid another translation.[3] Beware: The first time students get an assignment in their primary language, they may assume that you know the language, and off they go rattling their language to you.

For the most effective use of media like videos, explain ahead of time what students are going to view or give them an outline. In addition, there are many computer programs, some of them bilingual, available to aid in the teaching of reading. One of the most popular is Language First! (www.leapfrog.com) for Grades K–5. There is support in six different languages and evaluation in four proficiency levels. This program tries to make difficult aspects of English usage such as the correct use of pronouns, subject–verb agreement, and verb tenses interesting.

Most programs require students to reproduce words or phrases. More specialized equipment can evaluate how accurately the student reproduced the sounds. Older students especially appreciate the privacy of not having their mistakes noted by the rest of the class. These programs can increase confidence in speaking skills. If not available, try using individual tutoring with adult volunteers or older children.

Assessments

Using multiple sources such as commercial, state, and district tests, identify the priorities for improving student learning. Then follow up on the progress. Assessment of ELLs should be an ongoing process with the emphasis on what social studies content and skills they have acquired. Always give specific feedback on how they can improve, but concentrate only on one aspect such as verb tense or content. Constantly check for comprehension and use multiple methods of assessment—observation, portfolios, questioning, and the like. Ask simple questions that require only a simple response—yes, no, true, false. In all assessments, use positive rewards for improvement and praise success. Avoid correcting minor English mistakes but be a good model of English usage.

For tests, use any available accommodations such as encouraging the use of a dictionary when tests are being taken. Oral reading of the test plus visual representation of concepts can help ELLs. This is especially helpful for the more lengthy multiple-choice questions that are more difficult than the easier completion questions. Nevertheless, high-stakes proficiency tests are daunting for many ELLs even with relaxed, No Child Left Behind requirements. As much as possible, students should become familiar with test items they will encounter on high-stakes tests. They may need particular help in writing short-answer questions.

Small Group Work **10.1**

Actual Practice

Based on your experience, what type of education is being given to ELLs? Can you think of areas that need improvement? Are teachers using sheltered English or SDAIE approaches? ●

---

[3]George Sabato, "Translation Software to the Rescue," *Social Studies Review* 43, no. 1 (Fall/Winter 2003): 59–60.

Reading

*Y*ou have had or will have a course on teaching reading or language arts. Fourth graders in the United States had a higher average than their peers in a 2006 international study in reading. However, the nation's poor, Hispanic, and African American students still lagged behind other U.S. learners. Remember that even good readers also need to improve since reading (and writing) are evolving skills that everyone needs to continuously improve.

Reading difficulties in the social studies are not limited to only ELLs and students with disabilities. Starting around the third or fourth grade, students learn to use their reading skills to extract information from the text. Even students of average reading ability can be challenged by new vocabulary, longer sentences, lack of human interest, and high idea density in social studies materials. Trying to make sense out of abstract content is extremely frustrating for students, and their comprehension is often less than 50 percent accurate. This is because the reader must look for specific ideas rather than the narrative form of what will happen next.

Teaching reading in the social studies can be divided into three areas: **prereading** or **engagement, active reading,** and **postreading applications** (see Figure 10.2). Sometimes the activities of active reading and postreading applications merge together, as when students are filling in a graphic organizer or taking notes as they are reading. This contrasts with the traditional method of reading a certain number of pages and then answering the

Figure 10.2   Improving Reading Comprehension

PREREADING

Teacher as a Model
The Text Structure or Approach
Tap Prior Knowledge
Predicting
Vocabulary Up Front
Survey

READING

Monitor Comprehension
Working on Completing KWL, etc. while Reading
Strategies to Attack Difficulties

POSTREADING

Graphic Organizers
Reciprocal Teaching
Peer Assessment Questions
Drama

questions at the end of the section. Traditionally, the reading was done silently and the questions were answered individually.

Prereading is used to bridge student experience to content and to motivate the student. Let us examine these prereading or engagement strategies, keeping in mind that choosing content that is interesting and motivating to your students is the key.

Prereading or Engagement

Model a Person Who Reads   Students are helped to see you as a good reading model, especially if not much reading is taking place in their homes. Bring to class the novels, non-fiction, newspapers, or magazines that you are reading. Tell them that you are reading a very exciting book right now. Show them the book and give a little background information about it. You may want to read a few paragraphs from it. Bring in a newspaper and say you saw an interesting article in today's paper. Describe the topic. The article need not be on a social studies topic. Read quotations or poetry to your students. Inform them on what time you read. If true, tell your class that one of your favorite leisure activities over the weekend is to spend time reading the Sunday paper, or that one of the great things about summer vacation for you is going to the library to get a lot of good books. Share books with students and read to your students. Provide time for reading during the school day and engage in silent reading yourself instead of correcting papers. All of these activities can suggest to children that reading is both a fun and an informative activity.

Normally after a few weeks, most teacher learn how well their students read. But it is useful for students to make a self-assessment on their own reading outside of school. See Table 10.1 for useful questions concerning outside reading. Those who are already good readers are likely to read more than struggling, reluctant readers. Realize that many students actively try to avoid reading by doing fake reading or engaging in disruptive behavior. In reality, all students are doing some reading. They read TV listings, instructions for video games, ads, T-shirts, signs, and other environmental print. When teachers say their students do not read, they really mean that students are not reading narrative or especially expository text. Competency with these two types of texts is important for school success.

For younger students, determine which public library is closest to their homes and encourage them to obtain public library cards by having a librarian come to your class to explain how they can get a library card. Alternatively, you can secure the necessary forms yourself. More families, partly because they are so busy, are buying children's books instead of taking them to the public library. Try to arrange a book fair where children can buy

Table 10.1	Your Reading Outside of School

- How often do you read? Once a week? Every day?
- How much do you read outside of school? Give an amount of time.
- What do you read? The comics? Websites? Children's storybooks?
- Where do you read? Is the TV on when you read?

or trade books that they have already read. In addition, in many schools children can purchase books from major publishers by placing their orders. Giving recommended lists of books to students and parents is helpful. These techniques are most beneficial for the already motivated reader. In contrast, struggling readers often need help in selecting a book to read. They can easily spend a half hour aimlessly looking at the choices.

Try to raise motivation to read by spending a few minutes reviewing a few trade books or having book talks every week or so. First, find books with strong plots and characters. Hold up the book. Read an exciting part that relates to the students' own lives. Let the students hang in suspense on how it will end. The book should be available for immediate use by the students. Media experts and librarians can help you. Have a fair system ready to implement if more than one student wants to read the book.

Daily Silent Reading   Many schools have a requirement that there be a period of daily silent reading. Many teachers use the time after recess for this quiet silent reading time. Add books on social studies topics as choices for your students. Again, enlist the services of your librarian to help you acquire the many appropriate books. You will be amazed at how some students profit from the daily silent reading experiences if the books are of high interest to them and on the right reading level.

The Text Structure or Approach

Focus Questions   Always have focus questions to guide students in reading and understanding the assigned text. The focus questions typically include the following:

- Content
- Issues
- Skills like reading time lines
- Academic language—specialized social studies vocabulary plus more general words like *compare* and *evaluate*

Focus questions then allow students to read with a purpose. Otherwise, retention is a problem and students cannot summarize in their own words what they have read since they never knew why they were reading the text in the first place.

The Textbook   Social studies encompasses different types of text. You read differently if you are reading a catalog rather than a personal letter. Students should be oriented toward the structure of the text they are reading. The most common social studies text from the fourth to the eighth grades is a history text. Generally, history is written in a sequence or in chronological order, using common transition words. Words like those in Table 10.2 indicating a sequence or chronology are commonly found in history texts, as illustrated by the following sentences:

> *Initially* the colonists were loyal to their mother country, England. *Over the years* new tax laws were passed by Parliament. *Then* the colonists felt many grievances against England. *After* Lexington and Concord, many colonists *finally* wanted to separate from England.

| Table 10.2 | Transitional Words in History Texts | | |

when	in (a year)	then	initially
over the years	not long after	before	following
next	preceding	after	finally

Strong readers use these signal words to help them understand what the text is reporting. Poorer readers have to have these words pointed out to them. History texts also have many cause and effect words such as *because, consequently, as a result, for this reason,* and the like. These words contribute to understanding the text.

Although the traditional text is written in an objective tone, when reading primary sources, students must identify the tone or voice. For example, what viewpoint is being argued against or supported? Is the person denouncing the evils of slavery? Does the author promote women's rights?

Activate the Use of Prior Knowledge: KWL Chart   When reading, students should know what information they are seeking. Without a purpose, students often just read mechanically without much understanding of what they are supposed to do. One way to connect what they already know to the new material is to complete a KWL (What I Know, What I Want to Know, What I Learned). Give students a worksheet with a list of names or events. For the settling of the West and Southwest, you could include such names as Lewis and Clark, Daniel Boone, Indian reservations, Kit Carson, and the like. Students should fill out the first two columns, Know and Want to Know, prior to reading. Encourage students to ask questions. After their reading, listening, and viewing of content about the topics, they complete the chart. You may also have students write a summary of their KWL chart.

Predicting   After discussing, have students predict what the text will be about. This could be done in pairs. Predictions made by various members of the class can be placed on the chalkboard or on an overhead. Students should write predictions down and mark if they agree or disagree with each. After reading, students check and discuss to compare their predictions to what actually happened. The Taba strategy can be used with students listing as many words about the topic as they can. These can then be grouped and labeled. After reading, students add information that they have gained to correct their preliminary impressions.

Good predictions are based on what students already know. They can take the following format:

- I predict …
- I bet …
- I think that …

Vocabulary Frontload key subject-specific vocabulary or concepts—no more than three or four words. This means teachers must first identify the prereading vocabulary. Choose words that are important for understanding a particular content area or words that enhance general background knowledge. Use short explanations and numerous examples to illustrate concepts. Try explicit modeling by including the vocabulary in class assignments. If students are to retain words, the words must be used in future reading and writing assignments. Also hold students accountable for the key vocabulary. Generally speaking, students should not look up vocabulary in a dictionary or glossary at this point. Primary teachers use **word walls** with names of people or events on cards. When writing, students can refer to the word walls and not waste time wondering how to spell the words. Seeing the words also refreshes their memories. Hearing and seeing words are helpful, especially in context. Have students pronounce the word. If possible, show a visual representation of the word. For the American Revolution, vocabulary words like *independence*, *protest*, *patriot*, and *loyalist* are necessary for understanding.

Some teachers put the new vocabulary on the board and ask students to guess the meaning. Here there are no context clues and the student can be encouraged to look at the prefixes, root words, and suffixes. Some of the guesses would probably be wrong. Gradually building up the context clues by using the words in sentences is helpful. You could also use the word as used in the sentence in the textbook.

Using Text Features Guide students through a survey of the text by reading the title, chapter headings, first sentence of a new section, key words, captions under pictures, and any questions at the end of the text. These should give clues to the text's main ideas. The illustrations especially should be examined closely to help all readers get mental images and a vision of what is happening.

TECHNOLOGY

Reading on the Internet Whereas a textbook has organization, reading on the Internet with the jumble of ideas and styles can present a huge hurdle for weaker readers. First, the searcher needs to be somewhat knowledgeable about the topic being searched. Otherwise, these readers cannot recognize the relevance of what they are seeing and reading. As a result, they may exhibit little patience, have difficulty with the large amounts of text, browse instead of carefully reading, and be unable to assess the reliability of information found. These weaker readers need extensive supervision and guidance. Yet being able to gain information from the Internet is an important skill for all students to acquire. If at all possible, bring people in from the community to assist these weaker readers as well as student assistants to help them. Remember that equal access to technology is a goal for all students.

Active Reading

After the prereading activities, active reading helps students construct meaning from the text. Learners have to think while they are reading. Students must respond to ideas. They have to figure out what is important. Lastly, they must use strategies when they get stuck and things don't make sense. At first, teachers have the major responsibility for teaching these strategies. The teacher may think aloud and show how to gain meaning from an unfamiliar word. But gradually students learn these strategies without the help of the teacher.

Help students to realize that breakdowns in reading can be expected. Here are some guidelines: To figure out the meanings of unknown words, try to break the word into parts and silently sound it out. If this does not work, look at the context in the sentence and try to guess the meaning. Even better is to reread the whole paragraph to get more context clues to the meaning of the unknown word. Have students use a glossary to verify their guesses.

Here are some additional guidelines for helping to improve reading:

- Avoid round-robin oral reading from the text.
- Have students read with a buddy. The more capable reader can assist with unknown words.
- Encourage students to evaluate the content of their reading. Does it seem reasonable that an individual or people acted in a certain way?
- Use maps, globes, artifacts, photographs, and the like to supplement the text.

Postreading Activities

Particularly if students have been doing silent reading, postreading is the time to talk! Many of the activities suggested for postreading can be done in a group as well as individually (see classroom episode "Group Harmony"). At this stage, students should put it all together. The new material should be incorporated into their previous experiences and the learning reinforced.

- Complete charts, graphic organizers, cause–effect diagrams, and Venn diagrams to compare and contrast information from the text

Classroom Episode
Group Harmony

*M*s. Terri Musilek has organized her fifth-grade class into groups with each group having a wide mixture of abilities. Each group is filling out a graphic organizer after reading about Lewis and Clark's expedition.

Adeline: *Next we have to list the difficulties that Lewis and Clark ran into.*

David: *They didn't know if the Indians were going to be friendly.*

Other students in the group offer suggestions except Rabia.

David: *Rabia, can't you do any work?*

Her feelings hurt, Rabia goes to her teacher, Ms. Musilek, and says "They don't think I'm smart. I don't like that group."

Ms. Musilek than goes to the group and asks why Rabia is unhappy in their group. The students respond with the following comments: "She doesn't do her work." "She plays around." "She's no fun to work with." There are no positive comments. What do you think Ms. Musilek should do next? Does it make a difference if Rabia is a struggling reader?

- Dramatize part of the text
- Create a time line
- Make a poster of a historical person or event
- Defend a point of view with evidence
- Create a concept map
- Write in a journal (What happened? How did I feel? What did I learn?)[4]

These applications activities help to organize the content. They can also identify the unanswered questions at the prereading stage.

Graphic Organizers   After reading, students often fill out **graphic organizers.** Graphic organizers are a *visual* organization of information. Graphic organizers can take many forms. Often they are used to serve as a summary. You probably completed many graphic organizers during your elementary grades. Common are the following:

Countries France Britain	**Explorers**	**Date of Exploration**	**Achievements**
Religions Beliefs Texts	**Buddhism**	**Hinduism**	**Islam**
Continents Major rivers Highest point	**North America**	**South America**	**Asia**

Sometimes graphic organizers are hierarchical diagrams. For example, the words *legislative branch* may be on the top line. Below that, the students may fill out information for the terms *Senate* and *House of Representatives*.

The process for creating a Venn diagram can be explained by having two students stand up and then having the other students list characteristics about them while the teacher writes the characteristics in a Venn diagram. After explaining the process, the teacher can ask students to compare two presidents, two communities, two states, two nations, or similar categories.

Writing   Writing is also a common postreading experience. To make writing activities more interesting, use formats such as "If walls could talk," or have students write from the

---

[4]Thanks to Priscilla Porter, California State University, Dominguez Hills, California, for some of these ideas. Also Judith Irvin, *Reading Strategies for the Social Studies Classroom* (Austin, Texas: Holt, Rinehart and Winston, no date), and Brent Heath, "Releasing the Potential of Unmotivated Readers in 6–8 Social Studies." Presented at the California State Social Studies Conference, March, 2004.

perspectives of dogs and cats on what they have seen. Concept maps can be made by using boxes, circles, and arrows to show relationships. Creating a newspaper page is also a popular activity. When writing newspaper articles, students should remember to answer who, what, where, when, and why questions.

Reciprocal Teaching   Reciprocal teaching is an activity in which students can collaborate to understand a selection of content. This can be done individually, especially after students have internalized the steps in critical reading of a text. More often students in a group take on roles as summarizer, questioner, clarifier, or predictor. One student is chosen to lead the discussion of each section of the text that was read. Students take turns leading the discussion. The discussion leader asks questions and the rest of the group responds. Additional questions can be raised by any member of the group. If anything is unclear, the clarifier asks for discussion to clear up problem areas. The group also checks if their earlier predictions are accurate. Finally, the summarizer gives the summary with additional comments from the other members of the group. Meanwhile, the teacher monitors what is happening in the groups and notes any changes that have to be made to help students read with comprehension.

Peer Assessment Questions   After their reading, ask students in groups to write questions. Use Bloom's taxonomy so students will move beyond memory questions and will formulate higher-level questions. Then each group can orally ask the questions to the whole class. The class writes down the answers, and after giving some time for each response, the group gives the correct answers. This is a strategy that integrates test preparation into instruction and facilitates helping reading as students skim the text to design questions.

Looking at Multiple Perspectives   After reading a topic or selection, have the students check more than one medium or printed source to see what another source says about the same events or topics. This moves students beyond dependence on just the text and promotes looking at different perspectives.

Active Performance and Media   Often at the end of a reading experience, a good choice is to have a more active experience for your students. Can students react to any part of what they have read? More songs and music as well as videos are now available. Can they be used? Are there myths or stories about the culture being examined? All of these can be used to reinforce the reading experience.

Book Bags   One possibility for learning social studies is using **book bags**—taking home a social studies trade book or two with activities to support both the reading and social studies objectives. A reading buddy, parent, grandparent, older sibling, or other designated partner goes over the material with the student and fills out or checks what has been done and offers comments. The due date for returning the books must be clear. Children with disabilities have thrived with this activity and have gained in learning social studies. Of course, using book bags is not limited to just students with disabilities. Some classrooms rotate trade books every week with new books sent home on Fridays. This technique helps to emphasize that the formal education process involves the student, the student's family, and the teacher.

A goal for many teachers is for each child to eventually read a book a week independently. Few would discourage this goal since the more students read, the better readers they become. At first this goal may be mandatory but hopefully after several years, independent reading becomes part of a student's habit. Reading then is its own reward and does not have to be mandatory.

In summary, the three stages in reading—prereading, reading, and postreading—can help students to learn a social studies text as well as improve general reading skills. However, it is probably best to work on just one strategy at a time so students can easily incorporate the learning.

Small Group Work 1 0 . 2

Motivation

What do you think is the best way to motivate students to read a social studies text? Why? ●

Listening and Writing

Listening

Listening skills are critical in learning. A great deal of the school experience involves listening. Listening is stressed in many reading/language approaches. As children learn to listen, they can learn from others and expand their world. As in reading, the goal in listening is to grasp the main ideas. Students need to remember the most important things they hear.

Students must be encouraged to listen for the main theme—the major idea or thought that runs through the material. After students identify the main ideas and understand what has been said, the second stage in listening is to evaluate the content and ideas. Children often do not recognize that others may have a different frame of reference. When listening to a different frame of reference, students must identify the feel of the situation and see the problem the way the speaker sees it. This skill is called sensitivity or empathy. Before students hear a tape or record, assign to some of them roles such as labor leaders, American Indian tribal leaders, or Asian immigrants. Ask students to listen and react to the song or poem the way the individual in his or her assumed role would react. Compare their reactions to those of the rest of the class; in this way, many students become more aware of how their own frame of reference allows them to hear certain messages and ignore others. In addition, students realize that different people speak in different ways.

Teachers often use the rumor exercise in the classroom to illustrate how easily meaning can be distorted. The original message is whispered to one child and each person repeats this to the next person. The last member repeats the message as it has been received. Typically, the message, having passed through many versions, is likely to be very different from the original. This activity can be followed by a discussion of the difficulty people have in transmitting messages accurately and of the effects of poor listening habits and the insertion of bias.

The difficulty is that students think listening is boring; it's more fun to talk. In addition, biology works against attentive listening. Most people speak at a rate of 120 to 150 words a minute, but the human brain can process more than 500 words per minute, leaving time for inattention. (This has been pointed out as a disadvantage of direct teaching.) Furthermore, gender differences may play a role, with females being more sympathetic listeners than males and their interruptions more supportive than intrusive.

What can teachers do to encourage students' listening skills throughout the whole school day? Sometimes it is necessary to take time out for teaching these skills, as in debriefing in cooperative learning groups, to encourage students to be courteous listeners and not talk all the time. Check the amount of listening required in your class; young children have short attention spans. Try to vary the amount of listening with the opportunity for them to interact with others. Help students see the importance of listening by having them record the amount of listening they do both during the school day and outside school. Initially, tell your students what to listen for or to focus on and to look at the nonverbal clues of the speaker to help in understanding; later they can learn to listen without your assistance.

Writing

Writing is said to be neglected in the school and should be emphasized more in all subject areas across all grade levels. More than 50 percent of freshmen at U.S. colleges and universities are unable to produce good writing samples. NAEP data indicate that at grades 4, 8, and 12 about 20 percent of students are proficient, about 50 percent meet basic requirements, and about 20 percent are completely unsatisfactory in their ability to write.

It is estimated by the National Commission on Writing in America's Schools and Colleges (2004) that most fourth-grade students spend less than three hours a week writing. But what matters more than the amount of time given to a writing assignment is the kind of thinking that gets done. Asking students just to write answers to lower-level questions such as "Who was the president during the Civil War?" does not move beyond rote memorization. A report in which information is taken from one source without much thought encourages plagiarism as well as boredom. On the other hand, writing can be a powerful social studies tool. Writing can clarify students' ideas. Software is available to help students learn to improve their writing.

Throughout the previous chapters, you have noticed the many opportunities students have to write in the social studies. For example, many of the postreading activities involve writing as students fill in graphic organizers, Venn diagrams, concept maps, and KWL charts. Students answer questions, write reactions to trade books and biographies, make time lines, and label maps. Some of these activities have a visual component, such as posters and cartoons. However, typically, many more social studies activities are oral and listening. This includes listening to the teacher, having small-group discussions, viewing videos, role playing, and participating in simulations. Building on the broad oral and listening base allows social studies instruction to improve writing skills, an area of general concern.

Remember that writing depends on a spoken language base. Vocabulary is essential for the expansion of thought. Writing cannot be separated from an individual's language ability. Good readers have less difficulty with writing because they have been exposed to more of it. Furthermore, writing, like reading, is a learning process where improvement can take place.

Connecting Social Science Themes with Genres of Writing

Most state frameworks in language arts list the following four genres for writing: descriptive, narrative, expository, and persuasive. Using economics standards, let us examine how understanding and improving writing could be combined.

Descriptive Writing
1. Write an "I Know" poem—use examples of scarcity (familiar to all) or bartering
2. Write an "I Am" poem—focusing on economics, describe your own human capital
3. Write letters using descriptions of economic institutions such as banks
4. Design a sales receipt showing the item, price, and the like

Narrative Writing
1. Tell the story of bartering or costs and benefits of a decision
2. Tell the story of an inventor and the consequences of the invention
3. Write a newspaper obituary on a famous person

Expository Writing
1. Explain why a money system is better than bartering
2. Explain how cotton became so important (King Cotton)
3. Explain the difference between public and private property

Persuasive Writing
1. Create ads and posters—explain why a given ad is attractive
2. Write letters to the editor on a local economic issue, such as expansion of hospital or store
3. Write letters to an advice columnist on an economic issue

You can see the many opportunities for both increasing knowledge of economics and writing.

Written Assessment Tasks

An important area for written work in the social studies are assessments to see what students have learned. Notice that many of the writing samples in the four genres actually are a form of assessment to demonstrate if the student has identified the main understanding of an economic concept. Writing becomes a product to examine student achievement. The following is a sixth grader writing about the ancient civilization of Mesopotamia.

> Merchant Abdel, I would like to trade ten bushels of my barley for an equivalent value of your dates and pomegranates. Please send my messenger back with your offer by the rising of the coming moon.
>
> May the gods and goddesses bring you prosperity and peace.
>
> Merchant Qudar

Evaluating this writing sample, it is clear that the student knows several accurate facts about Mesopotamia: that merchants are active in the Mesopotamia society, the common crops that are grown, the reliance on the moon for telling time, the writing style used, and the beliefs in gods and goddesses. The student writer has been able to put together several items about Mesopotamia into a clear piece of writing. A rubric could easily be used to count each accurate statement in this example. This is just one example of how writing can be used in social studies assessment. Recall from Chapter 4 on assessment how students respond to short constructed-response questions, essays, and portfolios in the social studies.

Here are some writing prompts that can be used for the social studies.

- Awards—recommend someone for an award in a certain time period, such as India in the 20th century

- Take a stand—defend a position on a controversial topic
- Warning—supply information not available at the time to an historical person or group to warn of danger (Examples: Lincoln, don't go to Ford's Theater tonight; General George Custer, don't go to Little Big Horn; Serbs in 1914, don't assassinate the heir to the Austrian throne.)

Hints on Informal Writing Assignments

Please remember that students will usually write better on topics that are of interest to them. The following suggestions are premised on this idea.

Quick Writes   Using the "every student writing, every student thinking" strategy, ask students to do a "quick write" by taking a few minutes to write, for example, on why most Americans in the 1800s supported the idea of moving the American Indians onto reservations. After circulating around the room noting what students are writing, the teacher calls on several students to share and then asks who agrees or disagrees and why. In this way all students are engaged in thinking, writing, and evaluating instead of only a few students answering a question asked by the teacher.

Imaginary Diaries and Historical Newspapers   A popular writing activity is to have students pretend they are living in an another time period. For example, students can write a letter or journal entries in a diary. They can imagine that they are writing back home to a friend or relative about a historical event or about their trip in a covered wagon to the Gold Rush in California or to the Oregon Territory. It is necessary to know details about what was going on at that time and the likely responses of individuals at that time. Otherwise, the journal entry or letter merely states generalities (I miss you, I am fine or suffering hardships, etc.). Often a prompt and the required length of the letter or diary entry are given, for example:

1. Your task is to write a diary entry of approximately 100 to 200 words.
2. Write your diary entry as if you were living in Virginia around 1700 as an indentured servant. You can be either a male or a female.
3. Tell what work you are likely to do.
4. Explain what your hopes are.

Common diary entries include those about immigrants coming to the United States, including Irish, German, Amish, Catholic, Chinese, Mexican, and the like.

Historical newspapers written by a class can also be a good writing experience, especially with software designed to help with the format. Particularly interesting are those in which students take different perspectives on issues such as colonists moving into Indian territory. Students can write editorials or letters to the editor. Another idea is to produce two different newspapers such as one for the North and one for the South following the battles of Vicksburg and Gettysburg. Some students can draw political cartoons or maps of the area where the event took place. Students can include ads showing the latest fashions or want ads for desired articles of the time.

Splicing Videos into the Writing Process

TECHNOLOGY

Going further than a historical newspaper, students can make a documentary in which the digital video process is linked to the writing process. A popular format presents conflicting views about an event or an on-the-scene news report such as the discovery of gold in California in 1848. Another example could be Washington's victory at Yorktown or any other important battle. Students could interview General Washington, a British soldier, an American soldier, a French officer, a runaway slave with the British, General Cornwallis, and the like. The writing process would include prewriting such as researching, brainstorming, organizing, drafting and editing (revising, proofreading, peer editing, final editing). The digital video process would include preproduction (scripting, casting), production (rehearing, filming) and postproduction (editing, sound, and visual effects). The final showing often is a highlight for the whole class after working hard on the project. Typically using small groups responsible for different parts of the documentary, the documentary project probably works best for fifth graders and older.

Easier to do is a *podcast,* an audio or video file. For an audio file, software (available free for Windows or Macintosh operating systems) plus a microphone and a script are needed to produce a product that can be posted and available for others to listen to. Knowing that others may hear their podcast acts as an incentive for students to do their best. Along with writing the script, students also can practice using their voices to express emotion and to create an atmosphere.

Word Processing

TECHNOLOGY

Computers are being used more often for writing in the classrooms. More fourth graders are using computers for writing drafts and then final versions of a report. Students who can type welcome the computer's help in catching errors in spelling, grammar, and syntax and in being able to make corrections easily. Students with handwriting difficulties encounter less frustration. Using word processing encourages students to write one or more drafts and allows for improvement. As more students are able to use word processing, one can hope that writing skills will improve.

Blogs

TECHNOLOGY

E-mail has been widely used for pen pals, especially to classrooms outside of the United States. Blogging is now also being used as classes exchange information. You can use a free hosting service for yourself or your class from Blogger (www.blogger.com). It can be made private so it is only open to registered users. Other no-cost sites are Livejournal (www.livejournal.com), Xanga (www.xanga.com), and Edublogs (http://edublogs.org). Teachers have to decide if they want parents to be able to comment on the classroom blog. Most teachers still want to screen the content for appropriateness and to ensure Internet safety. Teachers have reported that students are motivated to reply.

Remember that a blog is a tool. It can be used properly or improperly. A blog should promote conversation. If the teacher only reads the blogs, and the discussion does not involve the class, some of the benefits of the blog are lost even if online journals spark students' skills in writing and critiquing alternative views.

Teachers have used blogging with social studies field trips, both real and virtual. They might show a photo of a log cabin, then ask students to write how their house is different. Students can also organize their reflections on visiting a museum or historical site. Again, make sure that the similarities and differences noted by the various students are brought back to the attention of the class.

Reports

Reports are more demanding than informal writing. Students are not frequently asked to write a report or anything longer than a page or two. Many teachers would consider three pages to be excessive. Part of the reason for not giving longer writing assignments is that teachers do not have time to correct such projects. Furthermore, many teachers are working hard just to get their students to write one good paragraph.

Written book reports are probably most common, but more teachers are now trying to make this an interesting learning activity for students (see Chapter 5 on biographies). The assignment may ask the student to write three key events in the person's life and why these events were important. With the Internet available for summaries of books plus readers' reactions (www.amazon.com), methods for probing details and checking if students have actually read their books are important. One possibility is for several students to make a co-operative biography of a given person's life, such as Martin Luther King, Jr. One student writes the first chapter on the birth and childhood of the person, the second student writes the second chapter on the person's young adulthood and higher education, and so on.

In addition, report writing from various sources is a classic obstacle for middle-grade students, especially if it is an individual report. Consider a fifth-grade assignment in which students are to choose and write about a European explorer of the Americas. To do this, a student needs to combine several skills. For steps on writing a report, see Table 10.3. Often these steps are not directly taught and the result is poor quality reports or un-completed work from some students. If writing is difficult for students, it is also hard work for teachers to correct. Yet corrective and positive feedback are necessary if students are to improve. This further discourages teachers from giving this type of written assignment. Teachers are more likely to move to oral reports but ask that students list their main ideas on index cards.

Table 10.3 Analysis of Report Writing
1. Locate information on the chosen topic in a variety of sources: use the Internet, reference books, textbooks, etc. In many cases, additional data will need to be gathered.
2. If available, use the index, table of contents, and headings.
3. Read for main ideas and supporting details.
4. Take notes (in your own words) to answer research questions.
5. Prewrite by reviewing notes and organizing an outline for the first draft.
6. Write (with word processing, if available) a first draft using the outline and notes.
7. Check to see that there is a topic sentence for each paragraph.
8. Edit the first draft for topic flow, organization, spelling, grammar, and mechanics.
9. Revise to rewrite the first draft.
10. Prepare the final draft.

Explicit directions and a checklist can improve written reports. Here are some possibilities:

1. Have each student include and label the following sections of the report: title, introduction, development, conclusions.
2. Divide the report into topic-specific sections. For example, in a report on explorers:
   a. Why did the explorer set out to explore?
   b. Where did the explorer go? Dates? Make a time line and a map.
   c. What were the results of the exploration?
3. Have a conference with the teacher or other students to proofread the report.
4. Have a venue for publishing the report to motivate some students to do a better job.

Small Group Work 10.3

Reports

Do you recall what types of reports you had to write while in elementary school? Did you get feedback on your report or did you learn to write a report by trial and error? What reports, if any, do you think are appropriate for the grade level in which you hope to teach? ●

Writing Is a Process

Students, and sometimes their teachers, often think of writing as a final product. Yet this neglects the importance of *prewriting*. Before they start to write, students need time to think about what ideas they will later put down on paper. Some teachers actually say, "Hold your pens up. No one is to start writing. First it is time to think." Sometimes before writing, it is a good idea for students to share their ideas with a peer or a group. Talking out before writing is helpful. Only after that point do students actually start to write down their thoughts in a first draft. Then they revise and edit their work to produce a final revision. After doing all these steps, the work should be presented to an audience. This could be posting to the bulletin board, reading to the class, or adding to their portfolios. Remember to assess the written work with a rubric or have students assess each other's work.

Daily Writing

Try to provide many daily opportunities for writing. If the idea of filling a page with writing appears to be an obstacle for students to write, first give them an index card to fill up. Initially the card does not have to contain complete sentences. In the beginning, students often will use large writing just to fill the index card, but with daily practice over the school year, they should become more fluent in writing. To encourage writing, some teachers ask students to fill out an index card at the end of the day or social studies period, writing what they have learned. This assessment also helps the teacher. For the social studies, you can have students keep a "Learning Log." Each day they write what they have learned in social studies for the given day, but it is not turned in daily. Or have students keep track daily by writing, "How and when did you participate in today's lesson?"

Of course many times students are writing when they fill out worksheets or chapter study guides that come with the social studies textbook to reinforce what has been presented in the chapter. If truly to function as a study guide, think about allowing students to use their guides in an open book type of testing. That way the students may see more purpose in writing and filling in the blanks. You also have to decide if these written assignments are to be turned in and corrected. Will students be marked down for misspellings and the like? Or will social studies content be the most important?

Five Paragraph Essay

As students become older, some teachers wonder if they should teach the five paragraph essay with the first paragraph to state the thesis, three paragraphs to support the thesis, and the final paragraph to restate the thesis. Some teachers believe this robs the creativity out of the writing process. Others think that this guide is helpful to students, especially for ELLs and students having difficulty with writing. Especially if a writing sample is going to be used in state testing, this issue becomes critical.

Study of Models

Along with using rubrics, students need to see models of good writing. Respecting the privacy of the student, use student work to analyze with the class what makes the writing clear and engaging. Is there a good summarization? In what ways could this sample of writing be revised and improved? This analysis also may help students better understand why some written work received higher grades than other pieces of writing.

Summary

Social studies learning is dependent on reading, listening, speaking, and writing. Teaching social studies can improve reading, writing, and critical thinking. English language learners can learn social studies with proper accommodations such as feeling welcomed in class, having appropriate materials, having sheltered English, using materials in their primary languages with machine translation software, using media, and having frequent assessments. The many strategies under prereading, reading, and postreading can help students better understand the text. Writing that is engaging can benefit all learners.

Suggested Readings and Websites

Alleman, Janet, and Jere E. Brophy. "Trade-Offs Embedded in the Literary Approach to Early Elementary Social Studies." *Social Studies and the Young Learner* 6, no. 3: 94.

Shorter version of book-length critique that examines limitations on social studies under some literature approaches.

Cruz, Barbara C., Joyce W. Nutta, Jason O'Brien, Carine M. Feyten, and Jane M. Govoni. *Passport to Learning: Teaching Social Studies to ESL Students: Bulletin 101.* Silver Springs, MD: National Council for the Social Studies, 2003.

Suggestions for Teaching ELLs.

Hoge, John D. "Improving the Use of Elementary Social Studies Textbooks." *ERIC Digest* 33 (1986): 2–3.

Lists ways to get more meaning from text reading.

Irvin, Judith L., John P. Lundstrum, Carol Lynch-Brown, and Mary Friend Shepard. *Enhancing Social Studies Through*

Literacy Strategies: Bulletin 91. Washington, DC: National Council for the Social Studies, 1995.

Fine overview of research on pedagogy made practical for middle-grade teachers.

Kornfeld, John. "Using Fiction to Teach History: Multicultural and Global Perspectives of World War II." *Social Education* 58 (September 1994): 281–286.

Author describes and analyzes personal experience of teaching sixth-grade literature-based unit including student bibliography.

O'Day, Kim. "Using Formal and Informal Writing in Middle School Social Studies." *Social Education* 58 (January 1994): 39–40.

Examples of using writing to learn in middle grades.

Pappas, Christine C., Barbara Z. Kiefer, and Linda S. Levstik. *An Integrated Language Perspective in the Elementary*

School: Theory into Action, 3rd ed. White Plains, NY: Longman, 1999.

Well-grounded curriculum/methods text for realistically implementing whole-language approach.

Websites

**Center on English Learning
and Achievement (CELA)**
http://cela.albany.edu

Research center dedicated to improving student learning and achievement in English as a subject and in the other academic disciplines.

Children's Books Online
www.cyberkids.com/Launchpad/TextPages/Books.html

Variety plus children's literature.

English as a Second Language
www.rong-chang.com

Website links as well as other help for ESL students.

ESL Lounge
www.esl-lounge.com

Lesson plans, worksheets, and teaching tips.

ESL Party Line
www.eslpartyland.com

Students can access interactive activities.

The Graphic Organizer
www.graphic.org

Best website for graphic organizers, concept maps, and visual tools.

Inclusion Press International Home Page
www.inclusion.com

Information on inclusion.

International Children's Digital Library
www.icdlbooks.org

National Science Foundation and the Institute for Museum and Library Services have created a free online collection of over 10,000 books in 100 languages.

International Reading Association
www.reading.org

Professional organization for reading.

Internet Public Library
www.ipl.org

Especially children's literature for librarians. Has a reference question section that may be helpful in answering questions.

**The Internet TESL (Teachers of English as a
Second Language) Journal**
http://iteslj.org

Games, conversation, questions, and more for ESL learners.

National Association for Bilingual Education
www.nabe.org

Professional organization promoting bilingual education.

Reading Quest
http://curry.edschool.virginia.edu/go/readquest

Help for teaching comprehension and content reading strategies.

Where the Classroom Comes to Life

VIDEO HOMEWORK EXERCISE

Writing Strategies for ESL

Go to MyEducationLab, select the topic **Literacy Connections,** and watch the video entitled "Writing Strategies for ESL."

In this video, a teacher uses the social studies topic of pygmies and their way of life to improve writing, reading, and listening skills of her ESL students.

Index